GENDER
AND
SLAVERY

UNSilencing
Slavery

TELLING TRUTHS ABOUT
ROSE HALL PLANTATION, JAMAICA

Celia E. Naylor

Published in partnership with the
Center for the Study of Southern Culture
University of Mississippi, Oxford
JAMES G. THOMAS JR., EDITOR

The University of Georgia Press
ATHENS

Published by the University of Georgia Press
Athens, Georgia 30602
www.ugapress.org
© 2022 by Celia E. Naylor
All rights reserved
Set in 10.5/13.5 Garamond Premier Pro Regular
by Kaelin Chappell Broaddus

Most University of Georgia Press titles are
available from popular e-book vendors.

Printed digitally

Library of Congress Cataloging-in-Publication Data

Names: Naylor, Celia E., author.
Title: Unsilencing slavery : telling truths about Rose
Hall Plantation, Jamaica / Celia E. Naylor.
Description: Athens : The University of Georgia Press, [2022] |
Series: Gender and slavery | Includes bibliographical references and index.
Identifiers: LCCN 2021056425 | ISBN 9780820362144 (hardback) |
ISBN 9780820362151 (paperback) | ISBN 9780820362137 (ebook)
Subjects: LCSH: Rose Hall Plantation (Jamiaca)—History. |
Slaves—Jamaica—Montego Bay—Social conditions. | Plantation
life—Jamaica—Montego Bay—History. | De Lisser, Herbert
George, 1878–1944. The White Witch of Rosehall.
Classification: LCC HT1099 .R67 2022 | DDC
306.3/62097292—dc23/eng/20211207
LC record available at https://lccn.loc.gov/2021056425

To my father, Cecil Anthony Naylor (1927–2017), a storyteller's storyteller who enjoyed hearing the stories in the musical notes of a jazz standard as much as he relished telling the stories of the old days in Jamaica.

To my mother, Fay Patricia Naylor, née Hornett (1929–2020), who listened to all of my father's stories and continued to tell her own stories about the past and present as a keeper of our family's history, traditions, and aspects of Jamaican culture.

To my daughter, Ayanbi Yejide Naylor Ojurongbe, who refuses expectations and assumptions about which stories should be told and conjures up her own in her poetry.

For Celia, Cecelia, and all the enslaved girls and women at Rose Hall, as well as all of my own ancestors enslaved in Jamaica whose names appear in Jamaican slave registers and those who remain unnamed in the archives yet recognized and remembered here.

And for all the free generations of Jamaicans in the future.

CONTENTS

ACKNOWLEDGMENTS

What a labor of love at the very end—trying to include everyone who supported and encouraged me during the process of writing this book and the journey of living my life. So many people to remember, and no doubt many who will erroneously not be mentioned in this offering of thanks. To truly do justice to everyone and everything would require countless pages. Innumerable persons and villages loved, supported, and nurtured me over the past several years as I worked on this book. Some of these people consistently inquired about how the book was progressing, and others were entirely unaware that I was even writing a book or taught at a college.

We sometimes do not recognize the impact one person, one teacher, one spirit has on our lives until they are no longer with us in physical form. Although that is the case for some who have joined with me on this journey called life, this is not the case for my first teachers, my parents, Fay Patricia Naylor and Cecil Anthony Naylor. They both passed during the time period I worked on this project, my father on August 23, 2017, and my mother on March 15, 2020. More than any archival document, poem, song, dance, book, or university course, they were my first teachers about the power of love, the magnitude of principles, and the importance of living a purposeful and joyful life. Even as I write this, I remain moved to tears by their physical absence, though still comforted by their infinite presence beyond their bodies. In their respective and collective passing, I have been reminded about the force of stories and storytelling, of the indescribable joy of loving others and being loved by others, and of the necessity of love, gratitude, and appreciation. My brother, Stuart, and my sister, Kathryn, are the only other people named here who have known me for my entire life. Even through the separation of physical distance and life circumstances, I hold them within me and beside me always, and whenever I am in their company, I am reminded of the healing I receive from them in shared stories, vivacious laughter, and a deep, abiding love. The family member I have known for her entire life is my daughter, Ayanbi. She is mentioned at different points in the book, and she was the person who encouraged this project from the very first tour at Rose Hall Great House. Beyond this project, though, Ayanbi has extended consistent encouragement and support. I will always be grateful for her loving, kind, compassionate, and fierce spirit, even though she is often "annoyed" by me.

Although they were seemingly not "directly" involved in this project, the seeds for this work were planted during my many moons as an undergraduate and graduate student. I extend my love, gratitude, and appreciation to my teachers in the traditional setting of universities. Now that I have been a full-time professor for over twenty years, I recognize more and more how much my teachers invested in me and so many others. I continue to feel truly fortunate to have been taught by incredible professors who were devoted to the practice and principles of teaching and learning with their students. As an undergraduate at Cornell University, I could not have asked for or possibly imagined a group of professors who demonstrated the art and absolute love of teaching in the classroom and beyond: Locksley Edmondson, Henry Louis Gates Jr., Robert L. Harris Jr., Carolyn "Biddy" Martin, Mary Beth Norton, Hortense Spillers, and James Turner. Not all of the teachers who inspired me at Cornell were professors. Although I did not have the pleasure of living at Ujamaa, I will always cherish the lessons shared by Ken Glover (then Ujamaa housing director) in intense discussions at Ujamaa and at the Africana Studies and Research Center. No matter how much I questioned and challenged him as I grappled with my place at Cornell and in the world, he remained a consistent supporter and demonstrated what it truly meant to be a teacher, an advocate, and a mentor.

When I began my graduate studies at UCLA, I continued to be in the company of and to learn from devoted professors such as G. Reginald Daniel, Robert A. Hill, Christine Ho, Anthony S. Parent Jr., and Richard A. Yarborough. While at UCLA for my first master's degree, I also learned a great deal while working on the Ford Ethnic Women's Curriculum Transformation Project. As part of this initiative, I benefited from the mentorship and guidance of the project manager, Norma Rice, who taught me about navigating all that settled in the crevices of academia as a woman of color and the politics of academia in general.

I could not have imagined a more extraordinary place for my doctoral studies than Duke University. First and foremost, I want to acknowledge Dean Jacqueline Looney, whose herculean recruitment and retention efforts, as well as extraordinary support, made it possible for me and many others to attend and graduate from Duke University. It was truly auspicious to be taught and mentored by Professors William Chafe, Jan Ewald, David Barry Gaspar, Karla F. C. Holloway, Sydney Nathans, the late Julius S. Scott III, and Peter H. Wood. Although these phenomenal professors were instrumental in my doctoral studies, the other graduate students with whom and from whom I learned not only informed my years at Duke but also continue to inspire me now. At the February

2020 event at Duke University to celebrate Professor Julius S. Scott and his influential work, *The Common Wind: Afro-American Currents in the Age of the Haitian Revolution*, I was reminded just how fortunate I and others were to be in a cohort of graduate students who were dedicated to learning about different aspects of the African diaspora as both an individual and a collaborative journey. Each and every one has been a teacher of mine in immeasurable ways: Professors Herman Bennett, the late Leslie Brown, Alexander X. Byrd, Rod Clare, Matthew Countryman, Kathryn Dungy, Christina Greene, Charles McKinney, Jennifer L. Morgan, Claudio Saunt, Stephanie Smallwood, Faith L. Smith, and many others. Due to the timing of when I left Durham, I did not meet Vincent Brown until much later, but I include him here as part of that extraordinary graduate student community at Duke, to which I am deeply indebted. In addition to learning with them and from them at Duke, I have been particularly grateful for the friendships sustained with some of them over three decades.

Colleges and universities have offered me unforgettable learning and teaching experiences, and I am particularly grateful for the countless gifts of friendship they have also bestowed upon me. I appreciate all of the loving relationships that began at various institutions of higher learning—at Cornell, the University of Ibadan, UCLA, Duke, Iowa State University, the University of New Mexico, Penn State Harrisburg, Dartmouth College, Barnard College, and Columbia University—as well as in spaces and places in between. So many people have come into my life through the medium of higher education and have been ardent supporters, whether for a few years or a couple of decades: Rachel Austin, Liz Beck, Felicia (Bishop) Denaud, Zanice Bond, Judith Byfield, Juba Clayton, Ayo A. Coly, Deirdre Cooper Owens, Joseph Cullon, Carol Dolan, Nnaemeka "Emeka" Ekwelum, Mary Ann Evans, Yvonne Gillam, Reena Goldthree, Sandrea Gonzalez, Janet Jakobsen, Roxanne Johnson, Jean Kim, Deborah K. King, Barbara Krauthamer, Modupe Labode, Ed Lewis, Natasha Lightfoot, Laura Lovett, David N. M. Mbora, Pat Miller, Dolores Morris, Annelise Orleck, Asata Ratliff, Russell Rickford, Vern Sakai, Mary Beth Snyder, Mary Tandia, Carlie and Gary Tartakov, Sasha Turner, Alex Watson, Craig S. Wilder, Meron Wondwosen, and Suzanne Zilber.

At different institutions I have cherished the kindness of colleagues, some of whom I also appreciate as friends. Being a faculty member in two departments can often be a burden, but at Barnard College it has been a double blessing. Colleagues in Africana Studies and History have demonstrated what I can only describe as love. I continue to appreciate their support and encouragement. All have been supportive in their own ways, and I am especially grateful to Yvette Christiansë, Abosede George, Kaiama L. Glover, Kim F. Hall, Maja Horn, Joel

Kaye, Dorothy Ko, Ady Matos, Monica L. Miller, Premilla Nadasen, Quandra Prettyman, Anupama Rao, Sully Rios, Michelle Rowland, and Lisa Tiersten. I have been forever moved by the consistent encouragement, unwavering support, and intellectual wisdom I have received from Professors Tina Campt, Yvette Christiansë, Dorothy Ko, and Lisa Tiersten, the chairs of my two departments as I worked on this project.

Throughout the research and writing process, I have received a tremendous amount of institutional assistance from Barnard College and Columbia University. Linda A. Bell, provost and dean of the faculty, has supported me in both the personal and professional aspects of my life. She has been not only a staunch advocate but also a compassionate leader. Barnard Faculty Research Grants served as the primary funding for my multiple archival research trips to Jamaica and England. A grant from the Barnard Committee on Online and On-Campus Learning (COOL) allowed for the development of my Rose Hall Digital Humanities Project.

My time in the archives and libraries in Jamaica and England proved to be invaluable not only because of the documents but also because of the assistance of staff members at the Jamaica Archives and Records Department (JARD) in Spanish Town and the National Archives in Kew Gardens, England. I appreciate the numerous ways the staff members of the Jamaica Archives and Records Department (JARD) supported my archival work; I extend special thanks to Kimberly Blackwin, Tracey Smith, Racquel Stratchan Innerarity, Crastareese Watson, and Margaret Williams. In addition, Mrs. Claudette Thomas, government archivist at the Jamaica Archives Kingston office, offered administrative support with this project and encouragement in finding out about the Naylor family's roots in Portland and the site of Naylor's Hill. Thanks also to Mr. Ahon Gray, senior researcher at the Jamaica *Gleaner*, who extended his assistance with the *Gleaner*'s archives.

Frequent trips to Rose Hall Great House were part and parcel of this journey. I am profoundly grateful to all of the Rose Hall Great House staff, working in various positions at this site, for their assistance and encouragement throughout this process. Whenever I experienced the tours, the tour guides always conveyed their enthusiasm, commitment, and engagement regarding Jamaican storytelling. Even as they expressed their utmost surprise about the actual history at Rose Hall, they remained steadfast about the significance of telling Jamaican history. Although I would have preferred to recognize each and every one of the Rose Hall tour guides in this section, in order to protect their privacy, I have not included their names here.

In addition to archival research trips, Barnard College funding also made it possible for me to hire an undergraduate research assistant in 2017. I cannot begin to express my appreciation to Monique Sophia Williams (research assistant extraordinaire of the Columbia University class of 2017) for her work in the summer and early fall of 2017. As an exemplary student in my Africana Studies colloquium—"Tongues on Fire": Caribbean Women's Articulations of Fracture(s), Freedom(s), and Futurities—in the spring of 2017, I was thrilled about her willingness to offer helpful suggestions on my book proposal, as well as to assist me with organizing and working through some of the archival material for this project. As I worked on the final revisions throughout 2020, Monique generously agreed to "reactivate" the research assistantship to review the manuscript, and she again provided excellent feedback and useful recommendations. In the spring, summer, and fall of 2020, when I was unable to travel to Jamaica due to travel restrictions related to COVID-19, Monique again assisted with last-minute final items and errands in Jamaica. Incalculable Barnard and Columbia students have encouraged me throughout the journey of this book. I initially wanted to name them all; however, leaving even one student's name out here would be unforgivable, and so I decided not to attempt to name every student who conveyed a reassuring word or asked about the progress of the book. They know who they are, and they also know they have individually and collectively encouraged me, taught me, inspired me, and motivated me in every phase of this process.

A number of intellectual communities and networks at Barnard College and Columbia University offered multifaceted critical engagement and encouragement over these past few years. It was a pleasure and honor to be a 2017–18 faculty fellow at the Heyman Center for the Humanities; my cohort of dedicated faculty and graduate students across the Columbia University community included Rachel Adams, JM Chris Chang, Brent Hayes Edwards, Robert Gooding-Williams, Robert Goodman, Anna Danziger Halperin, Matthew Hart, Joseph Howley, Andrew Jungclaus, Ana Paulina Lee, Mark Mazower, Sean O'Neil, and Dennis Tenen. Their generous comments on my work and on our collective projects enabled me to move forward in my writing process at a crucial time. Moreover, the comments and questions from people I know well and those I have only met once at conference presentations over the years became invaluable as I teased out various dimensions of this project. I am grateful for the encouragement from Barnard professor Rachel Austin (who primarily abides in the world of the "sciences"), who offered multiple times to read the manuscript, and when I finally shared it with her in March 2021, her responses were especially affirming.

I am grateful that I was selected as one of the inaugural fellows of Barnard's

Digital Humanities Summer Institute in 2019. The organizers and members of my cohort—Madiha Zahrah Choksi, Kaiama L. Glover, Corinth Jackson, Janet Jakobsen, Sylvia Korman, Miriam Neptune, Shannon O'Neill, Pamela Phillips, Katherynn Sandoval, Kimberly Springer, and Martha Tenney—demonstrated what could be accomplished with my limited digital humanities knowledge, a lot of willingness, and a supportive village. Other members of the Barnard College community, Fatimazohra Koli and Marko Krkeljas, also offered helpful advice, guidance, and lessons along the way. The Rose Hall Digital Humanities Project would not have been possible without the depth and breadth of expertise, creativity, and intellect of the Rose Hall Digital Project team: Kristen Akey (Rose Hall Digital Project undergraduate research assistant, 2019–20, Barnard College class of 2020), Madiha Zahrah Choksi (Columbia University, research and learning technologies librarian), Moacir P. de Sá Pereira (Columbia University, research data librarian), and Alex Gil (Columbia University, digital scholarship librarian). I always left our meetings entirely overwhelmed with new technodigital terms and processes, as well as new ways of thinking about the project.

Beyond the Barnard College gates, the CHAWWG gatherings with fabulous scholars Marisa Fuentes and Anne Eller heightened my understanding of the purpose of our collective work and the importance of creating a "beloved community" in the midst of that "work." Other sista-scholars in the struggle who continue to share the joys and challenges of our lives over decades within and without the academic world and who demonstrate the intimacies of friendship, the grace of resilience, and the strength of vulnerability in countless ways are Tiya A. Miles, Tanalís Padilla, Naaborko Sackeyfio-Lenoch, and Kimberly Stanley.

As grateful as I am for friends whose professional lives are deeply embedded in the academic world, I have to acknowledge that many of the lives of my longtime friends do not center wholly around academic institutions. Even as their professional profiles loom large in a range of sectors, some "old friends"—Joe Clark, Astrid B. Gloade, and Mariah S. Wilkins—have offered much-needed perspectives, insights, and refuge over the decades. My sistren Keecha Harris has served as a consistent, honest, and loving "sounding board" who has always sheltered me with the truth about myself and life itself, as well as walked with me for much of the ebbing and flowing of my adult life. She also welcomed me into her lovely home multiple times for much-needed time to simultaneously work on this project and revivify my spirit. Each of these "old friends" continues to be personal teachers to me of what friendship means and how loving, caring relationships endure over time and space.

Two friends whom I met while living in New Hampshire—Savitri Beharry and Karen Fisher-Vanden—have been sources of support in too many ways to delineate here. We could not have imagined that our friendship would have survived multiple moves, job changes, and life crises, and still we have supported each other and laughed out loud throughout it all. Thanks to Savitri, Jesse, Ashok, and Momo for offering me their guest space in Massachusetts for much-needed time to relax and focus on this project for a couple of weeks during the Rona summer of 2020 while enjoying their always delightful company, peaceful surroundings, and scrumptious meals!

Since my arrival in New York City, family members in this city have continued to be a source of love and laughter: Dimitri, Michelle, and Sascha Naylor, as well as Ursula and Brian Hornett. Others who have offered refuge from the academic world in New York City include Na'Im Ansar Najieb, Harriet/HT Love-Joy, and many other Mighty Companions, as well as Love 101 sistas and brothas in New York and beyond. Thanks to Na'Im for demonstrating/teaching love, freedom, and grace in relationships, in his thirteen books so far (beginning with *Love Is Not a Game*), and in all the ways he extends his loving purpose, mission, and blessings. Since my introduction to Integral Yoga Institute in New York City in 2013, it has also served as a consistent place of refuge. Founded by Sri Swami Satchidananda in 1966, IYI continues to embody his teachings and related goals for people to have "an easeful body, a peaceful mind, and a useful life." Special thanks to IYI instructors who have reminded me of these teachings in their own way—Alan, Bhakti, Gopala, Jayadevi, Kalyana, Lakshmi Scalise, Nobuko, Prashanti, Rashmi, and so many others.

I have tried, but I simply cannot fully explain the healing vibes of Jamaica for me. Even when spending day after day in the Jamaica Archives, still just being in Jamaica was always rejuvenating to my body, mind, and spirit. Although my immediate family members now reside outside of Jamaica, the Armstrongs—longtime family friends there—always reminded me they were "family." My mother's best friend, Aunty Flo Armstrong, and her and Uncle Harry's three children, Howard ("Chris"), Karen, and Robert, made these visits to Jamaica especially loving and joyful. Chris's wife, Margaret, and their two children, Tina and Luke, also created playful and fun times during many of those trips. My visits with my Armstrong family always included wonderful meals, intense, heated discussions on U.S. and Jamaican politics and politricks, religion and spirituality, controversial social movements, and much more! With them, as in Jamaica in general, I have always been able to show up and be loved exactly as I am. The Armstrong family always demonstrates with me and everyone that they are incredibly spirit-strong people. Their prayers and positivity over the decades have meant the world to me.

As the adage goes, last but certainly not least, the University of Georgia Press staff have been a source of immense support. My relationship with the press began with an invitation from Director Lisa Bayer to meet about my project during the Berks Conference in 2017. Although entirely unexpected, she attended my panel before our meeting. From the very beginning I have received only kindness and encouragement from her and the other UGA Press staff members who have been intricately involved with this book. Even though I do not know *all* of the members of the UGA Press team who assisted with publishing my work, I would like to extend my appreciation to those who personally assisted me along the way: Katherine La Mantia, Jordan Stepp, Mary M. Hill, and Nate Holly. Nate, in particular, offered useful feedback and consistent encouragement at critical periods. I am especially pleased that my work is part of the Gender and Slavery series, coedited by the illustrious scholars Jennifer L. Morgan and Daina Ramey Berry. Both conveyed their collective support for this project at various key stages in the process. In the manuscript review process, the three anonymous external reviewers provided extensive, thoughtful suggestions, and I am deeply grateful for the time and energy they invested in this book. Their feedback served only to improve the book overall. Due to the press's new collaborative project with the University of Mississippi's Center for the Study of Southern Culture, its associate director for publications, James G. Thomas Jr., also reviewed and offered helpful comments about the manuscript during the final revising stage. Two additional blessings were the permissions granted by Ntozake Shange's literary agent to include the excerpt from *For Colored Girls* in the epilogue, as well as celebrated Jamaican poet Olive Senior's generous gift of her permission for the inclusion of her poetry. While working on this book, I often returned to their work for inspiration, encouragement, and more!

In Love, Gratitude, and Appreciation to you and for you ALL!

unSilencing Slavery

Drawing of Rose Hall Plantation, ca. 1820–1821, by James Hakewell, Yale Center for British Art, Paul Mellon Collection. With the Rose Hall Great House pictured at the center, though at a distance, viewers may be initially drawn to the house and then perhaps to the two people on horses (considering their clothing, they are probably a white woman and a white man). There is another person in the drawing standing close to the right side of the entrance. Given the coloring of the person, this person is a person of African descent and most likely enslaved. This person's gender is unclear. It may be easy to miss the Black figure by the entrance. Even in this drawing the Black figure, the enslaved person, is visibly decentered / "invisible" / absorbed by and within the background.

INTRODUCTION

Initiation to Rose Hall Great House

In the summer of 2013, I decided to take my daughter, Ayanbi, to Jamaica for her first visit. I was born in Jamaica and raised there until I was ten, so most of my stories about the island have been childhood tales. Ayanbi was on the verge of teendom, willing and ready to travel internationally with me, and I felt it was important for her to have a better sense of this part of her family's history. Montego Bay (MoBay) was our destination, and though we visited different sites, our main excursion was to the Rose Hall Great House.[1] I admit I mentioned to Ayanbi that Rose Hall was a historic place, and to grab her attention I noted that when I was a child I had learned that it was a "ghost house." That, of course, intrigued her. As a child, I had also been captivated by *duppy* (ghost) stories.[2] However, I must confess that this was my first time on the tour. Growing up in Kingston, I had heard fleeting, disjointed stories of Annie Palmer, the "White Witch of Rose Hall," but I had never visited Rose Hall with my family or on my own.

Primarily because of Herbert G. de Lisser's 1929 novel, *The White Witch of Rosehall*, Annie Palmer is remembered as a particularly notorious mistress whose lovers included both Englishmen and men enslaved on her plantation.[3] Most stories emphasize her supposed numerous, heinous, and supernatural deeds: the murder of three English husbands, her excessively brutal treatment of the people enslaved on her plantation, and, as legend goes, her ghost haunting the Rose Hall Great House and grounds today. Indeed, as the novel and contemporary Rose Hall Great House tours highlight, Annie Palmer's life supposedly ended tragically when her previously enslaved lover, Takoo, killed her as an act of revenge for her lethal curse on his granddaughter Millicent. These details of Annie Palmer's legend have circulated widely in Jamaica and throughout the world; every year, more than one hundred thousand people visit Rose Hall. They have shared pictures and stories, keeping the legend alive into the present day.[4]

For our first tour of the Rose Hall Great House, Ayanbi and I arrived at Rose Hall at twilight—one of those evenings in the summer when the sun seemed to be resisting its own setting, seemed to want to linger as long as possible, seemed to be bargaining with the night before finally giving way to the inevitable darkness. As we drove along Highway A1 that evening, we entered the main gate of Rose Hall. The particular landscape of this plantation made the Rose Hall Great House appear quite far off in the distance. Popular photos of the Rose Hall Great House often create the appearance of the house being directly off the main road. This was not the case. Just inside the main gate on a mound were stones spelling out the words ROSE HALL. Arrows on a separate sign informed visitors to go to the left for the Rose Hall Great House and to the right for the White Witch Golf Course. A drive around the mound and then a few turns led to the main parking and welcome area. One might assume the house itself would be the welcome center, but that expectation was not initially realized. We had lost sight of the house after we entered the main gate, which only intensified the mysterious effect of the house and the legend on us. After perusing items in the gift store, Ayanbi and I joined the other guests awaiting the beginning of the tours. The house began to reveal itself again as we walked a short distance from the welcome area. Slowly the entire house came into view. Perhaps it was the final desperate glow of twilight, perhaps it was the brief stories I had heard of the myth, but the house seemed gloomy and unfavorable to the presence of strangers. It seemed to be already on guard against unwelcome guests.

As we gathered facing the stairs leading to the house, we were instructed by the tour guide to look closely at the windows on the upper level of the house. A woman's silhouette appeared in a window. And so the tour began with Annie Palmer's "ghost" looming above us, looking down on us and other guests as we prepared to walk up the stairs to the house. She did not beckon anyone inside. We all entered at our own risk. However, before ascending the long stretch of stairs, we were invited to have pictures taken by the staff photographer with the house in the background and the possibility of catching a glimpse of Annie Palmer's ghost as a memento of this moment. Once the photo session concluded, the tour guide finally gave us permission to climb the stairs and enter Annie Palmer's house.

As Ayanbi and I followed the tour guide, moving from one room to the next, I became increasingly incensed by how much the tour focused almost entirely on Annie Palmer and her malevolent actions as the White Witch of Rose Hall. Ayanbi and the other visitors, however, were entirely enthralled by it, especially the multiple attempts to scare us with startling sounds and sudden movements. To this day, even after many visits to Jamaica, when asked about her first visit, the Rose Hall tour remains Ayanbi's favorite part of that trip. As I walked away from my first tour of the Rose Hall Great House, however, the most pressing feeling that lingered for me was the disturbing absence of any essential information about slavery or the lives of enslaved people at Rose Hall Plantation. I was troubled by the conscious decisions made to use this plantation site to mesmerize and entertain in order to avoid the reality of the trepidation, trauma, and terror of previously enslaved people on these grounds. I was troubled by how the fabricated stories of Annie Palmer as the White Witch of Rose Hall provided an easy channel for white visitors (and everyone else) to circumvent the violences of slavery, offered them safe passage to enter the realm of slavery without any critical engagement, and allowed them to be apparently freed from the remnants of slavery's brutality and the suffering it caused. I was troubled by the pleasurable experiences of those visitors and by the fact that at the end many conveyed how much they appreciated all of the "history" presented throughout this tour. I was troubled by the ways in which the Black Jamaican tour guides (primarily women) were also seemingly enticed and entranced by the stories they told over and over again about the sexual and murderous exploits of Annie Palmer, without any stories about the women who were enslaved there—women who could have been their ancestors. I was troubled by my own state of being during and after the tour—simultaneously awake (read: "woke" in common parlance), aware of, and agitated by the silences, gaps, and inaccuracies regarding enslaved people and the peculiar institution of slavery itself. As a result of the ongoing legend of Annie Palmer's exploits as the White Witch of Rose Hall, this plantation has been reconstructed as a site of historical tourism, sexual scandals, and murderous tactics woven within the fabric of a ghost story. In the Rose Hall tours, as Annie Palmer's sexual exploits ground and captivate the narrative presented to visitors, enslaved women become "invisibly visible" and the ghostly embodiment of Gayatri Chakravorty Spivak's "historically muted subject."[5]

The choreography of these myths and silences in the Rose Hall Great House tours materialized from Herbert de Lisser's 1929 novel. Due to limited historical and factual information about Annie Palmer, de Lisser utilized the fertile ground of these historical gaps to concoct this legend about the White Witch of Rose Hall. As a result, the *only* historical facts included in de Lisser's novel and in the Rose Hall Great House tours are that a woman named Annie Palmer lived at Rose Hall Plantation between 1820 and 1830 and that she was the white mistress of Rose Hall during those years. All other details about Annie Palmer described in de Lisser's novel and the tours are entirely fictional, including (but not limited to) the information about Annie Palmer's and her parents' connections and time spent in Haiti; Annie Palmer being raised by a "voodoo priestess" in Haiti; Annie Palmer's marriage to three Englishmen; her murdering these three husbands; and her being killed by a previously enslaved man named Takoo during a slave revolt, the Baptist War/Christmas Rebellion of 1831–32. In addition to these fictional depictions of Annie Palmer in both the novel and the tours, the Great House tours also conclude at what is supposed to be Annie Palmer's final "resting place," a coffin on the Rose Hall property. Whether the remains of any person are in that coffin is unclear, but if there are any, they do not belong to Annie Palmer. Annie Palmer's final resting place is in the Montego Bay churchyard (though her grave is not marked or identified in any way). In a similar vein, visitors mistakenly assume that the Rose Hall Great House is a museum. Simply stated, it is not a museum. Instead, the Rose Hall Great House operates as a tourist site with fictional information presented as the "history" of the site.

Almost two years after that first tour, I vacillated between thoughts of how *someone* should write about this and, well, how *I* should write about this. Though clearly perturbed by the tour's narrative and the responses of other visitors, I walked away not haunted by the fabricated ghost of Annie Palmer. Instead, I was haunted by those who had an actual historical right to haunt this venue of terror and trauma—the enslaved people who labored at Rose Hall Plantation and directly experienced the horrors of bondage. As I ruminated about what exactly I would explore about Rose Hall, it became quite obvious that this would not be a "traditional" history book, nor would the research for this history project be entirely "traditional." It is important to note that my other primary motivation for undertaking this project centered on a long-deferred goal, established during my undergraduate years, to work on some facet of women and slavery in Jamaica. Over the years (and now decades), I never forgot about this goal, and I have experienced some measure of personal gratification in developing this Rose Hall project.

Telling truths about slavery at Rose Hall demands not only unearthing enslaved people's experiences out of limited archival records but also unveiling the afterlives of slavery embodied in the novel and the Rose Hall Great House tours. Even after I decided to include these aspects in this one book, I also recognized that the book would not be sufficient to demonstrate to a larger audience, in some small measure, the intricacies and nuances of the interlocking lives of enslaved people. Although I usually describe myself as a twentieth-century techie, early on I imagined a website that would offer another avenue, another form, to present these enslaved persons in order to counter the dominant master/mistress narrative in the "official" Rose Hall Great House website and other internet sources that centered on Annie Palmer and the legend of the White Witch of Rose Hall. It was crucial to move the enslaved people from the margin to the center of this history. I wanted to provide this information in an online format, one that would give visitors an opportunity to review selected historical documents about this plantation.

Overall, my interdisciplinary Rose Hall project centers on three specific outcomes: (1) a microhistory of enslaved people's experiences in the first decades of the nineteenth century at Rose Hall Plantation (with a focus on enslaved women's lives); (2) an interdisciplinary critique of two popular iterations of the legend of the White Witch of Rose Hall—Herbert G. de Lisser's 1929 novel, *The White Witch of Rosehall*, and contemporary manifestations of this myth in the Rose Hall Great House tours—in order to explore the poetics and politics of reconstructing and representing slavery in the modern era; and (3) a digital humanities project on Rose Hall to expand the critical discussion about this site to a transnational audience and provide the foundation for integrating substantive information about enslaved people and slavery in the materials and future tours at the Rose Hall Great House.[6]

IN THE WAKE OF ROSE HALL GREAT HOUSE

The Rose Hall Great House, the most renowned plantation house in Jamaica and located about fifteen kilometers / nine miles east of the town center of Montego Bay, has become a popular wedding venue and tourist destination.[7] This plantation has not been immortalized because of Jamaica's slavery past. Rather, it signifies for most local Jamaicans and visiting tourists a house in which the ghost of its most famous mistress, Annie Mary (sometimes identified as Annee Mae) Palmer (née Paterson), roams the grounds as the White Witch of Rose Hall. Plantations in the United States and the Caribbean, as well as slave forts in West Africa, have represented tangible, enduring monuments of slavery and have become accepted tourist destinations.[8] Even as they have served as historical sites of slavery, some of these spaces were refashioned in the twentieth century as settings for parties and weddings.[9] Though potential tools for educating visitors about slavery, these tourist sites (like the Rose Hall Great House) often present a fairly cursory, uncomplicated presentation of the world of slavery and the lives of bondswomen, bondsmen, and bondschildren. It is important to note that the particular challenges, strategies, and achievements of enslaved people often remain unexplored and grossly misrepresented at public memorial sites and in popular culture overall. Such sites and related tourist bureaus encourage visitation to these plantations by conveying a message about the beauty of slave sites in this neocolonial present.[10] Tourists and local Jamaicans too have the privilege of visiting previous plantation homes and reveling in the ongoing amnesia of slavery as they admire the beauty of these magnificent homes with breathtaking views, but without confronting the exploitation, violences, and trauma of slavery deeply embedded within these grounds.[11]

With the recent controversies surrounding Confederate monuments in the United States, it is telling that popular plantation homes that have long been used as tourist sites have not been publicly critiqued or castigated in the same intensely contested manner. Rather, plantation estates—one of the most iconic symbols of slavery—have, for the most part, operated outside the confines of passionate public scrutiny. However, these sites have not remained entirely below the critical radar of academic and social justice realms. In a September 2019 article in *The Nation*, entitled "Stop Getting Married on Plantations," legal scholar Patricia J. Williams pointedly confronts the "romantic allure" of monuments and plantation sites in order to elide the horrors of slavery.[12] In October 2019, Color of Change reached out to five wedding-oriented companies as part of a new campaign for such companies to reconsider their presentation and promotion of plantation weddings in their online and related materials.[13] How do we interrogate the complexities of history, public memorialization, and tourism directly related to sites of slavery? How do we tell the human story of plantation sites such as Rose Hall, invoking and integrating a sense of humanity in tourism and, in fact, in history? As historian Daryle Williams poignantly asked in 2018 at the "Slave Pasts in the Present: Narrating Slavery through the Arts, Technology, and Tourism" symposium, "How to tell a human story, in a humane way, about a crime against humanity?"[14]

Scholars from various disciplines have long examined the complexities of contemporary expressions and (re)constructions of history, trauma, memory, and suffering.[15] In her book *In the Wake: On Blackness and Being*, literary scholar Christina Sharpe asks us to consider the various manifestations of being "in the wake" of the "afterlives of slavery" in the "still unfolding aftermaths of Atlantic chattel slavery."[16] Sharpe not only explores her conceptualization of being "in the wake" but also posits that "we might make the wake and *wake work* our analytic, we might continue to imagine new ways to live in the wake of slavery, in slavery's afterlives, to survive (and more) the afterlife of property."[17] Sharpe describes "wake work to be a mode of inhabiting *and* rupturing this episteme with our known lived and un/imaginable lives. With that analytic we might imagine otherwise from what we know *now* in the wake of slavery."[18] She theorizes: "Just as wake work troubles mourning, so too do the wake and wake work trouble the ways most museums and memorials take up trauma and memory. That is, if museums and memorials materialize a kind of reparation (repair) and enact their own pedagogies as they position visitors to have a particular experience or set of experiences about an event that is seen to be past, how does one memorialize chattel slavery and its afterlives, which are unfolding still? How do we memorialize an event that is still ongoing?"[19]

This Rose Hall project consciously and purposefully moves in the direction of what Sharpe expresses as "wake work." In this endeavor, wake work translates into attending (and tending) to the presentation and examination of the actual lives of enslaved people who lived and labored at Rose Hall, as well as attending (and tending) to the erasure and recasting of slavery and of Black suffering and survival in the contemporary tours at Rose Hall Great House. It acknowledges, as Sharpe reminds us, that "in the wake, the past that is not past reappears, always, to rupture the present."[20] I consider what it means to work in the wake of the archives, piecing together the threads of stories and the shards of evidence of enslaved people's lived experiences, as well as working to disrupt, interrogate, and rupture the erroneous (re)presentations of their lives in the contemporary tours at Rose Hall. It is to begin to name those enslaved who have been unremembered and unmemorialized; it is to begin to reconstruct stories buried and deemed unworthy of telling and retelling; it is to begin to reimagine the struggles, suffering, and sanctity of people enslaved (though not entirely dehumanized); it is to begin to question the afterlife of slavery that is Rose Hall in content and in form; and it is to begin to ask *what* and *who* survive at Rose Hall in the mythical ghost haunting of a white witch, the pretense of memorialization, and the facade of slavery. In the literary and popular reincarnations of Annie Palmer, in de Lisser's novel, and in the contemporary tours at the Rose Hall Great House, what and who serve as witnesses, what and who are being witnessed, and what and who are being remembered and forgotten for what purposes related to the telling of the past, the living in the present, and the imaginings of the future?

Certainly, over the past several years (and, in some select cases, even decades), there have been concerted efforts at plantation sites in the United States (including Thomas Jefferson's Monticello and George Washington's Mount Vernon) to present more information about enslaved people during plantation tours and in the materials at the sites and on their respective websites.[21] The official Rose Hall Great House website, however, revolves around the myth of Annie Palmer. That focus extends into the Rose Hall tours, as Annie Palmer's experiences, "voice," and "presence" remain pivotal throughout the tours while enslaved women's experiences, voices, and presence are neglected, ignored, and silenced.[22] Yet it is not that these tours entirely discount the "presence" of enslaved women. At random moments during our tour, a couple of Black women appeared seemingly out of nowhere acting as ghosts of enslaved women engaged in household duties; they were dressed completely in white, and their faces were powdered white as well.

They expressed no words or utterances at any point in their performance. What were we to make of their ghostly appearances? How did their liminality function as a witness to slavery's past without personifying and demonstrating the horrors of bondage? How did their bodies simultaneously represent a palpable, corporeal marker for slavery while serving as neutralized, anesthetized tourist props? Why are the names of enslaved women and their actual lived experiences secretly cast into the shadows of the Rose Hall Great House?

I decided to research Rose Hall Plantation because of its historic importance and its contemporary usage. This critical interdisciplinary examination of the contemporary tours at Rose Hall Great House also includes an analysis of the principal source of the tours, of the legend itself: de Lisser's 1929 novel. By utilizing Rose Hall as a case study, my intentions (and interventions) are the particular voices and silences in the daily tours as a lens through which to understand how representations at Rose Hall Great House (and other such tourist sites of slavery) are neither innocuous nor incidental. Even though slavery's ritualized, routinized acts of terror and trauma are not presented during the Rose Hall Great House daily tours, these gaps and silences surrounding the stories of enslaved people in these tours today become a contemporary form of perpetual violence reified and reinscribed at this site of slavery.

FICTION PASSING AS HISTORY AT THE ROSE HALL GREAT HOUSE

The Rose Hall Great House tours present one striking example of the silences at a site of slavery. The tours represent fiction passing as history or in the process of being passed on as history; the tours serve to blur and blend history and fiction. They underscore and encapsulate in many ways the multiple meanings embedded in the French word *histoire*, including the historical accounting of events and the fictional telling of stories.[23] "History" is often understood in the public sphere as the "real," "truthful" accounting of past events, people, and places. It is frequently presented to the general public as an objective, authentic, and official rendering of the past, without any mention of how historians and other scholars create history and histories based on their subjective hypotheses, interpretations, and analyses of the past (embedded in and wedded to the usage and deployment of select sources and materials). Moreover, documents, specifically primary sources, are not necessarily presented as perspectives of the past.

Depending on our subjective valuation of respective authors and/or witnesses from the past, we identify and prioritize some materials and perspectives as definitive, reliable sources about the past, while we deem others as unreliable interlocuters of the past. As a result, the stories of eighteenth-century white male historians and enslavers have become a crucial foundation of the canon of Jamaican history, even as their reflections on Jamaica are inextricably linked to and vividly demonstrate their racist, sexist, classist, and ethnocentrist perceptions of people of African descent and the institution of slavery.[24] These works remain foundational primary source texts on slavery in Jamaica. Conversely, although there are numerous slave narratives of previously enslaved people in the United States, a similar extensive corpus simply does not exist in the Caribbean.[25]

As a result of the prolific writing of some white enslavers in Jamaica, the copious plantation records about slavery in Jamaica from the perspective of white witnesses of that era and with limited first-person narratives by enslaved persons in Jamaica (specifically, those of Abu Bakr al-Siddiq, James Williams, and Archibald John Monteath/Monteith), perhaps it is not surprising that these silences have been filled at Rose Hall Plantation with a legend about a white witch.[26] The historical production of narratives of slavery does not emerge only in the creation of sources penned or spoken into existence; instead, historical production also occurs in the creation of archives that house such materials, the creation of narratives and stories about these accounts, and the historical analysis about the events.[27] Moreover, although we often conceptualize history as happening in a chronological manner, historical production is not always linear but encapsulates interlocking processes of the creation of narratives and, indeed, the construction of silences within these narratives across different moments of time.

As Michel-Rolph Trouillot states, though, "not all silences are equal." The production of historical narratives also does not emerge out of a sociocultural, political, or economic vacuum. Instead, systemic forms of oppression and related power dynamics engender the establishment and positioning of narratives at the center or at the margins of history, if they are even deemed significant enough to be present at all. As Maboula Soumahoro, a French scholar of Ivorian descent, posits, it is important to understand the way "power operates through silence and invisibility." She questions: "Who is in charge of that narration of things past, and what is the current use of the past and this, of course, constructed, even construed, past for the present? . . . How does power unfold in this production, circulation, understanding, even memory (but all of that meaning), in the control, the narration, of the past?"[28] Due to the particular forces of and power relegated to white entitlement and white supremacy, narratives about slavery have long centered and prioritized the stories of whites, especially the perspectives of white men who enslaved people of African descent (and to a lesser extent the white women who also occupied this position of dominance). This specific centering of the white gaze has unleashed a particular unfolding of the production, circulation, understanding, memory, control, and narration of slavery's past, as well as the afterlives of slavery.

Along with the limited first-person narratives of enslaved people in Jamaica, the neo–slave narratives and slavery novels that appeared in the late twentieth century and that continue to appear in the twenty-first century have offered a creative gateway to restoring, reconstructing, and reimagining the lives of previously enslaved people in the Americas.[29] These neo–slave narratives and slavery novels constitute an integral aspect of the public memorialization of slavery.[30] Grappling with the particularities of memory and slavery, literary icon Toni Morrison engages in a form of "literary archaeology" in her novel (and neo–slave narrative) *Beloved* as a particular avenue to reimagine, repair, and redress "unspeakable" aspects of slavery. Morrison concentrates on the crucial work of "rememory"—of ripping, pulling, and drawing aside the veil in order to reveal slavery's "unspeakable" and "unspoken" memories.[31] As Morrison describes, "On the basis of some information and a little bit of guesswork you journey to a site to see what remains were left behind and to reconstruct the world that these remains imply. What makes it fiction is the nature of the imaginative act: my reliance on the image— on the remains—in addition to recollection, to yield up a kind of truth."[32]

This truth that Morrison summons functions as a historical and literary hinge between the past and the present, existing in a realm between history and fiction. In both Morrison's *Beloved* and de Lisser's *The White Witch of Rosehall*, fragments and traces of history (specifically the invocation of Margaret Garner and Annie Palmer, respectively) serve as the cornerstone of the fictional stories these authors weave around two specific women. However, Morrison's use of "rememory" in *Beloved* represents a reconstitutive process in a literary context that reconstructs the individual and collective lives of enslaved people in the African diaspora. In her exploration of the "unspeakable" and "unspoken" memories, Morrison unveils the corners and crevices of the interiority of enslaved people's lives.

Though Morrison's invocation of rememory in *Beloved* is often loosely defined and described as "memory" or memories of the past, her inclusion of rememory is not solely synonymous with memory. Instead, rememory involves a more capacious portal and process of remembrance related to the individual, collective, and intergenerational experiencing, forgetting, and remembering of a traumatic past inextricably linked to bondage. Rememories provide the characters in *Beloved* with a process through which to remember and reengage with past traumatic occurrences and experiences, as well as to initiate a process of navigating through and transcending these experiences. This reconnection with and reconstruction of their past provide the characters with a different reengagement with, although not necessarily liberation from, their past, present, and future experiences. Moreover, as poet and literary scholar Yvette Christiansë critically cautions, "Morrison's work, in making visible the active forgetting of some by others, complicates and resists our desire to read her fiction as a simple kind of memory work defined by the positive recovery of that which has been left out of the historical record."[33] Instead, from Morrison's novels, as Christiansë expounds, "each posing the question of how to witness, of who is eligible to witness and for whom, there is the insistent and visible inscription of gaps and silences, performing and redoubling what the diegetic aspiration of each novel stages, namely, the necessity of remembering forgetting."[34]

The "unspeakable" and "unspoken" silences related to Rose Hall emerge from interlocking myriad angles and moments. Given this conundrum, how do we engage in a process or processes of addressing and redressing these gaps and silences? How do we understand the blurred lines at Rose Hall between history and fiction? How do we comprehend the fixation on Annie Palmer and the simultaneous refusal to recognize the enslaved people who labored at Rose Hall in the tours? How do we critically process the relationship between real and fictionalized representations of slavery in these tours? How do we grasp the spurious speculations of history and the turn to fiction at this plantation site? In the wake of the Rose Hall Great House, history and fiction intermingle and deploy what notable Saint Lucian poet and playwright Derek Walcott aptly describes as a "deep amnesiac blow."[35] The presentation of the "history" of slavery at Rose Hall becomes a theatrical farce, with this particular "amnesiac blow" dominated by the enchantment and enthrallment of the legend of the White Witch of Rose Hall. Instead of the tours being utilized as a channel for rememory (processes of recognition, reckoning, recuperation, and redress with the troubled and troubling past of slavery and its afterlives), the tours present a refusal of rememory, a refusal of entry of the actual stories and experiences of enslaved people at Rose Hall. In the tours, enslaved people are only allowed entry in the form of real Jamaican women acting the part of enslaved ghosts who are silenced, not allowed to express any word or utterance at all.

FROM "GHOSTS" IN THE TOURS TO "GHOSTS" IN THE ARCHIVES

The ghostly presence of enslaved women in the contemporary Rose Hall Great House tours serves as an extension of the process of disavowal, which is often deeply entrenched in the archives, in the "historical record" of slavery. As Christina Sharpe asserts, "Those of us who teach, write, and think about slavery and its afterlives encounter myriad silences and ruptures in time, space, history, ethics, research, and method as we do our work."[36] "There are," Sharpe suggests, "specific ways that Black scholars of slavery get wedged in the partial truths of the archives while trying to make sense of their silences, absences, and modes of dis/appearance. The methods most readily available to us sometimes, oftentimes, force us into positions that run counter to what we know."[37] For Black scholars of slavery, she states, "our knowledge, of slavery and Black being in slavery, is gained from our studies, yes, but also in excess of those studies; it is gained through the kinds of knowledge from and of the everyday, from what Dionne Brand calls 'sitting in the room with history.'"[38]

Copious scholars have delineated the myriad challenges associated with mining the archives, as well as the ubiquitous experiences of "sitting in the room with history," attempting to tease out the individual and collective voices and perspectives of enslaved persons in the Caribbean and, indeed, throughout the African diaspora. The work of historian Marisa Fuentes reminds us of the oft-highlighted precarious position of enslaved women and their "dispossessed lives" and "mutilated historicity."[39] As Fuentes avows, "Enslaved women appear as historical subjects through the form and content of archival documents in the manner in which they lived: spectacularly violated, objectified, disposable, hypersexualized, and silenced."[40] Fuentes explains that the "violence is transferred from the enslaved bodies to the documents that count, condemn, assess, and evoke them, and we receive them in this condition. Epistemic violence originates from the knowledge produced about enslaved women by white men and women in this society, and that knowledge is what survives in archival form."[41] As a result, declares Fuentes, "the enslaved body, first damaged by the system of slavery, in the archive again succumbs to historical power."[42] Yet as Fuentes pointedly demands, "By reckoning unflinchingly with our methods and ethical practices as historians, our responsibility to our sources and subjects long dead, we might historically present what has typically been unrepresentable."[43]

By focusing on the early nineteenth century, I have grappled with elements of archival silence and archival violence that Fuentes highlights in her work, and I have sought to address the gaps, erasures, and silences of slavery at Rose Hall that are intricately rooted in the limitations of the archives. In this spirit, I not only illuminate the problematic ways slavery continues to be reconstructed and performed at the Rose Hall Great House tourist site (as symptomatic of a broader amnesia about slavery and enslaved people of African descent) but also utilize archival materials to name the bondswomen, bondsmen, and bondschildren at Rose Hall Plantation in order to begin to explore and reconstruct aspects of their lived experiences at this particular plantation.

Few records exist about the intimate personal lives and perspectives of enslavers of Rose Hall beyond random references to marriage, death, and property
ownership. Although a chapter on white enslavers might be expected, even assumed, no such chapter exists in this work. Instead, I offer a brief summary of the
enslavers of Rose Hall and its previous name, True Friendship, at the end of chapter 5, which covers the contemporary tours at Rose Hall.[44] I purposefully decided
this work would not contain a chapter dedicated to the white enslavers of Rose
Hall. Instead, their stories are integrated within the framework of those they
claimed as their human property, those enslaved Jamaicans who made Rose Hall
Plantation possible. For generations, histories about the institution of slavery
have underscored the development of white enslavers and their respective plantations, in some cases highlighting and centering their diaries and journals while
simultaneously pushing enslaved people's lives to the borders as background information in order to present the "central" story of white enslavers.[45] Instead, I
chose to focus on the lives of enslaved people and position the stories of white
enslavers, overseers, and bookkeepers in the margins as background information
and primarily within endnotes. In a similar vein, there has been heightened attention to white women enslavers over the past several years.[46] Due to the substantial and singular emphasis on Annie Palmer regarding Rose Hall Plantation, I did
not want to focus on white women enslavers in this book. They are an important
subject but not the central topic of this book. I leave this to other scholars to pursue in a thoughtful manner.

The purpose of this microhistory of Rose Hall is to consider multiple lenses to
explore both the history and the afterlives of slavery at Rose Hall. Even though
the Rose Hall Great House remains a popular tourist site, and even though there
is a directly related popular novel published by a prolific Jamaican writer, neither Rose Hall's history as a site of slavery nor the novel related to it has garnered significant scholarly attention. This work centers on revealing the names
and selected experiences of the enslaved persons who lived, labored, and, whenever possible, loved at Rose Hall Plantation. As a result of the looming tale of the
White Witch of Rose Hall, their own names and lives have been cast aside or at
times positioned in the background in order to highlight the myths about Annie
Palmer.

In her article "Venus in Two Acts," literary scholar Saidiya Hartman asks a
seemingly simple yet deeply provocative question: "And how does one tell impossible stories?"[47] In exploring this question, she poses other discerning queries
and reflections about the archive and history: "Is it possible to exceed or negotiate the constitutive limits of the archive? By advancing a series of speculative ar-

guments and exploiting the capacities of the subjunctive ... in fashioning a narrative, which is based upon archival research, and by that I mean a critical reading of the archive that mimes the figurative dimensions of history, I intended both to tell an impossible story and to amplify the impossibility of its telling."[48] Hartman describes her "method guiding this writing practice" as "critical fabulation."[49] She clearly affirms: "The intent of this practice is not to *give voice* to the slave, but rather to imagine what cannot be verified, a realm of experience which is situated between two zones of death—social and corporeal death—and to reckon with the precarious lives which are visible only in the moment of their disappearance."[50] For Hartman, it "is an impossible writing which attempts to say that which resists being said (since dead girls are unable to speak). It is a history of an unrecoverable past; it is a narrative of what might have been or could have been; it is a history written with and against the archive."[51]

In order to begin (re)positioning enslaved people from the margins to the center, the very first chapters of this book present the names and experiences of enslaved persons at Rose Hall. Because of the limited form and content of the archival record, I have portrayed enslaved persons by teasing out the bits and pieces of their stories in the records. In the spirit of Hartman's "critical fabulation," I have explored aspects of their lives by selectively and purposefully imagining what might have been their particular understandings of their individual and collective experiences. To be clear, these first chapters are historically grounded narratives; they are not fiction. Some scholars have invoked the moniker "speculative history" as a way of engaging in a process of legitimizing the imaginative, analytical processes of crafting history.[52] Although I understand the desire to name these processes with a particular term, I also recognize the need to directly define and describe these imaginative, analytical processes *as history*. As historian Mark Mazower posits, "History is, above all, ... an exercise in imagination based on facts, which is why it's not novel writing ... and without imagination the history people write is pretty dull."[53] In her own work on the Hemingses of Monticello, historian Annette Gordon-Reed avers: "History is to a great degree an imaginative enterprise; when writing it or reading it, we try to see the subjects in their time and space."[54] Even while "the connections will not be perfect—we cannot really know exactly what it meant to be [any person living in the past]—we have to reference what we know of human beings as we try to reconstruct and establish a context for their lives."[55] Although recognizing that historians "often warn of the danger of 'essentializing' when making statements about people of the past," as Gordon-Reed asserts, "there are, in fact, some elements of the human condition that have existed forever, transcending time and space. If there were none, and if historians did not try to connect to those elements (consciously or unconsciously), historical writing would be simply incomprehensible."[56]

(UN)SILENCING SLAVERY

With the legend and legacy of slave ownership at Rose Hall Plantation in mind, my archival investigation concentrates on Rose Hall Plantation in the early decades of the nineteenth century, ending with the Baptist War (also referred to as the Christmas Rebellion) of 1831–32. This slave revolt began on December 27, 1831, during the Christmas holiday period and continued into January 1832. In the actual revolt and in its wake, white planters murdered several hundred enslaved people.[57] They utilized brute force and "judicial executions" in order to punish enslaved people who were involved in (or thought to be involved in) this revolt. Moreover, in the aftermath of the revolt, whites seemed particularly motivated to kill enslaved people for minor offenses in order to demonstrate their power, as well as to deter enslaved people from engaging in any future rebellious acts. This slave uprising, conceived of and executed by enslaved people, served as the death knell for slavery in Jamaica and throughout the British slavocracy in the Caribbean. In fact, in 1833, less than two years after this revolt, the British Parliament declared the passage of the Slavery Abolition Act. On August 28, 1833, this act received royal assent, and it became effective as of August 1, 1834. Although this revolt, like many revolts and insurrections in Jamaica and the Americas, compromised the integrity of the institution of slavery, it was not the singular reason for the passage of the Slavery Abolition Act. Nonetheless, the revolt and the aftermath of violence certainly quickened the parliamentary process of abolition in Britain.

Examining these final decades of slavery in Jamaica, I am especially interested in unveiling the multifaceted aspects of enslaved people's lived experiences at Rose Hall, particularly enslaved women's experiences. In order to reveal the lives of enslaved people at Rose Hall, I examined the plantation records of Rose Hall during these early decades of the nineteenth century. In addition to sites in Jamaica, I examined materials on Rose Hall and slavery in Montego Bay housed in England at the National Archives in Kew Gardens and the Special Collections at the University College London Library. The archival materials for this period, located in Jamaica's National Archives in Spanish Town and the National Library of Jamaica in Kingston, provide information about the workings of Rose Hall Plantation (e.g., the annual Crop Accounts and triennial Registers of Returns of Slaves). The Registers of Returns of Slaves (often referred to simply as the slave registers), which are available at the Jamaica Archives in Spanish Town and the National Archives in Kew Gardens, provide specific information about individual enslaved people at Rose Hall. Following the Abolition of the Slave Trade Act in 1807 in Great Britain and responding to heightened pressures from abolitionists, the British government agreed to consider the enactment of a bill requiring a registration of enslaved people. Such a registration process was proposed to alleviate the possibility of illegal trafficking of African captives to British colonies. After implementing this registration in the Crown Colony of Trinidad in 1812, the British Parliament attempted to establish this slave registration process throughout its colonies. Some colonial legislative bodies in the British Caribbean, including the House of Assembly of Jamaica (often referred to as the Jamaican Assembly), initially resisted the Registry Bill. However, the Jamaican Assembly adopted this slave registration bill in 1816 and required these returns from enslavers in Jamaica beginning in 1817. This registration procedure generally transpired on a triennial basis in the British Empire; however, this was not consistent for all of the British colonies.[58] In Jamaica, slave registers began in 1817, and they continued on a triennial basis until 1832. Once instituted in Jamaica, the Registry Bill was not primarily utilized as a way to eliminate the illegal trafficking of African captives; rather, the Jamaican Assembly deployed it as a tool to apply heightened pressure on enslavers to achieve natural increase, or the increase in the number of live births, on their plantations and throughout Jamaica. Proprietors received tax breaks if they demonstrated they had achieved natural increase in their triennial registers. At the same time, however, penalties and fees related to incomplete registers did not result in complete compliance.[59]

As was the case with other Jamaican proprietors and enslavers, John Rose Palmer would have been expected to abide by the dictates of the Registry Bill for Rose Hall Plantation. Archival materials do not specify the exact date in 1818 that John Rose Palmer first arrived in Jamaica from his home in England. As the new proprietor of the plantations of his late great-uncle John Palmer, he may very well have brought with him ambitious plans for Rose Hall Plantation (as well as the neighboring Palmyra Plantation).[60] Certainly, he was greeted with a fairly substantial enslaved population. The first slave register for Rose Hall (the slave register for 1817) was completed the year before John Rose Palmer's arrival. This 1817 slave register lists 79 enslaved males and 73 enslaved females at Rose Hall, a total of 152 enslaved people.[61] Unlike a significant number of absentee slave owners who resided in England and not in Jamaica, John Rose Palmer chose to live at Rose Hall between 1818 and the time of his death in 1827. He was duly presented as proprietor and receiver for Rose Hall Plantation for the triennial slave registers of 1820, 1823, and 1826. The 1820 slave register for Rose Hall records 71 enslaved males and 71 enslaved females, a total of 142 enslaved people;[62] the 1823 slave register lists 71 enslaved males and 64 enslaved females, a total of 135 enslaved people;[63] the 1826 slave register lists 61 enslaved males and 62 enslaved females, a total of 123 enslaved people;[64] and the 1829 slave register lists 53 enslaved males and 62 enslaved females, a total of 115 enslaved people.[65] The final triennial slave register of 1832 for Rose Hall notes 51 enslaved males and 61 enslaved females, a total of 112 enslaved people.[66]

On my initial research trip in July 2014 to Jamaica's National Archives in Spanish Town, while reviewing the selected slave registers there, I encountered a three-volume set of weekly handwritten journal entries entitled the Rose Hall Journal (1817–32), penned by the white overseers at Rose Hall Plantation.[67] The time period of these journal entries coincidentally overlaps with Annie Palmer's time at the plantation, from approximately March 1820 (when she married John Rose Palmer at Mount Pleasant, in the parish of St. James in Jamaica) until she left Rose Hall in 1829–30, just a few years after John Rose Palmer's death in November 1827 in Jamaica.

Outside of the triennial slave registers providing a census of enslaved people at Rose Hall (including the total number of enslaved females and males, with additional notes concerning recent births and deaths on the plantation), the Rose Hall Journal represents the only other extant document revealing aspects of the daily routines at Rose Hall for enslaved people, as well as events deemed noteworthy on this plantation.

In approximately a thousand handwritten pages, the overseers who penned the Rose Hall Journal recorded information on the daily occurrences at this plantation, categorizing enslaved people who labored there based on their designated work groups (referred to as "gangs" in this journal and in other plantation records), as well as on their primary jobs and duties on the plantation (e.g., field worker, midwife, cook, cooper, carpenter, etc.). The overseers also noted on a weekly basis how many enslaved women were pregnant, how many enslaved people were "runaways," "invalids," "taking days," and "in the Great House." They did not record individual names of enslaved people in their charting of how many were assigned to which gangs and jobs in a given week. Only the additional brief notations included references to specific enslaved people who died, enslaved women who gave birth, and individual runaways in terms of when they departed and/or when they returned or were brought back to Rose Hall and whether they were punished for their actions.

In the Rose Hall Journal there is very little sense of enslaved people's lives outside of their work positions and related duties on the plantation. The overseers offered no information about the enslaved people's particular intimate experiences, for example, their individual or familial morning routines before they commenced their respective duties on the plantation. We assume that enslaved women with young children rose early to breastfeed their children and also perhaps to carve out time (no matter how briefly in the early hours of the morning) to commune with partners, friends, and other family members. Unlike other enslaved mothers in nearby or faraway plantations, these enslaved women did not have to serve as wet nurses to Annie Palmer's children, as she and John Rose Palmer did not have any children.[68] However, this fact in and of itself did not necessarily translate to enslaved mothers at Rose Hall receiving preferential treatment or extended time to breastfeed their children in the morning or at any other time of the day or night.[69]

As is often the case with such slave registers and plantation journals, limited information is offered about the intimate relationships between enslaved people. For example, in the triennial slave registers and in the Rose Hall Journal, notes about the births of enslaved children on the plantation specifically indicate their respective mothers; however, no fathers (whether enslaved or freed Black men or white men) are included in reference to any of these children. Certainly, this reflects the racialized, gendered, and classed dimensions of a slavocracy deeply embedded in the juridical doctrine of *partus sequitur ventrem*, a Latin phrase essentially meaning "that which is brought forth follows the womb/belly" or often simply as "offspring follows belly."[70] This principle dictated that the enslaved or free status of a child followed that of their mother. Besides the actual "status" of enslaved children, such records provide limited insight about the relationships, connections, and tensions between enslaved parents, as well as interactions with other members within Rose Hall's enslaved community.[71] What emerges, nevertheless, in the Rose Hall Journal and the slave registers is a sense of collective (and possibly communal) experiences of slavery that included the intergenerational presence of selected families at Rose Hall. The presence of multiple generations coexisting at Rose Hall reveals neither a harmonious nor a contentious enslaved community or even both aspects transpiring there simultaneously over time. The records do not provide explicit descriptions or references to the interactions, friendships, and other relationships between enslaved people outside of their individual and collective labor routines on this sugar plantation.

The archival sources I utilized are exclusively related to Rose Hall, and I do not intend to present any general conclusions about sugar plantations in Jamaica or in the Caribbean more broadly. Over the past several decades, there has been extensive historical work on plantations in Jamaica. Indeed, a frequent mantra in scholarly discussions is the ongoing need for more work still to be done on slavery in Caribbean countries other than Jamaica. For my part, and given the work already completed on slavery and sugar plantations in Jamaica, I was specifically interested in a focused case study on Rose Hall as a way to explore the archival material on this plantation and to offer a counternarrative to the myth and legend of the White Witch of Rose Hall.

What follows is not a "day in the life" of any enslaved person at Rose Hall. Part of the reason for this limitation revolves around the restricted and scattered pieces of enslaved people's daily routines in the Rose Hall Journal. The weekly journal entries primarily focus on the duties of those laboring in the sugarcane fields, with only partial references to the work of craftspeople such as the enslaved carpenters and coopers. In order to offer some sense of the individual and collective lives of enslaved people at Rose Hall, I present possible interconnected elements of their lives. I also wanted to contextualize the limited shreds of information provided in the Rose Hall Journal with possible questions and scenarios that could deepen readers' understanding and views of enslaved people beyond simply their names on the pages of a plantation journal. Instead of a day in the life of an enslaved person at Rose Hall, I reveal possible scenarios of enslaved people's connections and the meanings they may have ascribed to particular events. By doing so, I create potential narratives about their lives in order to display on the page how to move from bits and fragments of information to possible lenses of understanding. Instead of discussing how we write history with limited archival fragments, I use the early chapters and others in the book as a pedagogical and scholarly demonstration of the actual writing of history based on these archival fragments.

This book proffers Rose Hall Plantation from three different modes of history-making and history-telling.[72] The first three chapters center the archival research with historical interjections and interventions and tease out the possible individual and collective lived experiences of enslaved people at Rose Hall. The fourth chapter focuses on Herbert G. de Lisser's historical novel in his creation of the White Witch of Rose Hall myth and examines selected dimensions of his literary imaginings of particular themes and tropes related to bondage and freedom. The fifth chapter examines the histrionic enactment of these topics in de Lisser's novel within the ongoing contemporary tours at the Rose Hall Great House as these tours and weddings create a stream of income for the property owners, an elite white American family based in Delaware. These three modes of history-making and history-telling all evolve around the untold, interlocking, multiple erasure(s) of enslaved women, especially the physical, psychic, and sexual violences they endured, as well as the specific privileging of white supremacist, imperialist, heterosexist, capitalist frameworks.

Presenting a descriptive narrative of the labors of enslaved people in their various positions on this plantation and extracting additional information from scraps of archival material offer some semblance of their lived experiences as human beings, a way of "reminding all of us of the totality of black subjectivity."[73] How might they have understood their place, their sense of belonging, at Rose Hall Plantation? In what ways did they attempt to carve out and (re)claim aspects of their humanity by deploying individual and collective acts and processes of resistance? In what instances were they able to create and engage in different manifestations and expressions of their sociocultural identities? Can we utilize the records, specifically the Rose Hall Journal, as a medium and tool for articulating the experiences of enslaved people still shrouded in and buried by the legend of the White Witch of Rose Hall, even as the names and experiences of enslaved women, men, and children who labored at Rose Hall remain unspoken, unremembered, and unmemorialized at the present site? During the tours, we do not learn about Panella giving birth to her daughter Daisy a few days before Christmas in 1817.[74] Nothing is said about the time when "Kate Delivered of a Still Born child" in August 1824.[75] And there are no words uttered about the death of Celia's twenty-five-year-old son, Lewis, in 1818 when he was run over by a wagon or when sixty-year-old African-born Peachy took her last breath in early March 1818.[76]

Even as the voices of enslaved women such as Panella, Kate, Celia, and Peachy remain stifled and silenced in the contemporary Rose Hall Great House tours, even as enslavers of the days of yore denied their maximal humanity, the actual presence and experiences of enslaved women could not be entirely silenced. The first part of this book's title invokes Michel-Rolph Trouillot's *Silencing the Past: Power and the Production of History*, and I emphasize the process of what I refer to as "(un)silencing slavery." To be clear, slavery was not a quiet, secretive, or silent institution. Rather, it was resounding and deafening in its private and public, covert and overt demonstrations of pain, power, terror, torture, and trauma—in the notices of slave auctions and sales; in the regular, persistent, and often relentless advertisements for runaway slaves; in the accounting and calculations of the births and deaths of enslaved women, men, and children; in the refusal to grant the most fundamental human rights and civic privileges to enslaved persons; and in the practice of brandings, whippings, maimings, rapes, decapitations, murders, and executions, as well as other forms of emotional, psychic, psychological, physical, and spiritual violations and violences. The archives have often functioned and been deployed as "historical cover" for the depth and breadth of these violences.

The first chapter begins lifting the veil and "unsilencing" slavery at Rose Hall by uncloaking archival records and teasing out individual and collective refer-

ences to enslaved people in the Rose Hall Journal. Regardless of the systemic processes utilized to control and confine enslaved people and to silence any actions
not in the service of the purpose and objectives of the Jamaican slavocracy, enslaved people permeated and pierced through the archival records of Rose Hall
Plantation. Beginning in the first chapter, historical speculation serves as a com-
pass and medium of looking at, bearing witness to, listening to, and harnessing
what French scholar of Senegalese descent Mame-Fatou Niang renders as "the
noisy silences that have haunted" us.[77] Such "silences," she maintains, "can be as
eloquent as the noises." In the process of unsilencing slavery at Rose Hall Plantation I have purposefully integrated unanswerable questions and suppositions
about the lived experiences of the enslaved people who abided there. As you
experience the journey of the ideas and narratives within this book, know that
these queries serve as a way of broadening, of opening, our imagining(s) and un-
derstanding(s) about the vast humanity of enslaved people at Rose Hall. As one
of my mentors and eminent historian Mary Beth Norton often reminds her students, "You can't answer questions you don't ask." My sole corollary to this would
be that even if you cannot answer a question, still ask it. There will always be unanswered questions about the lived experiences of enslaved people. However,
the questions we pose and the stories we imagine, consider, and tease out about
their lives provide a vital lens in crafting a human and humane story of enslaved
people.

   History-telling itself serves as a modality to express some sense of the fullness
of enslaved people's spirits, the capaciousness of Black humanity, and a reclama-
tion, affirmation, and declaration that enslaved Black lives mattered at Rose Hall
Plantation and on all plantations in the Americas. The unrelenting timbres and
sounds of slavery and its silences permeate the Rose Hall Journal, and I ask you to
attend to these "silences"—the "noisy silences" of dehumanization and marginalization etched throughout the accounting of enslaved people's laborious routines
at Rose Hall. Yet not all silences were noisy and satiated with contempt and con-
demnation. Some enslaved people at Rose Hall may have generated, protected,
and maintained silences beyond the recognition and gaze of Rose Hall's enslavers
and overseers, beyond the veil of the documents housed in the archives—sacred
silences not to be shared or detected by those deemed outside the boundaries
of this knowledge and community of knowers. Even as the overseers scribbled
their brief notes and numbers in the Rose Hall Journal as a way of accounting for
the enslaved people and their respective duties and responsibilities, enslaved people at Rose Hall were also noting, cherishing, and attending to their individual
and collective thoughts, feelings, words, actions, realities, secrets, and dreams of
freedom.

Names	Colour	age	African or Creole	Remarks
Males				
Aaron	Negro	30	African	
Apollo	Negro	36	African	
Adonis	Negro	25	Creole	
Andrew	Negro	60	African	
Buck	Negro	40	Creole	
Bottom	Negro	48	African	
Bryan	Negro	32	African	
Charles	Negro	40	Creole	
Cæsar	Negro	25	Creole	
10. Craigie	Negro	50	African	
Colin	Negro	30	African	
Dublin	Negro	30	Creole	
Daniel	Negro	28	Creole	
Damon	Negro	38	African	
Fox	Negro	32	African	
George	Negro	25	Creole	
Gregory	Negro	40	African	Son to Hope
Gibbes	Negro	55	African	
Daniel	Negro	40	African	
20. Hannibal	Negro	40	African	
Henry	Negro	40	Creole	
Harder	Negro	21	Creole	
	Negro	53	African	Son to Cecelia
Hazard	Negro	50	African	

First colonial list of enslaved people at Rose Hall Plantation.
NA Kew, T71/202, fol. 540.

Names	Colour	Age	African & Creole	Remarks
	Negro	32	Creole	
Johnny	Negro	50	Creole	
John Parish	Negro	50	Creole	
Jannary	Negro	42	Creole	
Lewis-ney	Negro	70	African	
Lewis	Negro	35	Creole	
Luke	Negro	60	African	Son to Laha
Mackay	Negro	40	Creole	
Mereny	Negro	25	Creole	
Mac Quire	Negro	19	Creole	Son to Laha
March	Negro	50	African	
Nab	Negro	50	African	
Neath	Negro	45	African	
Nestor	Negro	40	African	
Orpheus	Negro	50	African	
Osenes	Negro	50	African	
40. Peurgen	Negro	40	African	
Patrick	Negro	45	African	
Plate	Negro	40	African	
Paton	Negro	50	African	
Perth	Negro	55	African	Son to Rachael
Peter	Negro	18	Creole	
Prague	Negro	70	African	
Ralph	Negro	40	African	
Ross	Negro	27	African	
Richard	Negro	43	Creole	son to brother
Sambo	Negro	40	Creole	
Smith	Negro	33	Creole	
Scott	Negro	41	African	
Shannon	Negro	28	Creole	

First colonial list of enslaved people at Rose Hall Plantation.
NA Kew, T71/202, fol. 541.

Names	Colour	Age	African or Creole	Remarks
Titus	Negro	55	African	
Ulysses	Negro	40	Creole	
Washington	Negro	45	African	
William	Mulatto	19	Creole	Son to Sambo Sarah
William Scot	Negro	30	Creole	
William	Negro	30	Creole	
60 Natt	Negro	45	African	
Ben	Negro	17	Creole	son to Augusta
Baxter	Negro	17	Creole	son to Rebecca
Pett	Negro	14	Creole	son to Augusta
Quaw	Negro	13	Creole	son to Dolia
Quipio	Negro	15	Creole	son to Polly
Hercules	Negro	9	Creole	
Archy	Negro	11	Creole	son to Zebra
Sam	Negro	11	Creole	Son to Dorinda
Mark	Negro	7	Creole	
70 Gloster	Negro	8	Creole	
Anthony	Negro	7	Creole	Son to Dorinda
North	Negro	6	Creole	son to Liddy
Parish	Negro	4	Creole	Son to Liddy
Paty	Negro	4	Creole	son to Susannah Johnston
James	Negro	4	Creole	son to Zebra
William	Negro	2	Creole	Son to Dorinda
Oliver	Negro	2	Creole	Son to Augusta
Thomas	Mulatto	1	Creole	son to Charlotte
79 Othello	Negro	1	Creole	Son to Quao
Females				
Augusta	Negro	38	African	

First colonial list of enslaved people at Rose Hall Plantation.
NA Kew, T71/202, fol. 542.

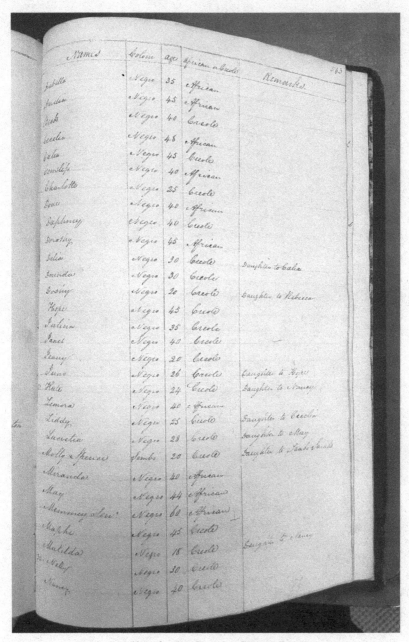

Names	Colour	age	African or Creole	Remarks.
Isabella	Negro	35	African	
Amelia	Negro	45	African	
Betts	Negro	40	Creole	
Cecilia	Negro	48	African	
Celia	Negro	45	Creole	
Conslife	Negro	40	African	
Charlotte	Negro	25	Creole	
Doves	Negro	40	African	
Daphiney	Negro	40	Creole	
Dorothy	Negro	45	African	
Delia	Negro	30	Creole	Daughter to Celia
Dorinda	Negro	30	Creole	
Dosiny	Negro	20	Creole	Daughter to Rebecca
Hope	Negro	45	Creole	
Juliana	Negro	35	Creole	
Janet	Negro	40	Creole	—
Jenny	Negro	20	Creole	
Juno	Negro	26	Creole	Daughter to Hope
Kate	Negro	24	Creole	Daughter to Nancy
Leonora	Negro	40	African	
Liddy	Negro	25	Creole	Daughter to Cecilia
Lucretia	Negro	28	Creole	Daughter to May
Molly & Spence	Sambo	20	Creole	Daughter to Sarah Sarah
Miranda	Negro	40	African	
May	Negro	44	African	
Mummey Leu.	Negro	60	African	
Mapha	Negro	45	Creole	
Malilda	Negro	18	Creole	Daughter to Nancy
Nelly	Negro	30	Creole	
Nancy	Negro	40	Creole	

First colonial list of enslaved people at Rose Hall Plantation.
NA Kew, T71/202, fol. 543.

Names.	Colour	Age	African or Creole	Remarks
Phœbe	Negro	25	Creole	
Polly	Negro	40	African	
Parthenia	Negro	20	Creole	Daughter to Zephney
Pavella	Negro	23	Creole	
Peachy	Negro	60	African	
Rosannah	Negro	30	Creole	Daughter to Celia
Ruth	Negro	40	African	
Rebecca	Negro	52	African	
42. Rachael	Negro	62	African	
Sarah	Sambo	40	Creole	
Susannah Scott	Negro	28	Creole	
Sabina	Negro	18	Creole	Daughter to May
Susannah Johnston	Negro	25	Creole	
Stella	Negro	32	African	
Mary	Negro	23	Creole	Daughter to Phœbe
Zebra	Negro	28	Creole	
Frances	Negro	19	Creole	
Frankey	Negro	18	Creole	
50. Gift	Negro	24	Creole	Daughter to Nancy
Susan	Negro	66	African	Daughter to Dorothy
Joan	Negro	19	Creole	
Hester	Negro	11	Creole	Daughter to May
Mary James	Mulatto	14	Creole	Daughter to Miranda
Betsy	Mulatto	13	Creole	Daughter to Rosannah
Bell	Negro	14	Creole	Daughter to Sambo Sarah
Fanny	Negro	14	Creole	Daughter to Celia
Mimmy Junr.	Negro	14	Creole	Daughter to Zephney
Flora	Negro	12	Creole	Daughter to Miranda
60. Peggy	Negro	14	Creole	Daughter to Stella
Justina	Negro	11	Creole	Daughter to May
				Daughter to Liddy

First colonial list of enslaved people at Rose Hall Plantation.
NA Kew, T71/202, fol. 544.

Names	Colour	Age	African or Creole	Remarks
Ironer	Negro	11	Creole	
Cynthia	Negro	11	Creole	Daughter to Augusta
Lisi	Negro	9	Creole	
Clara	Negro	11	Creole	Daughter to Zebra
Christianna	Negro	6	Creole	
Leanna	Negro	5	Creole	Daughter to Amanda
Hetty	Negro	6	Creole	Daughter to Zebra
Clarinda	Negro	5	Creole	
Doll	Negro	3	Creole	Daughter to Augusta
Jane Cranston	Mulatto	3	Creole	Daughter to Charlotte
Julian	Negro	2	Creole	Daughter to Sambo & Jacob
Helen	Negro	2	Creole	Daughter to Savannah ...

Males ...... Seventynine
Females ..... Seventythree
Total ...... One hundred fifty two

I Edward Mountague do swear, that the above List and Return, consisting of Three Sheets, is a true, perfect and complete List and Return, to the best of my knowledge and belief, in every particular therein mentioned, of all and every Slave and Slaves possessed by me as Receiver to Roll and Escroe, and reduced as most permanently settled, worked, or employed in the parish of Saint James, on the Twentyeighth day of June, one thousand eight hundred and seventeen, without fraud, deceit or evasion.

So help me God

Edw. Mountague

Sworn before me this Sixteenth day
of September 1817.

T. Phillpots.

First colonial list of enslaved people at Rose Hall Plantation.
NA Kew, T71/202, fol. 545.

A RETURN of SLAVES in the Parish of *Saint James on Rose Hall Estate* in the possession of *William Miller or William Heath* as *Receiver* on the *twenty eighth* day of *June* in the year of our Lord 1832.

MALES by last return — *Fifty three*
FEMALES — *Forty two*
TOTAL by last return — *One hundred and fifteen*

NAMES.	COLOUR.	AGE.	AFRICAN OR CREOLE.	REMARKS.	INCREASE, and cause thereof.	DECREASE, and cause thereof.
MALES.						
Edward Hall	Mulatto	2 5	Creole	Son of Mary Ann	By Birth	
James	Samboe	1 5	Creole	Son of Joana	By Birth	
Ned	Negro	5	Creole	Son of Bell	By Birth	
Duke	Negro	75	African			By Death
Hyde	Negro	70	African			By Death
Fox	Negro	65	African			By Death
Orange	Negro	64	African			By Death
Aleck	Negro	5	Creole	Son of Mary	By Death	
FEMALES.						
Joana	Negro	10	Creole	Daughter of Edward	By Birth	By Death
Jane	Mulatto	1 5	Creole	Daughter of Christiana	By Birth	
Sylvia	Negro	1 1	Creole	Daughter of Matilda	By Birth	
Beck	Negro	52	Creole			By Death
Lucretia	Negro	42	Creole			By Death
Roxana	Negro	5	Creole	Daughter of Bell		By Death
Nelly	Negro	45	Creole			By Death
					INCREASE. *Ten*	DECREASE. *Ten*

NUMBER of Slaves on the *twenty eighth* day of June 1832, *One hundred and eleven*
BIRTHS since last return *Ten*
DEATHS since last return *Ten*

I, *William Miller* do swear, that the above list and return, consisting of *one* sheet is a true, perfect, and complete list and return, to the best of my knowledge and belief, in every particular therein mentioned, of all and every slave and slaves possessed by me *as Receiver for Rose Hall Estate* considered as most permanently settled, worked, or employed in the parish of *Saint James* on the *twenty eighth* day of *June* in the year of our Lord one thousand eight hundred and thirty *three* without fraud, deceit, or evasion.

So HELP ME GOD.

William Miller

Sworn before me this *eighteenth* day
of September 1832.
George Cullen

Last colonial list of enslaved people at Rose Hall Plantation.
NA Kew, T71/223, fol. 91.

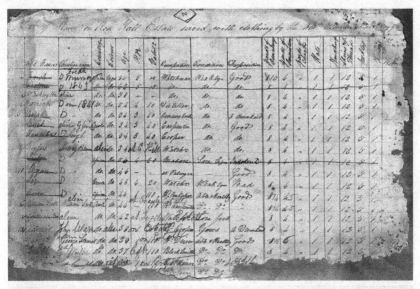

Annual clothing allowance list for Rose Hall Plantation, June 1828.
JARD, 1B/26, RHJ, vol. 3, fol. 2.

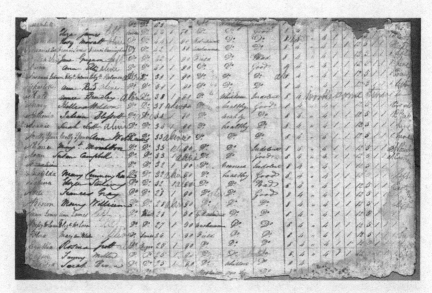

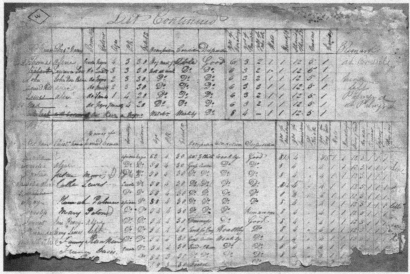

Annual clothing allowance list for Rose Hall Plantation, June 1828.
JARD, 1B/26, RHJ, vol. 3, fol. 3.

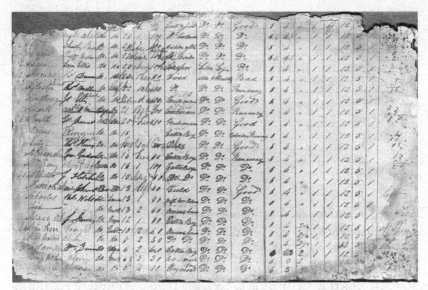

Annual clothing allowance list for Rose Hall Plantation, June 1828.
JARD, 1B/26, RHJ, vol. 3, fol. 4.

CHAPTER I

In the Wake of the Archive

As stated in my introduction, this book is not about all the intricacies and nuances of slavery at Rose Hall Plantation, nor is it a description of a day in the life of an enslaved person at Rose Hall. I do not have enough historical evidence to duly present either of those narratives. In the chapters that follow I provide some historical context about slavery in Jamaica, and I reference particular experiences and situations occurring throughout slaveocracies primarily in the Anglophone Caribbean. The purpose of this book is not to provide an in-depth contextualization of slavery in Jamaica. There are many comprehensive texts on the subject of Jamaican plantations, and I have highlighted a number of these major works in the endnotes of this book for your perusal. Whether this is the first book on slavery you are reading or whether you have read or even written articles and books on slavery, I recognize that you possess some basic information about slavery. You most likely know that slavery was a system that forced people of African descent into bondage, it was a system that restricted their rights and overworked and exploited them, and it was a system that incorporated whippings and other forms of violence. Some of this general information is provided in a cursory manner in secondary schools and, to a lesser degree, even in primary schools. Academic lessons on slavery in secondary schools often focus more on the jobs and labor of enslaved people, presenting them primarily as "field hands," and less on considering their full humanity and lived experiences.

I have chosen not to begin with the "usual" beginning, with information about white enslavers and the onerous duties performed by enslaved people at Rose Hall, including the range of socioeconomic functions they served at this plantation and other sugar plantations in the Caribbean. Part of the reason I do not start with the chapter on labor at Rose Hall is that I purposely want you to join with me (be alongside me) for the journey into the archival documents and what they reveal in a more holistic way. You may not have any sense of what it means to confront silences in the archives. I want you not only to enter the tour with me (and my daughter) as you did in the introduction but also to enter the archives and the documents with me—to see what is there and what is not. Given how much I rely on the Rose Hall Journal to construct this book, in this chapter I provide a lot of details about the journal, and I have included a few selected pages from the journal in this book for your perusal. It is important to note that not all plantation journals are the same; there is no universal format or template for plantation journals in Jamaica or across the sugar plantations in the Caribbean. As I have centered silences as part of the truths I am telling here, I want you to experience what I mean by silences in the documents, in the archives, in the novel, and on the tour. I want you to understand that although enslaved people were absolutely necessary for slavery to function at all, enslaved people were marginalized and objectified in the very documents that delineate the workings, profits, and accounting of slavery.

Like those on other plantations in Jamaica, Rose Hall's enslaved population included a combination of people born in communities in Africa and in the Americas. Nonetheless, from the archival documents, including the Rose Hall Journal, it is impossible to know how the lives of enslaved persons from different lands intermingled at Rose Hall outside of their regular work routines, which revolved around the harvesting of sugarcane for its profitable by-products. The Rose Hall Journal serves as a tangible reminder of what and who were deemed by white enslavers and overseers as important enough to be accounted for and recorded in the weekly journal entries. The columns of the Rose Hall Journal underscore what was considered valuable information as it related to the central purpose and productivity of Rose Hall as a sugar plantation. The weekly journal entries also reflected what and who were categorized as not valuable or only worthy of a cursory notation. Both the form and content of the Rose Hall Journal embody the denigration, devaluation, and disposability of enslaved people—the format of the journal, the organization of duties and responsibilities on this plantation arranged by rows and columns, and the brevity, placement, and marginalization of notes regarding the births and deaths of enslaved people.

It is truly impossible to re-create and reconstruct both the connections and the tensions between all of these enslaved people—the tribulations, traumas, and joys they may have shared (or withheld) at Rose Hall. Even so, by naming the enslaved persons who labored at Rose Hall, we at least begin to take one important and necessary step in identifying the people enslaved there beyond the mere numerical tallies of those alive and dead. In addition, in this chapter and in chapters 2 and 3, I also purposefully tease out possible narratives of the lives of these individuals in order to provide some contextualization of their individual lives, their humanity, and their communal lived experiences at Rose Hall.

Part of the purpose of chapters 1 and 2 and the book overall is to highlight the individual enslaved people at Rose Hall and some of their individualized experiences. Even though it would be sufficient to name some of the enslaved mothers and their children, which would provide a general sense of them, one of the purposes of this book is not solely to provide an overview of *some* of the enslaved women (and people) at Rose Hall. Rather, it is to name and include *all* of the information I have unearthed about these enslaved persons as individuals who had specific relationships and connections with others at Rose Hall and most likely at other Jamaican plantations. Every enslaved person at Rose Hall was special, though no more or no less special than any other enslaved person there. So each person's name is equally important in my telling of the story of Rose Hall, of the history of Rose Hall, of the truths of Rose Hall, no matter how much or how little information is available on each person. I include enslaved people whether their name appears briefly in one historical document or they are mentioned multiple times in several archival documents. In addition, providing these details for all named enslaved people, for all adults and children at Rose Hall (instead of a smaller, random group of them) between 1817 and 1832 serves as a way potentially to assist descendants of these enslaved people and others working on Rose Hall in the future to piece together the genealogies of countless families.

"DISTRIBUTION OF NEGROES" AND "DAILY OCCURRENCES" AT ROSE HALL

Spread out in front of me are pages and pages from the three volumes of the Rose Hall Journal. I have been looking at these handwritten pages for stretches of hours, days, weeks, and months. What I *want* to see and read are detailed and exhaustive letters, narratives, and stories written by enslaved people at Rose Hall Plantation about their experiences of labor, love, and life itself. Yet that is not what I have before me, and it is, of course, not what I expected to find in the plantation records housed in the Jamaican Archives in Spanish Town, Jamaica, and at the National Archives of the United Kingdom in Kew Gardens, London.

The Rose Hall Journal entries begin on Monday, March 17, 1817, and end on Saturday, November 10, 1832.[1] The varying penmanship styles indicate that several white overseers recorded information in the journal over the course of these fifteen years. The names of the overseers and bookkeepers are rarely recorded in the individual weekly journal entries. However, specific overseers and bookkeepers are mentioned in the journal when they are newly appointed, discharged, or transferred between the Rose Hall and Palmyra plantations.[2] It is possible that Rose Hall's white bookkeepers may also have contributed to some of these entries.[3] Although there are different overseers during this time period, the overall structure of the journal entries remains fairly consistent between Monday, March 17, 1817, and Saturday, January 17, 1829. However, a shift to a different overseer on Sunday, January 18, 1829, to the end of the journal entries on November 10, 1832, resulted in a change in the placement of sections of the entries.[4] In the final months of the journal, the overseer also included more comprehensive information about enslaved people (e.g., possible reasons why specific runaways might have absconded from Rose Hall, reasons why enslaved individuals were in the hospital, and a list of enslaved people in the great house and the overseer's house, including their name, age, and color). In addition, this overseer recorded visits by specific doctors, as well as the whites employed at Rose Hall.[5]

In these final months of the Rose Hall Journal, although no one recorded enslaved people's names systematically or consistently in the journal, whites employed on a short-term or long-term basis at Rose Hall are individually named in these entries under the heading of "White People Saving Deficiencies." Because of ongoing trepidation regarding the Black majority on Jamaican plantations (and throughout the British-controlled Caribbean islands generally), Jamaican deficiency laws required enslavers to employ a certain number of whites on their estates and businesses, and those proprietors who did not satisfy this law were required to pay deficiency fines on an annual basis. Although the laws were established because of the fear of slave revolts and as a defense against potential attacks from other European nations, the deficiency laws became viewed and deployed as a revenue-generating tool. The actual annual fees ranged over time; however, the required ratios remained constant in Jamaica—one white for every thirty enslaved persons. The Jamaican laws also stipulated one white for every 150 head of cattle and one white for every shop or tavern.[6]

Although the sporadic imperial and colonial surveillance of whites on Jamaican plantations became part of the workings of Rose Hall, the Rose Hall Journal concentrates on the systemic and persistent process of categorizing, controlling, surveilling, exploiting, and ordering human beings as human property based on the dictates of a slavocracy. In the Rose Hall Journal on the left side of page after page is the title "Distribution of Negroes." Immediately under that heading, overseers have noted specific months (with the years not consistently included on every page). On the very first full page of the journal (and this is the first entry of volume 1) are the words 1817 March. To the right of this month and year are six individual columns with dates, numbered from 17 to 22, Monday to Saturday. There is no seventh column for Sunday, March 23, seemingly out of respect for this day of rest from the usual arduous work routines on the plantation. Saturday, March 22, 1817, was a regular working day at Rose Hall. However, selected

Saturdays are often noted by the Rose Hall overseers as "Negroes Day," "Negroes Taking Day," or "Negroes in their Grounds." Enslaved people at Rose Hall were often granted selected Saturdays for cultivating their provision grounds; however, enslaved people at other Jamaican plantations often worked in their provision grounds on Friday afternoons.[7]

Jamaican laws required that enslaved people be granted, in addition to Sundays, particular periods of time or days away from working in the fields. These days were selected by resident enslavers and overseers.[8] In 1788 the Jamaican Assembly enacted the Consolidated Slave Law. This omnibus law addressed the treatment and punishment of enslaved people as a way to present ameliorative efforts with the intention of making slavery "more bearable" to encourage the natural increase of enslaved people in the colony.[9] Such laws neither reduced the number of hours enslaved people worked in the sugar fields and in other areas of Jamaican plantations nor dictated improvement in the deleterious working conditions on Jamaican plantations. This law, however, included specific rules and guidelines regarding the regular access of enslaved people to provision grounds.

The Jamaican Assembly passed other amendments related to enslaved people's access to provision grounds. Another law enacted in Jamaica in 1809 stipulated that in addition to Sundays, one day in every fortnight would be extended to enslaved people in Jamaica to tend to their provision grounds and not work in the fields. These were the days referred to as "Negroes Day" in the Rose Hall Journal. In 1816 the slave law of Jamaica barred any crop work on Sundays (specifically from 7:00 p.m. on Saturday evening to 5:00 a.m. on Monday morning). There was a twenty-pound fine for those proprietors and enslavers who broke this law. A law in 1826 established that there should be at least twenty-six of these days in each calendar year.[10] Rose Hall overseers, however, did not consistently record such notations about these days in the journal.[11] The description of "Negroes in their Grounds" in the journal reflects the actual intention of these "off" days— for the enslaved to work in the provision grounds, which would provide a substantial amount of the food to nourish their bodies.[12]

All along the left side of the "Distribution of Negroes" page are titles, duties, positions, and work sites—short descriptions of the primary work responsibilities of enslaved people distributed throughout the plantation. In each column, overseers included the number of enslaved people within that particular category on a daily basis. At the top of the list are the often referred to groups/gangs on sugar, cotton, and tobacco plantations in the Americas—first gang, second gang, and third gang.[13] In the Rose Hall Journal, depending on the overseers' individual choices and preferences, these gangs are listed independently, or the first and second gangs are often combined due to their similar, collective duties. Under the gangs is a list of specialized skilled positions and particular work venues at Rose Hall—carpenters, coopers, masons, blacksmiths, drivers and cooks (often a combined category), cartmen and boys, mulemen, those who attended stock, those who attended small stock, workers at the overseer's house and in the out offices, doctress (later on doctor) and gardener (often a combined category), young children and nurse, fishermen, and watchmen. These positions are followed by enslaved people in different temporary states of being, including positions of fugitivity—invalids, pregnant women, lying-in women (referring to pregnant women who were "lying in" the hospital for a limited time before giving birth and immediately following such births), runaways, and those who were taking days. The next lines are miscellaneous descriptions of enslaved people with different afflictions, sometimes mentioned as being in the hospital, as well as additional working venues depending on the harvesting and processing schedule, for example, in the great house, yaws (a chronic contagious skin infection that created ulcers and compromised bones, leading to disfigurement and disability), at the hospital (including attendants), and in the boiling house, mill house, and still house. Finally, the last items focus on general processes and places related to the sugar-harvesting and sugar-processing cycles—about the works, picking cane tops, and cutting wood.

The majority of the journal entries, which are listed on the right-hand pages opposite the "Distribution of Negroes" on the left-hand pages, are entitled "Daily Occurrences," which include descriptions of the general daily duties and sites of labor assigned to enslaved people. These pages contain notes about weather conditions, including rain showers, storms, and hurricanes. In addition to references to "Negroes Day" in the "Distribution of Negroes," notations regarding enslaved people working in their provision grounds are primarily included on Saturdays in the notes of the "Daily Occurrences." The corresponding page of "Daily Occurrences" for the week of March 17–22, 1817 (the first week of the journal), has been ripped out. Instead, the page of the following week's daily occurrences, from Monday, March 24, 1817, to Saturday, March 29, 1817, is positioned on the opposite page of the "Distribution of Negroes" for the previous week.[14] From the very first page of this journal, it is clear that the record itself will be neither entirely complete nor accurate.

The detailed and meticulous nature of this Rose Hall ledger, with specifics about duties and the number of laboring bodies associated with these responsibilities, also belies some of the overseers' actual mathematical skills. Racial, gendered, and classed elements of the slavocracy also shaped the range of overseers' abilities and different levels of literacy and mathematical abilities. The misspellings and miscalculated totals in the journal entries present the importance of

1817 March	17	18	19
First Gang	42	23	23
Second do.	7	5	5
Third do.	5	5	5
Carpenters	5	5	5
Coopers	2	2	2
Masons	1	1	1
Blacksmiths	6	6	6
Drivers & cooks	6	8	8
Cartmen & Boys	2	2	2
Mulemen	4	4	4
Attending Stock	2	2	2
do. small do.	8	8	8
Overseers House & out offices	2	2	2
Doctress & Gardner	19	19	19
Young Children & Nurse	1	1	1
Fishermen	15	15	15
Watchmen	6	6	6
Invalids	"	"	"
Pregnant	"	"	"
Runaways	"	"	1
Saking day	2	2	2
In the Great House	4	4	4
Yaws	7	7	6
Hospital & attendants	"	5	5
Boiling House	"	14	14
Still House	"	14	14
About the Works	4	4	4
Picking cane tops	2	2	2
Cutting Wood			
	153	155	155
By Isaac died of affection of the Brains ——	"	"	1
			154

First page of the journal and notation regarding
Isaac's passing on March 18/19, 1817, bottom of page.
JARD, 1B/26, RHJ, vol. 1, fol. 1a.

tracking enslaved people and maintaining meticulous records. However, those responsible for the written records and numerical calculations were not necessarily competent in the skills required for these practices. From the very first page of the Rose Hall Journal, the simple addition involved in totaling the numbers in a given column is at times inconsistent and inaccurate. Nonetheless, the descriptions in the columns and numbers recorded in the columns offer some sense of the range of duties at Rose Hall Plantation, as well as estimates of the number of enslaved people assigned to these respective duties.

No particular enslaved person is named in reference to any of the various duties until the very last line of that first "Distribution of Negroes" page for the week of March 17–22, 1817: "By Isaac died of affection of the Brains."[15] "Affection of the brains" was often associated with phrenitis (inflammation of the brain), which frequently included the symptoms of acute fever and delirium. Isaac's passing is also noted numerically in the column on March 19. In that column for that Wednesday, the total tally of enslaved people is reduced from 155 to 154. Isaac's individual identity emerges on this page. His passing serves as a final and solitary marker and recognition in the historical record that he existed at all. He only enters the archival record then as a note in reference to his passing; his sole presence in the journal registers his fatal absence. It is in death that Isaac's personhood emerges separate, though not entirely apart, from the usual distribution of other enslaved people at Rose Hall.

What this official record does not include or reflect in any way are Isaac's physical, psychological, and related experiences of his life and disease and the process of dying. Absent, too, are the other enslaved people's responses to Isaac's disease, duration of suffering, and eventual passing. In what ways did others enslaved at Rose Hall—perhaps people he identified as family and friends—witness the progression of his disease and mourn individually or collectively for him? How did they demonstrate their love for Isaac and all he meant to them beyond his economic value and the financial cost of this loss, beyond this one line at the bottom of this page of the Rose Hall Journal?[16]

Although the Rose Hall Journal does not list "death" as a category of "distribution," death most certainly served as a significant classification and state of being at this Jamaican estate and other Caribbean plantations. Throughout the Rose Hall Journal, disease and death figure prominently in terms of adult enslaved mortality, including fatal accidents that occurred in the harvesting and processing of sugarcane.[17] Over the course of the journal, from 1817 to 1832, the notes related to the passing of enslaved people at Rose Hall appear more frequently in the marginalia of these weekly reports. Earlier overseers often positioned this information at the bottom of the "Distribution of Negroes" section or interspersed it in the "Daily Occurrences" section. Yet in the final years of the journal, the overseers included this information in the marginalia, with the words written along the side, in the crevices from the bottom to the top of the page. It is important to consider the long history of these ledgers and the marginal references to people of African descent in the context of the transatlantic slave trade.[18]

The inclusion of Isaac's passing is one of countless individual references to enslaved people throughout the journal. In addition to the sporadic listing of individual enslaved people mentioned within the journal itself, official registration of the names and number of enslaved people at Rose Hall began in 1817. Growing concerns about amelioration in the British colonies in the Caribbean resulted in the Jamaican Assembly's passage of the 1816 Slave Registration Bill. This act required enslavers to maintain and submit a record of the births and deaths of enslaved people, as well as the number of enslaved people sold or manumitted. This first year of the Rose Hall Journal also coincided with the submission of the first triennial returns of slaves (also known as the slave registers) for Rose Hall. Attorney Edward Mountague signed the list of names of enslaved people at Rose Hall; this list was dated June 28, 1817.[19] Mountague's list includes the names of all 79 enslaved males and 73 enslaved females, a total of 152 enslaved people at Rose Hall.[20]

Unlike the weekly entries in the Rose Hall Journal, which primarily name enslaved people when referencing their birth, death, pregnancy, or state of fugitivity, the triennial slave register of 1817 (and the subsequent registers of 1820, 1823, 1826, 1829, and 1832) offers specific names of the enslaved women, men, and children at Rose Hall. The first triennial slave register of Rose Hall in 1817 lists all enslaved individuals at Rose Hall as of June 30, 1817; the subsequent registers list only those enslaved people who had been born and those who had passed in the three-year period between slave registers. Individuals are separated into two sublists, "Males" and "Females," with males consistently listed first. These slave registers present and reinforce this binary of males and females without any fluidity possible in the written records. It is important to point out that the absence of this fluidity in the archival documents should not erase the possibility of some sense of flexibility embraced by individual enslaved persons at that time. Although certainly not utilizing the terminology "queer," we can certainly hold the imaginative space for some enslaved people who might have recognized their resistance to this sharply defined gendered construct, as well as "a break in the line of gender."[21]

These slave registers also include an identification of each individual's "colour" (specifically noted as "negro," "sambo," "mulatto," or "quadroon"). These terms are included with particular meanings in regard to Blackness and whiteness or lightness: a "negro" was someone of African and/or Creole negro parentage who was not identified as being racially mixed; a "mulatto" had one negro parent and one white parent; a "quadroon" had one mulatto parent and one white parent; and a "sambo" had one negro parent and one mulatto parent.[22] Also included in these lists are each enslaved person's estimated age and their "country"—their place of birth in Africa or the Americas, as "African" or "Creole," respectively. Selected "remarks" related to their biological maternal connections are included, especially for those enslaved people who were twenty years old and younger (noted as the daughter or son of individual enslaved women at Rose Hall). Of these 152 enslaved people in 1817, 18 are African women, 34 are African men, 55 are Creole women, and 45 are Creole men, a total of 52 African-born people and 100 Creole people (approximately one-third African-born and two-thirds Creole).

In addition to notes scattered throughout the journal, individual names of every enslaved person at Rose Hall are provided in the journal with the annual disbursement of new clothing to enslaved people. This annual clothing disbursement was included in the dictates of the Consolidated Slave Law of 1788. At Rose Hall, this clothing disbursement usually occurred at some point between June and August. Although this list is not included every year in the journal, a list is included at the beginning of the journal entries for June 1828.[23] A similar list, dated August 18, 1832, again related to the annual clothing allowance, is included at the end of a 1911 monograph entitled *In Old St. James, Jamaica: A Book of Parish Chronicles*.[24] As was the case on plantations in Jamaica and on other plantations across the Americas, white enslavers granted enslaved people clothing that was considered practical and durable, given their plantation routines. Enslaved people's clothing was not of the same quality as the clothing of white enslavers. As noted in the June 1828 clothing allowance list for Rose Hall, the two main types of fabric enslaved people received at Rose Hall were osnaburg and peniston (sometimes spelled pennystone); both were cheap, coarse, plain fabrics worn by enslaved people in Jamaica.[25] In order to make the cloth into clothing, at Rose Hall enslaved persons also received twelve skeins of thread and five needles. As the 1828 annual clothing allowance list notes, eight yards of osnaburg and four yards of peniston were distributed to both enslaved women and men, with six yards of osnaburg and three yards of peniston allocated to enslaved children. Enslaved girls also received a smaller yardage (about two yards) of madras/bandana cloth (a plaid pattern that combined red usually with white, orange, or yellow).[26] Enslaved women received four additional yards of another cloth noted as "L. Ells." Although the "ell" was another measurement of cloth, the exact type of fabric is unclear in the records.[27]

A few enslaved women and men received extra yards of osnaburg and peniston, including Dorinda (midwife and hospital attendant), Cecelia (who attended to young children), Celia (grasscutter), George (head driver), William
Scott (head carpenter), and Aaron (head penkeeper). The particular positions
of the enslaved men probably resulted in their receipt of additional cloth. For
Dorinda, this may have been the reason as well. It is not as clear why both Cecelia
and Celia received extra cloth and why Dorinda and Celia specifically received
the most cloth of all the enslaved people at Rose Hall (fourteen yards of osnaburg
and five yards of peniston). The extent of Dorinda's and Celia's duties may well
have factored into this special allocation of cloth, as well as the number of children they bore at Rose Hall. It is important to note the exclusion of one particular item in the clothing lists: there are no shoes included in any of the clothing
allocation lists, as shoes were not deemed by enslavers as necessities for enslaved
people at Rose Hall and other plantations across the Americas.

Even though enslaved people primarily depended on these select items of
clothing as they labored, as historian Stephanie Camp reminds us, some enslaved
people in the United States also decided to relieve their enslavers of their own
clothing and jewelry without their permission and wore them at secret social
gatherings.[28] Enslaved people at Rose Hall most likely engaged in "borrowing"
particular items of clothing and jewelry from their enslavers as well. Furthermore, it is likely that enslaved women at Rose Hall created other clothing and
jewelry from items bartered, stolen, or crafted from other materials in their communities. Although the annual clothing distribution process functioned as another ritual of dominance and dependence, enslaved people at Rose Hall and at
other plantations throughout the Americas still forged pathways of artistry and
creativity in the articles and objects they fashioned to wear as distinct reminders
of their individuality and humanity.

These clothing allowance lists of enslaved people provide additional information about each individual at Rose Hall. The 1832 list in the *In Old St. James* book
identifies a total of 111 enslaved people: 51 males (with 15 born after the 1817 list
and alive in 1832) and 60 females (with 14 born after the 1817 list and alive in
1832).[29] Of the 51 males on the 1832 list, 8 are African, 42 are Creole, and 1 is unidentified in terms of country of origin. Of the 60 females on this list, 11 are African and 49 are Creole. Whereas in 1817 the African-born enslaved population is
one-third of the total enslaved population at Rose Hall, in 1832 the African-born
enslaved population drops to approximately 17 percent of the total enslaved population at this plantation. In addition to the identification of an enslaved person's "country" and "colour," noted in the triennial slave registers, the clothing
allowance lists (like the one in 1832) include "Christian names"; "married names"

for women if applicable; surnames for some children; estimated age; "P/R," the prime rating from one ("prime" and healthy) to five (for the elderly, often deemed superannuated); "valuation" in pounds in colonial currency; "occupation" (closely mirroring the titles and descriptions in the "Distribution of Negroes"); "condition" (e.g., "weakly," "able and healthy," and "venereal"); and "disposition" (e.g., "good," "drunkard," "indolent," "bad," "runaway," and "notorious runaway").

AFRICAN AND CREOLE KITH AND KIN AT ROSE HALL

As Isaac passed a couple of months before the creation of the 1817 Jamaican slave register, his name does not appear at all on the 1817 list. However, for those enslaved people at Rose Hall who were alive and included in the 1817 slave register, I have used this slave register, subsequent triennial slave registers, the 1832 list of enslaved people associated with the distribution of the clothing allowance, and the brief, random descriptions of specific enslaved people strewn throughout the Rose Hall Journal to piece together some sense of this enslaved community.[30] The racial, gendered, and classed tenets of the Jamaican slavocracy systematically truncated personal and familial connections in the archival record by excluding references to men who might have considered themselves and were considered by others to be part of familial frameworks and networks. Even though I am unable to include definitive references to biological fathers and/or to men who played nurturing roles in these Rose Hall families and the broader enslaved community as "other fathers," I have utilized archival documents to create family histories embedded within a communal context.

It is important to note that even as the archival record does not provide a comprehensive narrative of relationships between enslaved people and kinship connections, whether consanguineal (by blood) and/or fictive and expansive, the multigenerational presence of several enslaved families and the myriad multigenerational communal connections at Rose Hall reflect the branches and roots of a community tree.[31] The subject of enslaved family structures in Jamaica has been and continues to be an ongoing contested topic. Some have posited that enslaved Jamaican families lived primarily in nuclear families, and others have underscored more matrifocal and matrilineal family structures.[32] Even as the trajectory in slavery studies may still be moving generally along a fairly traditional heteronormative pathway in an attempt to reconstruct and highlight heteronormative relationships, partnerships, and marriages, there have been new initiatives related to "queering slavery" and moving beyond socially constructed and restrictive heteronormative parameters.[33] The matrilineages in this chapter (and throughout the book) are not offered as deficient family trees. Instead, they reflect core foundational elements of numerous familial and other intimate relationships that may or may not have included a significant nurturing male presence. The absence of a male presence and male lineage in the recording of births at Rose Hall and other Caribbean plantations in plantation journals does not necessarily or automatically translate into a crucial role that has been denied. We cannot assume that all enslaved children who were fathered by enslaved men emerged out of loving and monogamous heteronormative partnerships at Rose Hall. It is most likely that those enslaved children who were fathered by enslaved men were born due to multiple and complicated intimate relationships that might have been short lived or long lasting, monogamous or polyamorous, consensual or nonconsensual, and even beyond any of the monikers we use in the present day to categorize and simplify the complex interactions and intimacies between people. To consider a community framework and community tree in addition to individual family trees that include women, men, and children at Rose Hall offers an opportunity for us to move beyond linear lineages to community lineages and communal groundings. Some of these intimacies and interactions would have been not only biologically centered but also created because of gendered identities and within generational cohorts.

Multiple generations of enslaved families comprised of African-born and Creole relatives lived at Rose Hall. Although the lists for these individuals and families begin in 1817, some of the enslaved people on the 1817 slave register had probably lived and labored at Rose Hall for many years and even decades before 1817. Although the Rose Hall Journal specifically notes the births of enslaved people at Rose Hall, not all enslaved people described in the journal as "Creole" would necessarily have been born in Jamaica. Some may have been born in the Caribbean or in other areas of the Americas. Some of the enslaved people born in African communities may also have been initially transported to another Caribbean colony before their arrival in Jamaica. Whether African-born or Caribbean-born, they may have labored at plantations in other Caribbean colonies and at other plantations in Jamaica before they arrived at Rose Hall.

Given that England ended its formal, legal slave trade and importation of African captives to its colonies via the transatlantic slave trade in 1807, it is not surprising that a decade later, the eldest enslaved people at Rose Hall were Africans who were born in the 1740s and 1750s, lived into their sixties and seventies, and died before the abolition of slavery. Of the 152 enslaved people recorded at Rose Hall at the end of June 1817, the eldest were two seventy-year-old African-born men named Prague and Lewis-ney (listed also as Jemmy). The passing of both Prague and Lewis-ney/Jemmy was noted in the 1826 triennial slave register dated

June 28, 1826; Jemmy's name was listed immediately above Prague's name.[34] In the Rose Hall Journal, Jemmy's death was recorded on January 26, 1824, and less than five months later, Prague's death "of old age" was recorded on June 8, 1824.[35] Instead of being recorded at the bottom of the "Distribution of Negroes" page or on the "Daily Occurrences" page in the daily descriptions, the note regarding Prague's death was written in the left margin of the "Daily Occurrences."[36] The extant pages of the Rose Hall Journal, however, do not include the exact date and circumstances of his death.

It may have been coincidental that the two eldest members of the Rose Hall enslaved community died within five months of each other at the same recorded age of seventy. Archival records do not convey whether these men or any other enslaved Africans at Rose Hall might have been from the same African communities and even communicated in the same or closely sociolinguistically related African languages. However, we also cannot deduce definitively that there were no enslaved Africans at Rose Hall who shared similar cultural backgrounds, languages, and cosmologies. Perhaps Prague and Lewis-ney/Jemmy shared a camaraderie, brotherhood, and intimacies that had lasted for many years at Rose Hall, and perhaps this resulted in their respective passing within mere months. At the time of the first slave register in 1817, had Prague and Lewis-ney/Jemmy been enslaved at Rose Hall for several years or for decades? Had they shared similar circumstances of being enslaved at different plantations in Jamaica and on other Caribbean islands? Had they been shipmates during the Middle Passage or come from the same region in West Africa or West Central Africa and "become dear to each other"?[37] Were they from the same ethnic group, or did they share knowledge of the same African language or languages, and might they have appreciated the opportunities, however random or infrequent, to speak to each other in a shared mother tongue or in an African language with which they were both familiar?

As with Isaac's passing, the journal does not include any information about how other members of the Rose Hall enslaved community responded to the deaths of Prague and Lewis-ney/Jemmy. As the eldest members of this community, were their deaths marked with any particular celebratory rituals, including mourning songs or ceremonies? As African-born elders in this community, had they previously shared and guided such ceremonies of others who had passed before at Rose Hall and those living on neighboring plantations? Were there particular African-centered mortuary practices that might have been invoked and observed when these two elders passed? With their own deaths, had special ceremonies been included and even been created as a way to observe and celebrate their possible significance by African-born and Creole people enslaved at Rose

Hall and other plantations who might have deemed them their kin or even "family" and by the enslaved community overall at Rose Hall?

Following Prague and Lewis-ney/Jemmy, the oldest enslaved person at Rose Hall was an African-born woman. She is identified as sixty-six-year-old Jreen in the 1817 slave register for Rose Hall.[38] Six years later, her death was recorded in the 1823 slave register; her name in this register is spelled Green. Her age at death is noted as seventy. Jreen/Green probably died of old age on Saturday, May 4, 1822.[39] Although she was the oldest enslaved woman listed at Rose Hall in 1817, Jreen/Green was not the only African-born sexagenarian at that time. Other enslaved sexagenarians included three other African-born women and two African-born men: Rachael (age sixty-two in 1817), Memmy Sen (shortened for Senior, age sixty in 1817), Peachy (age sixty in 1817), Andrew (age sixty in 1817), and Luke (age sixty in 1817).[40] As Prague and Lewis-ney/Jemmy might have developed a certain connection as the eldest African-born men at Rose Hall, did Jreen/Green, Rachael, Memmy Sen, and Peachy create intimate connections of their own that were particular to their gender, age, and duties at Rose Hall? Did this community of African-born elder women extend to those African-born women in their fifties and forties—Rebecca (age fifty-two in 1817), Cecelia (age forty-eight in 1817), Amelia (age forty-five in 1817), Dorothy (age forty-five in 1817), May (age forty-four in 1817), and Janet/Jannet (age forty in 1817)—as well as the six African-born women who were forty in 1817—Cowslip, Dove, Miranda, Polly, Ruth, and Lenora?[41] And were the three other younger identified African-born women—Augusta (age thirty-eight in 1817), Arabella (age thirty-five in 1817), and Stella (age thirty-two in 1817)—included within these networks? Did this transgenerational group of African-born women share their cultural knowledge, practices, and customs about family, community, relationships, resistance, pregnancy, childbirth, child-rearing, and various aspects of womanhood and motherhood with each other and extend this knowledge to Creole enslaved girls and women at Rose Hall and surrounding Jamaican plantations?

This transgenerational presence at Rose Hall endured into the emancipation era in the 1830s in Jamaica. Many of the elder African people listed in the 1817 slave register sustained their presence into the 1820s and a few into the 1830s: Jreen/Green passed in 1822 at the age of seventy, Andrew passed in 1822 at the age of sixty-five, Rachel passed in 1823 at the age of sixty-six, Memmy Sen passed in 1824 at the age of sixty-nine, Gibbes/Gibs passed in 1827 at the age of sixty-five, Luke passed in 1829 at the age of seventy-two, Hyde passed in 1830 at the age of seventy-one, Fox passed also in 1830 at the age of sixty-five, and Craigie passed in 1831 at the age of sixty-four.

At the time of the 1832 clothing allowance list, the eldest women and men at Rose Hall remained African born (and were also listed on Rose Hall's first 1817 slave register). In 1832, African-born March was the eldest person at Rose Hall; on the 1832 list, he is described as sixty-four and a watchman.[42] The other elder African men on the 1832 list include Bolton at sixty-two and Washington at fifty-nine; they all are described as weakly and serving as watchmen at that time. The remaining five African-born men on the 1832 list ranged in age from fifty-six to forty-four: Ross at fifty-six, Garrick and Ralph at fifty-four, Bryan at forty-six, and Aaron at forty-four.

In 1832 the eldest African-born woman was Cecelia, who is listed as sixty-two on the 1832 clothing allowance list. She was the only African-born woman in her sixties at Rose Hall in 1832. Described as "weakly," she is identified in 1832 as primarily attending to young children at Rose Hall. In addition to Cecelia, in 1832 there remained ten more African-born women: Amelia and Dorothea at fifty-nine; May at fifty-eight; Cowslip, Janet/Jannet, Miranda/Maranda, and Ruth at fifty-four; Augusta at fifty-two; and Julina and Arabella at forty-nine. Unlike the eldest African-born men who were watchmen, most of the eldest African-born women—Amelia, Dorothea, May, Cowslip, and Ruth—remained relegated to agricultural-related duties as "grasscutters," or a combination of field work and grasscutting (in the case of Augusta). In 1832 the youngest African-born women, Julina and Arabella, worked solely as field workers. One of the African-born women, Janet/Jannet, is identified as the only "driveress" at Rose Hall at the time (with George being described as the "head driver" and Harry as the "second driver").[43] In addition, Miranda/Maranda's primary duty is noted as "cook for gang." The 1832 list also contains information in the "disposition" column related to fugitivity. Two of the African-born women—Cowslip and Arabella—are described as "runaway." Indeed, given her numerous runaway attempts documented in the Rose Hall Journal, Arabella should have been described as a "notorious runaway." None of the African-born men is noted as a "runaway" on the 1832 list, but four Creole men—Gloster, Alick, Oliver, and James—are categorized as "runaway," with James being specifically described as a "notorious runaway."[44]

The eldest Creole enslaved people listed in the 1817 slave register were the enslaved men Johnny and John Parish; they were both fifty years old. They did not survive long enough to be included in the 1832 list. The Rose Hall Journal describes Johnny's death at age fifty due to dysentery on May 5, 1819, and the 1820 slave register notes his passing.[45] The Rose Hall Journal also mentions the passing of John Parish at age fifty-eight on June 11, 1824; the 1826 slave register also records his death.[46]

The eldest Creole enslaved women at Rose Hall—Hope, Maphe, and Celia—
are all listed as forty-five years old in the 1817 slave register. Hope's passing at age
fifty-six is recorded in the 1829 slave register. However, both Maphe and Celia,
though they are listed in 1832 as fifty-nine years old and "weakly," remained working as "grasscutters" at Rose Hall. Although the triennial slave registers and other
related plantation documents delineate the "country" of enslaved people as either
"African" (born in Africa) or "Creole" (born in the Americas), this did not necessarily translate into enslaved people working in groups at Rose Hall solely on
the basis of their country or region of origin. As grasscutters, Maphe and Celia
would have worked alongside the elder African-born women grasscutters: Amelia, Dorothea, May, Cowslip, Ruth, and Augusta.

All of these African-born and Creole enslaved women could have developed relationships beyond their work routines and gang groupings. As enslaved
women who had been present at Rose Hall since 1817 (and, for some, possibly
several years before that time), they would have been living in close proximity
for years and even decades. They experienced the challenges of bondage and the
hardships of laboring at this particular plantation, as well as giving birth and
(perhaps individually and collectively) raising their children and grandchildren
at Rose Hall. In the specific case of Celia, she remained at Rose Hall over the
years and decades, witnessing the growth of her family from generation to generation and, most likely, sharing her experiences with some of her children, grandchildren, and great-grandchildren who also resided at Rose Hall.

Transgenerational, consanguineal, and probably expansive and extended kin
relationships transpired between African-born and Caribbean-born enslaved
people at Rose Hall. Archival records of the African-born enslaved people at
Rose Hall do not specify any African community or region of birth; however,
those who were African-born probably shared elements of their birthplace and
related cultural customs with others at Rose Hall. This sharing would probably
not have occurred solely between those who were African born; instead, aspects
of African-born people's lives might have been shared with those born in the
Americas and living at Rose Hall, perhaps especially with their respective Creole
descendants. It is unknown what might have been selectively and consciously disclosed by African-born enslaved people about their African cultural beginnings
and groundings. They may have revealed information about their memories of
their African connections, histories, families, and communities selectively and
purposefully—not every experience, custom, tradition, skill, and memory might
have been disclosed to those they called family or friends at Rose Hall or other
nearby plantations. Such individual and collective knowledge would not have
been one directional. Those who were Creole and not born in African communi-

ties would also have had experiences, customs, traditions, skills, and memories of their own that might have been shared or withheld based on various reasons and circumstances.

Enslaved people would have created definite familial and other relationships and networks that were not dictated by Rose Hall's enslavers and overseers; they would have forged intimacies beyond the columns, rows, and notations in the Rose Hall Journal. Due to a range of factors, relationships between enslaved African-born and Creole people would have informed their interactions during times of arduous labor and in guarded moments beyond the gaze and scrutiny of Rose Hall's enslavers and overseers. Even though all of their daily, particularly their intimate, interactions remain unrecorded in the archival documents, we can glean some sense of their relationships by extricating details out of the archival records and imagining and integrating a sense of the fullness of their humanity within and beyond the lines of these records. Building on this overview of enslaved people at Rose Hall, the next chapter explores the experiences of enslaved girls and women as linked to productivity and reproductivity, as well as the conditions of enslaved mothers and enslaved children. These experiences offer a particular lens for examining what might have transpired in the spaces betwixt and between the columns and rows of the Rose Hall Journal, inside and outside of their responsibilities shackled to the agri-industrial plantation complex at Rose Hall.

CHAPTER 2

Bondage, Birthing, and Belonging
at Rose Hall Plantation

A legacy of racialized, gendered, and classed conceptions and caricatures of Black women's bodies and sexuality throughout the African diaspora shaped and informed the lived experiences of Black women at Rose Hall in the nineteenth century. In the sixteenth and seventeenth centuries, Europeans began framing Africa and Africans as sites for exploitation and extraction. African women's bodies and their sexuality in particular became aligned with what historian Jennifer L. Morgan describes as "mechanical and meaningless childbearing."[1] By the beginning of the seventeenth century, with England joining other European countries (especially Portugal and Spain) in the transatlantic slave trade, African women became sources and resources to be tapped to address England's socioeconomic needs and desires. As a result, "African women's reproductive work embodied the developing discourses of extraction and forced labor at the heart of England's design for the Americas."[2]

That design for the Americas, including Jamaica and other British colonies in the Caribbean, had been deeply ensconced by the time John Rose Palmer left England and arrived in Jamaica in 1818. In early nineteenth-century Jamaica and throughout the Americas, Black women's dual and intersecting productive and reproductive functions served as the foundational tenets of chattel slavery. This did not translate into an enhanced double or even multiple socioeconomic or cultural valuation of enslaved women in the Americas. Instead, enslaved women were simultaneously valued and devalued within agri-industrial slavery economies based on their interlocking racial, gendered, and classed positionalities. They were valued for their productive and reproductive labor solely in the service of the slavocracy while they were systemically and unequivocally devalued due to their supposedly inferior and innate racial and gendered classifications. In addition, the fruits of their productive and reproductive labor became clearly demarcated by laws and claimed within the parameters of slavery. The doctrine of *partus sequitur ventrem*, dictating that the enslaved or free status of a child followed

that of her or his mother, provided the unequivocal passage through which enslaved women's children became part and parcel of the fruits of racial capitalism
and the machinations of the institution of slavery.

The valuation of enslaved motherhood and enslaved childhood in Jamaica
was neither consistent nor absolute; instead, it changed from the final decades
of the eighteenth century into the early decades of the nineteenth century. With
heightened attention garnered by British advocates of the abolition of the transatlantic slave trade, Jamaican enslavers duly recognized and reckoned with their
burgeoning awareness of some transformation of slavery in their midst. As historian Colleen A. Vasconcellos explains, in the years leading up to the abolition of
England's official involvement in the slave trade, "ideas of child worth and value
also shifted as planters realized the need for change in the management and treatment of the women and children on their estates."[3] Jamaican enslavers and the
members of their plantation management networks (including managers, attor-
neys, and overseers) categorized enslaved people who were fifteen and younger
as children.[4] Even though enslaved children were not fully engaged in the laborious work in the sugar fields until they were fifteen or sixteen years old, from the
age of five or six on Jamaican sugar plantations such as Rose Hall, most young
enslaved children became indoctrinated into the less arduous duties of the agri-
industrial plantation complex and the expectations of what lay ahead for them
as enslaved adults. A number of factors influenced the growing attention to the
roles of enslaved children on Jamaican plantations. "As abolitionist sentiment
gained both momentum and strength," as Vasconcellos posits, "the white community assigned ever changing subcategories to childhood based on the perceived value, need, and place of enslaved children in the system."[5] Specific terms
also reflected changing notions and the continuum of enslaved childhood and
adulthood, including the labels of infant, boy, girl, man-boy, and woman-girl.[6]
Once Britain ended its official involvement with the trade slave, "enslaved children become more important commodities in Jamaica."[7]

Enslavers' evolving, expansive notions of childhood in Jamaica in the early decades of the nineteenth century also permeated ideas about the transitional age
from enslaved girlhood to enslaved womanhood and, by extension, to enslaved
motherhood. As enslaved children "became more important to the struggle
against natural decrease on the island, the term women-girls occasionally referred
to pubescent girls below the age of sixteen." On Jamaican plantations, notions
of "womanhood" could encompass girls who were as young as ten. This conception of womanhood also characterized young enslaved girls as sexually available
and accessible to white men on a plantation—enslavers as well as bookkeepers
and overseers—through rape and sexual harassment. "By the time enslaved girls

reached the delicate age of eleven" on Jamaican plantations, Vasconcellos proffers, "they were women; more specifically they were breeding wenches."[8]

Both the productive and reproductive valuation and devaluation of enslaved
girls and women appeared in the pages of the Rose Hall Journal in the scattered
notes about enslaved African and Creole mothers and their enslaved children residing at Rose Hall. The blood lineage of enslaved women and the very wombs
of enslaved women established the veins and arteries of slavery's multigenerational enterprise. Yet enslaved African-born women who could trace their lineage back to an African homeland and to particular African communities did
not wield any immediate economic or sociopolitical currency within Jamaica's
nineteenth-century slavocracy or its related, document-based archive. As a result,
there are no traces in the Rose Hall records of the African parents (or any known
African ancestors) of African-born persons enslaved at Rose Hall. In these records the African-born women enslaved in Jamaica become the source, the origin,
the "Eve" of a new Creole population.[9] These African women (and their Creole sisters in struggle and bondage) enter as *the* first identifiable female ancestors at Rose Hall. As a result, this absence denies the presence of the longevity
and breadth of their actual African familial lineages, as well as their historical,
cultural, and sociological groundings—the copious generations of Africans from
countless communities existing on the other side of the Atlantic Ocean.

Although the Rose Hall Journal does not reveal the ancestral connections of
the older African-born enslaved people, the journal contains notations of familial
connections between African-born and Creole enslaved people at Rose Hall. It is
likely that some elder African-born enslaved women at Rose Hall were mothers
or "other mothers" who nurtured and guided other enslaved African-born and
Creole women whether or not they shared consanguineal or affinal kinship ties.
Following the doctrine of *partus sequitur ventrem*, notes in the Rose Hall Journal identified enslaved African and Creole mothers and their enslaved children
residing at Rose Hall. Ninety-nine enslaved girls and women lived at Rose Hall
between 1817 and 1832; these girls and women were part of multigenerational
relationships between great-grandmothers, grandmothers, mothers, children,
grandchildren, and great-grandchildren all residing at Rose Hall. Twenty-seven
enslaved girls were born between 1817 and 1832. The eldest of this generation of
enslaved children who remained alive in 1832 was Daisy/Daizy; she was fifteen
at the time of the 1832 register. Her birth is recorded in the Rose Hall Journal
on December 22, 1817.[10] The remaining seventy-two were adult enslaved women:
nineteen African-born women, fifty-one Creole women, one woman (Julina)
who is categorized in the 1817 list as Creole but in the 1832 list as African, and
one female named Mariah who is noted as a runaway in the Rose Hall Journal

but does not appear in any of the slave registers.[11] As a result, there is no indication of Mariah's age or whether she was African born or Creole.

Of the four eldest African-born women in 1817—Jreen/Green, Memmy Sen, Rachel, and Peachy—only Rachel is specifically identified as being the mother of a child at Rose Hall. She is described as the mother of eighteen-year-old Peter in the 1817 list. As Rachel is listed as sixty-two years old in 1817, Peter was probably not her first child, though he may have been her last child. No other children at Rose Hall are described as being daughters or sons of Rachel. Rachel and the other enslaved sexagenarian women may well have had children located at Rose Hall and/or at other plantations, although those children are not recorded in the registers and the journal. Indeed, Memmy Sen may have been the mother of another African-born woman at Rose Hall named Miranda, and if she were Miranda's mother, then she would be the only African-born woman who became a grandmother and great-grandmother living with her kin at Rose Hall from 1817 to 1832. It is certainly likely that all (or most) of these African-born enslaved women had given birth to children who may have died at an early age or were living at other plantations in Jamaica or in other areas of the Americas or the African continent. The Rose Hall Journal does not include any notations about enslaved mothers at Rose Hall Plantation having enslaved children residing at other Jamaican plantations. Furthermore, as only enslaved mothers of children are listed in the Rose Hall records, African and Creole men who were the fathers and grandfathers of children and grandchildren at Rose Hall or any other Jamaican plantations were not identified as such in the Rose Hall Journal. However, the mothers and grandmothers of these children probably recognized these children and grandchildren as their kin. Even though these children and grandchildren of African and Creole men may not be documented in the archives with specific biological and familial connections, that did not foreclose these children and grandchildren from being recognized as part of these individual lineages, multiple family roots, and communal frameworks.

Of the fifteen enslaved African-born women of childbearing age at Rose Hall in 1817, the records describe approximately eight of them as mothers of children at Rose Hall: Rebecca, Cecelia, Dorothy/Dorothea, May, Miranda/Maranda, Polly, Augusta, and Stella. Augusta and Cecelia had not only children but also grandchildren at Rose Hall. The remaining seven African-born women of childbearing age were not explicitly identified as mothers in the records: Amelia, Cowslip, Dove, Janet/Jannet, Lenora/Leonora, Ruth, and Arabella.

The thirty-one enslaved Creole women who are listed as mothers of children at Rose Hall were Celia, Hope, Maphe/Maph, Daphney, Nancy, Sarah/Sambo Sarah, Delia, Dorinda, Rosannah, Zebra, Juno, Charlotte, Liddy, Giss/Gift,

Kate, Mary, Panella, Susannah Johnston, Jeany, Chance, Matilda, Bell, Mary James, Memmy Jun, Bessy, Cynthia, Glister/Glissom, Christianna, Brown, Dianna/Diana, and Jane Cranston.[12] Six of these mothers became grandmothers at Rose Hall: Celia, Hope, Maphe/Maph, Nancy, Sarah/Sambo Sarah, and Rosannah. Only one of these Creole women, Celia, became a mother, grandmother, and great-grandmother at Rose Hall.

There were nineteen Creole women who were of childbearing age and not specifically identified as mothers of children at Rose Hall: Beck, Nelly, Lucretia, Susannah Scott, Doshy, Molly Spence, Parthenia, Joan, Frankey/Frankie, Sabina, Flora, Pastora, Rose, Kitty, Clarinda, Fanny, Phoeba/Phibba, Peggy, and Doll.[13] In addition, one young girl, Clara, died at the age of eleven. Julina, who is listed as Creole in the 1817 slave register and African in the 1832 clothing allowance list, is also not identified as a mother. It is possible that one or more of these women had children who were living at other plantations. Moreover, as other scholars have noted, the specific conditions at sugar plantations in the Caribbean adversely affected the reproductive potential of enslaved women and increased the possibility of infertility.[14] It is also possible that one or some of these women chose not to have any children while enslaved; as a result, they may have engaged in gynecological as well as medical and herbal practices that limited or completely eliminated the possibility of pregnancies. Some scholars have utilized the term "gynecological resistance" to highlight different ways that enslaved women resisted exploitative and forced reproductive practices. Such practices included extending breastfeeding periods as a partial form of birth control, abortion, and infanticide.[15] However, historian Sasha Turner notes the importance of not equating gynecological resistance with what she characterizes as "maternal resistance." Gynecological resistance centered around biological processes that should not be conflated with the range of maternal acts, rights, and practices.[16] In addition to considerations regarding gynecological resistance, Africana studies scholar Felicia Denaud posits "Black gesturgency" as "practices and strategies of slave revolt concerning or coordinated by pregnant rebels across the African diaspora."[17] Perhaps older African-born and Creole women provided guidance and knowledge about specific practices and strategies and effective substances regarding reproductivity rooted in African and/or Caribbean cultural epistemologies as well as medical and healing practices. We do not know definitively whether these factors contributed to the decisions these women made individually or even collectively among a select group about their reproductive choices at this Jamaican plantation. However, it is important that we recognize enslaved women's possible strategies and decisions about accepting or resisting pregnancies and childrearing at Rose Hall Plantation.

LYING-IN AND DYING AT ROSE HALL:
MOTHERHOOD, MORTALITY, AND MOURNING

Scholars writing about enslaved maternal mortality and infant mortality on Jamaican plantations have long described enslaved women in Jamaica dying in childbirth or during the days and weeks following childbirth, as well as enslaved pregnant women who miscarried, delivered prematurely, or had stillborn children.[18] Whether enslaved women labored in Rose Hall's sugar fields or labored as "domestics" in and around the great house as cooks or washerwomen, they joined other enslaved women on Jamaican plantations who navigated motherhood while engaged in the laborious duties of the agri-industrial plantation complex. The cursory descriptions in the Rose Hall Journal offer evidence of the toll the arduous quotidian duties of enslaved girls and women took on their physical, psychological, and emotional well-being, including descriptions of the birth and death of enslaved children. Information in the triennial slave registers for Rose Hall is fairly consistent in the recording of births and deaths between 1817 and 1832. Given the heightened value of the reproductivity of enslaved women in these early decades of the nineteenth century, there was some attempt to track pregnancies in the Rose Hall Journal.[19] At different points in the journal, some of the overseers created separate columns for women who were pregnant and for those who were lying in, while other overseers combined these two categories (e.g., "pregnant and lying in with midwife"). "Pregnant and Lying in with Midwife" became one of the recurring permanent categories on the "Distribution of Negroes" pages. Only the number of women appears in this category from week to week. It is not until these women had given birth to their children that the mothers' names appear in the journal with the reference to the delivery of a female or male child.

The names of these newborns are often not included in the initial mention of their respective births in the journal. There could have been multiple reasons for not including the names of newborns at birth. This absence may have been based on enslaved parents' individual, familial, and cultural practices and traditions regarding naming processes, rituals, and ceremonies. Different naming practices and ceremonies existed across West African and West Central African societies, and these cultural customs were not replicated in their entirety on Jamaican plantations. Even with different cultural customs, due to the conditions of bondage, shared conceptions still coalesced about allowing "a seven-to-nine-day period before incorporating babies into the community."[20] Some enslaved newborns might not have been named in the first several days after their arrival due to the stark recognition and reality that many enslaved newborns did not live past the ninth night.[21]

Notation regarding Glister's birth of a baby girl who passed within nine days of her birth, last line of March 27, 1824 entry. JARD, 1B/26, RHJ, vol. 2, fol. 41b.

There were a number of overseers' inconsistencies in the recording of newborns' names in the journal. One overseer noted that on March 27, 1824, "Glister delivered of a Female Child which died within the Nine days."[22] Within a year before or after her daughter's birth, Glister, also referred to as Glisson, had also given birth to a son named Sam, who died at ten days old.[23] Sam is the only child of Glister/Glisson listed as dying in the three-year period after the 1823 slave register. Due to the missing and unreadable pages in the journal between late June 1822 and May 1823, it is likely that Sam's birth and death occurred within this time period. Yet Glister's female infant who died within the oft-referenced nine-day period is not included in the 1826 slave register. It is possible that, having survived to the tenth day, Sam had been named, and thus his death is recorded in the triennial slave register. Though the birth and death of Glister's newborn daughter are noted in the journal, they are not recognized in the official slave register.

Glister's daughter was not the only newborn who died within the nine-day period and whose birth and death were not recorded in the slave register.[24] Indeed, the journal also mentions the deaths of other unnamed newborns. In the daily notes for Friday, August 27, 1824, the overseer noted that "Kate Delivered of a Still Born child."[25] Kate's newborn does not appear in the 1826 slave register in the list of deaths at Rose Hall. On Wednesday, July 2, 1823, the overseer recorded, "Gift Delivered of Dead Child."[26] There is no other mention of Gift/Giss having other children. However, two years after this infant's passing, the overseer noted on September 28, 1825, in the marginalia that "Gift died in Childs bed."[27] It is possible that this infant's passing, though unrecorded in the official slave register, made an indelible mark on her mother, Gift/Giss, and that the death of her infant was not marginal to Gift/Giss's own life and might have contributed to her own passing.

In addition to listing stillborn infants, the journal also mentions the miscarriage of Mary, who is described as being in the hospital the week of September 9, 1832. Mary remained in the hospital during the week of September 16. She is no longer listed as being there the week of September 23. It is unlikely that this was the only incident of a miscarriage at Rose Hall. Pregnant women who had miscarriages may not have disclosed this information, and/or such cases might not have been recorded on a consistent official basis at Rose Hall.[28]

Not all newborns who died within nine days of their birth were unnamed and unrecorded.[29] The 1826 slave register notes that the baby girl Lydie, daughter of Jane Cranston, died at seven days.[30] Although Lydie died within the nine-day period, she was named perhaps by her mother, by her father, or by other members of the community. As a result, her birth and death within the nine-day period are recorded in the 1826 slave register. Her name in the slave register appears as Lydie in the line regarding her birth and Leddie in the line noting her death at seven days (both lines note that she is the daughter of Jane). Jane is listed as a three-year-old mulatto in the 1817 slave register, and she would have been between the ages of nine and twelve when she gave birth to Lydie/Leddie sometime between late 1823 and early 1826. Her young age at the time of her daughter's birth and the unstated circumstances related to conception possibly contributed to the death of her newborn.

Even though the creation of these triennial slave registers was supposed to provide an accurate accounting of the number of enslaved people and a more systematic way of monitoring enslaved people in the British colonies in the Caribbean, the absence of some of these newborns in the slave registers underscores the incomplete nature of this recording system. As a result, the deaths of days-old infants are not fully captured in the official records, and the infant mortality rate overall based on such records does not present the entirety of this fatal reality at Rose Hall and at other Jamaican sugar plantations.

Moreover, even as their respective infants are unnamed and unrecorded in the official slave registers, we do not know whether Glister/Glissom, Kate, Gift/Giss, or other family members privately named these infants. We also do not know whether any or all of these enslaved women engaged in any mourning practices or customs by themselves or involving other family or community members at Rose Hall in recognition of the loss of these infants. The absence of any accounting and registering of these infants' deaths in the official slave registers did not necessarily translate into a similar absence of recognition, mourning, and grief for the loss of these souls for their mothers and other members of the Rose Hall community.

Even with the absence of notations regarding stillborn infants in the triennial slave registers, these registers reflect enslaved mortality realities at Rose Hall, including acute infant and child mortality, with the particular births and deaths of specific infants being recorded in the same register. These triennial slave registers consistently list the names of recently born children first, followed by the names of recently passed persons (of all ages). For example, the birth of Morris (one of Dorinda's children) and then his death at the age of two are listed in the 1820 slave register.[31] The birth and death of John at age one (one of Mary's children and one of Maphe's grandchildren) are listed in the 1823 slave register.[32] The Rose Hall Journal includes John's birth on April 16, 1822; however, due to missing pages in the journal in 1823, the specific date and cause of John's death are not included in the journal.[33] The birth and death of Marcus (one of Matilda's children and one of Nancy's grandchildren) are also recorded in the 1829 slave register. Matilda, a Creole woman listed as eighteen in 1817, had three children at Rose Hall.[34] Two of her children remained at Rose Hall in 1832. Her son Adam was noted as age one in the 1826 slave register and six in 1832.[35] Matilda's daughter Sylvia's birth is recorded in the journal in June 1831 and in the 1832 slave register.[36] Between the birth of these two children, Matilda's son Marcus died; his birth and death at age two are included in the 1829 slave register.[37] The birth and death of another infant named Maxwell (one of Bell's children and one of Celia's grandchildren) are also listed in the 1829 slave register. Marcus's age at death is listed as two years old, and Maxwell's age at death is noted as one year old.[38] Some of the children born at Rose Hall only lived for months. Charity (one of Brown's children and one of Augusta's grandchildren) is listed in the 1829 slave register; the record notes her birth and then her death three months later.[39]

Even though the slave registers indicate that a number of enslaved women had one child who died within the first couple of years of life, there were enslaved women at Rose Hall who had experienced the deaths of multiple young children. Mary, a Creole woman who was twenty-three in 1817, had at least five children.[40] Three were alive in 1832: Ned, described as sambo and age two in 1820 and then as mulatto and age thirteen in 1832;[41] Sally Rose, described as sambo and age one in 1823 and then as mulatto and age eight in 1832;[42] and Jimmy, sambo and six months old in 1826 and age five in 1832.[43] Mary also had two sons who passed. Her son John is described as sambo, and both his birth and death at age one are recorded in the 1823 slave register.[44] Allick, described as negro, was three months old in 1829, and his death due to fever at age two is noted in the journal.[45]

Creole Dorinda had at least four children who died before reaching the age of five. Her son Morris, as previously noted, died at age two, and two additional sons, Allick and Surry, died around their first birthdays.[46] One of her daughters, Eliza, died at age four.[47] Indeed, three consecutive triennial slave registers—1820, 1823, and 1826—list the death of at least one of Dorinda's children. Before and after these deaths, Dorinda had given birth to at least five additional children who had survived from birth to the 1832 final list of enslaved people who received their clothing allowance at Rose Hall: Sam, who was eleven in 1817 and twenty-five in 1832;[48] Anthony, who was seven in 1817 and twenty-one in 1832;[49] William, who was two in 1817 and sixteen in 1832;[50] Venus, who was one in 1826 and six in 1832;[51] and John, who was three weeks old in 1829 and two in 1832.[52]

Dorinda is referred to as the midwife in the Rose Hall Journal in 1830 (and probably the only midwife at Rose Hall at that time).[53] She is also described in the slave registers and other lists as "hospital attendant."[54] It is unclear how long she was a midwife at Rose Hall and what her particular duties and responsibilities were. Some enslaved midwives in the Anglophone Caribbean received remuneration for their skills and services.[55] There is no indication in the journal or other archival documents that Dorinda received any form of cash payments for her duties as midwife at Rose Hall. However, as stated earlier, the additional clothing she received during the 1828 clothing allowance might have represented partial recompense for her midwifery services. Her combined responsibilities at Rose Hall as a midwife and hospital attendant centered on her prenatal care of pregnant women, guidance and support during their laboring processes, and postnatal assistance with newborns.[56] It is important to consider the particular burdens of enslaved women such as Dorinda who had given birth to several children and experienced the deaths of a number of them as well. As previously noted, the records indicate that Dorinda had given birth to at least nine children, four of whom died between the ages of one and four. Perhaps Dorinda having given birth to the most children at Rose Hall during these early decades of the nineteenth century led her to be deemed a suitable midwife. It may also have been the case that Dorinda was interested in midwifery and doctoring in general, and those interests encouraged her to be in this particular position at Rose Hall. She might also have realized that even when dealing with the complications of pregnancy and myriad illnesses, she preferred this labor instead of joining other enslaved mothers (described as "worker-mothers" by Sasha Turner) in the fields day after day. Having experienced the loss of four of her children, Dorinda would have been keenly aware of the realities of infant mortality and the psychological, emotional, and physical reverberations for enslaved mothers in the wake of their children's deaths. Yet even as she dealt with the loss of multiple children, Dorinda still remained responsible for assisting and guiding other women through the birthing processes and care of their infants. We can reasonably assume that Dorinda experienced complicated and contradictory feelings and emotions as a result of all of these experiences.

Despite Dorinda being the only woman identified as a midwife at Rose Hall, the first reference to her as a midwife in the journal is in regard to her "neglect" of her midwifery duties. The journal entry for Wednesday, April 21, 1830, states: "Dorinda the midwife being ordered to the field for general neglect in the performance of her duty that proper [unclear handwriting] to abscond." The entry for the following day, Thursday, April 22, 1830, notes: "This Evening Dorinda returned."[57] And almost eight months later, in the journal entry on Saturday, December 11, 1830, it is noted that one of Elizabeth Palmer's children died a couple of days after being born due to "neglect of Dorinda—the midwife, being the fourth child in succession."[58]

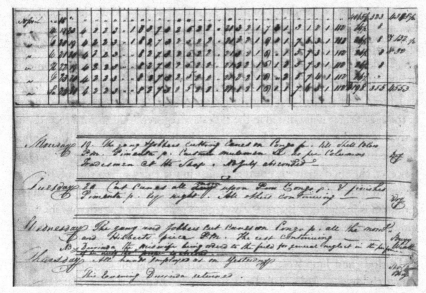

Notations regarding Dorinda, the midwife, running away on April 21, 1830, when
she was ordered to work in the field for "general neglect" of her duties, as well as her
return the following evening on April 22, 1830 (bottom of this cropped page).
JARD, 1B/26, RHJ, vol. 3, fol. 72a.

The reasons for Dorinda's "neglect" of her duties are unknown. It is possible
that Dorinda's own children demanded additional time and that her children's
requests and her responses compromised her time and attention related to her
midwifery duties. The cumulative effects of the loss of Dorinda's four children
between 1818 and 1824 might also have informed her "neglect" of her duties related to other enslaved mothers and pregnant women. She might have been particularly neglectful with pregnant women with whom she did not get along and/
or did not particularly like. No matter what the reasons for her "neglect" of her
duties, the harsh reality of her punishment of "being ordered to the field" un-
deniably resulted in her decision to abscond quickly from Rose Hall. Yet her
decision to return the following day may well have been guided by her familial
and communal connections to Rose Hall. Even if she had to serve temporarily
as a field worker, she would still be physically close to her five children—one of
whom, her youngest, John, was not quite one at the time Dorinda ran away. Indeed, Dorinda's "neglect" may not have involved any "neglect" whatsoever, given
the brutal, deleterious elements of slavery that reflected and exacerbated the precarity and disposability of Black life in the agri-industrial plantation complex in
Jamaica.

Of the forty-one enslaved mothers identified at Rose Hall, the majority of women—most of whom were also field workers—experienced the loss of a child, and several endured the death of multiple children. Like Dorinda, Juno had multiple children who died in infancy, although others lived.[59] Archival documents disclose the deaths of four of Juno's children. The 1823 slave register notes Juno's daughter Cecelia's birth and death at the age of one.[60] Her daughter Prue's death at the age of three is also listed in the 1823 slave register.[61] The journal records the arrival of another daughter of Juno's, named Lydia, on May 3, 1824.[62] The journal also mentions the death of Juno's child from lockjaw (tetanus) on January 6, 1826; however, the child's name is not mentioned in the entry. Given the information provided in the records, this is most likely Lydia.[63] The birth of Juno's daughter Susan is included in the 1832 slave register; she is noted as ten months old.[64] However, this register should also have included Susan's passing, as the journal notes that Susan died of fever on September 26, 1831.[65]

Dorinda and Juno were not alone in experiencing the loss of infants and young children at Rose Hall. Bell's first three children, Lewis, Maxwell, and Rosanna, had died between the ages of one and five. Her fourth child, Ned, five months old in 1832, perhaps lived into the postemancipation era. Brown's one daughter, Charity, passed when she was three months old, as listed in the 1829 slave register.[66] Charlotte's daughter, Doll, was seventeen in 1832;[67] however, her son, Thomas, died at nine years old in 1826.[68] Christianna's daughter, Jane, was born in 1831 and was noted as one in 1832;[69] her son, Henry, died at the age of two.[70] Glister/Glissom experienced the loss of two children, Sam, who died at ten days old, and an unnamed daughter, who died within the nine-day period. Glister/Glissom's daughter Marinda/Naranda was four in 1832.[71] As a result of the persistent presence of infant and child mortality, mourning itself might have been experienced and even understood as a painfully integral rite of motherhood at Rose Hall (and other Caribbean plantations). The enslaved women who experienced the deaths of their infants and young children at Rose Hall may have collectively offered each other compassion, comfort, and condolences, given their shared experiences of this particular loss and grief.

In 1831, on the eve of emancipation, African-born May possibly believed that the worst had passed in terms of the loss of a child. It had been over a decade since her daughter Peggy had passed; Peggy was fourteen in 1817, and she died at the age of seventeen.[72] May had two adult children in their thirties: Joan, who was nineteen in 1817 and thirty-three in 1832, and Sabina, who was eighteen in 1817 and thirty-two in 1832; both were field workers at Rose Hall.[73] Neither Joan nor Sabina was noted as having any children. There were also no children mentioned for May's eldest daughter, Lucretia. Unlike her younger sisters, Joan and

Sabina, Lucretia would not have the possibility of having any children at Rose Hall, as she passed in the year before the final triennial slave register of 1832. Lucretia was twenty-eight years old in 1817 and forty-two when she died.[74] We do not know whether Lucretia had been ill for some time or if her passing occurred suddenly due to an accident. In 1832 fifty-eight-year-old May was still working as a grasscutter, and she perhaps had been envisioning life beyond bondage with her three adult daughters. When Lucretia passed, May perhaps was grateful that at least two of her four children would live to experience abolition, but still she probably grieved for the loss of Peggy and Lucretia. At no point could enslaved mothers rest easy about their children's mortality; long after the ninth day of their children's births, even after several decades, enslaved mothers could still be confronted with the passing of their adult children.

No matter what comfort and support mothers at Rose Hall received, for some mothers of deceased children, the loss of a child perhaps hastened their own passing. Liddy, a twenty-six-year-old Creole woman in 1817, had three children. Pastora, Liddy's daughter, was eleven in 1817 and twenty-five in 1832.[75] North, her son, was six in 1817 and twenty in 1832.[76] Her youngest child, her son Parish/Paris, was four in 1817. However, both Liddy's and Parish/Paris's deaths are recorded in the 1823 slave registry. Liddy's age at death is noted as thirty, and Parish/Paris's is four. Parish/Paris's death as a result of worms is described in the journal on January 6, 1819.[77] For some reason, Parish/Paris's death is not recorded in the 1820 slave register. There is no specific information about Liddy's passing in the pages of the journal, and thus we do not know the circumstances surrounding her death. Although two of her children had survived their early years of life, perhaps when Parish/Paris passed at a young age, Liddy could not navigate her way through her mourning for him. Given Liddy's age at the time of her death—thirty years old— she would have passed a couple of years after Parish/Paris had died.

African-born elder Cecelia would outlive Liddy, her only daughter, at Rose Hall, and in 1832 Cecelia continued to labor at Rose Hall into her sixties. Two other African-born women, Dorothy and Rebecca, experienced the passing of their adult children. The death of Dorothy's daughter, Giss, at age thirty-two is noted in the 1826 slave register. Unlike Cecelia, who had two sons still alive at Rose Hall in 1832, Giss was the only recorded child of Dorothy's at Rose Hall. It is possible that Dorothy may have had other children living at other plantations. Even if that were the case, this may still have been a significant loss, possibly compounded by the fact that Giss's only recorded pregnancy resulted in a stillbirth. Perhaps Giss had benefited from the support of her mother and other enslaved women in the Rose Hall community when she experienced her own loss of a child. With Giss's passing, perhaps members of the enslaved community at

Rose Hall and other plantations would have comforted, supported, and loved
Dorothy as she continued to live at Rose Hall in the years after Giss's death. Dorothy was still working as a grasscutter at the age of fifty-nine in 1832.[78]

Giving the approximate timing of Giss's passing, Dorothy may have been
sharing her grief and mourning with one other enslaved woman in particular.
At the same time Dorothy was mourning Giss's passing, Rebecca was also grappling with a similar, though perhaps to her a compounded, loss. Rebecca, who
was fifty-two in 1817, had two children at Rose Hall.[79] Though she, too, may have
had other children living at Rose Hall and other plantations during her lifetime,
the 1817 slave register identifies her as the mother of Doshy, a daughter who was
twenty years old in 1817, and Exeter, a son who was seventeen in 1817.[80] The Rose
Hall Journal references the passing of Doshy on November 8, 1823, and the 1826
slave register notes Doshy's passing at the age of twenty-eight.[81] Exeter's passing
at the age of twenty-seven is recorded in the triennial register of 1829.[82] Given
Exeter's death at age twenty-seven and the placement of his name on this slave
register, he probably died between the end of 1826 and the beginning of 1827.[83]
As Doshy had absconded from Rose Hall on numerous occasions, Rebecca may
have expected Doshy eventually to run away successfully. Rebecca, however, may
not have anticipated or been prepared for Doshy dying before her at Rose Hall.
Indeed, Rebecca may still have been mourning the loss of Doshy when Exeter
passed. Exeter's death may have exacerbated her feelings of loss and perhaps even
regret. We do not know who may have shared Rebecca's feelings about her children's individual and joint deaths. What we do know is that Rebecca's passing is
recorded in the journal on July 15, 1828, and the reason for her death at the age
of sixty-three is noted as "old age."[84] As Rebecca labored at Rose Hall for at least
twelve years and possibly for much of her life, her age most certainly contributed
to her passing. However, her age may only have been one of several factors that
affected her passing in 1828; Rebecca's mourning for her two adult children and
possibly an extended collective mourning for other children at other plantations
with perhaps even older children in West Africa or West Central Africa may well
have been a significant cause for the timing of her own death.

Although the Rose Hall Journal documents the passing of children of all ages
for enslaved adult women at Rose Hall, not all of the mothers at Rose Hall had
experienced the loss of a child as adults. Jane Cranston is described in 1817 as
a three-year-old mulatto and daughter of Creole Sarah (also known as Sambo
Sarah and Sarah Spence).[85] As previously stated, the 1826 slave register notes the
birth and subsequent death of Jane's daughter Lydie/Leddie at seven days old.[86]
Jane's age in 1832 is noted as seventeen.[87] Given the three-year time period between slave registers, this meant that Jane would have given birth to her daughter

when Jane was between the ages of nine and twelve. We have no record of the biological father of Jane's daughter; and as the conditions of conception are also unknown, we do not have any indication of how Jane responded to this pregnancy or the death of her newborn. However, Jane's pregnancy and the subsequent birth of Lydie/Leddie illustrate one poignant example of the sociosexual vulnerability, fragility, and precarity of enslaved young girls at Rose Hall Plantation and other plantations in the Caribbean. Jane's feelings about the death of her child may have been complicated by a sense of mourning and grieving related to violations of her own innocence. We can neither understand nor begin to explain what these enslaved mothers experienced and felt with the loss of an individual child or several children, and no mourning rites and processes may have addressed the layered, profound dimensions of Jane's and other enslaved women's experiences and respective feelings.

Even as enslaved people abided in the shadow of death, not all enslaved women experienced the death of their children. The archival records do not have any information associated with the deaths of children for eighteen enslaved women (almost half of the worker-mothers) at Rose Hall: African-born women Augusta,[88] Polly,[89] Rachel,[90] Stella[91] as well as Creole women Bessy,[92] Chance,[93] Cynthia,[94] Daphney, Delia,[95] Dianna,[96] Hope,[97] Jeany,[98] Maphe,[99] Memmy Jen, Nancy,[100] Panella, Rosannah, and Sarah. Even as many enslaved mothers at Rose Hall lived to witness some of their infants survive beyond nine days or even nine years and beyond, not all of these mothers would endure long enough to see their children cross into adulthood. When she was seventeen years old, Memmy Jun gave birth to one son, Isaac.[101] However, only a couple of years after she gave birth to Isaac, Memmy Jun died at nineteen years old. The cause of death is not mentioned in the record.[102] Isaac was still alive in 1832 at age twelve. Panella was twenty-three when she gave birth to her daughter in 1817.[103] Her daughter Daizy is listed as two years old in 1820.[104] Even though Panella's life ended in 1822 due to consumption/tuberculosis, her daughter Daizy remained alive in 1832 at age thirteen.[105] Considering that Panella died when Daizy was four years old and that Isaac was even younger when his mother, Memmy Jun, passed, it is clear that another woman (or women), as well as other people in the Rose Hall community, mothered and nurtured both Daizy and Isaac in the physical absence of their respective biological mothers.[106]

The notes about the brevity of some of these mothers' lives offer evidence of the toll their quotidian duties and schedules took on them as worker-mothers who tended to sugarcane fields and, in a few cases, domestic duties in the great house or in the overseer's house. Daphney was forty years old in 1817, but her name appears in the next slave register, as she passed a year later. The overseer noted

that Daphney "died of natural decay." It is important to mention that Daphney's age at death was recorded as forty—a reflection of the deleterious, onerous effects of slavery on her and other enslaved people at Rose Hall.[107] Although
Daphney passed at forty, she lived to see both of her daughters enter different
stages of adulthood—her daughter Parthenia was twenty in 1817 and thirty-four
in 1832.[108] Her daughter Fanny was fourteen in 1817, though she passed at the age
of eighteen, a few years after her mother's death.[109] Like Daphne, Rosannah, one
of Celia's daughters, also died at the age of forty.[110] Rosannah's one child, Mary
James (mulatto), appears in the 1817 and 1832 registers.[111] Four of Mary James's
children remained alive at Rose Hall in 1832.

Even while they may have lived and labored at Rose Hall together over a
stretch of years or decades, enslaved worker-mothers were not always working
in close proximity to their children, no matter what their ages. Laboring as a
"domestic" at the great house or as a field worker did not necessarily translate
into enslaved mothers being in close proximity to their younger or older children. The four children of Sarah Spence (sambo and forty years old in 1817)[112]
at Rose Hall were all alive in 1832, and each worked in different areas of Rose
Hall's agri-industrial plantation complex: Molly Spence (sambo and twenty in
1817 and negro and thirty-three in 1832),[113] William (mulatto and nineteen in
1817 and thirty-three in 1832),[114] Bessy (mulatto and thirteen in 1817 and twenty-
seven in 1832),[115] and Jane Cranston (mulatto and three in 1817 and seventeen in
1832).[116] Both of Sarah's two grandsons (Bessy's sons) were also alive in 1832: quadroons Richard Mabon and Robert. With the categorization of her first child,
Molly Spence, as sambo/negro and her following three children as mulatto, it
is most likely that multiple men fathered Sarah's children and that at least one
father was a white man. Molly Spence was the only child of Sarah's who was a
field worker in 1832. William was a cooper, and Bessy was a washerwoman. In
1832 Jane was described as "with Mrs. Palmer." This probably included tending to
Mrs. Annie Palmer's needs and overall well-being; thus, Jane's position centered
on Mrs. Palmer in the great house.

It is likely that Sarah Spence's primary duty was not field work, especially
given her color categorization and the duties assigned to most of her children.
Even though she probably did not have to contend with the physically taxing labor of field work, Sarah may still have been responsible for a range of domestic
duties. Perhaps the onerous nature of those duties took a particular toll on her, as
Sarah's death at forty-seven is noted in the 1826 register (along with the death of
her youngest daughter Jane's infant, who died at seven days old). Although described as sambo in the 1817 list, Sarah is described as mulatto in the 1826 slave

register noting her death. There is no reason included in the slave register for Sarah's death. We do not know what could have caused her death at the age of forty-seven. We cannot be certain of the particular psychological, emotional, physical, and sexual burdens she experienced as the child of an unspecified enslaved woman (and possibly a white man), as the mother of three children who were fathered by one or multiple white men, as the mother of a daughter who gave birth to her first child between the ages of nine and twelve, and as the mother of another daughter who gave birth to two children described as quadroons (and thus also fathered by one or two white men).

It is possible that although Sarah and other enslaved women might not have had children with recorded deaths during their lifetimes, they might still have experienced the loss of children who are unrecorded in the official registers for Rose Hall—stillbirths and newborns who died within nine days of birth. The older women may have experienced the passing of their children at different ages while they labored at other plantations before their arrival at Rose Hall and even while they lived at Rose Hall physically separate and apart from other children. With the likely presence of "other mothers" (women who mothered and nurtured people who were not biologically related to them), even if these women did not experience the loss of their own biological child or children, they could still have been overcome with feelings of deep loss with the passing of "fictive kin" and "other children." Furthermore, even as some of these women lived to witness their children enter into adulthood, others also experienced the loss of grandchildren. Nancy's daughters entered their thirties while she was alive in 1832, though Nancy experienced the loss of two grandchildren, Leddy (Kate's daughter was six months old in 1826 and then dead at the age of eight months old in the subsequent slave register of 1829) and Marcus (Matilda's son, whose birth and death at age two are noted in the 1829 slave register).[117] Moreover, though this section focuses on motherhood, as is often the case in discussions of slavery and parenthood, we must also at least recognize the loss that some enslaved men experienced at the passing of children whom they fathered and nurtured and who may or may not have been their biological children.

We do not know the circumstances surrounding the conception and birth of any enslaved child born by an enslaved woman at Rose Hall or the specific biological father for any of these enslaved persons at Rose Hall. As on other sugar plantations throughout Jamaica and the Americas, the sexual violation of enslaved girls and women represented one of the deeply embedded tenets of chattel slavery.[118] After England's abolition of its involvement in the legal slave trade in 1807, the economic value of enslaved girls and women rose due to their potential reproductive capabilities. At Rose Hall, the records reflect the certainty of inter-racial sex between enslaved women and white men. Given the racial, gendered, and classed power dynamics of the slavocracy in Jamaica, we cannot assume "consent" of enslaved women in these circumstances. Some families may have experienced multiple generations of interracial rape at Rose Hall. Although the majority of enslaved people of all ages at Rose Hall were categorized as negro, in the records, as previously mentioned, there were a few enslaved people who were classified as mulatto or quadroon.

Mere references to the categorization of enslaved people as mulatto and quadroon do not reveal any sense of the conditions of conception. Just as the archival documents for Rose Hall fail to disclose the circumstances surrounding the conception of people referred to as negro, they also remain silent on the nature of the acts and processes that resulted in the births of those categorized as mulatto and quadroon. Due to the particular racial, gendered, and classed power dynamics on sugar plantations such as Rose Hall, it may be difficult to imagine the complexities, nuances, and simultaneity of such acts and processes of coercion and coitus. Evidence of white male enslavers' acts of sexual violation has been explored through their diaries and miscellaneous plantation records.[119] Although one enslaver provided detailed information of the acts from his perspective, the extent and depth of enslaved women's responses to these individual and collective acts remain unknown.

There are also no known diaries or journals and no sentences or words left behind written by any enslaved women at Rose Hall about any of their experiences that resulted in the birth of children sired by white men (or any men) at Rose Hall. We know that Celia's daughter Rosannah had one child, daughter Mary James, who was a fourteen-year-old mulatto in 1817 and a twenty-eight-year-old in the 1832 clothing allowance list. We do not know about Rosannah's specific responsibilities and jobs at Rose Hall; in 1832, though, Mary James's primary job was as a great house attendant. Mary James had five children living at Rose Hall: Peggy (quadroon, and her birth and death at age two are included in the 1823 register); John, also known as John Kerr (described as quadroon and age one in 1823 and ten in 1832); Henry (mulatto and age one in 1826 and six in 1832); Eliza Hill (mulatto and eighteen months old in 1829 and four in 1832); and Edward Hill (mulatto and two years and five months old in the 1832 slave registry). Although Mary James is categorized as mulatto, which indicated that her father was a white man, we do not know who Mary James's father was or what conditions led to Rosannah giving birth to Mary James. In a similar vein, with Peggy and John categorized as quadroon, we also do not know which white man (or white men) sired these two children of Mary James. When Mary James's daughter Peggy died at the age of two, did Mary James experience degrees of mourning or relief or both? Mary James's last three children (Henry, Eliza Hill, and Edward Hill) were described as mulatto (not quadroon or sambo), so it is unclear whether they were miscategorized as such or if the biological father or fathers of these children were also mulatto.

Evidence of transgenerational interraciality also exists in the records for another enslaved family at Rose Hall. Sarah Spence, also referred to as Sambo Sarah, is described as a forty-year-old woman in 1817. We do not know any information about her mother or father. Although she is described as sambo in 1817, she is recorded in the 1826 slave register as mulatto and dead at the age of forty-seven. Her first child, Molly Spence, is also categorized in two different ways in the slave registers (as sambo and twenty years old in 1817 and then as negro and thirty-three years old in 1832). Molly Spence was Sarah Spence's eldest child and the only one who was identified as a field worker. Given her primary duty, it is possible that Molly Spence was defined as negro in 1832 to be consistent with the color designation of the other field workers at Rose Hall. Sarah Spence's other three children are identified consistently as mulatto: William (nineteen in 1817 and thirty-three in 1832, cooper), Bessy McLaren (thirteen in 1817 and twenty-seven in 1832, washerwoman), and Jane Cranston (three in 1817 and seventeen in 1832, job with Mrs. Palmer). Sarah had two grandchildren living at Rose Hall in 1832; these were Bessy's children. Both are described as quadroon—Richard Mabon (one in 1823 and nine in 1832) and Robert (one in 1829 and three in 1832). As with Rosannah and Mary James, we do not know the circumstances resulting in the birth of Sarah Spence, her children, or her grandchildren.[120]

Without any diaries or journals or scraps of paper left behind by Rosannah, Mary James, Sarah, or Bessy, we do not know what transpired between these enslaved women and the white men for whom they bore children. At Rose Hall Plantation between 1817 and 1832, possible white fathers would have included the overseers and bookkeepers, as well as enslaver John Rose Palmer himself. Some scholars have downplayed the characterization of acts of sexual violation during slavery, especially in the discussion of enslaved mothers of mulatto or quadroon children. It is critical to recognize that whether sexual violation occurred only one time or occurred over decades between a white enslaver or overseer and an enslaved woman, the simultaneity of power, domination, and violence exercised through sexual acts must be directly recognized and addressed.[121] Without the words of these enslaved women who bore the children of white men, we perhaps can look to one fictional representation of sexual violation from the vantage point of an enslaved woman, Lilith, at Montpelier sugar plantation in Jamaica. Marlon James's novel *The Book of Night Women* offers a glimpse into one example of rape:

> Outside, the girl spin round two times and laughter rush in one ear and outside the other. The darkness giving her nothing. She can't make out shapes. Her left eye swell and her cheek wet from either sweat or blood. A driver they call McClusky grab her and she stop spinning. He set her good. The girl standing now but she teetering. She didn't see it coming. McClusky punch her straight in the face, between eye and nose. The girl fall back flat on the ground and near knocked out. She bite her tongue. . . .
>
> The girl only seeing a blur of white hands and faces and the faces have no eyes or nose or mouth. A hand grab her by the foot and drag her for a bit. Dirt scrape under her skin and rock cut up her legs. A hand grab her wrists and pull her up again. . . .
>
> The girl hear laughter running in and out of her ears again. Two hands grab two ankles and she try to scream through all the blood in her throat choking her. . . . Two hands drag her to what look like a stable. They pull her up to her feet again and start to push her from one set of hands to the other, and again and again and up and down until she lose balance with the ground and fall again. Two hand catch her. More laughter. The girl feel her dress rip off her body and cold air rush into her bruises. More laughter. McClusky say something about first and another voice say something violent. The girl hear a scuffle and a shout.
>
> —Mince her up, a voice say.
>
> One hand grab the girl left leg and the other grab her right and pull them as far apart from each other as sun and moon. She feel the air crawl between her. More laughter. A man pull down him pantaloon and slap him cocky till he ready. He throw himself on top of her to more laughing and shouting. The girl feel the whole weight of the man crushing her chest and forcing between her legs. A man with yellow hair, straight and sour. He grab her neck and her eyes go black.
>
> The ball still going and people still eating, drinking and merry-making. . . . The girl on the ground in the stable not moving, the dust making more sound than her.[122]

James's fictional description of the rape of Lilith should not be read as either entirely fictional or wholly exceptional. Indeed, in 1816 the Jamaican Assembly directly addressed the sexual abuse of enslaved girls who were under the age of ten. That the Jamaican Assembly dictated that any sexual activities with a female slave under the age of ten were punishable by death "suggests that the rape of enslaved girls under the age of ten was so prevalent that the Assembly enacted a law to prohibit it; it is also another indication that there was no consideration of childhood or girlhood on Jamaica's estates before the creation of the law."[123] Vasconcellos also presents cases in this category after the enactment of this law that were not adjudicated and concluded without any punishment at all. In fact, such cases only reified that "slaves were chattel, no matter their age," and thus entirely available and accessible to be exploited and sexually abused according to the desires, needs, and whims of whites.[124] Although archival records document the sexual abuse of enslaved women of African descent at the hands of white men with whom they interacted on a quotidian basis in Jamaica and throughout the Americas, an explicit description of such acts does not exist for Rose Hall. Nonetheless, the racial and color categorizations of enslaved people, especially enslaved children born at Rose Hall, provide evidence of such circumstances and the convolutions of slavery and sexuality. The recorded births of enslaved children at Rose Hall not only intimated conditions of bondage but also offered the naming of enslaved children as a lens for uncovering individualized and collective elements of belonging at Rose Hall.

NAMES AND NAMING PRACTICES

Even though the records provide limited information regarding the paternity of enslaved children and the circumstances surrounding respective conceptions at Rose Hall, the naming of enslaved people might offer some sense of the connections of kith and kin at Rose Hall. As discussed previously, the (un)naming of newborns who passed within days of their birth represents an aspect of enslaved infant mortality. It may have also reflected elements of disposability related to Black enslaved lives; however, this was only one dimension of the naming processes of enslaved people at Rose Hall. Indeed, scholars have long engaged in multiple interpretations of the meanings of names and naming practices among enslaved people and their descendants in the Caribbean.[125] Names and the processes of naming are deeply layered and textured within the African diasporic kaleidoscope. In some communities, names are also part of an elaborate constellation of familial and communal systems of belonging to respective lineages and communities. Naming practices among the Yoruba in Nigeria, for example, allow family, friends, and community members to offer their suggestions for names of the new members of their respective families and communities. These names might refer to circumstances related to the birth of children (e.g., twins named Taiwo (firstborn of twins) and Kehinde (second-born of twins), irrespective of

gender, though it is culturally believed that Kehinde is in fact the firstborn who
pushes Taiwo out into the world first), as well as honor and wealth bestowed on
the family (e.g., Folasade means "honor earns a crown" or "crowned with wealth
and honor"). These names frequently include connections to other family members, the timing of a child's birth, and namesaking (e.g., Yejide and Babatunde for
when a child is born relatively soon after the passing of a female or male elder in
the family such as a grandmother or grandfather as a way to pay homage to and
honor that passing elder).[126] Among the Akan of Ghana, birth order and special circumstances also shape the naming of children. Furthermore, day names
are often included in the naming process. For example, Sunday-born males are
called Kwasi or Kwesi, and Sunday-born females are called Akosua; Wednesday-
born males are called Kwaku, and Wednesday-born females are called Akua and
Akuba.[127] For the Yoruba, Akan, and Ga peoples, the eighth day after birth is
often the day designated for the naming of newborns.[128] These represent only
a couple of examples of the naming-related practices in West Africa; however,
these are by no means the only West African naming practices. Moreover, it must
be clearly declared that there was (and is) no monolithic, singular African naming practice in West Africa or for enslaved and free African-descended people in
the Caribbean.

The institution of slavery and the miasma of bondage compromised African
naming practices throughout the Americas and in many ways limited the enslaved parents' decision-making processes about what names parents (and enslaved community members generally) wanted for their children, including what
names they (as children or later as adults) would be referred to by enslavers. It
is not possible to know exactly who named individual enslaved people at Rose
Hall or what complicated processes of naming transpired in the days and weeks
following the birth of an enslaved infant (whether or not that infant survived beyond nine days of life). However, some of the names in the archival record might
offer a glimpse into enslaved people's use of names as a way of demonstrating familial connections grounded in community relations, recognition, and remembrance.[129] Names at Rose Hall might even serve as a way to determine a few instances of maternal and paternal connections that were neither specifically nor
directly stated in the triennial slave registers. Was the reference to infants living
beyond nine days (and possibly being named after that period of time) similar to
or even based on the Yoruba, Akan, and Ga practices of waiting until the eighth
day before a newborn's name was shared as part of a naming ceremony? Waiting
until the eighth day to name newborns in these West African contexts emerged
as a way to make sure the newborn had completely transitioned from one realm
to another and survived the first week of life before being named. This practice

also allowed some time for the family and community to get to know the newborn and to decide on appropriate names for the child. This practice and related West African and West Central African customs of naming might have been reshaped and utilized by African-born and Creole enslaved people in Jamaica partially in response to the deleterious circumstances and conditions of the plantationscape (including references in the archival documents about the ninth day after birth representing a particular kind of final gateway to a new realm of being).

Just as some naming practices may have been transformed due to the spatial shift from West Africa and West Central Africa to the Caribbean, we cannot assume that temporal consistency prevailed in any naming practices of enslaved people from the seventeenth century into the nineteenth century in Jamaica. Moreover, we simply do not know the multiple and even contradictory motivations of why enslaved people utilized names that might have been given by white enslavers or names chosen for themselves. Even when previously enslaved people chose "white" or "English" names in Jamaica, we cannot conflate that, neither clearly nor definitively, to a desire to be white. We can, however, consider that previously enslaved people wanted to shed the inferior meanings ascribed to Blackness and may have partially utilized names as a way to affirm and demonstrate their humanity, volition, and freedom. We still need to consider how enslaved people's understanding and use of names (like their invocations of naming practices) may have changed or been altered from the seventeenth century to the nineteenth century, from West Africa and West Central Africa to the Caribbean. Furthermore, at Rose Hall there were possible patterns of naming children after loved ones who had passed or in honor of an elder family or community member by whites or by enslaved people and/or even some combination of these two aspects. For some, too, Christian rituals (such as baptismal practices) might have created additional names for some enslaved people.

At Rose Hall there was only one clearly identifiable African or African-derived name in the official slave registers—Quaco. Quaco is considered a creolized form of the Akan day name for a male born on Wednesday; the name is Kwaku in the Twi language.[130] In the 1817 slave register, Quaco is the thirteen-year-old son of thirty-year-old Delia.[131] He is also the grandson of forty-five-year-old Creole Celia. We do not know what meanings Delia or other community members associated with the name Quaco itself. Quaco's family members could have chosen that name as a way of invoking familial history linked to the Akan people of West Africa. Celia's mother was probably African born, and she may have been Akan. Perhaps Celia or African-born members of the Rose Hall community became involved in Quaco's naming process and purposely decided to utilize an African-centered name in honor of the family's possible Akan connections. Although

Quaco's "Christian name," Robert Williams, is included in the 1832 clothing allowance list, the official slave registers only refer to him by the name Quaco. It is also possible that Quaco's family members were not aware of the Akan meaning of the name Quaco at all. They may have utilized it to convey a connection to an African past, with or without any familial or ancestral link to a particular region or cultural background.

In addition to the distinctly Akan-related name Quaco, there are also English familial references that might offer additional information about kinship bonds at Rose Hall. In the nineteenth century, the use of Junior and Senior reflected a familial relationship, specifically indicating one person being younger or older than another person. At Rose Hall there are two women's names presented in this Senior-Junior manner: Memmy Sen (short for Senior) and Memmy Jun (short for Junior). These designations might have been utilized simply as an efficient way for using the same name and including a reference to distinguish between the older Memmy (Memmy Sen) and the younger Memmy (Memmy Jun). This naming pattern might even have reflected the choice some enslavers claimed as a right to name enslaved people on their farms and plantations. Perhaps, though, these particular names were created as a way of honoring an elder by invoking the name again for a younger member of a family (namesaking) or another person in the enslaved community generally. In the 1817 slave register, Memmy Sen is described as a sixty-year-old African-born woman. Seven years later, the journal entry for November 1, 1824, includes a notation that "Old Mimmy an Invalid died" on October 30, 1824.[132] In the 1826 slave register, Memmy Sen's death is also recorded (at the estimated age of sixty-nine).[133]

In the 1817 slave register, Memmy Jun is a fourteen-year-old Creole (negro) girl, and she is identified as the daughter of Miranda, a forty-year-old African woman. If there were no relationship between Memmy Sen, Miranda, and Memmy Jun, why was this name repeated in this way? There is no archival confirmation that Memmy Sen was Miranda's mother and Memmy Jun's grandmother. However, it is possible that Memmy Jun was named by Miranda and perhaps by Memmy Sen, Memmy Jun's father, and other members of the community. This name choice might have represented a way of honoring one of the elder African women members of a family or of this community. But why does Miranda's daughter in particular have this name and not another enslaved child at Rose Hall? Although not specifically noted in the records, it is possible that Memmy Sen and Miranda were biologically related as mother and daughter or in some other familial relationship. Even if they were not biologically related, Memmy Sen might have nurtured and mothered Miranda as an infant or young child who may have been separated from her biological mother during the process of captivity, during the Middle Passage, or after they arrived in the Caribbean. Even if Memmy Sen was not Miranda's biological mother, she might have become for Miranda an "other mother" who helped her to navigate life at Rose Hall.

In this same family, Glister/Glossom (one of Miranda's daughters) named one of her daughters Marinda/Naranda. Before this child's birth, as noted earlier, Glister/Glossom had given birth to a son and a daughter, both of whom died within only a few days of their respective births. This third child of Glister/Glossom, Marinda/Naranda, is recorded as eighteen months old in the 1829 slave register, and she is four in the 1832 clothing allowance list. Glister/Glossom may have named this child with a derivative of the name of her mother, Miranda, as a way of honoring her African-born mother, as well as with the possibility that this name might also protect this child and allow for a longer life. In fact, Glister/Glossom's African-born mother, Miranda, remained alive in 1832 at the age of fifty-four and worked as the "cook for gang."[134]

This was not the only example of a younger Creole girl bearing the same name as an elder African woman at Rose Hall, whether they were related by blood or not. In the 1817 slave register, Cecelia is described as a forty-eight-year-old African-born woman, and in 1832, Cecelia is recorded as sixty-two years old and of "good" disposition, though "weakly."[135] On February 5, 1822, thirty-one-year-old Creole Juno gave birth to a daughter named Cecelia.[136] The following year, the 1823 slave register, however, records both this infant Cecelia's birth and her death at the age of one.[137] Although the elder Cecelia's life lasted for the entirety of the triennial slave registers from 1817 to 1832, the younger Cecelia's life, like that of many infants born into slavery in Jamaica, lasted but one year.

Seven years after Cecelia's birth and death in 1822 and 1823, another daughter of Juno, Hope, is noted in the 1829 slave register as two and a half years old.[138] Three lines below the listing of Hope's birth, the name Hope is repeated. This listing, though, is on the first line in the section on deaths. This elder Hope's age at death is noted as fifty-six in the 1829 slave register; the Rose Hall Journal records her death on December 7, 1828, due to "debility."[139] This elder Hope was Juno's mother, who appears in the 1817 slave register as a forty-five-year-old Creole woman. A record of the younger Hope's exact birth date does not appear in the readable pages of the journal. Given the younger Hope's age in 1829, she was probably born in 1826 or 1827 before her grandmother Hope passed. Perhaps given the elder Hope's declining health, Juno decided to name this daughter in honor of her mother, Hope. Unlike Juno's daughter Cecelia, young Hope survived her first year, and she is described in 1832 as four years old, "healthy," and of "good" disposition, working in the hogmeat gang or the children's gang, which was assigned to a range of cleaning and clearing duties on the plantation.[140]

The reasons for the naming of two of Juno's daughters after elder enslaved women at Rose Hall—one African born and the other her Creole mother—are not included in any of the slave registers or other plantation documents. With her infant daughter Cecelia dying within a year of her birth, Juno's next child after Cecelia (recorded in the slave registers) was daughter Lydia. The journal notes Lydia's birth on May 3, 1824.[141] This Lydia does not appear in the 1832 list of enslaved people at Rose Hall, and the journal notes the death (due to lockjaw) of an unnamed child of Juno's on January 6, 1826.[142] For Juno and possibly other members of the enslaved community at Rose Hall, another daughter's birth in 1826 or 1827 offered an opportunity to honor another enslaved woman in the community and, in this case, Juno's ailing mother, Hope. Perhaps the birth and death of two daughters one after the other and the arrival of another daughter in 1826 or 1827 served as another reason for naming this newborn Hope. In 1827 there may have been mounting hope not only for this daughter's survival but also for the possibility that this Hope's future (and the entire enslaved community at Rose Hall) would not be bound by the shackles of slavery.

The repetition of names reflects perhaps a marker of belonging and kinship within the Rose Hall enslaved community. This repetition occurred not only with the names of women but also with the names of a few men. In the 1817 slave register, Lewis is the name of two men, seventy-year-old African-born Lewis-ney and twenty-five-year-old Creole Lewis. As was the case with all African-born enslaved men at Rose Hall, the elder Lewis-ney (a.k.a. Jemmy) is not mentioned with any familial descriptions or family relationships at Rose Hall. Though he was not recorded as a father in the slave registers or in any of the other archival material, this does not necessarily mean that Lewis-ney/Jemmy did not have biological kin and/or create expansive kinship networks at Rose Hall. Given the age of the younger Lewis, it is possible that Lewis was named for the elder African Lewis-ney/Jemmy and even had a possible familial connection to him. With the forty-five-year age gap, Lewis-ney/Jemmy might even have been younger Lewis's grandfather.

In the 1817 slave register, the younger Lewis is noted as being the son of forty-five-year-old Creole Celia. If Lewis-ney were biologically related to younger Lewis, then Lewis-ney might also have been related to Celia—possibly Celia's father. Just as the records do not reveal Celia's mother or father, Celia may have given birth to other children who may have died at Rose Hall or lived on other plantations. The 1817 slave register includes references to Celia's five living children at Rose Hall: Rosannah (age thirty), Delia (age thirty and possibly a twin of Rosannah), Lewis (age twenty-five), MacGuire (age nineteen), and Bell (age fourteen). The 1817 slave register and subsequent lists include notes concerning

Celia's five grandchildren (Mary James, Quaco, Lewis, Maxwell, and Rosanna) and four great-grandchildren (Peggy, John, Henry, and Eliza). Moreover, the records only reference Celia's daughters' children and grandchildren. It is most likely that Celia's sons, Lewis and MacGuire, fathered children at Rose Hall and/ or other plantations. Celia may also have had other grandchildren and great-grandchildren living on other plantations if she had additional children who re-sided at other plantations.

Celia's son Lewis is specifically mentioned in the journal on December 8, 1818. When a Rose Hall wagon was in the process of running errands (including trans-porting shingles from another site to Rose Hall), Lewis is noted as "falling under the Wheel it Crush'd him so much as to cause his death."[143] The 1820 slave reg-ister notes Lewis's death at the age of twenty-five. After Lewis's death, another Lewis is mentioned in the records: Bell's son Lewis (and Celia's grandson), who is one year old and categorized as sambo in the 1823 slave register. The invocation of the name Lewis for this infant in this family was not necessarily coincidental. This Lewis is the first recorded child of Bell at Rose Hall. Bell was described as a fourteen-year-old Creole girl in 1817, so she was old enough to remember her uncle Lewis and even to have developed a connection to him before his fatal acci-dent in 1818. It is also possible that Bell, her mother, Celia, and other members of the community collectively decided to name Bell's son Lewis in the wake of Lew-is's untimely death and perhaps in honor of elder (and possibly family member) Lewis-ney/Jemmy, who passed in January 1824, only a short time after the birth of Bell's son.

Bell's son Lewis appears in the 1829 slave register; his death is noted at the age of five in this register. In this same slave register, another son of Bell named Max-well is also included; his birth and his death at age one are also recorded. After Maxwell's death, Bell gave birth to a daughter named Rosanna. It is possible that, given the similar name, Bell's daughter Rosanna was named in connection with Bell's aunt Rosannah. Infant Rosanna's birth is noted in 1829. Her birth is men-tioned in the Rose Hall Journal on May 11, 1829.[144] The journal also notes her death on March 6, 1832, at the age of two due to fever.[145] Although Bell may have had other children living on other plantations, in the Rose Hall records, only one of Bell's children was alive in 1832: her son Ned, who is described as five months old in the 1832 slave register. In 1832 Bell was described as twenty-eight years old, working in the field, "healthy," and of "good" disposition. Although Bell is char-acterized as being of "good" disposition, this did not necessarily or accurately re-flect Bell's state of mind, that of a twenty-eight-year-old woman whose primary duty was in the fields and who had experienced the death of three children (and possibly more unrecorded) over the course of a decade.

Like the repetition of the name Lewis, the appearance of another name in Memmy Jun/Mimmy's family might also indicate a familial connection. The journal notes that on Thursday, April 13, 1820, "Mimmy deliver'd of a Male Child." In the 1820 slave register, this son of Mimmy is identified as Isaac.[146] Is it possible that this child is named in honor of Isaac who died in March 1817? And if so, Isaac, whose name only appears at the bottom of the first page of the journal, announcing his passing, may have been connected to Memmy Jun's family. It might well have been her family, in addition to other community members, who mourned Isaac's passing.[147]

As in the case of Memmy Sen, the invocation and repetition of "Sen" for one other enslaved person might also refer to a familial connection. A forty-five-year-old African-born man named Patrick is noted in the 1817 slave register. The one and only time his name appears in the journal is in reference to his passing. A note in the journal on October 28, 1828, in the margin on the left side of the page states, "Patrick Sen died on the 28th Inst from eating a pisonus fish."[148] Patrick's death is included in the 1829 slave register.[149]

Patrick is also the name of one of the sons of African-born Miranda, who was forty years old in 1817. Miranda's son Patrick was born on September 8, 1818.[150] Records indicate that Miranda gave birth to three daughters before the birth of this son, Patrick (i.e., Memmy Jun, who was fourteen in 1817; Glister/Glissom, who was eleven in 1817; and Christianna, who was six in 1817). That Miranda's son is named Patrick may suggest a connection with African-born Patrick Sen—Patrick Sen may have been his father. Indeed, Patrick Sen may have fathered other children of Miranda who lived at Rose Hall (and possibly at other plantations). It is also possible that Patrick Sen, even if he were not the father of the younger Patrick, could have been an "other father" to the younger Patrick; he may have represented an important nurturing presence in his life.

The records do not allow for definitive answers regarding enslaved people's naming processes and name choices at Rose Hall. Even though Quaco is the only seemingly identifiable African name at Rose Hall, the names written on the official slave registers might only have included some of the names linked to enslaved people at Rose Hall. Other names—African-derived and/or newly created creolized names—might well have been invoked and utilized by enslaved people beyond the white gaze and hearing. It is possible that enslaved people created, adapted, and utilized African or African-derived familial naming processes and communal structures as avenues for the recognition of consanguineal connections, as well as for the remembrance of dead and/or elder members of Rose Hall's enslaved community. It is also critical to consider how enslaved people used naming as a process of reclaiming their humanity and their control over themselves and their family members.[151]

Even as enslaved people at Rose Hall may have developed and utilized particular naming practices, cultural customs, and communal processes to carve out moments and spaces that affirmed their humanity and their relationships at Rose Hall, the oppressive and consuming nature of the agri-industrial sugar plantation complex still infringed upon and compromised their individual and collective lives. The routine weekly listing of duties and responsibilities in the journal exemplifies the emphasis on the valuation of the jobs assigned to enslaved people and the erasure of the individual enslaved people who were responsible for the successful completion of these duties by any means necessary. The next chapter provides a sense of those individual enslaved persons who were relegated to the gangs laboring in the sugar fields, as well as those who were engaged primarily in other aspects of the workings of Rose Hall Plantation. The regular groupings of individual enslaved people in work gangs may have not only constituted a laboring unit but also engendered other interactions and relationships beyond the categorizations of being part of the "first gang," "second gang," or "third gang" or performing other jobs not solely centered on the harvesting of sugarcane (e.g., midwife, blacksmith, and cooper).

Interspersed throughout the litany of laboring in the Rose Hall Journal are references to enslaved women, men, and children who challenged the force of bondage. The next chapter highlights the persistent and continuous acts of those enslaved persons who risked their lives for even a few hours of freedom. As a result, overseers included a row in the journal for runaways—the row usually positioned at the bottom of the list of jobs and duties. Whether absconding for a few hours, days, or months or never caught, these recorded episodes of fugitivity present only one mode of resistance of countless acts and processes of resistance hidden seemingly behind veils of submission and masks of subjugation—often undetected and unrecorded in the extant archival records.

CHAPTER 3

"Till Shell Blow"

Labor and Fugitivity at Rose Hall Plantation

"Cane Gang"

Torn from the vine from another world
to tame the wildness of the juice, assigned
with bill and hoe to field or factory, chained
by the voracious hunger of the sugar cane

the world's rapacious appetite for sweetness

How place names of my servitude mock me:
Eden, Gold Vale, Friendship, Green Valley,
Hermitage, Lethe, Retreat, Retirement, Content,
Paradise, Pheonix, Hope, Prospect, Providence

Each with the Great House squatting
on the highest eminence
the Sugar Works overlooking
my master's eye unyielding
the overseer unblinking
not seeing
the black specks

                              floating across
                                        their finely crafted
                                                  landscape

At shell blow assembled the broken-down
bodies, the job-lots scrambled into gangs
like beads on a string O not pearls no just
unmatched pairings the random bindings
like cane trash no not like the cane pieces
laid out geometric and given names
and burning.[1]

"DAILY OCCURRENCES" OF
LABORING AT ROSE HALL

Even as enslaved people at Rose Hall engaged in personal intimacies centered on familial and communal activities, their lives revolved around their individual and collective duties and responsibilities, which were inextricably embedded in the harvesting of sugarcane, as well as the critical commodities and by-products of sugar and rum. Dereliction of these duties and responsibilities on plantations in Jamaica and throughout the Americas often elicited different modes of punishment, terror, and trauma. Acts and processes of violence and violation were inextricably linked to the routines and rhythms on plantations in the Caribbean. Violence was anticipated, threatened, or implemented at any particular moment, and specific, scheduled routines structured the laborious days of the plantationscape.

The phrase "till shell blow" appears frequently throughout the weeks and years of the overseers' summations of activities and incidents recorded in the Rose Hall Journal. The blowing of the shell was one of the signs (and often a primary sign and sound) of a transition from one physically arduous activity to another at different sections ("pieces") of the vast estate of Rose Hall. During the busy season of harvesting and processing sugarcane and due to the crucial element of timing after cutting sugarcane, enslaved people at Rose Hall (as on other sugar plantations) often worked well into the night. Indeed, at the peak periods of harvesting, shifts of enslaved people often worked around the clock in the various stages of the sugar-harvesting process. The recorded activities in the Rose Hall Journal for the weeks between March 1817 and November 1832 reflect the fairly regimented work schedule of enslaved people at Rose Hall. As on most sugar plantations, enslaved labor centered on the agri-industrial plantation complex of sugar and rum production. It is perhaps easy to imagine the monotony of each day at Rose Hall Plantation. The journal reflects the rituals, routines, and repetition of each day, week, month, and year of the sugarcane-harvesting processes.

The grueling processes on sugar plantations involved every possible woman, man, and child being charged with specific duties related to the sowing, tending, and harvesting of sugarcane, followed by extracting, boiling, and processing the juice for the production of sugar and rum. Beginning in June, the first and second gangs worked on preparing sections at Rose Hall for planting, which involved cutting grass, clearing sections, and burning and removing trash. From July to October and often extending into November, enslaved laborers continued to work on clearing/weeding sections, removing trash, carrying dung from livestock pens, dropping dung in sections, as well as digging cane holes (cane-holing) and planting cane. November and December often provided time for necessary repairs and maintenance activities involving both field workers and craftspeople (e.g., carpenters and masons). From January to May (the harvesting and sugar- and rum-making season), enslaved field workers focused on cutting the sugar- cane, and, once cut, it was taken promptly for the processing stages in the mill house, boiling house, and still house. Even while enslaved people cut sugarcane tops on several sections of the plantation at this harvesting time, they were also planting cane, "dropping dung" (fertilizing), and cleaning other specific pieces, demonstrating some degree of staggered cultivation at Rose Hall. By the end of May, work in the boiling house and the mill house usually ended. May and into June saw cleaning and clearing sections for planting, as well as the height of trans- porting wagonloads of sugar (in hogsheads and tierces) and rum (in puncheons and gallons) from Rose Hall to the Montego Bay wharf for exportation to En- glish cities such as London and Bristol.[2]

Although there is no extant record of the location of all of the specific plan- tation sections at Rose Hall, the names of the targeted "pieces" or sections of the plantation recur each year in the daily entries of the journal regarding work sites (e.g., Juba, Sheep Pen, Mahomet, Commodore, Monkey, Sula, Garden, Dog- wood, Horse Stable, Congo, James, Pimento, Fruittree, Hibbert, Cassava, Lamb, Rocky Hill, George, Neasberry Pasture, Quarrie Pasture, and Little Hill Pas- ture).[3] Enslaved workers at Rose Hall would have become familiar with the reg- ular rotation from one section of the plantation to the next. They would have been keenly aware of the feel of the soil when it was ready for planting the cane cuttings, how deep to dig the holes for the cuttings, how much and what mixture of dung to use for manure, when the cane was optimally ready for cutting to be taken expeditiously to the mill house, when the juice had been adequately re- duced and purified, when it was ready to be treated and purified with lime juice, and when it was finally ready for the crystallization process.

The enslaved persons on the official triennial slave registers for Rose Hall did not constitute the entirety of the enslaved laborers at Rose Hall. Every year from the first year of the Rose Hall Journal, additional enslaved people described as "Hired Negroes" appear as a supplemental enslaved workforce.[4] In the journal, there are regular notes about "Hired Negroes" (and in the final years of the jour- nal about "Jobbers") from specific enslavers working at Rose Hall during the har- vesting season. Many of them were identified as "Joseph Ridley, Esq's Hired Ne- groes" and "Mr. Kerr's Negroes."[5] They were often at Rose Hall during the har- vesting season. They were not described individually by name, only collectively as "Hired Negroes" or "Jobbers." It is possible some may have regularly worked at Rose Hall year after year and become part of the overall enslaved community there (and even developed relationships with the enslaved people who had been connected to the plantation for years and decades).

The 1832 clothing allowance list of enslaved people at Rose Hall specifies the range of positions and responsibilities on sugar estates, and it indicates the respective primary assignments for all enslaved people at Rose Hall (excluding these "Hired Negroes"). It delineates the gendered division of skilled work, with enslaved women's primary positions centered on field work and many of the enslaved men's positions as skilled craftsmen and in specialized jobs related to the sugar and rum production processes. It is important to note the various duties and responsibilities of enslaved children that were not specified in the clothing allowance records. In her work, Vasconcellos delineates that younger enslaved children, often between the ages of five and nine, in the hogmeat or children's gang on Jamaican plantations worked the same twelve-hour days as adults, and some of their duties included carrying manure, disposing of trash, weeding and picking grass, collecting food for livestock, and other chores. After the hogmeat or children's gang, enslaved children beginning at the age of nine or ten would then become part of the second gang. Vasconcellos states: "Comprising mainly children between the ages of nine and fifteen, the second gang usually performed the same tasks as the adults."[6] A smaller cadre of enslaved children between the ages of nine and fifteen who labored primarily as domestics and not in the sugar fields "assisted with food preparation and cooking, cleaned pots and kitchen utensils, and attended their master's or mistress's every whim."[7] Usually at the age of fifteen or sixteen, enslaved children then joined the first gang, composed of enslaved adults, unless they were selected to continue working as domestics (e.g., cooks and washerwomen) or, for a small group of enslaved young men, as craftsmen or tradesmen (e.g., carpenters, coopers, and blacksmiths).

Visitors from England who were unfamiliar with the workings of Jamaican plantations might have been surprised by the duties enslaved women were responsible for at Rose Hall. As Sasha Turner notes, "By the closing decades of the eighteenth century, enslaved women formed the bulk of field workers on the majority of Jamaican sugar estates."[8] The majority of enslaved women at Rose Hall worked in the sugarcane fields for an average of twelve hours each day, except for the selected "Negro Days," when they labored in their provision grounds. Of the 111 enslaved people on the 1832 clothing allowance list, 60 are identified as female, and 51 are identified as male. Of the sixty females, thirty-seven—ranging from the ages of twelve to forty-nine—are categorized in positions directly connected to the planting and harvesting of sugarcane. Of the sixty, twenty-seven are defined solely as field workers: Julina (age forty-nine), Arabella (forty-nine), Delia (forty-four), Zebra (forty-two), Juno (forty), Susanah Johnson/Elizth. Palmer (thirty-nine), Charlotte (thirty-nine), Kate (thirty-eight), Mary (thirty-seven), Pathenia (thirty-four), Jeanie (thirty-four), Molly Spence (thirty-three), Chance (thirty-three), Joan (thirty-three), Frankie (thirty-two), Matilda (thirty-two), Sabrina (thirty-two), Bell (twenty-eight), Brown (twenty-eight), Flora (twenty-six), Cynthia (twenty-five), Glissom/Glister (twenty-five), Pastora (twenty-five), Kitty (twenty), Clarinda (nineteen), Diana (nineteen), and Frances (twelve). These twenty-seven females would have been regularly grouped in and assigned to the first gang or great gang. At Rose Hall, one African-born woman named Jannet was the driveress in 1832. Due to their age (in their early fifties), two additional women, Creole Nancy and African-born Augusta, are described as field workers and grasscutters. The other seven enslaved women in their fifties in 1832 are described only as grasscutters. These women were not part of the first gang, and depending on age, health, and ability, they would have been part of the second gang (and a few possibly were in the third gang). This group included African-born women Amelia, Dorothea, May, Cowslip, and Ruth, as well as Creole women Celia and Maphe. These thirty-seven enslaved women who were field workers represented approximately 60 percent of all the enslaved women at Rose Hall.

African-born Cecelia, the oldest woman at Rose Hall (sixty-two in 1832), is the only person described as "attending young children." Cecelia most likely had labored in the cane fields of Rose Hall for many years, probably multiple decades, before transitioning to this particular duty. The eight youngest enslaved female workers, categorized as part of the hogmeat gang, were all Creole children between the ages of four and nine: Eve, Sally, Bess, Elizabeth Chambers, Venus, Suckie, Hope, and Naranda. Duties of the hogmeat gang included collecting trash, weeding, helping with livestock, and performing other ancillary duties on the plantation.[9] The three youngest girls, who were classified as "not at work," were four-year-old mulatto Eliza Hill, one-year-old mulatto Jane, and one-year-old negro Sylvia. Although a first gang designation was often associated with a group of younger, healthier enslaved people engaged in the most physically intense aspects of the sugar-planting and sugar-harvesting processes, in the Rose Hall Journal the overseers consistently describe the combination of enslaved people in the first and second gangs as being responsible for these shared laborious duties, especially during the planting and harvesting months.

Selected enslaved people (both adults and children) attended to the needs of enslavers and overseers and were included in the Rose Hall Journal based on these positions or generally as "domestics." The number of domestics assigned to the great house ranged from one to seven, the smaller number reflecting the absence of enslavers and the larger number of additional whites in the house (not only enslavers but also guests at Rose Hall). In the final years of the journal, two domestics were regularly singled out in a separate category as being "With Mrs. Palmer." In addition, there were five to eight enslaved people assigned to the overseer's house (with some additional references to the bookkeeper's "out offices"). Other persons included in the category of domestics are the washerwomen. The early years of the journal include these women in the category of "domestics"; however, in the later years of the journal, overseers created a separate category for the one or two "washerwomen" at Rose Hall. In 1832 the three people assigned to the great house were all Creole women: twenty-eight-year-old mulatto Mary James as "Great House attendant," seventeen-year-old mulatto Jane Cranston as "with Mrs. Palmer," and thirteen-year-old negro Daizy as a "domestic." Although the number of women often varied, in 1832 one woman, twenty-one-year-old Creole Christianna, was assigned to the overseer's house. There were also two Creole women who are described as "washerwomen": forty-two-year-old Creole Susannah Scott and twenty-seven-year-old mulatto Bessy McLaren. The cook for the gangs was fifty-four-year-old African-born Maranda.

Although the number of enslaved women "lying-in" and the number of sick enslaved people varied from day to day and month to month, there were always a couple of enslaved people assigned to "the hospital." One of the most consistent enslaved people in the hospital was forty-four-year-old Dorinda, described as the midwife and as "hospital attendant."[10] In 1832 the other enslaved woman assigned to the hospital was twenty-three-year-old Rose, who is also described in 1832 as having "one leg." No doubt this physical circumstance (which is not described further) limited her ability to perform agricultural duties. Only two Creole young women are not described as field workers but as "attending small stock": seventeen-year-old sambo Doll and thirteen-year-old Philis.

Unlike the majority of enslaved women, the majority of enslaved men did not work in the cane fields at Rose Hall. Instead, they were involved in sugar and rum production, including the boiling and distilling processes. They also worked as craftsmen, referred to as "tradesmen" in the journal in the final years, for example, as coopers and blacksmiths.[11] Some men were placed in titled gendered positions associated with tending livestock or auxiliary jobs in the agri-industrial plantation complex (specifically as cattleboys, cartmen, mulemen, and watchmen). Of the fifty-one enslaved males at Rose Hall in 1832, only four were solely field workers: Hercules (age twenty-three), Gloster (twenty-two), July (eighteen), and Patrick (thirteen). Two enslaved men are identified as drivers: George (thirty-nine) was head driver, and Harry (thirty-five) was second driver. Due to their ages, two enslaved boys were in the hogmeat gang: five-year-old Jennie/Jimmie and four-year-old Thomas. An additional six enslaved boys were "not at work": six-year-old mulatto Henry McLean, three-year-old quadroon Robert, two-year-old negro John, two-year-old mulatto Edward Hill, one-year-old sambo James, and seven-month-old negro Ned.

Of the fifty-one enslaved men at Rose Hall in 1832, thirty (approximately 60 percent) were assigned duties primarily outside of field work. There were six cattleboys (all Creole): James (eighteen), Oliver (sixteen), William Kerr (sixteen), Othello (fifteen), Isaac (twelve), and Adam (six).[12] The three (Creole) cartmen were Pitt (twenty-eight and head cartman), Mark (twenty-one and a cartman), and Ben (thirty-one and a cartman and field worker). There were two mulemen: Creole Anthony (twenty-one) and Creole North (twenty). African-born Aaron (forty-one) was the head penkeeper. There was one fisherman—Creole Peter (thirty-two). The seven watchmen were African-born March (sixty-four), African-born Bolton (sixty-two), African-born Washington (fifty-nine), Creole Ulysses (fifty-four), Creole Joe (forty-six), Creole Shemonth (forty-two), and Jack (connected to the estate of Mr. Kerr and no country of origin or age noted). Eight craftsmen are identified: African-born Ross (fifty-six) as mason, Creole Smith (thirty-seven) as blacksmith, Creole William Scott (forty-four) as head carpenter, Creole Bush (fifty-four) as carpenter, Creole Adonis (thirty-nine) as head cooper, and three additional coopers: Creole Hannibal (fifty-four), Creole William (thirty-three), and Creole Sam (twenty-five). Three enslaved men are noted as holding other specialized jobs related to the boiling and distilling processes: African-born Garrick (fifty-four) as distiller, Creole Scipio (twenty-nine) as distiller and field worker, and Creole Quaco (twenty-seven) as head boiler.

Five enslaved boys and men are noted as being assigned to the great house and the overseer's house. Sambo Charles (thirteen) is the only male described as being "with Mrs. Palmer." African-born Ralph (fifty-four) is identified as the overseer's cook, and three younger Creole enslaved boys were based at the overseer's house: mulatto Ned (thirteen), quadroon John (ten), and quadroon Richard Mabon (nine). And only one enslaved man, African-born Bryan (forty-six), was working away from Rose Hall, "at Palmyra."

The 1832 clothing allowance list provides some sense of the range of duties of enslaved girls, boys, women, and men at Rose Hall; these and similar categories of labor also defined the official parameters of enslaved people's labor on sugar plantations throughout the Americas. It is clear from this list of names and respective duties that enslaved women, especially worker-mothers, were encumbered with the majority of work related to the arduous planting and harvesting processes of sugarcane at Rose Hall. Not only were enslaved women responsible for most of the planting and harvesting of sugarcane at Rose Hall, they were entirely responsible for the reproductive labor involved in pregnancy, childbirth, and childcare processes. Furthermore, enslaved worker-mothers at Rose Hall were particularly burdened with field work, as they also attempted to breastfeed and take care of their children. As the white mistresses at Rose Hall did not have any children, enslaved women did not serve as wet nurses or nannies for any white children of their enslavers. This allowed enslaved worker-mothers to focus on breastfeeding their own infants (and, when necessary or requested, the newborns of other enslaved women).[13]

Pregnancy, childbirth, breastfeeding, and related childcare practices did not automatically result in significant changes to enslaved women's duties as laborers in the sugar fields or in other areas of the agri-industrial plantation complex in Jamaica. As Colleen Vasconcellos states, "Pregnancy and childbirth did not guarantee immunity from their plantation duties, and most enslaved women worked until a few days before their due dates only to return to work a few days after giving birth."[14] Some enslaved pregnant women delivered their babies in the midst of working in the sugar fields.[15] Even though there are no direct references in the journal to a consistent designated amount of lying-in time granted to pregnant women before or after the delivery of children, the overseers fairly consistently note the number of pregnant women and the number of women lying-in at the hospital. The names of pregnant women, however, are rarely included in the "Pregnant" category or the combination category of "Pregnant and Lying in with Midwife." Only a couple of overseers included the names of women who were pregnant and lying-in; for the most part, though, only the number of women is included in this category. As a result, the inconsistencies with bookkeeping make it difficult to calculate how much time was granted to enslaved mothers at Rose Hall individually and collectively for a lying-in period before and after childbirth. The descriptions of overseers, however, of such allowances for a lying-in period for enslaved pregnant women at Rose Hall are neither delineated solely within the limits of the Rose Hall Plantation nor dictated only by the perspectives of these overseers at Rose Hall Plantation or other Jamaican plantations.

As Sasha Turner critically discusses, the final decades of the eighteenth century and the early decades of the nineteenth century in Jamaica represented a time of intense surveillance and regulation of enslaved women's practices related to pregnancy, breastfeeding, and caretaking of their young children.[16] Early on in the journal, beginning on March 17, 1817, the term "Doctress" appears on the "Distribution of Negroes" page.[17] The overseer included a combination column for "Doctress & Gardner." Although these two separate positions held by two different people might not seem to be linked due to their differing purposes, perhaps the overseer understood the doctress's ability to attend to enslaved people as rooted in doctoring skills via the usage and prescription of natural remedies and cures from herbs, seeds, leaves, flowers, and bark. The term "Doctress" continues to be noted through the week of November 3, 1817.[18] The following week, the week beginning on November 10, 1817, the category changed to "Doctor & Gardner."[19] The overseer mentioned neither the name of the enslaved woman who served as "Doctress" during this time in 1817 (and possibly for an extended period before March 1817) nor the name of the enslaved man who became the "Doctor" at Rose Hall. The name of the gardener is also not specified. A few months later, on March 16, 1818, this category was slightly adjusted to "Doctorman and Gardner."[20] The overseer reinstituted the combination category "Doctor and Gardner" beginning on November 9, 1818.[21] The position "Doctor" (combined with "Gardner") remained in the "Distribution of Negroes" list until the week of March 20, 1820.[22] After that week, only the term "Gardner" was included, without the term "Doctor." There is no indication of whether the enslaved man who served as "Doctor" continued to perform the same duties and was simply no longer singled out in a separate category in the "Distribution of Negroes" or if this enslaved man stopped serving (or was ordered to no longer serve) in this capacity. It is also unstated in the journal whether unnamed enslaved people and/or white people served in this role after this point. However, in the final months of 1832, the overseer created a separate, new boxed section at the bottom of the weekly entries entitled "Doctors Visits," with specific doctors named on selected days of each week (e.g., Dr. Larson, Dr. Chambers, and Dr. Spencer).[23] The specific patients of these white male doctors and the respective illnesses they were treating are not included in the entries.

This shift from the position of enslaved doctress or doctor at Rose Hall to regular visits by official white male doctors (a couple of times a week) reflects a broader transition beginning in the latter half of the eighteenth century and extending into the early nineteenth century. Before the enactment of ameliorative laws in Jamaica, enslaved mothers returned to the sugar fields within days of childbirth with their children on their backs. However, amelioration resulted in the establishment of nurseries on plantations where other (usually older) enslaved women attended to enslaved infants while their mothers labored in the sugar fields.[24] In addition to these newly established nurseries due to ameliorative efforts, the Consolidated Slave Law of 1788 also required regular monitoring of enslaved people on plantations with visits of white doctors and a reward system to incentivize overseers and enslavers to encourage natural increase in Jamaica. Some Jamaican enslavers and overseers also engendered reward systems for enslaved women that included the possibility of extra food, clothing, and even colonial currency in order to encourage additional births of healthier infants and reduce enslaved infant mortality.[25] An 1801 amendment to the Consolidated

Slave Law of 1788 stated that enslaved mothers who had six or more living children should receive an exemption for all labor on Jamaican estates. It is unclear how many enslavers in Jamaica abided by this amendment and how enslaved worker-mothers perceived such stated rewards and incentives. These legislative maneuvers were not grounded in the elevation of the individual and collective humanity and well-being of enslaved women and their children; instead, these acts centered on encouraging the natural increase of enslaved people in the service of the racist, capitalist enterprise of the Jamaican slavocracy.

Instead of the doctoring linked to enslaved women's reproductive and child-care processes being focused on and controlled by enslaved women, the doctoring of enslaved women on Jamaican plantations moved further into the hands of white male doctors. The respective differing perceptions and agendas of abolitionists, enslavers, doctors, the imperial and local Jamaican governments, and enslaved persons (especially enslaved women) generated and exacerbated conflicts due to differences, as Turner posits, "in skills and approaches to caring for the bodies of laboring women. . . . Rivalries between doctors, planters, and enslaved women further developed over the meaning of work associated with childbirth. The economic motivations of planters to reform plantation medicine competed with enslaved people's expressions of independence and social belonging developed around the clinical acts of caring for mothers."[26] Furthermore, Turner states, "power struggles were also at play. Control over childbirth gave women access to power, even if brief and informal. For doctors, monopolizing plantation health care boosted their professional authority and generated revenue." As Turner maintains, "In conflict similar to the gendered class struggles in England between poor, rural midwives and mostly urban man midwives, doctors and enslaved women in Jamaica further clashed because the social nature of childbirth within enslaved people's communities contradicted the individualized, scientific approach that doctors believed was necessary to improve plantation medical care."[27] However, Turner argues, "Unlike the British conflicts that pivoted around concern by the male-dominated medical establishment about women's control over childbirth," the divergences in Jamaica "included those gendered conflicts in addition to the concern of [the] Jamaican ruling class to maintain slavery by boosting population growth." Thus, tensions and "rivalries between midwives, and doctors over the treatment, care, and healing of enslaved women's reproductive bodies, or what we may call *reproductive body work*, politicized black midwifery. The child-care work of enslaved women defined how black reproductive bodies ought to be treated and contested slaveholders' reduction of childbearing to the production of a marketable commodity. In addition, maternal labors of enslaved women affirmed their social connectivity."[28] It is important to note, however, that the duties and responsibilities extended to white midwives in early modern Britain were not granted to enslaved Black midwives in the colonial Jamaican slavocracy. [29] Moreover, the duties and related benefits afforded to midwives were not consistent across different plantations within the British Empire; responsibilities and remuneration for midwives reflected racial, gendered, and socioeconomic status positionalities.

How particular rivalries played out at Rose Hall is not included in the multiple overseers' notes. However, it is clear from the Rose Hall Journal entries regarding Dorinda that as the midwife and one of the hospital attendants, she served as a significant (if not primary) person responsible for the care of pregnant women at Rose Hall. Dorinda may have acutely experienced the heightened integration of white male doctors' presence and authority within the hospital at Rose Hall. Her own responsibilities and what she may have perceived as partial control and authority in the hospital may have been compromised and significantly reduced over time by the increasing role(s) of white male doctors. Indeed, it is wholly possible that Dorinda's previously mentioned "neglect" of her midwifery duties in 1830 may have partially reflected a response stemming from her discontent with the burgeoning presence of white male authority in the hospital, including possible changes to her duties and evolving procedures related to the overall care of pregnant enslaved women at Rose Hall. Although not being assigned to the fields was one benefit of Dorinda being a midwife, the archival records do not indicate any special benefits or payments extended to Dorinda for her midwifery duties.

Although Dorinda held a primary position in the hospital taking care of pregnant women before, during, and after childbirth, she was not alone in taking care of infants and young children, given that sixty-two-year-old African-born Cecelia, the eldest woman at Rose Hall in 1832, was "attending young children." We have no information about whether Cecelia was responsible for attending to all of the infants and young children who were "not at work." We also do not know whether she considered this duty a blessing, a burden, or both. Given that enslaved women in their late fifties continued to labor as field workers and as grasscutters, perhaps for Cecelia, attending to the young children was not only a labor of love but also an opportunity to be rid of the fetters of field work. We do not know how she attended to these young children. Did she solely attend to making sure they were fed and safe? As the eldest African-born woman at Rose Hall, Cecelia may have understood her job attending to young children as an avenue for sharing information about African history, stories, lessons, and cultural practices with these young children (and others at Rose Hall). Even as she attended to the young children, did Cecelia also attend to the worker-mothers at Rose Hall, aid-ing and guiding them in the care of their children in ways that integrated cultural customs based in West Africa or West Central Africa?

Even as Cecelia's primary duty in 1832 involved attending to the young children, not all young children may have been under her care. Notations in the Rose Hall Journal and in the 1832 clothing allowance list refer to enslaved children who worked in the great house and the overseer's house. Both adults and children were assigned to the great house to attend to the needs and desires of those who lived in both spaces. Enslaved children and adults categorized as mulatto and quadroon often held domestic positions within the great house. In the Rose Hall overseer's house in 1832, the two enslaved adults associated with that house are fifty-four-year-old African-born man Ralph, who was the overseer's cook, and twenty-one-year-old Creole woman Christianna, who was noted simply as at the overseer's house. Christianna's duties may well have been as "housekeeper" at the overseer's house; this role often included a presumed sexual accessibility and availability of the enslaved women in this position. Christianna had two children at Rose Hall, and both were categorized as mulatto. Her son, Henry, is two months old in the 1829 register, and in the same register his death is recorded at age two.[30] The birth of her daughter, Jane, is recorded in the journal on January 23, 1831, and Jane is one year old on the 1832 clothing allowance list.[31] Jane was "not at work" in 1832 due to her age; she most likely was also living at the overseer's house with her mother.

The four children officially described as at the overseer's house were Ned (thirteen, mulatto), John Kerr (nine, quadroon), Richard Mabon (eight, quadroon), and Henry McLean (six, mulatto). There were multiple enslaved mothers of these children. Creole Mary (a field worker in 1832) was the mother of Ned. Creole Mary James (Great House attendant in 1832) was the mother of both John Kerr and Henry McLean. Creole Bessy McLaren (mulatto washerwoman) was the mother of Richard Mabon. Although Bessy's position was not directly at the overseer's house, it is likely that her association with the overseer at Rose Hall at that time resulted in her son Richard Mabon being assigned to the overseer's house.[32] Given the multiracial descriptions of these enslaved children at Rose Hall and the respective positions of their mothers, the overseers were probably the father(s) of all of these children. Furthermore, it is possible that Robert McLaren, who served as an overseer at both Rose Hall Plantation and Palmyra Plantation at different periods between 1803 and 1821, was Bessy McLaren's father, and she may well have been associated with this overseer during her lifetime.[33]

No singular attribute determined enslaved people's placement in specific jobs in particular venues at Rose Hall. Gender, age, color, abilities, disabilities, familial connections, interactions with enslavers and overseers, and a range of other perceived, assumed, and actual characteristics and relationships established the particular kinds of duties they held at Rose Hall over time.[34] For young children, witnessing family members and others in the enslaved community at Rose Hall at work in various positions served as a primary mode of education about what their own duties would probably be as they transitioned from childhood to young adulthood, possibly to elderhood, and eventually death. The types of labor performed and the particular settings for these duties also created additional opportunities for risk, danger, and even fleeting moments of relief. No matter what duties they performed at Rose Hall, every enslaved child, woman, and man understood that their lives were not entirely their own. They recognized that even as they developed relationships with other enslaved people at Rose Hall, these relationships and people's experiences and lives were deeply embedded in and bound by slavery. As on other plantations across the Americas, enslaved people at Rose Hall were keenly cognizant of the reality that for them and possibly for generations of their families, Rose Hall would be a site of their bondage until and unless they freed themselves.

FUGITIVITY AND OTHER "CRIMES" OF FREEDOM

"Shell Blow"

For we—as you know—
are master engineers when it comes to

scratching out a living on vinyl, on dutty
or plantation. We is Ginnal at the Controls!
Nansi Nation. We can rib it up, dibble it,

rub it, dub it and fracture it. Splice it. Spice
it up. But like a spite, we still can't find
a way to erase not one word. They say,

that is how History stay. Say you bound
to re-live it on and on. Unless you can find
a way to shell it out; pass it on.

PASS IT ON![35]

Whether slaves primarily worked as field workers in the three gangs in the sugarcane fields of Rose Hall, as "domestics" in the great house or overseer's house, as a midwife in the hospital, as coopers or other craftsmen, as cattleboys or mulemen tending to livestock, or in a range of auxiliary positions underpinning the agri-industrial plantation complex, sites of labor often shaped and informed enslaved people's avenues to—"rib it up, dibble it, / rub it, dub it and fracture it. Splice it. Spice / it up"—resist.

Fugitivity has been a central dimension of slavery studies for generations of scholars.[36] Digital humanities projects have been one particular venue for the presentation, exploration, and analysis of fugitivity, especially the examination of runaway slave advertisements in the Americas.[37] Although they are a particularly useful source of information and a record of countless enslaved people who absconded from plantations, such advertisements do not capture all runaway attempts. Moreover, even as penal institutions developed as central sites of incarceration for those residing in St. James Parish, for enslaved people at Rose Hall, it was the jail within the bowels of Rose Hall's great house itself that operated as the primary venue for the punishment, containment, and confinement of those enslaved at this plantation.[38]

The Rose Hall overseers utilized the journal as a way to record daily labor routines on the plantation, as well as to track individual enslaved people who attempted to abscond from Rose Hall. Journal entries illustrate the pervasive nature of runaway attempts at Rose Hall. Like enslaved people on plantations throughout the Americas, some at Rose Hall demonstrated their resistance to bondage by running away on their own or with others for short periods of time, often hidden by loved ones near or far, with the intention of returning (often referred to as lying out or *petit marronage*). For others, their objective was to run as far away as possible and never return (described sometimes as *grand marronage*). They, too, could be hidden by loved ones in the area of Rose Hall or head farther out (thirty kilometers or almost nineteen miles) to Maroon Town or even a few kilometers farther into other Maroon communities in Cockpit Country.

In addition to recording the births and deaths of enslaved people, Rose Hall overseers designated space regularly within the journal for the individual names of enslaved people who absconded from Rose Hall. For the majority of the journal, there are no specific reasons provided by the overseers for these individual and even collective decisions to leave the plantation. However, for the final two years of the journal, selected overseers (not identified by name in the journal) offered additional reasons for these actions and, in many cases, simply noted "without reason" or "habit." Such notes throughout the journal provide an additional lens and contextualization for exploring some of the choices enslaved people at Rose Hall made about whether to run on any given day and for what reasons. These weekly journal entries serve as a source, a record, of a particular manifestation of fugitivity at Rose Hall from 1817 until abolition in the 1830s.

Just as there are weeks of the Rose Hall Journal that are missing or are unreadable due to the weathering of pages or the illegibility of penmanship styles, the recording of the incidents of fugitivity are also incomplete in the journal. Yet carefully working through the journal entries reveals significant accounts of multiple runaway attempts, returns, and captures of specific enslaved people (often referred to at the time as "notorious" runaways) and, for others, seemingly singular attempts to leave the plantation. Enslaved people left Rose Hall for short periods of time (for hours) or extended intervals of time (for several months), and some never returned. In addition to the listing of particular positions and places related to the exacting work regimen at Rose Hall, the journal often includes a regular column for "Runaways." The names of runaways are usually indicated on either the "Distribution of Negroes" pages (with the specific number of runaways included in the column) or the "Daily Occurrences" pages. Although most overseers included the individual names of runaways, there are also journal entries where only the number of runaways appears without any individual names being mentioned. In most cases, overseers not only indicated when individual enslaved people ran away from Rose Hall but also when these individuals either returned or were brought back to the plantation.

In the journal, there are many instances when enslaved people are noted as the only runaway on a given day and other instances when multiple runaways have absconded at the same time. Certainly, there were enslaved people at Rose Hall who decided, perhaps strategically planned, when they would depart on their own, whether or not they told others, or whether they remained silent about their plans. It is also possible some of these runaway attempts were decided or implemented in a collective manner. There were some enslaved people who often absconded either at the same time or during the same time period. In the Rose Hall Journal, Mondays often served as the primary day of reckoning regarding those who might have left over the course of the weekend. The regular absence of a Sunday column in the journal ledger as a "day off" for enslaved people often translated for some as a day to take off from Rose Hall.

It is important to note the language consistently utilized by the overseers to describe these runaway attempts and the overseers' recorded conclusions. Such attempts are listed simply with the person's name and "runaway" or "absconded." The descriptions of enslaved people's return to Rose Hall are noted either as the person having been "brought home" or as the person simply "return[ing]." In the journal entries, those who ran away are never "brought back"; they are always "brought home." For the overseers, that wording may well reflect their understanding of Rose Hall as the "home" of enslaved people. However, those who chose to abscond from Rose Hall may not have defined or claimed Rose Hall as their "home" whether or not they had family or friends there or had developed close relationships with other enslaved people at Rose Hall.

The weekly entries of the Rose Hall Journal illustrate that the majority of enslaved people who absconded from Rose Hall, as on other plantations in the Americas, were enslaved men. Of the 208 enslaved women, men, and children at Rose Hall Plantation between March 1817 and November 1832, notations in the journal indicated that forty-nine of them absconded during this time period. However, given the significant number of children under the age of ten at Rose Hall during this period, the percentage of runaways of the population over ten years of age represents approximately 30 percent (almost one-third) of the enslaved adult population. Of the forty-nine enslaved people at Rose Hall who ran away, thirty-four were men and fifteen were women—women comprised 30 percent (almost one-third) of the total number of enslaved people who absconded from Rose Hall. Of the forty-nine runaways, thirty-six were identified as Creole (twenty-five enslaved men and eleven enslaved women), twelve were categorized as African (nine enslaved men and three enslaved women), and one woman (Mariah) was not specifically noted as either Creole or African in the journal and does not appear in any of the slave registers. All of these enslaved people who ran away from Rose Hall between 1817 and 1832 (except for Mariah) are listed on the 1817 slave register.

Almost 25 percent of the total enslaved population were identified as running away from Rose Hall at least once during this time period. Twelve enslaved men ran away only once: Creole Adonis, Creole Ben, African-born Colin, Creole Dublin, African-born Garrick, Creole George, African-born Glasgow, Creole Harry, Creole Joe, Creole Ned, Creole Shemoon, and African-born Washington. The eight enslaved women who were recorded as absconding only once were Creole Beck, Creole Christianna, African-born Cowslip, Creole Dorinda, Creole Mary, African-born May, Creole Nancy, and Mariah (unidentified by region of birth). Five of them were specifically identified as mothers of enslaved children at Rose Hall: Christianna, Dorinda, Mary, May, and Nancy. Twenty-eight (almost 60 percent) of the forty-nine enslaved people who ran away engaged in multiple runaway attempts during this time period at Rose Hall. Those who ran away between two and ten times included nineteen enslaved men— Creole Anthony (eight times), African-born Bolton (three times), Creole Caesar (two times), Creole Charley (six times), Creole Gloster (two times), Creole James (five times), Creole January (four times), Creole Johnny (two times), Creole July (two times), African-born March (two times), Creole Mercury (six times), African-born Oserus (two times), Creole Peter (two times), Creole Pitt (eight times), African-born Plato (two times), African-born Scott (three times), Creole Smith (three times), Creole William (four times), and Creole William Kerr (two times)—and five enslaved women—Creole Cynthia (four times), Creole Elizabeth Palmer (two times), Creole Juno (four times), Creole Kitty (four times), and Creole Rose (four times). Three of these five women were mothers of enslaved children: Cynthia, Elizabeth Palmer, and Juno. And there were five enslaved people who absconded over ten times: two women—African-born Arabella (thirteen times) and Creole Doshey (sixteen times)—and three men—Creole Mark (twelve times), Creole Archey (fifteen times), and Creole Hercules (twenty-six times). Neither Arabella nor Doshey was identified as having any children at Rose Hall; however, their runaway attempts may have been due to their desires to be with loved ones on other plantations (possibly including lovers, children, and other family members) and/or for the purpose of self-emancipation (on their own or perhaps to connect with Maroon or other communities of free people of color).

The majority of enslaved people running away were field workers, and enslaved craftspeople are often identified specifically by their position in the notes regarding their runaway attempts. For example, the journal entries regarding Creole William running away also refer to him as Cooper William.[39] Described as the "Head Cooper" in 1832, Adonis ran away in May 1830, with the overseer noting Adonis's attempt to avoid the punishment of "being orderd to work in the field."[40] The overseer does not mention the reason(s) for his punishment. As Adonis is also described in 1832 as a "drunkard" and with the debilitating disease called "yaws," it is possible that both of these conditions might have partially compromised his regular cooper duties, and this resulted in him being punished with field work.[41]

Overseers also mention enslaved men in other positions who ran away in response to avoiding punishment related to a particular transgression. On July 10, 1829, the overseer noted that "George, Harry and Smith absconded on the 10th Inst. cause Theft."[42] In 1832 all three of these men were described in specific positions at Rose Hall: Creole George (Hope's son) was the "head driver," Creole Harry (one of Cecelia's sons) was the "second driver," and Creole Smith (also one of Cecelia's sons) was the blacksmith. Although there is no indication of what item(s) were stolen, it is likely that the men collectively engaged in this "crime." It is unclear whether one or all of these men were punished for their involvement in this theft and/or for absconding from Rose Hall. Enslaved adults were not the only perpetrators of theft and other infractions on plantations; enslaved children also channeled their energies into such crimes as theft, vandalism, arson, and generally disturbing the peace on plantations.[43]

Enslaved women in specialized positions also absconded in response to specific incidents or with no noted reason at all. As previously mentioned, Dorinda ran away in order to avoid being sent to the fields as punishment for her "neglect" of midwifery duties. In November 1830 Rose, who (like Dorinda) was a hospital attendant in 1832, "ran away making her Escape thro the roof of the Hospital for no cause."[44] This is the third time overseers mentioned Rose running away. Her first runaway attempt was in September 1818; at the time, she was nine or ten years old.[45] She returned the following day.[46] Her second recorded runaway attempt was several years later; she ran away on January 5, 1829, and she returned within a week.[47] No reasons are stated for any of these runaway attempts. When she made "her Escape thro the roof of the Hospital" in 1830, it is unknown whether she was injured in the process. She also ran away on March 22, 1831, and she was "caught" on March 29, 1831.[48] However, in 1832 Rose was described as having "one leg." It is possible that her having one leg could have resulted from her previous escape attempts. Even if this were not the case and she had one leg for most or all of her life, the fact that she ran away at least three times demonstrated her desire to run even with this physical limitation.[49] As one of the children of Zebra, she had a number of siblings living at Rose Hall, and still Rose may have absconded to be with other loved ones or in an attempt to free herself entirely from being bound to Rose Hall.

Just as enslaved people working in different positions at Rose Hall absconded from this plantation, enslaved people from different age groups also ran away. The age range for those who decided to abscond was from eight years old (Creole Mark at the time of his first recorded runaway attempt in 1818) to sixty-two years old (African-born March at the time of his second recorded runaway attempt in February 1829).[50] Some waited for months and even years between runaway attempts. For others, soon after they were "brought home," they absconded again within a few weeks or even the next day.[51] After his first runaway attempt at the age of eight, Creole Mark continued to abscond from Rose Hall; the journal entries indicate that he ran away at least eleven more times between 1818 and 1832.[52] Given that Mark's mother is not identified in any of the slave registers or in the journal, it is possible that one of Mark's reasons for leaving Rose Hall repeatedly was to be with family members who were not enslaved at Rose Hall or to be entirely free of bondage itself. In 1832 Mark was twenty-one years old, and his status on the 1832 clothing allowance list is "runaway," as he had absconded at that time. He may never have returned or been brought back after this final runaway attempt in April 1832.

The circumstances surrounding runaways being "brought home" or "returned" are usually not mentioned in the journal, except in one specific case. In Decem-

ber 1820 enslaved African-born man Bolton (forty-eight in 1817), whose attempts
to run away were noted in March and April 1821 and again in April 1830, is identified as the person who "brought home" the enslaved Creole man named January in December 1820.[53] January was approximately forty-five years old in 1820.
Except for this instance, overseers did not include any information about who
exactly "brought home" runaways to Rose Hall. However, in the weekly entries,
beginning the week of December 5, 1825, the "Runaways" category changed to
"Runaways and Looking for d⁰."[54] A week later, the week of December 12, 1825,
in addition to the "Runaways" category, there is a separate category solely entitled "Looking for Runaways."[55] It is possible that selected enslaved watchmen
served in this capacity; however, the specific enslaved (or free) people associated
with this duty are not named in the journal entries. Enslaved watchmen's duties
included guarding the different areas of the sugar plantation (including crops, factory buildings such as the boiling house and the mill house, and smaller ancillary
structures in which carpenters, coopers, and other artisan enslaved men worked).
Watchmen also served to monitor and surveil other enslaved people and provided
some degree of security against any intruders (including setting traps on some
sugar plantations). Older enslaved men who had labored as field workers often
served as watchmen.

In the 1832 list African-born Bolton is identified as one of Rose Hall's watchmen, even though he attempted to run away in April 1830 (at the age of sixty-
one). His time at Rose Hall and his age perhaps led to him being chosen for this
position, even though he himself had absconded from Rose Hall. Perhaps his status as someone who had attempted to run away might have affected the decision to select him as one of the watchmen for Rose Hall. In 1832, in addition to
Bolton, five other enslaved men served as watchmen: sixty-four-year-old African-
born March,[56] fifty-nine-year-old African-born Washington,[57] fifty-four-year-old
Creole Ulysses, forty-six-year-old Creole Joe,[58] and forty-two-year-old Creole
Shemoon.[59] All six men had resided at Rose Hall since 1817, and some (perhaps
all) may have lived there for many more years (and possibly decades) before being included in the 1817 slave register. Of these six men, five had also absconded
between 1817 and 1832: Bolton, March, Washington, Joe, and Shemoon. Even in
1832, the year of the last triennial slave register, a journal entry mentions Joe as
having run away in June of that year. It is possible that their duties as watchmen
afforded them additional knowledge of the area and additional opportunities for
such runaway attempts.

Other enslaved men at Rose Hall who also shared responsibilities may have
collectively decided to run away. Although overseers often did not include (or
necessarily have knowledge of) the specific reasons why enslaved persons chose

to run away at any given moment, specific consequences of enslaved people's run-away attempts are mentioned in the journal. On August 21, 1826, the overseer referred to three young enslaved Creole men running away and the ramifications of their absence beyond simply their physical absence from Rose Hall. The over-seer states, "Ben, Pitt and Anthony absconded in consequence of their absence from watch from which the cattle broke the pen and destroyed the canes con-siderably."[60] At the time of this runaway attempt, Ben (son of African-born field worker Augusta) was twenty-five years old, Ben's younger brother Pitt (also one of Augusta's sons) was twenty-two years old, and Anthony (son of Creole mid-wife Dorinda) was sixteen years old.

It is possible that while Ben, Pitt, and Anthony were supposed to be watching the cattle, they were not being closely supervised. They may have been deemed trustworthy enough to monitor the cattle, and when they believed they were not being watched, they decided to abscond together. All three young men also may not have decided to run away together at all. This may or may not have been a premeditated attempt by one, two, or all three of them. However, given that Ben and Pitt were brothers, they might have planned this escape together, and An-thony, the youngest of the three, might have decided to join in. Before this run-away attempt, Anthony had run away and been "brought home" at least three times between September 1821 and June 1822.[61] Due to his previous attempts, he could have been the primary planner for this joint escape. However they de-cided to take advantage of their situation and abscond from Rose Hall, what was recorded was seemingly a collaborative, coordinated runaway attempt. Ben and Pitt returned to Rose Hall by Friday, August 25, 1826.[62] However, Anthony re-mained away for a longer period of time. His return date is not specifically men-tioned, but he had returned to Rose Hall by September 18, 1826.[63] On one previ-ous occasion, on June 5, 1822, Anthony is noted as having absconded at the same time as Pitt.[64] The records do not mention Anthony, Ben, and Pitt running away again together, though Anthony ran away multiple times in 1828 and 1829 with-out either Ben or Pitt.[65]

As other cattleboys are also mentioned as running away from Rose Hall a few years later, this position may have offered particular conditions and chances for such attempts. One of Dorinda's sons, Creole William, is noted as a cattleboy on the 1832 clothing allowance list. He is also described as being a runaway at the time of this 1832 list. William is not the only cattleboy listed as a runaway in 1832; both Creole Oliver (age sixteen) and Creole Othello (age fifteen) had also absconded from Rose Hall by the time of the 1832 list. In addition, the other cattleboy, James, was also on the run and noted as a "notorious runaway" on the 1832 list. All four cattleboys are described as "able and healthy."[66] Given that all of them worked on tending cattle (and possibly other livestock) at Rose Hall, it is likely that they also took advantage of their situation and generated a plan for individual and/or collective escape.[67]

Although many of the runaways at Rose Hall were younger Creole men, Bolton and March were not the only older African-born people to abscond from Rose Hall. African-born Scott (referred to also as "Old Scott" in the journal) was forty years old in the 1817 slave register. Scott attempted to run away from Rose Hall on at least three separate occasions in March 1821, May 1822, and May 1823.[68] About two months after his third recorded runaway attempt, Scott died, with no reason for his passing included in the journal.[69] It is unclear why Scott ran away at this particular age. Since there are no extant runaway records for Rose Hall before 1817, it is possible that he ran away at other times earlier in his life.

Two older enslaved Creole people also ran away and died only months after being brought back to Rose Hall—Beck and Charley. Like Scott, Beck and Charley were noted as being forty years old in the slave register of 1817.[70] Beck's name only appears once in the journal as a runaway. On February 15, 1829, the overseer noted that Beck absconded, "causes unknown."[71] Beck was "Brot home" on February 24, 1829.[72] Beck would not live into the next year, as she passed due to "debility."[73] Between 1817 and 1822, Charley ran away at least five times.[74] On August 1, 1825, Charley ran away for the sixth time, as noted in the journal.[75] On November 9, 1825, the overseer relays, "an old Negro Man named Charley found dead in the Woods, absconded from here on 1st of August 1825—an Inquest was held. Verdict died by the Visitation of God."[76] There must have been some question about the circumstances of Charley's death to warrant an inquest. This is the only time in the journal that an inquest is recorded. Charley's death in the woods may have resulted from his own physical condition and the hardships he encountered in the woods. It is also possible that Charley's death may have occurred as a result of self-inflicted injuries or injuries that appeared to be caused by the actions of others. In the end, Charley's passing was deemed as divinely orchestrated. Perhaps Scott, Beck, and Charley had some indication that their time was limited and wanted to choose their final resting place as free people and not in bondage at Rose Hall. Did they leave in an attempt to pass from this life in the company of those they considered family, who may not have lived at Rose Hall? Or perhaps they simply wanted the sense of moving about freely on their own volition for their final days.

The search for freedom was certainly not only understood by enslaved people at Rose Hall who were in the final stages of their lives; many of the runaways were younger enslaved women and men and, in a few cases, enslaved children. The name of one enslaved man, Creole Caesar (twenty-five in 1817), appears only briefly in the journal related to his fugitivity and death.[77] On January 12, 1818, the overseer noted that "Ceasar [sic] & Glasgow still away."[78] The following day, January 13, 1818, the overseer indicated that "Ceasar [sic] brought home."[79] Approximately five months later, in June 1818, Caesar ran away.[80] A month later, in July 1818, Caesar was "brought home."[81] Two weeks later, the overseer recorded Caesar's death with no reasons included.[82] It is unclear whether Caesar, who had been brought back a short time before his passing, sustained injuries while on the run or as punishment upon his return to Rose Hall. Although not stated in the journal, Caesar may have become ill before, during, or immediately in the wake of his return. It is also possible that having unsuccessfully attained his freedom, Caesar decided to seize his life from the hands of others and to utilize his own hands to end his time of bondage at Rose Hall and free himself.

For African-born and Creole enslaved women, as with enslaved men, ideas about freedom may also have run deep in their minds, hearts, and souls. Even though the majority of runaways were enslaved men, enslaved women also absconded from Rose Hall. As previously mentioned in chapter 2, motherhood, as well as complications related to childbirth and motherhood, might have informed the decisions of some enslaved women to abscond from Rose Hall. While pregnant, Creole Elizabeth Palmer (also known as Susannah Johnston) ran away twice in the summer of 1830 (in July and August), and she returned to Rose Hall in October 1830.[83] Only a couple of months after her return, on December 5, 1830, she gave birth to a daughter. This baby died on December 8, 1830.[84] Elizabeth Palmer was not the only pregnant woman at Rose Hall who ran away. A couple of days after Elizabeth Palmer left Rose Hall in July, Creole Juno (who is described in the journal as "being pregnant") also ran away from Rose Hall.[85] Even before this pregnancy, Juno had engaged in previous attempts to run away from Rose Hall in 1826 and 1829.[86] For Elizabeth Palmer, Juno, and perhaps other enslaved pregnant women at Rose Hall, being pregnant may have encouraged (not discouraged) them from trying to pursue freedom for themselves and their unborn children (even if that meant leaving their other children behind at Rose Hall).

The decision of one woman, Creole Christianna, to run away may have been related not to the forthcoming birth of a child but to the passing of her child. Her son Henry, her first child recorded in the journal, was born on December 10, 1826.[87] However, both Henry's birth and his death at the age of two are included in the slave register of 1829.[88] Although this is not stated in the journal, given Henry's age at the time of his death, he probably passed in 1828 or even in the first few months of 1829. Christianna's only runaway attempt is noted in the journal on July 16, 1829, though the date she returned or was brought back is

not included.[89] Although Christianna had at least one more child in subsequent
years (daughter Jane in 1831), Henry's passing might have precipitated her need
for some time to mourn him away from Rose Hall (either temporarily or permanently). Given that Christianna's job was at the overseer's house and that both
Henry and Jane were categorized as mulatto, it is possible that her circumstances
related to the overseer might also have contributed to her desire to run far away
from Rose Hall.

Although no reasons were offered for Juno's decisions to run away in 1826 and
1829, in March 1830, the overseer specified, "Juno absconded on being ordered
to the field with sore foot."[90] Juno returned to Rose Hall two days later.[91] Perhaps this short time away from Rose Hall provided some reprieve for her foot
to heal. It is unclear whether Juno was forced immediately to work in the field
when she returned or was punished in additional ways for running away. Juno
was not alone in attempting to avoid field work for health reasons and other circumstances. Indeed, being ordered to field work in and of itself served as a severe
form of punishment for those whose duties were not inextricably connected to
field work. For midwife Dorinda it was being ordered to the fields that resulted
in her running away in April 1830.[92] As previously mentioned, Adonis (the head
cooper) also chose to run away from Rose Hall to avoid the punishment of working in the fields.[93]

For enslaved people who regularly worked in the fields at Rose Hall, running
away also served as an avenue for circumventing other forms of punishment (such
as being whipped or sold to another enslaver). The laborious nature of field work,
usually beginning early in the morning and ending in the evening hours, resulted
in incidents of either accidental or purposeful "late rising." Although Creole
Cynthia ran away at least three times between February 1829 and June 1830,[94] the
overseer noted that in May 1830 "Cynthia absconded from dread of punishment
for late rising."[95] Two days later, Cynthia was "brot home."[96] Cynthia was not exceptional in "late rising." Although it is highly likely that many others may have
risen late for field work, the overseers mentioned only one other enslaved person
in this predicament. In June 1830 the overseer relayed that "James runs for fear
of punishment for late rising."[97] Although references concerning James running
away commenced in 1829 (when he was nineteen years old), he ran away before
and after this attempt involving his late rising.[98] It is telling that in both of these
cases involving "late rising," overseers specifically mentioned that the "dread,"
the "fear," and the trepidation related to punishment motivated the runaway attempts of Cynthia and James.

Even though the overseers did not elaborate in any way on the actual forms of
punishment due to their "late rising" or their running away, Cynthia, James, and

Notations about Cynthia absconding on May 25, 1830, from "dread of punishment for late rising" and "Brot home" on May 27, 1830, and on the night of May 27, 1830, Hercules "after receiving Chastisement for his late desertion escaped once more" and on May 29, 1830, Hercules "returned" and "was forgiven" (words in this sentence are unclear in the entry). JARD, 1B/26, RHJ, vol. 3, fol. 74b.

other enslaved people were certainly duly aware of the range of consequences of these transgressions. As it was on other plantations, punishment was not meted out primarily in secret spaces. Instead, in order to deter other enslaved people from similar infractions, punishment often involved other enslaved people witnessing the flogging and other forms of torture inflicted on enslaved people's physical bodies and psychic states of being.

Although a number of enslaved women such as Dorinda, Elizabeth Palmer, Juno, and Cynthia absconded either once or only a couple of times, other enslaved women at Rose Hall became notorious runaways, absconding multiple times even in light of the punishment(s) they received if they were caught. Indeed, one woman, Creole Doshey, daughter of African-born Rebecca, was the woman who made the most recorded runaway attempts at Rose Hall between 1817 and 1832. In the five-year-period between April 1817 and June 1822, Doshey ran away from Rose Hall at least sixteen times.[99] Doshey is described as twenty years old in the 1817 slave register. We do not know with certainty whether Doshey was a field worker; however, as the majority of enslaved women at Rose

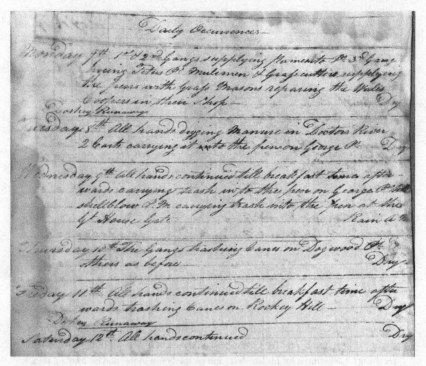

One of many notations regarding Doshey's at least sixteen
runaway attempts, last line of January 7, 1822 entry.
JARD, 1B/26, RHJ, vol. 1, fol. 238b.

Hall labored in the fields, Doshey probably worked in this capacity. Although
Doshey had other biological kin at Rose Hall (her African-born mother, Rebecca, and her brother, Creole Exeter), neither the triennial slave registers nor
the journal include any notations regarding Doshey having any children at Rose
Hall. However, her children may have lived at another plantation or plantations.

The majority of Doshey's runaway attempts were for relatively short periods
of time, usually for a couple of days to one week. If she was not visiting her own
children, she may have run away during these times to visit a lover or lovers living
at other plantations. Most of her attempts ended with Doshey being "brought
home," so she may have visited a specific, known plantation or area and then been
quickly identified and "brought home." On one of her runaway attempts in December, she left on December 10, 1821, and returned (not "brought home") on
Christmas Eve, December 24, 1821, in time for the annual holiday break (usually two or three days) granted to enslaved people at Rose Hall and plantations
throughout Jamaica. Given her decision to return to Rose Hall for that holiday

time, it is also certainly feasible that Doshey may not have run away to visit any-one at all but that she decided to abscond to live more freely for a few days every few months. There is no indication in the journal that Doshey was ever sent to a workhouse or jail, though she may have been punished with "confinement" in the Rose Hall jail cells (often referred to in the Rose Hall great house tours as its dungeon).[100] Given the frequency of Doshey's attempts to leave Rose Hall, even for short periods of time, she may have continued to do so for much longer than five years. However, the journal notes her passing on November 8, 1823; the entry includes no cause of death.[101]

In addition to Doshey, one other enslaved woman made frequent runaway at-tempts: African-born Arabella. In 1817 Arabella was thirty-five years old, and in the 1832 clothing allowance list, she was forty-nine years old and a field worker. In 1832 she was also noted as having absconded from Rose Hall and not present for the annual clothing allowance distribution. Between 1817 and 1832 Arabella ran away at least thirteen times.[102] Unlike the relatively short periods of time of Doshey's attempts (perhaps more of an example of *petit marronage*), Arabella ab-sconded from Rose Hall for much longer absences. The records do not mention Arabella having any children at Rose Hall. As is the case with Doshey's runaway attempts, Arabella's decision(s) to run away may have been motivated by her de-sire to be with her children, lover(s), or other loved ones at other plantations and/or to free herself completely from enslavement at Rose Hall.

There is no indication in the journal that Arabella was punished by confine-ment or sent to the Montego Bay workhouse or jail. However, with two jail cells on-site in the lower level of Rose Hall, and given her numerous runaway at-tempts, Arabella may well have been punished with internal confinement there for short or lengthy periods of time. Just as her return and those of other run-aways are not consistently recorded in the journal, it is also possible that confine-ment and other forms of punishment were not mentioned (and simply assumed) in the journal's weekly entries. It is difficult to imagine that Arabella's frequent absences would not have resulted in some form(s) of punishment. Though un-stated in the journal, flogging would have been one of the primary options for discipline and torture. No matter what Arabella endured during her numerous runaway attempts, her final runaway attempt is recorded on June 3, 1832; this rep-resented her own personal act of abolition before the British Parliament's enact-ment of the Slavery Abolition Act in 1833. It is unclear whether Arabella returned to Rose Hall as a freed woman. Although Arabella's punishment for her runaway attempts is not stated explicitly in the Rose Hall Journal, the journal certainly de-lineated aspects of punishment for others who absconded from Rose Hall.

Enslavers in Jamaica deployed corporal and capital punishment (including flogging, mutilation, and executions) alongside the use of penal institutions, which had become deeply embedded within the Jamaican slavocracy by the time Doshey and Arabella had made a "habit" of running away from Rose Hall. The period from the late eighteenth century into the early nineteenth century has garnered significant attention in relation to the development and expansion of the penal system in Europe and the United States; this was also a time of substantial growth in Jamaica's penal institutions. Much earlier, though, in the late seventeenth century, as historian Diana Paton explains, "Jamaican legislators had passed an act authorizing workhouse building in 1683, but this did not lead to the establishment of penal institutions. Instead, during this period the colonial state delegated day-to-day authority over slaves to slaveholders, placing little constraint on their power to inflict violence."[103] According to Paton, enslavers in Jamaica also received significant support from the British imperial state through the regiments stationed in the Caribbean. These armed forces attacked the Maroons and were also involved in suppressing slave rebellions and defending this British colony from other imperial forces. Enslaved people in Jamaica "could be tried for serious crimes in slave courts, which inflicted severe punishments, including death, mutilation, transportation (organized with minimal state support), and flogging."[104] As Paton explicates, "state agencies did not, however, take responsibility for imprisoning slaves; nor did they provide substantial resources for organizing their punishment or for facilitating their private punishment by masters."[105]

Until 1759, only one penal institution existed in Jamaica: the Middlesex County Gaol in Spanish Town, as Spanish Town served as the Spanish capital from 1534 to 1655 and the British capital of Jamaica from 1655 to 1872. Jails for the other two counties of Surrey and Cornwall were established in Kingston and Savanna La Mar, respectively, in response to legislation for additional structures throughout the island.[106] During the 1770s, the Jamaican Assembly enacted a number of laws charging parish authorities to establish penal institutions, including jails within parishes, and then a workhouse ("house of correction") was built in Kingston. Subsequent workhouses were established throughout Jamaica. By 1780 there were at least eleven parish or county jails and a workhouse in Kingston. The workhouses served as the core of the Jamaican penal system for the confinement and punishment of enslaved people, and jails primarily confined free people imprisoned for debt.[107] By 1820 the number of Jamaican workhouses had increased to sixteen, and most parishes had their own jails.[108]

Unlike prisons erected in London in the early nineteenth century, prisons in Jamaica's slavocracy served a specific purpose related to confining, disciplining, and punishing enslaved people. Enslaved people who had run away from plantations and been captured were often sent to workhouses by their enslavers as punishment for running away. The singular decision of enslavers to utilize work-houses as punishment was sufficient cause for confinement; no external judicial process was deemed necessary for enslaved people to be committed to work-houses.[109] Moreover, as Paton states, the "symbolic function of the prison did not work easily in an unfree society. A punishment whose premise was the depriva-tion of freedom faced problems in maintaining its reputation for severity when most of the people who suffered it were already unfree." Furthermore, "the idea of reforming the inmate's character or transforming his or her soul, which was be-coming dominant in British prisons in this period, made little sense in a society that denied the personhood of the vast majority of people. In the context of slave society, reform and rehabilitation meant enslaved people's acceptance of their subjection."[110] Newspaper notices, however, demonstrated that enslaved prison inmates not only rejected being reformed but also continued their attempts to escape while confined to workhouses and jails in Jamaica.[111]

As this web of houses of correction developed throughout the island, these workhouses made it easier for runaways to be identified and returned to their respective enslavers. Prior to the establishment of these workhouses, private indi-viduals were responsible for identifying owners of captured runaways. As a result of the creation of workhouses, runaways were taken to these sites, and the work-houses regularly advertised information about the runaways being held in the re-spective parish workhouses. Jamaican newspapers such as the *Royal Gazette* reg-ularly and consistently included designated sections listing the names of people who were confined in parish workhouses and jails.[112]

Although Doshey and Arabella may have been spared punishment in a work-house or jail, for particular enslaved men at Rose Hall Plantation, the journal specified their partial punishment in nearby workhouses and jails.[113] Two Creole enslaved men, Mercury and Archey (son of Zebra), were punished by being sent to these formal, external structures of confinement—Montego Bay jail (fifteen kilometers or a little over nine miles from Rose Hall) and the Falmouth work-house (twenty kilometers or about twelve miles from Rose Hall), respectively. In 1817 Mercury was described as a twenty-five-year-old Creole man. Between Feb-ruary 1818 and November 1820, Mercury ran away at least six times. During this period, he absconded on his own, as well as possibly with other enslaved men and women. Indeed, both Doshey's and Arabella's names appear linked with Mercury in a number of their simultaneous runaway attempts. Overseers recorded Mercu-ry's absence (as well as Creole Charley's absence) on Monday, February 9, 1818.[114] Almost seven months later, on Friday, August 21, 1818, the overseer noted, "Mer-cury Came hom [*sic*]."[115] Within two months, on October 19, 1818, the overseer

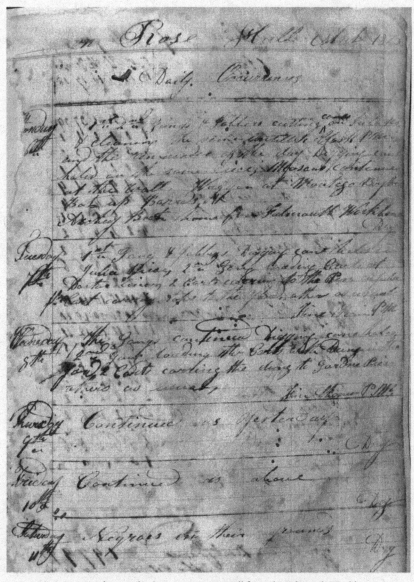

Notation regarding Archey's return to Rose Hall from the Falmouth Workhouse ("house of correction" or prison), last line of October 6, 1823, entry. JARD, 1B/26, RHJ, vol. 2, fol. 17b.

recorded, "Mercury & Arrabella Got away at Shell Blow."[116] Due to overseers in late 1818 not consistently noting names but only the number of runaways in the journal, it is unclear when Mercury returned or was brought back after that runaway attempt. Yet on Monday, February 7, 1820, Mercury was noted as having run away.[117] Two months after this attempt, Mercury was "brought home" on Saturday, April 22, 1820.[118] The journal entries indicate that Mercury ran away at least three more times in 1820.[119] On January 15, 1821, the overseer noted that "Mercury sent to Montego-Bay Goal [sic]."[120] Two weeks later, on January 30, 1821, the overseer recorded, "Mercury died in Montego-Bay Goal [sic]."[121] The 1823 slave register also confirms Mercury's death. Being sentenced to the Montego Bay jail served not only as a form of correction for Mercury but also as a fatal punishment for his pursuit of freedom.

Although Mercury did not survive the Montego Bay jail, this form of punishment failed to correct or kill other enslaved men who were confined in "houses of correction." The journal noted Creole Archey's attempts to run away at least fifteen times.[122] Although Archey may have attempted to run away before the first entry in the journal, the first note about Archey running away appears on November 19, 1821.[123] Archey was approximately fifteen years old at that time. After Archey had made at least eleven runaway attempts and after he had been "brought home" on August 18, 1823, a note in the journal states that on August 20, 1823, "Archy [was] sent to Falmouth Workhouse for punishment."[124] Six weeks later, the journal mentions on October 6, 1823, that "Archey [was] Brot home from Falmouth Workhouse."[125] It is certainly plausible that to exacerbate his punishment, Archey was sent not to the closer Montego Bay workhouse but to the Falmouth workhouse twenty kilometers or about twelve miles away from Rose Hall (and in a different parish). After Archey's departure to the Falmouth workhouse on August 20, 1823, no additional runaways are mentioned in the journal until early October 1823. Given that runaways may have been routinely punished at Rose Hall, Archey being sent to the Falmouth workhouse may have informed other enslaved people's reticence about running away in the weeks following his departure to Falmouth. No one also ran away from Rose Hall in the weeks following Archey's return from the Falmouth workhouse.

For Archey, though, even after his six weeks of punishment in the Falmouth workhouse, he remained determined to leave Rose Hall. On Tuesday, November 11, 1823, a little over a month after he was released from the Falmouth workhouse, Archey ran away again.[126] Although his return is not noted in the journal, on Thursday, November 13, 1823, there are no runaways mentioned; so it appears he returned or was brought back within one or two days of absconding from Rose Hall.[127] For the rest of the year, no runaways are recorded at Rose Hall. In the new year, the overseer notes Archey's absence on October 11, 1824, and his return a few days later on Thursday, October 14.[128] In 1825 the journal includes a note about his runaway attempt on February 28.[129] Two other runaway attempts are mentioned. The first is on October 11, 1825.[130] On another occasion when Archey's departure is not specified in the journal, he is noted as being "brought home" on December 26, 1825.[131] No other runaway attempts for Archey are noted in the journal after that date. However, in the 1826 slave register, it is clear that Archey's attempts resulted in a final separation from any family and friends in Jamaica. At the age of twenty, he is described in the 1826 slave register as being "transported."[132] This punishment of "transportation" translated into an enslaved person being sold and transported off the island.

We do not know what the process of being transported from Rose Hall involved logistically. We also do not know how Archey's family, including his mother, Zebra, and loved ones at Rose Hall and other plantations, may have responded to Archey's multiple runaway attempts, his punishment at the Falmouth workhouse, and his transportation off the island. What we do know is that one of Archey's younger brothers, James (one of the cattleboys and another son of Zebra), was also determined to leave Rose Hall. Only a couple of years after Archey's departure from Jamaica, possibly following in his brother's footsteps, James absconded from Rose Hall on August 11, 1829, and on March 16, 1831.[133] The final note regarding James appears in the journal entry on March 20, 1832, which states that he had absconded.[134] James's ongoing absence is also noted on the 1832 clothing allowance list, where he is described as a "notorious runaway." Given the timing of his final runaway attempt, James could have claimed his freedom and, after abolition, even returned to Rose Hall to be with loved ones as a freedman.

Although not classified in the archival records as a notorious runaway, the enslaved person who absconded from Rose Hall the most times between 1817 and 1832 was Hercules.[135] Hercules may have been aptly named, as he ran away from Rose Hall at least twenty-six times.[136] Hercules was described as Creole and nine years old in the slave register of 1817.[137] No enslaved woman at Rose Hall is identified as Hercules's biological mother in the documents. Indeed, in the list of nineteen boys between the ages of one and seventeen in the slave register of 1817, there are only three boys not described with any biological mothers at Rose Hall: Creole Mark (seven years old in 1817), Creole Gloster (eight years old in 1817), and Hercules (nine years old in 1817).[138] As in Mark's case, Hercules may have absconded in order to see or visit loved ones, including his mother and other family members possibly located at other Jamaican plantations, or to free himself. In only two of Hercules's runaway attempts did overseers note that Hercules had "returned" and not been "brought home."[139] His first runaway attempt is noted

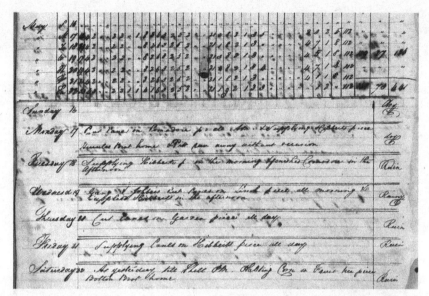

Notations regarding Pitt running away "without occasion" on May 17, 1830, Hercules "Brot home" on May 17, 1830, and Bolton "Brot home" on May 22, 1830.

JARD, 1B/26, RHJ, vol. 3, fol. 74a.

in the journal on July 31, 1821; Hercules was approximately thirteen years old at that time. His final runaway attempt was on January 24, 1832. Although there is no indication of when Hercules was brought back or returned to Rose Hall after this January 1832 attempt, he is recorded as back at Rose Hall by the time of the clothing allowance distribution in August 1832.[140]

Even though Hercules ran away at least twenty times between July 1821 and May 1830, it is not until May 1830 that the overseers officially noted in the journal some form of punishment for Hercules's numerous runaway attempts. On May 27, 1830, the overseer stated that "Hercules after receiving Chastisement for his late desertion escaped once more from his [illegible word] this night."[141] The overseer did not comment on the nature of the "chastisement" Hercules received and from whom at Rose Hall. Whatever the form and content of the "chastisement," it did not curtail Hercules's desire to continue to run away, and his response was to abscond again. Three days later, on May 30, 1830, the overseer stated that "Hercules returned was forgive [*sic*]."[142] Again, the journal does not mention what was involved in Hercules being forgiven. Hercules again absconded two weeks later, on June 14, 1830, "without cause."[143] Hercules was "Brot home" on June 28, 1830.[144] Within three months, on September 13, 1830, the overseer recorded, "Hercules absconded cause unknown."[145] No notation in the jour-

List of runaway-related activities (running away, "caught," and "Brot home") for July, James, Nancy, Rose, Hercules, Cynthia, and Mary, from February to April 1831 (bottom of page). JARD, 1B/26, RHJ, vol. 3, fol. 97b.

nal indicates when Hercules was brought back or returned to Rose Hall. Nevertheless, a month later, on October 24, 1830, the overseer relayed that "Hercules made his Escape from Confinement."[146] This is the only reference concerning Hercules being punished via confinement at Rose Hall. There is no description of the prescribed length of Hercules's punishment in this manner and how long Hercules remained away from Rose Hall. Within a month of Hercules escaping confinement, on November 16, 1830, the overseer noted, "Hercules after being pardond for his last offence again made his exit without cause."[147] Just as Hercules had been previously forgiven and absconded, now he had been pardoned (though the nature of the "pardoning" is not delineated in the journal entry); however, he remained steadfast in his consistent response. No specific date is included for Hercules's return to Rose Hall at the end of 1830 or at the beginning of 1831. However, Hercules ran away again on March 29, 1831, and he was "caught" a week later. While on the run in 1831, Hercules and other enslaved persons in the area may well have heard, witnessed, or been involved with preliminary deliberations and movements setting the stage for the Christmas Rebellion / Baptist War of 1831–1832.

THE CHRISTMAS REBELLION / BAPTIST WAR
OF 1831–1832 AND THE AFTERMATH OF ABOLITION

Initially staged as a peaceful general strike of enslaved people with the objective of attaining a working wage of "half the going wage rate," the strike escalated quickly into a full-blown rebellion: the Christmas Rebellion / Baptist War of 1831–1832. This rebellion involved an estimated thirty to sixty thousand enslaved people (out of a total enslaved population of over three hundred thousand in Jamaica at the time). After almost two weeks of intense resistance, at least two hundred enslaved people were murdered during the rebellion, hundreds were executed (including Sam Sharpe, the enslaved Baptist deacon of a Montego Bay Baptist chapel, deemed the leader of the rebellion), and at least thirty-five were transported off the island. The rebels' actions resulted in massive destruction of property on Jamaican plantations, including estate homes and sugar works buildings; the estimated value of property destroyed during the rebellion was £1,132,440 or over $111 million today.[148] In the wake of the rebellion, whites continued to kill and execute hundreds of enslaved people for myriad actual or imagined crimes. As other scholars have highlighted, part of the rationale for the Christmas Rebellion involved enslaved people's belief that the British government had abolished slavery and that enslavers in Jamaica had not abided by these dictates.[149] The Christmas Rebellion represented a striking, monumental spark in the British abolitionist movement, a forceful implosion strategized and implemented by enslaved people in Jamaica. Less than two years following this revolt, on August 28, 1833, the Slavery Abolition Act—an Act for the Abolition of Slavery throughout the British Colonies—received royal assent and went into effect on August 1, 1834.

In the days and weeks leading up to the Christmas Rebellion / Baptist War, which commenced on December 27, 1831, the Rose Hall overseers did not explicitly mention in the journal any heightened trepidation at Rose Hall. Two weeks before the rebellion, the overseer noted seven runaways (no names included) on Monday, December 12, 1831; then on Tuesday, December 13, the number of runaways decreased to five. By Friday, December 16, that number had decreased further to three, and it remained at three for Saturday, December 17.[150] The following week, on Monday, December 19, two runaways were recorded for every day that entire week (again with no names included).[151] As was often the case in the days before the Christmas holiday break, the overseer noted fairly general cleaning duties for enslaved people in the fields the week of December 19. Their duties included "cleaning Great House Pasture" on Monday, December 19, and Tuesday, December 20; on Friday, December 23, they were "Cleaning the yard." No notes were written for Christmas Eve, Saturday, December 24.

Although the white residents at Rose Hall Plantation might have been looking forward to the festive Christmas holidays, the slave rebellion during the Christmas holiday of 1831 wreaked havoc in Montego Bay and all across the north coast of Jamaica. Rose Hall would not have remained unscathed. Given the chaos that ensued throughout Montego Bay and surrounding areas, enslaved people from Rose Hall may well have been involved in either an individual or a collective manner in the rebellion. Had Archey not been transported off the island, he would probably have been engaged in or at the very least he would have utilized the revolt as an avenue to abscond from Rose Hall. Doshey, too, might have been encouraged to run away during this time had she survived to witness this moment.

The journal does not reveal any specific information about what transpired at Rose Hall during this slave rebellion. The last extant entry for 1831 is for the week of December 19 (ending with Christmas Eve).[152] There are no journal entries for January 1832. The next page of the journal, following the week of December 19, 1831, is for the week of February 6, 1832.[153] The loose pages of the journal for this time period at the Jamaica Archives offer no indication of whether no entries were crafted during the rebellion and in the weeks following the rebellion or whether entries were intentionally removed or simply misplaced. The last journal entry for 1831 (for the week of December 19, 1831) includes a total of 113 enslaved people at Rose Hall. The first journal entry for 1832, for the week of February 6, includes the same total of 113 enslaved people. The weekly entry beginning on February 6, 1832, makes no references to the rebellion, and it does not give any sense of the situation at Rose Hall in the aftermath of the rebellion. Three runaways are noted for that week of February 6 (again with no names mentioned). However, at the bottom of the entry for the week of February 6, 1832, the overseer stated, "Hercules absconded 24 Jany."[154] Appearing two weeks after the date Hercules absconded, this is a rather irregular note about a runaway. This note provides some indication that, indeed, no journal entries were created from December 25, 1831, until February 6, 1832, due to the absolute disruption and disorder caused by the rebellion. This timing may also have reflected the end of martial law, which had been proclaimed on January 1, 1832, and ended on February 5, 1832.

When Arabella, Doshey, Archey, and Hercules ran away from Rose Hall in the years and decades before the formal abolition of slavery in the British colonies, they could not have expected or known that the formal abolition of slavery in Jamaica would occur in 1834. No doubt they and other enslaved people in Jamaica—for years, decades, and generations—had imagined a time when slavery would exist only as a memory for themselves and the generations to come. However, instead of waiting, seemingly endlessly, for whites to abolish slavery, they set a course for self-emancipation. Absconding from Rose Hall meant the possibility of an experience of freedom for one moment, one hour, one day, one week, one month, perhaps forever. Yet due to consanguineal and other intimate relationships at Rose Hall or even at another nearby plantation such as Palmyra, for some enslaved women and men who also had children at Rose Hall, unbearable thoughts of leaving without them (or perhaps with only one of them) meant they would not consider making any attempt to run away from Rose Hall at all. They might have engaged in individual and communal processes that represented what historian Stephanie Camp posits as the "rival geography"—"alternative ways of knowing and using plantation and southern spaces that conflicted with planter's ideals and demands."[155] They may have explored other manifestations of resistance that did not even involve physically running away or mobility at all. They could have created or carved out sites of freedom within themselves—in their minds, hearts, and spirits—while their physical bodies labored in the sugar fields. Although scholars often still focus on running away, marronage, and slave revolts as emblematic of resistance, alternate modes of resistance beyond tangible physical acts of mobility need to be further considered, imagined, and probed in the twenty-first century, even without any trace in the archives.

The Christmas Rebellion of 1831–1832 represented a watershed uprising against slavery, and in the long century following the abolition of slavery, the afterlives of slavery in Jamaica birthed additional uprisings centered on Black Jamaican laborers' rights in the evolving economic, social, and political landscapes. In the wake of abolition, many landowners witnessed the decline of their sugar plantations due to the reduction in sugar productivity and the falling price of sugar throughout the island, especially with heightened competition from Cuban sugar plantations. No longer legally enslaved, recently emancipated people who had labored on sugar plantations could stay at their current location (or relocate to another sugar plantation) and negotiate for wages and terms of residence. For others, it was important to distance themselves not only from sugar harvesting and production but also from the respective plantation sites of their bondage.

Whether they remained to work on a sugar plantation or attempted to carve out another way of life through subsistence or cash crop farming, previously enslaved persons recognized that abolition had not materialized into their acquisition of all rights and privileges extended to white colonists. While formerly enslaved persons represented a significant Black majority in Jamaica, the election of 1864 signaled that they would remain disenfranchised due to poll taxes established to limit suffrage primarily to those elite (white and brown) denizens of the country. Indeed, out of a total population of over 436,000, only approximately 2,000 Jamaican men were eligible to vote in 1864.[156] Furthermore, in the decades after abolition, the ongoing systemic injustices on economic, social, and political fronts only intensified with long episodes of drought, the frequency of floods, and outbreaks of smallpox and cholera. During such a period of devastating natural occurrences and illnesses in the 1860s, the Morant Bay Rebellion erupted in October 1865 as a demonstration of collective refusal of the oppressive conditions of neoslavery and restricted landownership for Jamaican laborers. It ended with martial law and mass executions, including two people who would later be honored as Jamaica's national heroes, Paul Bogle and George William Gordon.[157] During this rebellion, the controversial and heinous decisions of the then governor of Jamaica, Edward John Eyre, and British reckonings with its colonies generally resulted in Jamaica being designated as a Crown Colony in 1866. It was no longer administered by the local Jamaican Assembly; instead, it was under direct rule by the metropole of Great Britain itself.

This change of rule, however, did not significantly alter the penurious conditions of Black Jamaicans in the subsequent decades, and they pressed for British imperial assistance in bolstering their livelihood as laborers. With the declining position of Jamaica in the sugar industry, white planters confronted ongoing challenges of bankruptcy. Many of the large sugarcane plantations became consolidated and owned by large British companies such as Tate & Lyle, which continued to profit from the labor of Black Jamaicans on sugar estate factories. Yet Jamaica's new position as a Crown Colony and the Crown Lands Settlement scheme offered recently freed people an opportunity to purchase small plots of land (usually two to four hectares) not deemed of any prime importance.

Although sugar reigned as king during the slavocracy, in the final decades of the nineteenth century, bananas became Jamaica's principal export. The focus on another agricultural product for profit, one that was not linked to sugar and sugar estates, also resonated with Black Jamaican peasant farmers who were interested in charting a different path toward their economic independence. In the late 1860s, peasant farmers from the parishes of St. Mary and Portland and individual merchant-agents working on behalf of American schooner captains collectively fashioned the beginnings of the banana industry in Jamaica. Due to the profitable nature of banana production, by the first decade of the new century, the American-based United Fruit Company (UFC) had bought out and eclipsed other companies and established a monopoly in the banana trade in Jamaica.[158] The heightened position of the UFC and the declining influence of Jamaican peasant farmers in the banana industry resulted in the creation of the Jamaica Banana Producers Association in 1929, a farmer-owned cooperative established to wield more local Jamaican control over the different aspects of the banana trade and challenge the monopoly of the UFC. The Great Depression exacerbated the precarity of the livelihood of peasant farmers and laborers in general. The uprisings of the 1930s foregrounded Jamaican laborers' demands for heightened British economic investment and development in the country; simultaneously, a rising tide of Jamaican nationalism also surfaced during this era. As someone deeply ensconced in Jamaican history and politics, observing the mounting labor challenges in the 1920s may have served as a catalyst for writer Herbert G. de Lisser to look to uprisings of the past and the Christmas Rebellion of 1831–1832 as the backdrop of his fictionalized story of the "White Witch" at a plantation called Rose Hall.

CHAPTER 4

The Fictional Fabrication of the Myth of the White Witch in Herbert G. de Lisser's *The White Witch of Rosehall*

Some contemporary visitors to the Rose Hall Great House hope to experience what they have been told is a haunted house. For others, especially local Jamaican children, field trips to Rose Hall are presented as a way for them to also learn more about Jamaican history and about slavery in Jamaica. The "official" Rose Hall Great House website caters to the desires of tourists and visitors from near and far. It presents the fictional (and entirely untrue) stories of multiple murders and a legend about a ghost house haunted by Annie Palmer, the White Witch of Rose Hall.

As mentioned in the introduction, my idea for this project started when my daughter and I experienced the Rose Hall Great House evening tour. Due to the disturbing silences regarding enslaved people and slavery, I felt compelled to seek out whatever information I could about the actual enslaved persons at Rose Hall. I wanted to present something, anything, about who the enslaved people were at Rose Hall. Utilizing archival records, the previous chapters represent my efforts to tell truths about enslaved persons at Rose Hall. In addition to offering these narratives about enslaved persons at Rose Hall in the early decades of the nineteenth century, it is imperative to explore what remains problematic and ahistorical about the tours themselves. The script used for the Rose Hall Great House tours did not emerge out of a sociocultural and political vacuum. Rather, the information for the script was extracted and compiled from Herbert G. de Lisser's novel about Annie Palmer.[1] De Lisser's fictional creation provided the foundation and fodder for these tours. As I did with the archival path to Rose Hall's history, I ask you to join me in the journey of this novel. I recognize that most readers will not have read the book or be familiar with it, so in this chapter I have included extensive quoted sections from the novel in order to provide some sense of the language, storyline, and major highlights of this fictional work as I present critical commentary about selected elements of the novel. Note that de

Lisser changed the two-word form of the name of the plantation, Rose Hall, to one word, Rosehall, in his novel. I follow his usage in my discussion of the novel.

By the time Herbert G. de Lisser (1878–1944) published his novel *The White Witch of Rosehall* in 1929, he was a prominent journalist, prolific author, and editor of Jamaica's most influential daily newspaper, the *Gleaner*.[2] It had been almost a century since the abolition of slavery in Jamaica, and the country was on the verge of becoming engulfed in one of the most significant labor movements in its history. Indeed, earlier sparks in the 1920s contributed to the labor movement in the 1930s. These early sparks may well have inspired de Lisser to revisit one of the most critical slave revolts in Jamaica, the Christmas Rebellion of 1831–1832, as one of the focal points of his novel. The reasons for the 1930s labor movement in Jamaica and throughout the Caribbean centered on the ongoing exploitation of Black workers, with its socioeconomic and political roots grounded in slavery.[3] Even with de Lisser's legacy as the editor of the *Gleaner* for four decades and the range of his other literary writings, it is this singular novel that has attracted the most popular attention over the past several decades. Before exploring the contemporary Rose Hall tours, it is critical to consider this text, because it is this fictional work that serves as the "historical" source for the narrative of the Rose Hall Great House tours. Reflecting similar dimensions of white entitlement/ dominance and Black exploitation/suppression woven throughout the Rose Hall Journal, de Lisser's novel also centers white elite individuals and marginalizes enslaved persons. The following critical reading of themes embodied in this novel's major characters reveals the novel's depictions of whiteness and Blackness, of visibility and invisibility, in ways that exacerbate the erasures of enslaved women's experiences while accentuating and concentrating on the journeys of white enslavers and other white denizens generally in the Jamaican plantationscape.

A CAUTIONARY TALE OF ROSEHALL
BY ROBERT RUTHERFORD

In this novel, Herbert G. de Lisser offers readers a sense of white characters' individual stories and societal positions within a nineteenth-century Jamaican slavocracy on the eve of abolition. Readers are privy to these characters' present realities, which are linked to their past circumstances and histories. Although the title of his novel directly focuses on the "White Witch," Annie Palmer, the book's protagonist is Robert Rutherford. The book centers this fictional character's ex-

periences at Rosehall and his introduction to slavery and to enslaved and free
people of color, as well as his tortured relationship with Annie Palmer. It is in the
novel that de Lisser created a fictional portrayal of the historical person Annie
Palmer, and his fictional portrayal also invented her seduction of men, torture of
enslaved persons, and use of metaphysical powers. It is through Robert Rutherford's interactions with this fictionalized Annie Palmer and other characters that
readers learn about this fictional rendition of Annie Palmer's personal history
and her various "witcheries."

From the very beginning, in the title of the first chapter ("The New Book-
keeper"), de Lisser describes the central character of the novel. The book opens
with Rutherford's arrival at Rosehall:

> Robert Rutherford reined in his horse at the stone and iron gates that opened
> into the estate; half a mile away, on an eminence that commanded a wide,
> sweeping view of canelands, hills and sea, stood a building, the fame of whose
> magnificence he had heard when in the town of Montego Bay, some ten miles
> to westward.
>
> White in the gold light of the sun it stood, the Great House of Rosehall. It
> dominated the landscape; it imposed itself upon the gaze of all who might pass
> along the road that ran in front of the property; it indicated opulence. Young
> Rutherford knew that it represented the pride and arrogance of the planter
> caste which still ruled Jamaica, and whose word, on its own plantations, car-
> ried all the authority and sanction of an arbitrary will scarcely curbed by laws
> passed in recent years for the protection of the bondsmen. Behind him, a few
> paces from the outer edge of the road, rolled and glittered a vast expanse of sea,
> all blue and purple, with snowy breakers rolling lazily to the shore. Above him
> stretched a vault of azure flecked with clouds. It was eight o'clock in the morn-
> ing. The month was December; the year, 1831.[4]

Rutherford's first impressions of the great house reflect and reify the grandeur
and authority deeply ensconced in the house itself and how the house exhib-
ited the mastery and entitlement of Jamaica's white planter class. From the first
chapter to the final line of the book, de Lisser allows Robert Rutherford to guide
readers along the fault lines of slavery. Readers follow him as he enters the Jamaican terrain and claims his role(s) within this peculiar sociopolitical and cultural
plantationscape. Throughout the novel, de Lisser presents Robert Rutherford's
voice and his point of view as neutral, objective, and essentially omniscient. Robert's voice embodies the "master narrative" of history, of slavery, dictated and directed from an elite, white, male perspective deemed as being unlimited and un-
fettered by the machinations of bondage and Blackness.

As the novel progresses, we witness Robert Rutherford's rite of passage through Jamaica. We discover within the first few pages that Robert's presence at Rosehall is part of his father's strategy for his son to have firsthand experience with the business of slavery and mastering at a sugar plantation in the West Indies. As an absentee planter for a substantial plantation in Barbados, Robert's father decides it is time for his twenty-five-year-old son to learn about estate management as a "future West Indian proprietor" (8). Instead of sending his son to the family's estate in Barbados, the father thought a preliminary training ground elsewhere would be best; by going to Jamaica instead, his son might not be taken advantage of by the Barbados estate's attorney, overseers, and bookkeepers. His father determines that "Robert should go to some other West Indian colony to acquire the knowledge he would need for the management of a sugar plantation, whether he should afterwards decide to reside permanently on his own in Barbados or to visit it at frequent intervals" (8). Due to his connections, his father makes all necessary arrangements for his son to be the "new book-keeper" at Rosehall.

The novel unfolds with the experiences of Robert Rutherford as he navigates the world of slavery. It begins with his arrival, and only a few weeks later, it ends with his survival (the lone survivor of the other central characters) and departure on a ship heading back to England. As Robert arrives at Rosehall, he begins to identify the range of buildings on the plantation—the sugar works (including the mill house and the boiling house), the overseer's house, and the slaves' quarters. His focus on the buildings then moves to the enslaved, "clothed in coarse blue osnaburg, busy cutting canes in the fields, women as well as men armed with scythes and machetes, and hacking at the roots of the slender green-topped plants." In addition to noticing the wagons operated by enslaved people and drawn by oxen and mules, he is struck by the Black slave drivers, who are armed with whips. They were "sturdy fellows whose duty it was to see that the slaves did not loiter or slacken at their work; yet in spite of them some of the labourers lifted curious eyes to gaze for a moment at the strange white man who seemed to be going up to the Great House where lived the lady owner of these domains." They noticed Robert "also, but asked no directions, for he was white and therefore one of the masters who gave commands and put questions, and was not there to be interrogated by such as they" (2).

What the Black slave drivers understood about the racial, gendered, and classed power dynamics at Rosehall also extends to Robert Rutherford's awareness. Even as a stranger to Jamaica and the slavocracy there, within minutes of his arrival at Rosehall, Robert interrupts a slave driver whipping an enslaved young woman. De Lisser describes the intensity of this clarifying moment. Robert observed "a stout black fellow lift a whip and bring it sharply down on the shoulders of a girl who was stooping to lift a bundle. The girl howled and crouched, but did not dare to move, for the whip hovered menacingly over her. Three or four women in the vicinity trembled violently, bent over their tasks with feverish intensity; the moment was one of tension." Moments later, "Robert remembered that he was a book-keeper, and, as such, the boss of the driver who seemed to be about, in a spirit of brutal enjoyment, to strike the girl again. 'Stop that and go and attend to some other business!' he shouted to the man peremptorily. The fellow started to give some explanation; he was evidently astonished. The girl turned appealingly to her unexpected protector" (18–19). In the midst of Robert's orders, "Burbridge [the senior bookkeeper] said nothing. The driver hesitated; yet he still held the whip above the young woman. Angered by his attitude, Robert rode up to him and kicked the whip out of his hand, the man uttering an exclamation of pain as he did so. Then Robert and Burbridge passed into the stillhouse" (19).

In a conversation following this incident, Robert asks Burbridge about the possible reason for this whipping. Burbridge replies, "Some neglect of duty, perhaps . . . but I guess he was really taking it out on her for a private reason; possibly she wouldn't have him and he is showing her what she might expect for her rejection." As Robert attempts to understand the actual racial, gendered, and class power dynamics of this new country, he asks, "But these people are not allowed to flog without express permission from white men, are they? I thought that in these days only the white men on the estate could give a flogging order." Burbridge explains clearly that "practice and theory are sometimes different . . . and if you prevented these drivers from using the whip altogether you would soon have every slave raising the devil. There's plenty of flogging on Rosehall, Rutherford—more perhaps than on any other estate" (19).

This exchange underscores the multiple vulnerabilities of enslaved women at the hands of men, both enslavers and enslaved. It also hints at the heightened abuse of enslaved people at Rosehall at the hands of the white mistress, Annie Palmer, an aspect of this plantation developed later in the novel. Power dynamics on such plantations involved not only white masters and mistresses but also some enslaved men who wielded a limited degree of authority over other enslaved people. In this scene, de Lisser points to the expectations and assumptions about the assumed availability and accessibility of enslaved women's bodies and sexuality, though he does not present any direct examples in the novel about the sexual violation and abuse of enslaved women on sugar plantations perpetrated by white men. In this instance, Burbridge's assumption centers on the enslaved woman rejecting the physical sexual advances of this Black male slave driver. De Lisser does not explore the perspectives of either the enslaved woman or the enslaved slave driver in this scene, and both are unnamed in the novel. Instead, the deliberations about the slave driver's attempt to whip this enslaved woman and any judgments regarding this situation are reserved as a conversation between two white men. Furthermore, in just one episode, within mere minutes of his arrival, Robert recognizes, claims, and deploys his power and entitlement as a white man—and white savior—on this plantation. The first instance of violence against an enslaved person in this novel is at the hands of another enslaved person, and it is a white man who intervenes and "protects" the enslaved woman/victim from the force and pain of the whip, one of countless tangible and quotidian manifestations of the violence of slavery.

The following morning Robert's intervention is quickly corrected and subverted when this enslaved woman and two additional enslaved people are summarily whipped in "a sort of ceremonial punishment" before "some twenty persons assembled to witness it, clearly the more obstinate of the bondspeople" (25). In attendance, too, is Mrs. Palmer. This whipping scene serves as Robert's (and readers') introduction to Annie Palmer, who questions his presence. Robert's mounting disgust for this public whipping ultimately leads to him quickly leaving the scene before the flogging recommences: "As he moved away he shuddered, for a long, terrible cry broke from the girl's lips and continued until her flogging ceased, though only eight lashes were administered to her. She was flogged to her knees" (27).

Revolted by these events, Robert reflects on a similar position and treatment of laborers, soldiers, and sailors who were whipped in England. He understands that "the use of the whip was believed to be indispensable if discipline was to be maintained. But he himself had never seen a human being flogged before, and a woman at that; and the circumstance that another woman, young, of good breeding, and presumably of ordinary humane feelings, should stand by and see such punishment inflicted startled and shocked him" (27). Robert reasons that at "Rosehall the evil, reckless spirit of former days seemed to manifest itself; the danger that threatened was ignored; here he was back in the eighteenth century instead of being in the early nineteenth. And a woman was the mistress of this estate. . . . Only a devil would willingly watch the agony of others as she had done, was the thought that ran in his mind" (28).

In this scene, de Lisser does not offer any sense of what the enslaved woman experiences physically, psychologically, or emotionally; only Robert's reactions to her "long, terrible cry" and Annie's willingness to witness the flogging become the central elements of this flogging. The enslaved woman's thoughts about her whipping and the acts that may have precipitated this punishment are not even mentioned in passing. Was this her first time being whipped, or had such whippings and other forms of punishment become painstakingly familiar and even a regular aspect of her life and the lives of other enslaved people there? Her flogging and her cry play a role only as far as they present a moment for Robert's reflections. De Lisser, here and throughout the novel, privileges the entitled point of view and positionality of Robert and the other white characters over this and any other (unnamed) enslaved women in the novel. De Lisser presents a sense of Robert's innocence at never observing a "human being flogged before" and his distance from neither observing nor, it would seem, practicing corporal punishment. His startled and shocked response emerges not only from the enslaved woman being whipped but also from seeing a white woman of "good breeding" like Mrs. Palmer witnessing and overseeing such a whipping. Being so repulsed by this incident, he chooses to leave before the flogging commences to protect and maintain his innocence and distance from this demonstration of brute force and torture.

Even with his initial thoughts of Annie Palmer's devilish nature, Robert's more formal introduction to her later on results in his attraction to her, as well as his eventual seduction by her. In their first conversation after this flogging, she expresses some of her perspectives on enslaved people. When he is taken aback as she speaks openly to him with enslaved people nearby, she quickly defends herself: "'They don't matter,' she said indifferently; 'we are practically alone here. They don't count; they have no feelings.' There was supreme if unconscious contempt in her voice, in her look. The people about might have been sticks and stones so far as they affected her" (33). Annie Palmer's pronounced rejection of enslaved people mattering in any significant way persists throughout the novel; she treats enslaved people as things, as tools, to be utilized in the service of her basic needs and desires. Annie Palmer clearly denigrates enslaved people and explicitly dismisses their sapience, sentience, and humanity. Intoxicated by the charms of Annie Palmer, Rutherford integrates her ideas about enslaved people into his own consciousness. Following his intimate time with her, he reflects: "Annie said that they had no feelings, spoke of them as if they did not matter. And indeed they did not matter; what they might think could have not the slightest sort of significance" (37). As his father had planned, Robert is, indeed, learning about mastering in Jamaica; however, his father would neither have expected nor have imagined his most influential teacher to be a white woman—mistress Annie Palmer.

As Annie Palmer elevates herself above enslaved people at Rose Hall, early on she describes the deep, enduring trepidation of whites amid a Black majority in Jamaica. She relays to Robert that he is unaware of "the difficulties we are having now with our people. Unless we inspire them with a proper dread they may rise at any moment and cut our throats" (31). She poignantly declares the necessity of the potential and realized force of coercion and torture as the only possible panacea for Black rebellion. Her use of the plural possessive pronoun in her description of "our people" does not reflect her shared human identity with enslaved people. Instead, it illustrates the idea of enslaved people belonging to her, as well as her rights and rites of ownership over enslaved people. During the course of their conversations, she attempts to convince Robert that she is a kind mistress. And he is swayed to believe that "elsewhere, to some men, she might seem bold and forward as she herself has suggested she must appear in his eyes. But here it seemed that everything she did was natural, inevitable, for her circumstances were not normal and the hardships and distresses of her life were surely a warrant for her splendid independence" (55). The formidable forces of Jamaica serve as the rationalization for such abnormal circumstances and responses being naturalized and normalized. Indeed, throughout the novel, de Lisser establishes Jamaica itself as a core presence and "character" in the white figures' individual and collective consciousness that molds and transforms their sense of themselves and others solely in deleterious ways.

With his encounters with Annie Palmer and his shifting perspectives, Robert begins to recognize that the "West Indian *ethos* was already affecting him. He felt at once inclined to live gaily, riotously, dangerously today and let the morrow take care of itself" (34). Robert allows himself to be sexually intimate with Mrs. Palmer; de Lisser presents this moment as Robert submitting to her. His submission occurs as a result of being overcome by Annie Palmer and the potency of her charms. In the early morning, after spending the night with her, the "elevation of the hours before had vanished; he was secretly startled that he had so quickly succumbed to what he had heard at home were the manners and customs of this country, with a disregard of all concealment, a careless acceptance of any condition and circumstances that might appeal at the moment, however flagrantly might be violated every principle of circumspect conduct" (61). Robert recognizes his own transformation as a result of the effects of "the manners and customs of this country." In this novel, the tropical setting of Jamaica accounts for part of the inherent incivility of the country; however, the pervasive Blackness enveloping Robert and other whites in this Black majority embodies the pivotal ingredient for the violation of civility and principled codes of conduct.

Annie Palmer cannot be blamed for her devilish and seductive ways; rather, it is Jamaica and all of its Blackness that permeate, corrupt, and poison her and all of her white, womanly sensibilities.

These sentiments about Jamaica are not presented as exceptional but rather as commonplace. Having been in Jamaica for a much longer time and having served as one of the temporary bookkeepers, Rider worries about Robert remaining in Jamaica, and he ruminates on the effects of staying in Jamaica from day to day, month to month, and year to year. Rider, also a clergyman, surmises: "A lifelong liaison with the girl, and children, and drink, and no real obligation to work (which might mean more drink and other liaisons), what was there in all this save the deterioration of a young fellow who had fine instincts and was a gentleman? In the tropics some men throve; those were the men of stern fibre or a sort of brutal hardness." Rider deduces that Jamaica's "tropics, with their large servile population and small aristocracy of proprietors who lived in a world of the narrowest mental and moral horizons—what a horror they actually were! If they did not become physically the white man's grave, they formed for him as deadly a spiritual sepulchre. It was death anyway" (196). The "manners and the customs of this country" seemingly contribute to white men's deterioration and degeneracy, as well as the overall ruination and death of white male sensibilities. Rider's description of the country, of this world, with "the narrowest mental and moral horizons," buttresses Robert's earlier reflections about Jamaica's devoid state of civility. Rider's particular emphasis on the combination of "the girl, and children, and drink" underscores the specific intoxicating influences of enslaved women's sexuality, the inevitable "mulatto" products of such unions, and the eventual drowning in one of the very by-products of sugar plantations. His musings on the corrupting elements of Jamaica paint a precarious paradise in the West Indies.

Historians have long explored this conception of ruination in terms of (white) Creole degeneracy of Englishmen and English colonists in the Caribbean partially as a result of sexual contact with Black women in the Caribbean.[5] In addition, scholars of slavery have analyzed the "seasoning" processes enslaved people experienced in the Americas.[6] De Lisser presents a different kind of seasoning process for Englishmen as they adjust to their new lives in the Caribbean. De Lisser chooses not to explore a seasoning process reflecting the racial, gendered, and classed hierarchical Jamaican slavocracy, which resulted not only in white men's projected (and realized) entitlement to and exploitation of the natural resources via colonization and slavery in the Caribbean but also in their accessibility to (and penetration of) Black women's bodies and sexuality.

In recounting his medical rounds to aid the ailing in Jamaica on September 22, 1798, Dr. John Williamson described this sense of entitlement: "Black or brown mistresses, are considered necessary appendages to every establishment: even a young bookkeeper coming from Europe, is generally instructed to provide himself; and however repugnant may seem the idea at first, his scruples are overcome, and he conforms to general custom."[7] In journaling about her experiences in 1803 in Jamaica, Lady Nugent (wife of George Nugent, who served as governor of Jamaica from 1801 to 1805), scoffs at the ways "white men of all descriptions, married or single, live in a state of licentiousness with their female slaves; and until a great reformation takes place on their part, neither religion, decency nor morality, can be established among the negroes."[8]

Instead of these particular historical lenses of discernment, in the novel de Lisser portrays Englishmen as under the undue and unnatural carnal influences of Black women; thus, these men have been led astray by their desires for these women. Even as de Lisser highlights the sexual improprieties of Englishmen living in Jamaica, he mitigates Englishmen's desires for controlling, penetrating, and exploiting enslaved women in the Caribbean. Just as Annie Palmer's devilish ways are unduly influenced by the forces of Blackness, so too are Englishmen characterized in the novel as manipulated and guided by the unrelenting presence and pressures of Blackness and Black sexuality, which are acutely rooted in Jamaican women and the Jamaican plantationscape.

As part of Rutherford's settling-in process—his seasoning process—at Rosehall, the senior bookkeeper, Burbridge, introduces him to his new living quarters and the presence of the "housekeeper." In the Jamaican context, this word and this role served at the time as a euphemism for a woman of color whose association with a white man involved domestic duties and sexual interactions. After noting that Rutherford "can't afford to be a gentleman" here, Burbridge says that he will "get Psyche to look after your room till you get a housekeeper, Rutherford. Psyche is a good girl, but you will have to get your own, for she has a lot to do for me, besides doing her ordinary work in the trash-house" (15). Rutherford recognizes that this arrangement may be more than "housekeeping," and he probes for additional information from Burbridge on this point:

> "She's your servant?" But even as Robert asked the question he knew from something in Burbridge's attitude and from his praise of Psyche that the girl, whoever she was, was something more than a servant to his colleague. His eyes lifted themselves automatically and again he spied opposite to him, hanging from a nail in the wall, that fluttering female garment.
>
> "She's my housekeeper and a very good girl." (15)

Once Burbridge introduces Robert to Psyche, they engage in a lighthearted exchange:

"This is Mr Rutherford, Psyche, the other book-keeper," explained Burbridge. "He is going to live in the next room, like Mr. Fanbourg did, and I want you to fix it up for him till he gets somebody of his own to do it. It won't be too much for you?"

"No," grinned Psyche, looking Robert over with an appraising and appreciative glance. "An' it won't be long."

"That's so," agreed Robert. "I suppose they allow a servant, don't they?"

"Yes, you are allowed a servant to do the necessary things," said Burbridge, "but not for all the time. She will have other work to do."

"An' dem all is tief," said Psyche decisively. "Dem all rob you, except you is their sweetheart. But you will get a sweetheart, massa, specially as you is such a pretty gentleman. There is Millie, my cousin; she is just twenty and she have good ways and is pretty. You want to know her?"

"No, no, Psyche," laughed Robert with real enjoyment. (The eagerness of Burbridge's lady to find for him a special helpmeet, and her unabashed frankness about it, affected his sense of humour keenly.) "I think it would be much more proper for me to select my lady-love myself: don't you agree?"

"Yes," agreed Psyche, "for, after all, what I t'ink may suit you mightn't like; you' taste may be different. But Millie really a good-looking girl and can work, an' she is a free girl, massa. I bring her over to see you soon; dat will be no harm, for you needn't teck her if you don't like her. What you say?"

"Just as you please," laughed Robert. "There can be no objection to the lady calling on me, if that is a custom of the country. And of course I shall like her, though that does not mean that I shall take her. And here is something for you, Psyche." He handed the girl a dollar, at the same time glancing at Burbridge to see how he would regard the gift. He noticed that it was by no means resented by Burbridge. As for Psyche, she crowed with delight. Robert perceived that the advent of Millie was likely to be hastened.

"I live here," said Psyche, pointing to Burbridge's room, "an' Millie could live dere," and she pointed to Robert's room; "an' bote of us could keep dis place nice and convenient, and we could be happy an' virtuous."

Robert stared. Then he remembered that virtuousness must mean to Psyche something quite different from what it signified to persons with a better knowledge of the English language, though not necessarily with a higher appreciation of the value of virtue. That Psyche was convinced that she was living a highly virtuous life he did not doubt for a moment. As for Burbridge, Robert realized that virtue meant nothing to him; he would have said that it could not possibly have any part in the life of a book-keeper—which was indeed the universal view.

(15–17)

Psyche is the only enslaved woman character to whom de Lisser grants a voice, a perspective, and an inkling of her persona in her exchange with Burbridge and Robert. She is described as a "middle-sized, pleasant-looking damsel of about nineteen years of age, light chocolate in complexion, and therefore sambo, with bright black eyes and a merry smile." Robert notices, "She wore a single robe that reached to the knees, but it was not coarse osnaburg such as Robert had seen on the women in the fields; it was of much better material and must, Robert concluded, have been purchased with Burbridge's money. Her head was taste-fully covered with a large scarf looking like a chequerboard of bright diverse co-lours; her feet were bare." He also recognizes that "she had nothing of a slouch-ing, timid demeanor; on the contrary, she flashed Robert a merry glance, bade him good day, then touching Burbridge lightly on the shoulder, asked what he wanted" (15). It is unclear whether de Lisser's attention to Psyche emerges due to her position as Burbridge's housekeeper (primarily charged with domestic duties, catering to all of his "needs"), her "light chocolate" complexion, her "sambo" cat-egorization, or some combination of these attributes. As previously mentioned, the majority of enslaved women at Rose Hall were not domestics but field work-ers. The majority were not light-colored sambos or quadroons; they were darker-complexioned and categorized as "negro."

Unlike the enslaved woman who is whipped at the beginning of the novel, and unlike all of the other enslaved women, Psyche is physically visible and vocal; yet it is her intimate proximity to white masculinity and the particular ways she is at the service of Burbridge that allow her visibility and vocality in the novel. Those enslaved women who are not directly and purposefully attending to the domestic needs of white men (including their sexual needs) remain visibly invis-ible and emerge only as part of the backdrop of the Jamaican plantationscape. In the conversation between Psyche and Robert, there is no indication of the power dynamics deeply embedded in and informed by the racial, gendered, and classed codes of conduct of the Jamaican slavocracy. Furthermore, readers, again, are not permitted any insight into Psyche's actual, complete thoughts and feelings about Robert or her serving as Burbridge's "housekeeper."

What Psyche verbalizes to Robert and Burbridge in this scene constitutes the entirety of readers' understanding about herself and this housekeeping arrange-ment. Even without any indication of Psyche's internal thoughts and feelings in the text, her ability to freely engage in a jovial conversation with Robert and his willingness to participate with her in this manner certainly reflect the fictitious nature of this storyline of slavery. The lightness and freeness of Psyche's physi-cal movements and verbal comments would not have been possible for enslaved women working in the fields at Rose Hall. It is also uncertain if this would have been the case for any enslaved women at Rose Hall Plantation, women such as Christianna, whose primary venue of labor was as a domestic in the overseer's house at Rose Hall, which probably translated into her being a "housekeeper" for one of the overseers at Rose Hall Plantation.

Because de Lisser describes and characterizes Psyche in this manner, readers may well erroneously conclude that Psyche's character exemplifies the experiences of enslaved women laborers at Rose Hall Plantation early in the nineteenth century. They might mistakenly deduce that enslaved women's volition entirely (or primarily) dictated what they articulated, where they moved on and off the plantation, what duties they were responsible for, and with whom and how they interacted with other denizens (whether with other enslaved and free people of color or whites). De Lisser's focus on Psyche's free voice and spirit might also be interpreted by uncritical readers as emblematic of a fairly relaxed environment, a leisurely work regimen, and a benign form of bondage. They might even misconstrue the "fluttering female garment" as a metaphorical representation of the ease and freeness of Psyche's movements and status on the plantation. Such characterizations belie the reality of the onerous, quotidian work regimen the majority of enslaved women endured at the actual Rose Hall Plantation. It also inaccurately frames enslaved women's labor within a primarily domestic realm and outside the actual, historical constrictions of field work, which dictated the labor routines of the majority of enslaved women at the Rose Hall Plantation. Moreover, it entirely glosses over the racial, gendered, classed, and sexual power dynamics that enabled, legitimized, and normalized the sexual violations enslaved women experienced due to preconceived notions of their sexual accessibility and availability, as well as white, entitled, and supremacist conceptions and practices.

In addition to the enslaved woman character Psyche, de Lisser also offers a complicated presentation of a free woman of color called Millicent (also referred to as Millie in the novel), who is cast in the role of the "housekeeper" for Robert Rutherford. Through the character of Millicent, de Lisser presents a compelling tale of a free woman of color who exercises free will, including mobility on and off the plantation, and who directly expresses her desires for Robert Rutherford. The initial conversation between Robert and Millie reflects a similar playfulness like the one between Robert and Psyche, as well as one that is shaped and directed by Millie's intentions.

"Good morning, Squire."

Robert noticed that she did not say "massa."

"So you are Millie, eh?" he replied. "But how did you get here so soon? You don't live on this estate?"

"No Squire; but I come here nearly every day, an' me cousin tell me that you—you want to see me. I was here yesterday, too, an' I saw when you ride in. So I know you already, Squire."

"And you want a job to look after my part of this house?"

"I think I could look after you well, Squire."

"I don't need looking after, Millie; but the place does. I am told that I can be supplied with a servant here, but perhaps you would do much better."

"A servant?" asked Millie. Her face was troubled, disappointment plainly expressed in it.

"A housekeeper," corrected Psyche.

"A housekeeper?" echoed Millicent. "You like me, Squire?"

"Of course I do; you seem quite a nice, tidy girl, but liking has hardly anything to do with our arrangement, has it? You are a free girl, aren't you? How much wages do you expect?"

"We don't need to talk 'bout wages now," said Millicent hastily. "I can read and write, an' I saw you yesterday, Squire, an' like you." She paused not wishing to say much in the presence of a third party, and without definite encouragement from the Squire. (38–39)

Although de Lisser only discusses enslaved women in a limited way in the novel, he develops the character of Millicent, who is a free woman of color. Readers become more familiar with Millicent throughout the novel due to her interactions with Robert and Mrs. Palmer. From her initial meeting with Robert, Millicent directly and freely conveys her interest in him. She also clearly and decidedly presents herself as a free woman (and not a servant) and a literate woman. As he was with Psyche's ease with expressing herself, Robert is surprised by the way Millicent openly conveys her attraction to him. Millicent discloses that she noticed when he arrived and was aware of his presence at Rosehall. In their exchange, she is the person who encourages the potential arrangement between them. She overtly demonstrates her interest in him and urges him to consider choosing her as his housekeeper. She is so determined to convince him of her suitability for this role that she expresses a lack of interest and no sense of urgency in finalizing her actual wages for this housekeeper position.

Throughout the novel, de Lisser portrays Millicent as sexually available and sexually willing to be with Robert. She wants him to choose her as his housekeeper; however, she is also self-assured as she encourages him to make this choice. After Robert returns to his abode, the morning after his night spent with Mrs. Palmer, Millicent greets him with concern about his whereabouts. When Robert again uses the word "servant" to describe Millicent, she corrects him and proclaims her feelings for him: "'I came here as your housekeeper, not as a servant,' she retorted, emphasizing the word housekeeper, giving it the significance of its Jamaican meaning. 'And,' she boldly added, 'I wouldn't care what you did, or whether you live or die, if I didn't love you. So there!'" (70). Immediately after her declaration of love, Millicent serves Robert with a good tot of rum. De Lisser writes, "His head swam, for the rum was potent and the quantity plentiful, but it put him in good spirits. He was not disposed to be harsh with Millie now; indeed he suddenly realized that he rather liked this brown spitfire who dared to go to great lengths because she was 'free and educated' and her grandfather was a man of great wealth and power" (71). Though Robert initially attempts to circumvent her efforts to be with him, he eventually succumbs to Millicent. They kiss, though they do not have an intimate sexual relationship. After a couple of brief encounters, Robert's feelings for Millicent intensify.

After their conversation in which she pronounces her love for him, Millicent contemplates and clarifies her intentions for him and with him. Just as de Lisser allows readers access to Robert's thoughts and feelings about Mrs. Palmer and Millicent and his impressions about life in Jamaica, he also offers Millicent's thoughts and perspectives about her life, her choices, and her desires. She muses that the "young 'massa'—she called him so in her mind, yielding to custom, in spite of her freedom and education—had kissed her, and, in spite of all that she had said about Mrs. Palmer, had decided to let her stay on in his service." She feels emboldened by the fact that he "had confessed that he might come to like her. But he had been with the white lady all the night before, as other men had been, and she had heard a great deal about the fascination which that woman exercised over those who loved her until she wearied of them." She decides that if "she could break that enthralment at once, the young, handsome squire would be saved and would leave Rosehall, taking her with him, as she was absolutely determined that he should do. He was not the first young white man that had liked her; others had suggested an establishment to her, and they were not mere overseers either, but owners of their own properties." Indeed, she reckons that if "she had remained 'single' up to now, it was of her choosing; none of her suitors had touched her heart, or, as she put it, 'filled her eye.' But Robert Rutherford did; he stood forth in her imagination like a god. She had seen and loved him, just as Annie Palmer had done. She was resolved to fight for possession of him as Annie Palmer was" (75).

De Lisser specifically elaborates on Millicent's decision not only to choose Robert but also to deny the proposals of other white men of authority and power in Jamaica. Millicent's intentions are not exclusively centered on her attraction to Robert; she also strategizes that Robert will be "taking her with him." Millicent's interest in Robert is not simply about his pleasing physical characteristics but what his position of entitlement will facilitate for her possibilities and options beyond Rosehall. Again, de Lisser imparts a sense of this woman of color being able to liberally choose and refuse any white suitors solely according to her desires and volition. Although legally not enslaved and although afforded some rights and privileges due to this status, the majority of actual free women of color who had limited resources were not in a position to be able to wield this degree of control over all aspects of their lives, including choosing all of their sexual partners and dictating all sexual interactions in colonial Jamaica.[9] De Lisser chooses not to present any sense of the actual racial, gendered, classed, and sexual dynamics of power and privilege that ensured the rites of white elite manhood, including the rights of white male enslavers and other white male denizens as manifested in their rapes of enslaved Black women in the Jamaican slavocracy. Rather, de Lisser portrays Psyche and Millicent as willing and consensual sirens wielding their sexual powers to manipulate and coerce Robert Rutherford into cohabitation and sexual intimacy with Millicent.

Millicent not only acknowledges her desire for Robert directly to him and to herself but also brazenly divulges her feelings for him to Mrs. Palmer. In one of the most dramatic scenes in the novel, Millicent confronts Annie Palmer and refuses to submit to her in any way. When Annie Palmer arrives at Robert's place, she verbally bashes Millicent and accuses her of being a thief. Millicent lashes back and rejects Annie Palmer's attempts to denigrate her. In the midst of their fight, Millicent launches into her verbal attack on Annie Palmer:

> "An' the reason why you don't want the Squire to have me for his housekeeper is because you want him for you'self an' you are jealous!"
>
> "Jealous of you, a creature like you—*you*? Girl, are you mad? Do you want to be whipped within an inch of your life? Do you remember who you are talking to? Dirt that you are, how dare you! Leave Rosehall this minute, or—"
>
> "I won't!"
>
> "You won't?" shrilled Mrs. Palmer, and that shrilling voice was new to Robert and shocked him. "You won't! Surely you must be mad!"
>
> "I am not one of your slaves. Dis place is yours, but the Squire is a free man, an' a white man, an' if he say I am to stay here tonight I can stay. And you can't flog me. You can't!"
>
> "We'll test that now," said Annie softly, narrowing her eyes. She lifted her riding whip and brought it down sharply on the girl's shoulders. Swiftly she raised it again for another blow.
>
> Robert darted between them.

"Annie, Annie," he implored, "remember your position."

"I am a mistress of slaves, that is my position," she retorted; "and this woman is little better than a slave. Leave me to deal with her, Robert. I know her kind."

"If you touch me again I will dash your brain out," shrieked Millicent, seizing a chair. "I am free like you are, and, so help me God, I rather die than let you beat me!" (104–105)

Millicent keenly articulates what she believes to be her right as a free, literate woman of color to act as such, and she also unequivocally equates her freedom to the freedom wielded by Annie Palmer and Robert Rutherford. Empowered with the sense of her rights as a free woman, Millicent unhesitatingly defends herself and announces her willingness to physically attack Annie Palmer. Although Robert pleads with Annie not to strike Millicent again, he is unsuccessful.

However, just as Annie gets ready to hit Millicent one more time, Millicent's grandfather Takoo enters and persuades her not to continue. When Takoo appears on the scene, he admits that he had been observing Annie Palmer's movements, and he intervenes in order to protect his granddaughter. Takoo then escorts Millicent away, though she leaves unwillingly and continues to verbally abuse Annie as they depart.[10]

Readers were introduced to Takoo before he appeared in this scene. Earlier, Millicent described him to Robert as "black, coal black, and he tall and old, very old; he is a Guinea man and wise! He can talk to spirits, like the old witch in de Bible, who call up Samuel. Me gran'father is very great; everyone here 'fraid for him—even Mrs. Palmer! . . . [H]e's more than an obeahman. More powerful" (71).

De Lisser's integration of Obeah and Myal practices in this novel serves as a way of highlighting one critical dimension of the supposed dangers associated with the enslaved people of Jamaica, one of the sundry perilous "manners and customs of this country." The term "Obeah" primarily appears in the Anglophone Caribbean. As anthropologists Jerome S. Handler and Kenneth M. Bilby posit, it is difficult to definitively define Obeah, especially as its meanings and perceptions about it have changed over time and space. In addition, "there is little consensus among scholars on its meaning and significance, although many conceptions of obeah, both in the past and in more recent years, stress its antisocial and evil nature as witchcraft or sorcery."[11] Obeah, as Bilby and Handler explain, "is not an organized religion. It lacks a more or less unified system of beliefs and practices involving, for example, deities or gods, communal or public rituals and ceremonies and the physical spaces or sites where they occur, or spiritual leaders of congregations/congregants, as in Haitian Vodun/Vodoo, Brazilian Candomblé, Cuban Santería, or the Orisha religion (formerly known as Shango) in Trinidad."[12] Instead, they describe Obeah as a "catch-all term that encompasses a wide variety and range of beliefs and practices related to the control or channeling of supernatural/spiritual forces by particular individuals or groups for their own needs, or on behalf of clients who come for help."[13] Obeahwomen and Obeahmen often utilize charms and articles, as well as healing salves, to resolve specific ailments and problems.[14]

In addition to the spiritual and healing elements related to Obeah, it is important to note that from the perspective of British colonial authorities, these practices were deemed as a significant threat to the integrity of the colonial system. As a result, colonial authorities enacted legislation targeting those who engaged in such supernatural practices. In the 1760 rebellion, often referred to as Tacky's War or Tacky's Revolt (named after one of the leaders), an Obeahman was instrumental in preparing Tacky and other rebels for battle; his assistance protected them from any shots fired at them and heightened their sense of their powers against their enemies. As Vincent Brown postulates, during "the 1760s two bodies of spiritual practice, obeah and myal, came to the attention of Jamaican authorities. Often conflated in the minds of whites and in their descriptions, these two spiritual arts held a supernatural political authority among the enslaved." Both were utilized "to mediate conflict and to instigate it; they were both a threat to communal equilibrium and a powerful social discipline. Sometimes too, they provided an axis for insurrectionary action, for, as John Newton discovered in 1751, supernatural beliefs emboldened slaves to resist the dominion of their masters and allowed blacks to believe more generally that they could challenge whites."[15] As celebrated Jamaican scholar and novelist Patricia Powell avers, "Black people have always used Obeah in the service of justice."[16]

Although a binary and oppositional relationship between Obeah and Myal often permeates discussions of Jamaican metaphysical discourse, with Obeah as "black magic" and the "antithesis of Christianity" and Myal linked with "healing practices" and "good magic," this particular "distinction was initially established during the Myal Revival of the 1860s, when Myal practitioners engaged in a systematic anti-Obeah campaign."[17] However, Obeah and Myal "practitioners' skill in herbalism, the healing aspects of both practices, their preparation of fetishes and other objects for the purpose of influencing behavior, assuring protection, and reaching one's goals—are all aspects in which the two practices are almost identical." However, Myalism, "as a group practice with a spiritual leader, brings a new dimension to the practice of Jamaican Obeah, one absent from the Obeah practiced in other Caribbean territories, which are characterized primarily by solo practitioners working with individual clients."[18]

The depth and breadth of Takoo's powers in Obeah and Myalism and the ways his African identity magnifies his metaphysical powers emerge at different points in the novel. A young enslaved boy who escorts Annie Palmer later on in the novel provides a comparative evaluation of Takoo's power in relation to Annie Palmer's. The young boy "was afraid of this woman, who was hand in glove with Takoo, with Takoo who was dreaded by every man and woman on Palmyra and Rosehall. As dreaded as Mrs. Palmer, and even more in a peculiar sort of way." Indeed, "the slaves believed that Takoo could read their minds; he was African, a witch-doctor, and it was madness to try to deceive him. They had often deceived Mrs. Palmer, and though she was dangerous she was less so, to them, than the gaunt negro of whom even some white men stood in awe" (142). Takoo's powers are severely tested, however, when Annie Palmer decides to do away with Millicent forever. It is because she considers Millicent to be a threat to her relationship with Robert that Annie Palmer devises a plan to eliminate her.

De Lisser devotes significant attention in the novel to the way Mrs. Palmer utilizes her wrath and "witcheries" and puts a fatal curse on Millicent. He locates the central source of Annie Palmer's powers in her past in Haiti. In order to reveal more about the rumors of Annie Palmer's past and powers, de Lisser integrates a conversation between three characters (the three fictional bookkeepers at Rosehall—Rider, Burbridge, and Rutherford) about her racial heritage and related ramifications. Burbridge, the senior bookkeeper, suggests that Annie Palmer may be "both French and negro. . . . I hear there is a lot of mixture of blood in Haiti; she may have some. That might account for her witcheries." Rider, in response to this, adamantly claims: "No; you are quite wrong about Annie Palmer's origin. Her mother and father were said to be Irish; she herself was born in England or Ireland—both countries have been mentioned—but they took her over [to Haiti] while she was yet a little girl" (128). Though Rider challenges any notion of Annie Palmer's blood connection to Blacks, he continues, "She must have heard and seen some strange things in Haiti; it was there, if anywhere, that she discovered she had powers out of the ordinary. . . . White, lovely, imperious, strong, fearless: don't you see she was just the sort of girl that a superstitious people would have worshipped?" (129).

Rider further deduces, "The voodoo priests there, who are versed in all the old African sorcery, and who do understand how to influence the minds of their dupes in all sorts of extraordinary ways, may have seen in this wonderful young girl great occult possibilities, and have taken pleasure in teaching her how to develop those possibilities." As a result, he continues, "she knows how to terrorize the people on her own estates; she has always known it. She can beat down the resistance of white men weaker than herself." He highlights, "As a matter of fact, the priestesses of Haiti are quite as powerful, in every way as influential, as their male colleagues. Given a woman of that description thrown in contact with Annie Palmer when she was growing into womanhood, when her mind was maturing, when her curiosity was at its keenest, and anything might happen." He further concludes, "She may have had a voodoo priestess for nurse when her parents took her to Haiti; it is quite likely. And Haiti, we all know, is the very stronghold of devil-craft in this part of the world. There the people see visions and the dead are brought out of their graves, or seem to be" (129).

With or without a blood connection to Haiti (or Blackness in general), the mere mention of Haitian influences on Annie Palmer serves as partial justification for her "witcheries" and subversive sexual sensibilities. The invocation of Haiti itself reifies the perils of a world beyond civility and civilization, a world that symbolizes the particular dangers of unleashed Blackness and Black freedom, and a world that ought to be avoided if at all possible (both Haiti itself or even the potential of Jamaica emulating Haiti at that time in 1831 and becoming a free Black republic). As Rider underscores, the powers of Haitian "priestesses" could not be trivialized; instead, the potency of their vital position, especially over an innocent white girl like Annie, could not be minimized or denied.

Just as the three bookkeepers discuss her past in Haiti, Annie "often thought of her youth in the nearby island." Her memories centered on "a high priestess" there who "had been no nurse of hers, as Rider had suggested; she had been a woman of position and property in Cape Haitian [sic], a woman who had marched with the armies of Dessalines and Christophe when these set out to free Haiti from the French domination" (137).[19] This woman gave Annie beautiful gifts. De Lisser writes that this woman "seemed to care for the girl; she was childless, and her husband was dead. Annie's parents thought it more advantageous than otherwise that a woman, whose husband had actually been born a baron of King Christophe's black Court, should be kindly disposed towards Annie, and consequently towards them." As a result, the friendship of this priestess "was well worth having. Its benefits were seen in the number of Haitians who patronized the Irish merchant—for he was Irish. Her enmity might have been a thing unpleasant to contend with" (136–137).

De Lisser creates this Haitian woman as not only culturally and historically grounded in the new republic of Haiti but also deeply rooted in the Haitian Revolution (especially with the invocation of Jean-Jacques Dessalines and Henri Christophe). He emphasizes the power that she wields in different realms of Haitian society, and this power reflects the dynamism of her fortitude and the range of her metaphysical abilities. Over a period of years, "this woman, whose title in northern Haiti was that of baroness, gradually won an ascendancy over Annie. In her way she loved the girl, though, on principle, she hated the white race, whom she regarded as the natural oppressors of her people." Annie herself "remembered how the Baroness—she had taken the title seriously when she lived in Haiti—had talked to her about the spirits that wandered about the earth and the air, the spirits who inhabited and animated everything, and how human beings, by determination and practice, and especially by belief and faith, could acquire power over these spirits" (137). Annie "had been fascinated" by all that the baroness told her and showed her. Without the protection and guidance of her parents in Haiti, Annie Palmer, as de Lisser depicts her, is particularly vulnerable to this Haitian woman's metaphysical powers and the boundless dangers of Haiti overall. The combination of the perils of Haiti and the powers of this baroness compromise the integrity of Annie's innocence. This Haitian baroness entices Annie and captivates her with powers previously unknown to the impressionable young Annie.

Like the "manners and customs" of Jamaica, Haitian customs and practices also epitomize a space of earthly and unearthly perils. In de Lisser's description, Haiti is "an atmosphere charged, so to speak, with the supernatural, where white as well as black believed in the occult, in the mysterious, in the traffic of earthly beings with those who were disembodied or of unearthly origin; in a strange, dark land where, among the mountains, in the dead of the night, and in spite of the king's decrees, the eerie sound of the voodoo drum could be heard stabbing through the silence and the darkness." Thus, "it was not surprising that Annie should believe what she was told, especially as the Baroness showed her how the common people worshipped those who called them to the midnight orgies or blasted the disobedient into insanity or death." It was also not surprising that "the Baroness told her that she too had the capacity to do wonderful things, and taught her the secrets of the Voodoo. And Annie came to believe that she possessed the power of a god" (137–138). Indeed, Annie not only believes in but also repeatedly demonstrates her supernatural powers in the novel. Throughout the novel, Annie Palmer reveals her sense of her supreme dominion over everyone and everything at Rosehall according to her will and desires. Her position as mistress of Rosehall and her role as its sole slave owner (having killed her three husbands) exacerbate her awareness and deployment of her distinct powers. Moreover, these powers are not only sourced by knowledge from this Haitian baroness but also extracted from Jamaica's metaphysical world of Obeah.

Due to Annie Palmer's decision to possess Robert for herself and Millicent's overt resistance to Annie's wishes and demands, Annie resolves to eliminate Millicent as a threat in any way. De Lisser strikingly describes Annie preparing her fatal curse for Millicent: "From the parcel in her hand, she now drew forth a queer round object; it was a child's skull smeared with blood. To it was attached, by a piece of wire, a bit of white cardboard. She herself was completely merged in the environing darkness, but her movements were as noiseless as those of a cat." Having placed the object on a nail on the door, she focused "her gaze upon the door, as though she would pierce with her vision through the solid wood, she stood there tense and erect. Her hands were clenched. . . . Her rigidity was that of a cataleptic." She waited until "there came a cry from within the little dwelling, a cry of agony and terror and despair. Again and again it rose; someone was crying out in mortal fear, in heart-stricken panic." Upon hearing the cry, "a smile of triumph wreathed her lips as she caught the sounds and exclamations of confusion that now broke out in the house; sharp calls and questions succeeding to those terrifying screams that had issued from the lips of a frightened, startled woman within" (140–141).

Annie's "witcheries" continue to work successfully on Millicent. Millicent's health quickly declines, and by the next morning news has spread about her condition. When a concerned Robert arrives at Takoo's house, a weakened Millicent describes her dream the night before and Annie's part in it all: "'It is she, I know it is she!' broke in Millicent wildly. 'I didn't see her face when she or her spirit come into the room, but I feel it was she. She was here, sucking all me blood; she is an Old Hige, a witch, a devil. She want to kill me because she want you for her own self'" (152).[20]

Takoo explains to Robert that an "Old Hige was a woman with the power to divest herself of her skin, and to render herself invisible. She sought out people whose blood she desired, babies as a rule, and sucked them to death. A grown person could not so easily and quickly be deprived of his or her blood; but to show that Millicent's death, a death by occult means, had been determined upon, Takoo added, an obeah spell, a curse, had also been put upon her the night before. The proof of it was there" (152–153). Takoo then presents the skull as evidence of the deed committed; when Robert questions the idea that Annie Palmer is the source of this curse, Takoo vehemently proclaims, "I believe, I know that that dam' white woman, that witch, that Old Hige was here last night, an' that she was in dis room sucking me gran'child blood! She was here; she come to commit murder—it is not the first time she done that. But, so help me God, it is going to be the last. If I can't save Millie's life, I will revenge her!" (153).

Recognizing that he must do whatever he can for his granddaughter, Takoo leads a special ritual/ceremony in order to save Millicent from the fatal consequences of Annie Palmer's curse. Having colluded with Mrs. Palmer in the past, though he is not sexually intimate with her in the novel, Takoo recognizes the strength of her metaphysical powers. This cleansing and healing ceremony involves the community of enslaved people at Rosehall. Hiding among the trees, Robert and Rider witness Takoo's Myal ceremony; readers observe and experience the ceremony from their vantage point.[21] De Lisser writes: "About twenty yards away a concourse of people crouched upon the ground, forming a rude circle, and within this circle blazed a great fire.... Bodies swayed to the right and left in unison with the rhythm of that chant, and the drum-throbs marked the cadences of the hymn of exorcism" (205). What transpired before them "was nothing that even Rider had ever heard before, no Christian words or air; it was something that had come out of Africa and was remembered still. There were people in the swaying crowd who had been born in Africa, and in their minds and emotions they had travelled back to that dark continent tonight." As they swayed and chanted, they "were worshipping again some sinister deity with power and will to harm, one to be propitiated with sacrifice and one who would not be turned aside from his designs by mere appeals and prayers for mercy" (206). A signal at midnight from one of the women ended the chanting. Where they all gathered, "a lane was rapidly made, and from among the sheltering trees came a girl, walking with stiff, short steps, and a tall, gaunt man behind her. He himself was followed by a youth who bore something in his arms" (207).[22] With the entrance of Takoo and Millicent, those gathered shifted their attention to the new arrivals.

De Lisser's invocation of Africa in this section reflects connections between Myalism and West African spiritual belief systems. In such ceremonies, note Margarite Fernández Olmos and Lizabeth Paravisini-Gebert, "Myal dances linked the Jamaican slaves to the worship of a West African pantheon of gods from which they had been separated when transported to the New World, and which used drums, dancing, dreams, and spirit possession as a part of organized veneration of both deities and ancestors." Moreover, they explain, the "ritual of the Myal dance, a hypnotic dancing in circles under the leader's direction, involved as well a mesmerizing opening for the entrance of the spirit in the body of the initiate, providing a bridge between the spirit possession characteristic of Afro-Creole practices and the filling with the Holy Spirit found in some variants of New World Christianity."[23] As Kwame S. N. Dawes posits, "De Lisser relishes the gory detail and sensationalism of the obeah ritual of cleansing. Seen through the eyes of Rutherford the scene becomes evidence of a diabolic struggle that is fully grounded in African magic and spiritism. Christianity sits in the bushes and watches the Afrocentric religions destroy each other. Contained here is the metaphor for the entire novel: the expatriate representing Britain, sits and watches the colony destroy itself through a demonstration of its inability to rule itself."[24]

This ceremony continues for a few pages, including various incantations and Takoo's sacrifice of a young white goat. After the sacrifice, Takoo begins to think he has defeated the curse: "The victory was his, he proclaimed triumphantly; his power was greater than that of anyone who had brought his granddaughter to this state; the battle was won and the girl was free" (210). De Lisser continues:

> And then, startlingly incongruous at such a gathering, a new cry rose upon the air and was heard about the shouting. It came from the voices of a dozen people who had leapt to their feet, and the word cried aloud was "O Christ!"
>
> For the first time since these people had assembled the name of Christ was uttered. It was shrieked out in an agony and spasm of fear. Men and women who had sprung upright were pointing in one direction with outstretched arms. Their motion attracted universal attention and from Robert's lips also came that same exclamation—"O Christ!"
>
> For there, about the spot whence Millicent and the witch doctor had emerged into the light, stood the grotesque figure of a mighty, ill-shapen bull, twice the natural size of any creature that these people had ever seen, and about its neck hung a chain that glowed as though it were of fire, and its eyes were like balls of fire as they rolled menacingly in the hideous head. The brute pawed the ground slowly as it stared at the gibbering crowd, it was as though it were about to advance upon them. But they waited for no more. It all happened in a moment or two. Everyone was on his or her feet. Through the trees they all rushed, screaming; vainly, Takoo, for a brief instant, sought to stay them; they did not heed him, did not even see or hear him; their one thought, their only impulse, was to flee to safety. And as they fled Robert heard the words, "Rolling Calf!" And still the monster stood there, though already it seemed to be vanishing. (210–211)

In mere minutes it disappears, and Rider explains to Robert that a "Rolling Calf" is "an evil spirit or devil that is supposed to take the form of a gigantic bull. Even to see it is dangerous. To be attacked by it is certain death" (211).

Robert listens to Rider attempt to explicate what they had witnessed, and suddenly they are faced with another undeniable sight: "Into the now deserted space, where the fire still burnt brightly, stepped a slight figure clothed all in black and like a man. They knew it at once. There was no mistaking it. Annie Palmer walked over to where Millicent had been sitting and looked down upon the dead body of the kid." Annie then "cast her eyes slowly around her, standing still for a minute. . . . She heard nothing. The men holding their breath as they looked, saw her kick contemptuously the kid's carcass that lay at her feet, then she laughed. The utmost contempt was expressed in that peal of laughter, contempt and a consciousness of triumph. She turned and went the way she had come" (212).

The next morning as tensions mount on the plantation and throughout Mon-

tego Bay about the eruption of a slave revolt, Robert confronts Annie Palmer
about her actions the night before. She mocks him and denies she was present at
all. Robert threatens to tell the officials of her practice of Obeah, and she explains
how he will be the subject of ridicule with such ludicrous stories. Once Robert
leaves, she decides to have one of her previous lovers (the white overseer Ashman) murder Robert for her. She proposes that either Ashman kill Robert or it
may be possible to simply have him killed during the slave revolt itself. While Annie Palmer plans Robert's demise, he and Rider continue to try to save Millicent.
They enlist the services of a doctor from Montego Bay; however, the doctor confirms that nothing further can be done. In retaliation for Annie Palmer's lethal
curse on his granddaughter Millicent, Takoo decides to murder Annie Palmer
during the slave revolt.[25]

As enslaved people, including Takoo, charge the great house, Rider and Robert return to the house and try to convince Takoo and other enslaved people not
to kill Annie Palmer. Takoo refuses to spare her, and he strangles Annie Palmer to
death. Capitalizing on white trepidation in Jamaica about slave revolts, de Lisser
purposely and vividly describes Annie Palmer's murder by Takoo in the midst of
the Christmas Rebellion in December 1831, thus intensifying the extensive effects
of such a monumental slave revolt as not only a fatal end to an individual mistress, Annie Palmer, but also a fatal threat (and possible end) to the institution of
slavery in Jamaica.

After murdering Annie Palmer, Takoo then turns to Rider and Robert and
states: "We could kill both of you, Squire, if we want. . . . But both of you are
kind. We may have to fight you tomorrow, but for Millie's sake you can go tonight" (253). Takoo and his men depart for the hills, and Robert and Rider remain behind for a few moments before also heading out. In the end, Robert decides to go on foot to Montego Bay, and he lets Rider use his horse. To punish
Robert for challenging her, Annie had instructed Ashman to have Robert killed.
This plot against Robert, which Annie Palmer had crafted and shared with Ashman, comes to fruition. While Rider is on Robert's horse, he is mistakenly killed.
In the final lines of the novel, the rector, Mr. McIntyre, bids farewell to Robert
in February 1832. As Robert "took his seat in the boat which was to bear him
out into the stream to the ship whose destination was England," Parson McIntyre
asks: "'Do you think you will ever come back to the West Indies?' 'Never,' was the
reply" (261).

In this novel de Lisser has created a fictitious melodramatic story centered on
the trope of a notorious white woman in the form of Annie Palmer.[26] His novel
focuses on the telling of a fictitious tale of a malevolent mistress and her subversive nature, yet slavery exists in this novel as a backdrop against which de Lisser

exposes Annie Palmer's wayward witcheries. De Lisser explores some aspects of Annie Palmer's mythical, spiteful disposition, but the lives of enslaved people remain undisclosed and deeply embedded solely within the background of the Jamaican slavocracy. The purpose of de Lisser's novel does not revolve around any substantive telling regarding the lives of enslaved people at Rosehall Plantation. Instead, they appear as markers of slavery and Blackness—working in the sugarcane fields, being whipped for some transgression, or witnessing and participating in a healing Myal ceremony. As a result, in his novel enslaved people are discounted, disavowed, and disposed of within the master/mistress fictional narrative of Annie Palmer as the White Witch of Rosehall. The fictional perspective, storyline, and context in de Lisser's novel represent *the* source of the contemporary Rose Hall tours.

CHAPTER 5

The White Witch and Enslaved Ghosts

Reinscribing Silences of Slavery in the
Contemporary Tours at Rose Hall Great House

The fabricated stories of paradise and peril in Herbert G. de Lisser's novel offered considerable fodder to fuel rumors and myths surrounding Rose Hall Plantation. They also provided the foundation for the contemporary Rose Hall Great House tours. Such stories involving Jamaican metaphysical beliefs (such as Obeah) had been wholly entrenched by the late 1950s, when John Rollins Sr. (former lieutenant governor of Delaware, entrepreneur, and philanthropist) purchased the seven-thousand-acre Rose Hall property in the 1950s; at the time, the house itself had been uninhabited for over one hundred years.[1] In the 1960s Rollins then invested between $2 million and $3 million to renovate the great house to its former glory; this renovation was completed in 1971. Beginning in the 1970s and extending into the present day, the Rollins family has constructed major hotels in Montego Bay.[2] Following John Rollins Sr.'s death in 2000, his wife, Michele Rollins, became the owner of Rose Hall and other Jamaican properties owned by him.[3] Indeed, she provides her own personal online invitation to guests, summoning visitors to experience the legend of the White Witch of Rose Hall.[4] These significant purchases and development schemes by the Rollins family reflect the ongoing U.S. imperialist presence in the Caribbean.[5] Jamaica and other Caribbean countries often represent oases of escape and hedonism for foreigners, including prime venues for destination weddings, and these countries have also become targets for neocolonial business ventures.[6] Even as England has relinquished socioeconomic and political control of some of its former Caribbean colonies, some Americans have manifestly reinforced and wholly embraced the idea of the Caribbean as the United States' "backyard"—and, as Karen Wilkes posits in her work, as "paradise for sale."[7]

For almost fifty years, the Rollins family has generated extensive and impressive marketing strategies for Rose Hall Great House and its expansive hotel/resort properties.[8] Visitors to Montego Bay are inundated with tour information about the Rose Hall Great House at Sangster International Airport in Montego

Bay, as well as at hotels along Jamaica's north coast. At the Norman Manley International Airport in Kingston (as of November 2019), a picture of the Rose Hall Great House serves as the prominent, central image in the featured poster on St. James Parish—one of several posters in the airport presented courtesy of the Jamaica Tourist Board. There are also cruise ship companies that highlight Rose Hall Great House, with some creating combination packages that include a day tour of the Rose Hall Great House.[9] Before and after the tours, visitors are also encouraged to purchase items at the gift store to enjoy the pleasures of Rose Hall beyond the boundaries of this plantation.

The Rose Hall Great House operates as a tourist attraction with fictional information presented as the "history" of the site. It is often mistaken by visitors as a museum; to be explicitly clear, the Rose Hall Great House is *not* a museum. From the limited information available in the old office files housed at Rose Hall Great House, the tour narrative has not changed since the late 1960s or early 1970s. The tour guides are not "educators" or "curators." The Rose Hall Great House tour guides are trained by the Tourism Product Development Company, Ltd. (TPDCo). Rose Hall Developments, Ltd., is also an accredited TPDCo company and registered with the Ministry of Tourism. Established in April 1996, the TPDCo is the "central agency mandated by the Government of Jamaica to facilitate the maintenance, development and enhancement of the tourism product." It is officially a "private company under the jurisdiction of the Ministry of Tourism."[10] The Rose Hall Great House tour guides are also trained by the TPDCo as part of Team Jamaica. Created in 1997, Team Jamaica programs (as part of TPDCo) provide basic, general information about the history of the tourism industry and offer professional skills and expertise in hospitality services and programs. Over the past few years, Team Jamaica has been working on the development of new programs for supervisors and administrators in culinary, spa, and hospitality management.[11] All Rose Hall Great House tour guides are certified by the Ministry of Tourism via the TPDCo certification programs. In addition, senior guides and supervisors at Rose Hall teach the script to new employees. New employees start at Rose Hall engaged in other tasks, and they are given as much time as necessary to learn and memorize the script. They are required to adhere to the script; however, a few of the more senior tour guides who have been Rose Hall Great House tour guides for over ten years have added their personal touches by integrating a couple of additional comments and reflections at different moments during the tour.

The Rose Hall Great House tour guides are not volunteers. There are no unpaid workers at Rose Hall. Staff members are also not contract laborers; instead, they are full-time employees of Rose Hall Developments, Ltd., and they are paid in accordance with the labor laws of Jamaica. Tour guides receive health insurance, group life insurance, maternity leave, and pension benefits. They also receive free lunch, overtime, shopping vouchers, uniforms, paid vacations (between two and four weeks per year), and up to ten sick days per year. In addition to paid employees, Rose Hall Great House hosts several high school students every year who are involved in community service. These students are paid a stipend through the Ministry of Tourism, and they also receive free lunch at Rose Hall. Their duties often involve filing and assisting in the Rose Hall Great House Gift Shop.[12]

INSIDE THE ROSE HALL GREAT HOUSE TOUR

The tour itself begins at the bottom of the stairs that lead up to the entry of the Rose Hall Great House. The tour guides briefly introduce the house as a "mansion once dominated by a vast sugarcane plantation. The land was six thousand acres with two thousand slaves working on it."[13] The tour narrative inaccurately notes the total population of enslaved people at Rose Hall as two thousand when Annie Palmer resided there. The correct number would be closer to two hundred enslaved people during Annie Palmer's time at Rose Hall. The tour narrative includes the various owners of Rose Hall, ending with the current owners, the Rollins family of Delaware. Even though the day and evening tours center on Annie Palmer's adult life at the house, the tours begin with the mythical story about Annie Palmer's early years in Haiti, including the fictitious information regarding her parents' time in Haiti. The tour guides describe Annie Paterson Palmer's parents as British merchants who moved to Haiti when Annie was ten years old. However, a year after their arrival in Haiti, her parents died after contracting yellow fever. After they passed, Annie was adopted by her Haitian nanny, whom the tour guides describe as a "voodoo priestess." According to the tour guides, the nanny "taught Annie everything about witchcraft. When she was eighteen years old, her nanny died. She left Haiti, came to Jamaica in search of a wealthy husband. Annie lived within the house for eleven years and within nine years murdered her three husbands along with countless slave lovers." Being nurtured (and groomed) by this Black nanny/"voodoo priestess" in Haiti, the tour guides explain, planted the initial seeds of Vodou within the young and innocent Annie's mind and soul. Visitors learn that young Annie's intimate proximity to this Haitian woman tainted her purity and innocence and that this Haitian woman thus initiated Annie Paterson into a transgressive and subversive world of Vodou. The tours highlight a Haitian woman's influence on young Annie Paterson without any direct reference to Annie Paterson herself being of African descent in any way. As mentioned in the previous chapter, the invocation of Haiti in the novel and in the tour reinforces a particular threat of Blackness, of danger for whites in a Black world.

The majority of the Rose Hall tour narrative repeats Annie Palmer's numerous mythical, murderous deeds in detail. As stated in the introduction, all of these details about multiple husbands and murders are entirely fictional. However, the tour guides present this information as factual. In the tours, guests move from one room to the next as they are informed about the lavish furnishings and decorations within each room. In the explanations of the bedrooms, tour guides describe how Annie Palmer killed each of her three husbands either by herself or by ordering enslaved people to work with her to end her husbands' lives. Annie Palmer informed people that her first husband, John Rose Palmer, "died of yellow fever," but as the tour guides point out, she poisoned him "by pouring arsenic in his coffee." The tour guides explain that Annie killed her second husband as she "stabbed him several times while he was sleeping and, then to make sure he was dead, she poured hot oil in his ears. Blood stains could be seen on the wall from 1905 to 1965. This husband, she said, was abusing her, so she had to defend herself by killing him." She murdered "her third husband, with the help of her freed slave lover Takoo, by strangling him." Annie "then had her slaves come and get the bodies and get rid of them for her." The slaves would go through an underground tunnel and bury the bodies.[14]

The tales of murder are interwoven with stories of her sexual adventures. The tour guides describe Annie's sexual relationships with both white men and enslaved Black men. Annie Palmer's various sexual and murderous deeds reflect the subversive nature of her exploits, given the specific historical and sociocultural contexts. Having been portrayed as closely connected to and guided by a Haitian nanny early on, Annie Paterson relocates to Jamaica and then extends the influence of Blackness in her life and world. While the tours underscore her subversive hypersexualized expressions, Jamaica and, by extension, the Caribbean serve as the venue and catalyst for this sexual exploration and her wild desires for multiple loves of different racial identities.

Moreover, in the absence of a permanent white husband at Rose Hall, Annie Palmer supposedly released and channeled her unstable, malicious nature in her brutal treatment of enslaved people. White male protection cannot be extended to Annie Palmer in this case due to her own efforts to eliminate multiple white husbands when they are of no further use to her. Her fictional Haitian connections and maleficent nature serve as the means of weaponizing white womanhood. Furthermore, in his novel, Herbert G. de Lisser integrates descriptions of Annie Palmer riding at night in men's clothing, which reinforces the sartorial invocation of masculinity in the presentation of her power and authority as master and mistress of Rose Hall. So while the mythical Annie Palmer disrupts conceptions of elite white womanhood and respectability, she embodies material evidence of the contaminating power and potency of Blackness, especially in its corruption of white female innocence. Furthermore, the dramatic recounting of Annie Palmer's endeavors by the tour guides generates a sense of awe regarding her sexual and murderous accomplishments. Instead of personifying elite white womanhood embedded in notions of purity, piety, and innocence (often characterized as Victorian attributes and moral standards), Annie Palmer's legend creates a counternarrative to assumed and projected nineteenth-century racial, gendered, and classed codes of conduct of white femininity, sexuality, and womanhood.

Although Annie Palmer's sexual involvement with multiple men is an integral element of his novel, de Lisser does not include any sexual relationship between Annie Palmer and the previously enslaved man Takoo. However, the tour narrative specifically mentions Takoo as a former lover of Annie Palmer's. The inclusion of a sexual relationship with Takoo intimately expands the vortex and scourge of Blackness in Annie Palmer's life. In the tour, Takoo becomes the epitome of unbridled Black male sexuality and brutality in need of containment and confinement. If what he stands for is not contained, then white womanhood (literally in the hands of Black men) becomes more vulnerable, in danger of being compromised and even destroyed.[15] During the tour, visitors learn that Annie Palmer was murdered by Takoo; this is presented in the tours and in de Lisser's novel as an act of revenge and retribution for Annie Palmer's "curse" on Takoo's granddaughter Millicent. Takoo, as the quintessential "Black brute," then extinguishes the life of this elite white woman, precipitated by her refusal to adhere to the societal codes of conduct. In the evening tour, a Black man (acting the part of the ghost of Takoo) runs wildly down the stairs; he screams as he heads to the lower level of the house. In the tour, the brief mention of Takoo's murder of Annie Palmer during a slave revolt is almost incidental compared with her litany of murderous acts, even though the murder is an important aspect of de Lisser's novel. The portrayal of Takoo as an Obeahman (in the novel and the tours) also reflects the deleterious (and even fatal) effects of Annie Palmer's ongoing engagement with Blacks (and their related metaphysical dimensions) in the Caribbean.

Though the tours focus on Annie Palmer's legend, Takoo's "story" is included in the tours in ways that provide an avenue for the demonstration of his agency and his engagement in the performance/acts of masculinity (e.g., his attempts to protect his granddaughter Millicent, his decision to avenge her death, and even the actor [as the ghost of Takoo] in the evening tour screaming freely through the house in rage). Due to Takoo's position as a freedman of color (and an Obe-ahman), both the tours and the novel portray him as a man who wields a certain amount of control over his life and attempts to protect his loved ones based on his position as a freeman of color in this slave society. As he screams throughout the house, the spirit of Takoo articulates his rage, as he refuses to be silenced in life and in death.

Even as Takoo's presence is felt and heard during the tour, no white male in any form makes an appearance at any point during the tour. As the tours center on how Annie Palmer's experiences in the Caribbean (in Haiti and then later in Jamaica) engender and empower her subversive acts during her lifetime, the tours do not touch on these experiences and ramifications for white men in the Ca-ribbean. Although de Lisser's novel's central character is an Englishman, Robert Rutherford, the tours only present information about Englishmen as unnamed victims of a pernicious, poisoned, and warped white womanhood and sexual-ity (vis-à-vis Annie Palmer murdering her multiple husbands). Englishmen's acts of exploitation, abuse, and torture of enslaved people in Jamaica's slavocracy are muted in the tour narrative; instead, the tours reify the victimization of white men based on their seemingly innate innocence. In some of the tours, Annie Palmer's only husband, John Rose Palmer, is only briefly mentioned by name, and she is then linked with two additional fictional husbands.

With Annie Palmer's legend as the "White Witch" as the primary focus of the lore about Rose Hall, questions about possible abuse of enslaved women by white male enslavers at Rose Hall (including Annie's husband, John Rose Palmer) are not mentioned. Given that the triennial slave registers for Rose Hall include the birth of a few children described as "quadroons" (during the time of John Rose Palmer's presence at Rose Hall), and even with Rose Hall's overseers and book-keepers being potential biological fathers of these children, it is possible that John Rose Palmer could have fathered one or more of these children. Informa-tion regarding John Rose Palmer's granduncle John Palmer is even more lim-ited. Without any documentation describing the enslaved people at Rose Hall during John Palmer's time in residence there (between 1767 and 1797), we have no evidence of him having fathered enslaved children. John Palmer had no chil-dren with Rosa Palmer at Rose Hall.[16] And after Rosa Palmer's death in 1790, two years later, John Palmer (probably in his late fifties to midsixties at the time) married twenty-year-old Rebecca Ann James. Certainly his interest in Rebecca Ann James might not have been his only sexual interest on either Rose Hall Plan-tation or his neighboring Palmyra Plantation. The tours and de Lisser's novel ex-clude the presence and stories of John Palmer and John Rose Palmer, as well as any mention of their potential sexual abuse of enslaved women, and the tour nar-

rative does not include any information about enslaved women being sexually violated as an integral tenet of slavery.

There is no specific information in the official tour narrative about the particular individual or collective lives and experiences of enslaved women at Rose
Hall. Millicent is only briefly mentioned as Takoo's granddaughter in some of
the tours, and her status as a free woman of color is not mentioned. Indeed, she
is often not named at all and solely referred to as "Takoo's granddaughter." Limited information on slavery is offered by the tour guides. These guides highlight a
bucket during the tour, and they mention that the heavy bucket when filled with
water was carried by enslaved children. The bucket is offered for guests to pick up
to get a sense of its weight. Yet the full weight and gravitas of slavery remain untold in the tours.

At the very end of the tour, guests enter the lower level of the house, the dungeon of the great house. It is at this point in the tour that guests can peruse pictures on the walls of the dungeon. The room includes photos of members of the
Rollins family at different gatherings (including family weddings at Rose Hall)
and pictures of important public figures who have visited the house. These large
glassed displays command the attention of guests; they are entitled "Weddings
at Rose Hall, Jamaica," and "Our Special Guests at Rose Hall." One of the titles of the wedding section is "A charmed life begins at Rose Hall." There is also
one section with photographs of the house before it was renovated, and another
case includes photographs with John Rollins Sr. in front of the house in the process of being renovated (dated 1960). A large case includes other photos of John
Rollins Sr. with a feature article on him entitled "The John Rollins Story" and a
newspaper article on Michele Rollins entitled "People in Paradise: Michele Rollins." Throughout this room, there are a number of random articles on display
outside of the glass cases; some of them are labeled (e.g., "Door Lock and Key"
and "Key"). One possible remnant of slavery, or at least of the labor involved at a
sugar plantation, is the undated tool marked as "Hoe." Another large item is described by the tour guides as a "bear trap" previously used to capture runaways.
The majority of the items in this section of the lower level are old plates, bowls,
utensils, and other household wares.

Most guests stop only briefly in this area to look at the photos before they
head to the area currently named and refashioned as "Annee's Pub."[17] A decora-
tive sign hangs in the bar inviting guests to "try our HOUSE Special 'WITCHES
BREW.'" An image of a fullish glass with a straw is positioned in the middle
on the left side of the sign. Most of the words are in black, but the two words
"WITCHES BREW" are in red. Under that title is a description in smaller, cap-
italized letters: "BLENDED FROM THE FINEST JAMAICAN RUMS AND

TROPICAL FRUIT JUICES!!!" In the bar area, there is a specially framed picture of Michele Rollins with Charles, Prince of Wales, and Camilla Parker Bowles, Duchess of Cornwall, posing in front of the Rose Hall Great House. All of the photos of members of the Rollins family and the royal family displayed throughout the dungeon/bar area reinforce the centering of a white presence, white pleasure, white power, and white entitlement.

There are places in the bar area for guests to sit and enjoy their drinks. If any guests need to use a restroom, the dungeon area has two restrooms (one for women and the other for men). Beautifully renovated in the 1960s, these restrooms were originally the two jail cells at Rose Hall Plantation—the areas described in the Rose Hall Journal for "confinement" to punish enslaved people (including those who had absconded from the plantation). Originally utilized for punishment and torture during slavery, these two renovated spaces have been refashioned as venues for the personal ease, comfort, and release of Rose Hall Great House guests.

Although the tour narrative has basically remained the same over the years, the Rose Hall Great House has made one significant change inside the dungeon area. In late 2018 large poster panels were installed in the dungeon area with general overviews—"The Rose Hall Great House," "Trans-Atlantic Trade in Africans," "African Slavery," "The Rise of King Sugar," "Maroons in Jamaica," "The British Movement Towards Emancipation," "Post Emancipation Jamaica," "A History of St. James," "Traditional Music and Dance," and "Out of Many One People." There is also a photo of Johnny Cash, who was a friend of John Rollins Sr. and who also lived with his wife, June Carter-Cash, at the nearby plantation called Cinnamon Hill.[18] There are a couple of paragraphs of information on each panel. As of November 2019, there was still no specific material in any of the panels about the enslaved people who labored at Rose Hall.

Though Rose Hall was a site of slavery, these tours do not engage critically with the tenets of slavery or the lives of enslaved people. Silencing slavery in these tours also serves to silence enslaved women—their presence, their challenges, their lives. By focusing on Annie Palmer's legend, her ghost speaks through the tour guides, who provide a "voice" and medium to convey her story. Annie Palmer forces her presence into the present, leaving an indelible mark on contemporary visitors. However, during the tours, enslaved women's voices and experiences are bound and confined by death. Black women are not only historically bound and silenced by the tenets of slavery and white supremacy but also disembodied as silenced ghosts in these ongoing contemporary Rose Hall evening tours. The evening tours underscore enslaved female corporeality as a marker of slavery, with enslaved women appearing as ghosts throughout the night tours as

the embodiment of slavery's past, as well as incomplete, liminal, and ghostly beings. During the evening tours, a few Black women acting as enslaved women are
dressed in white, and their faces are powdered white as well. They appear at random moments throughout the tour. They do not utter any words; instead, their
movements reflect only their household duties as enslaved people (e.g., cleaning
up rooms). These women, who move silently throughout the tours, reflect the
"invisibly visible" presence of enslaved Black women. They become reinscribed
as property, as props, as objects that appear and disappear throughout the tour.
They are ghostly accessories to the story of Rose Hall. Like the other props and
objects in the house, they represent part of the "staging" of the house as a site of
slavery and for the delivery of the master/mistress narrative of slavery that presents them as objects to be acted upon and not as subjects in their own right. In
both de Lisser's novel and the contemporary Rose Hall Great House tours, the
experiences of enslaved women in Jamaica remain obscured, unexplored, and interpreted through a white supremacist, imperialist lens.

That a plantation like Rose Hall would be linked with a ghost story is not exceptional. Indeed, as Tiya A. Miles critically examines in her book *Tales from the
Haunted South: Dark Tourism and Memories of Slavery from the Civil War Era*,
"African American lives, and Black slavery in particular, seemed to be fair game
for the dark-tourism industry, so much so that deceased Black slaves are main
characters of the southern ghost tour."[19] Miles explains, "Ghost stories make it a
point to render what is taboo, frightening, and alien to mainstream society. This
means that the ghost story is not only a form of historical narrative; it is potentially a form of radical historical narrative that can dredge up unsettling social
memories for reexamination."[20] Though often dismissed as improbable and friv-
olous, ghost stories can "call to mind disturbing historical knowledge that we feel
compelled to face, but they also contain the threat of that knowledge by marking
it as unbelievable." As Miles states, "Just as hauntings are about the return of the
past, or time 'out of joint,' ghost stories are a controlled cultural medium for recognizing *trouble* in that past, for acknowledging the complexities and injustices
of history that haunt the periphery of public life and leave a lingering imprint on
social relations."[21]

In the case of plantations serving dual purposes as historic sites and as ghost
stories highlighting Black ghosts in bondage, Miles thoughtfully proffers:

> The recuperated black slave in the form of a ghost is presented in caricature on
> these tours, positioned outside black cultural contexts, and stripped of the his-

torical realities of American slavery. . . . Rather than finding an opportunity to learn about the antebellum past, to empathize with enslaved human beings, or to connect with a rich troubled regional and national heritage, tourists encounter narratives that temper the history of slavery and race relations, assuage guilt, and feed fascination with the racialized other. The use of slaves' lives, likenesses, and experiences for the grist of this economic enterprise seems to amount to a virtual recommodification and recommercialization of black bodies in the modern moment.[22]

Unlike the named enslaved ghosts highlighted in Miles's book, who seem to avoid the gaze of visitors to these southern haunted spaces, the "ghosts" of unnamed enslaved women at Rose Hall Great House appear (though randomly) for visual consumption for all visitors throughout the evening tour, and they offer ample time for photographs and videos of their ghostly presence. Throughout the Rose Hall tours, Annie Palmer (the only actual historical figure at the center of the tours) becomes the ghost—the White Witch of Rose Hall—and actual Jamaican women become ghosts during the tours who reflect the facade of slavery.

Due to the range of ages of visitors to plantation sites such as Rose Hall, white-centered tour narratives often present this facade of slavery with shared details of the lives of the enslaved based on what would be considered palatable and "appropriate" information for children and adult visitors. Reenactments are usually limited to actors and actresses dressed up as domestic slaves, with reenactors only demonstrating bondage in some relatively "benign" form. Reenactors often are engaged in domestic duties, and they take time away from these duties to interact with visitors and answer questions about the plantation.[23] Thus, visitors to these sites do not witness the quotidian acts of coercion, trauma, and terror that were deeply embedded in and foundational to the institution of slavery itself. There are no displays of people being punished or suffering in any way; such plantation sites do not reenact brandings, whippings, rapes, and other acts and processes of violence. As a result, examples of the systematic physical and psychological torture of enslaved people are not included within many plantation tours. With these vital and essential aspects of the institution of slavery being deemed unsuitable for reenactment at plantation sites, visitors move through these plantation tours with relative ease and comfort (and even entertainment, in the case of the Rose Hall Great House evening ghostly tours). Echoes of slavery during these tours reinforce popular, ahistorical notions of a benign institution with only benevolent slaveowners and sustain the ongoing amnesia, ignorance, and silences about the institution of slavery.

The tours and staging of the Rose Hall Great House itself encourage visitors

to welcome and accept this facade of slavery, this illusion of history. In staging
fiction as history, the contemporary tours present Rose Hall as a museum, with
museum cords used to guide visitors throughout the house and to protect sections of the house from guests touching or getting too close to specific objects on
display. Though presented as (and assumed by most visitors to be) a museum in
form, Rose Hall Great House represents a pretense of a museum in content—a
mimesis of a museum, of history.[24] Rose Hall embodies instead a mausoleum of
mythical memories. Herbert G. de Lisser's novel informs the tour narrative from
beginning to end, with this fictional story deemed by Rose Hall visitors as a history lesson on slavery in Jamaica. Rose Hall represents a remarkable transformation from the historical presence of this plantation and the enslavers and enslaved
who resided there to their fictitious and ghostly portrayal in the contemporary
tours.

Even though slavery's ritualized, routinized acts of terror and trauma are not
presented during the Rose Hall Great House daily tours, can we understand the
gaps and silences surrounding the stories of enslaved people in these tours as a
contemporary form of perpetual violence reified and reinscribed at this site of
slavery? When we consider the significance and meanings of particular representations of slavery and enslaved people at Rose Hall Great House, Saidiya Hartman reminds us of the crucial examination of "scenes of subjection." "By defa-
miliarizing the familiar," Hartman explains, we "illuminate the terror of the mundane and quotidian rather than exploit the shocking spectacle." As she pointedly
argues, "what concerns me here is the diffusion of terror and the violence perpetrated under the rubric of pleasure, paternalism, and property."[25] The essential "spectacle" of slavery at Rose Hall at the cornerstone of the tours is not the
enslaved people or the horrors of slavery; instead, it is the white mistress Annie
Palmer and her mythical sexual and murderous exploits. Simultaneously, the silent, ghostly figures of enslaved women appearing at arbitrary moments in the
evening tour obviate and eliminate the terror of bondage in these tours. As a result, visitors to Rose Hall can participate in the awe and glorification of Annie
Palmer's life, relish the stories of her multiple sexual partners and murderous
feats, and experience the pleasure of roaming the house accentuated by the sensa-
tions of surprise and spectacle throughout the evening tours. On the other hand,
the enslaved beings in these tours appear as apparitions who are not presented
as subjects in any meaningful ways; instead, the public performance of slavery
via the tours mounts a contemporary scene of subjugation. It is through enslaved
women's ghostly reincarnation in the tours, in their seemingly "mundane" appearances in front of visitors, that their enslavement and experiences of bondage
become fleeting moments, conjuring up otherworldly persons and places, void of

any sense or sensation of the violence, suffering, and trauma of their bondage at Rose Hall.

Though there may be guests who ask about enslaved people and slavery at Rose Hall, I must admit that no one has posed questions about enslaved women or the institution of slavery during the numerous tours I have attended over the past several years. The one question that is often asked concerns the reasons why Takoo killed Annie Palmer and how he was able to do so. In de Lisser's novel, he describes Takoo's murder of Annie Palmer as directly related to Annie Palmer's fatal curse on his granddaughter Millicent. However, as previously noted, in the Rose Hall tour, Takoo is also described as Annie Palmer's freed slave lover. As her lover he has access to her bedroom, which is where he supposedly kills Annie Palmer as an act of retribution for her fatal curse on his granddaughter.

Although the lore of Annie Palmer alludes to the intricacies of gender, sexuality, and power within a Jamaican plantationscape, the Rose Hall tours prioritize the mythical "lovings and killings" of an elite white mistress and neglect the stories of enslaved women, who far outnumbered white mistresses on Jamaican plantations. Visitors leave with a titillating story about Annie Palmer, yet the names and experiences of enslaved women who labored at Rose Hall remain unspoken, unremembered, and unmemorialized. The intentional neglect and silencing of enslaved women's perspectives, stories, and experiences in the tours reflect a long and deep legacy of the disavowal of enslaved women and enslaved persons overall within white supremacist, heterosexist, imperialist ideologies and praxis.

WHO WAS ANNIE PALMER?

So what is the actual historical narrative about the enslavers and owners of Rose Hall Plantation, including Annie Palmer? In concert with the myth of the White Witch of Rose Hall, the inaccuracies regarding the ownership of Rose Hall Plantation continue to be shared and disseminated during the tours and in popular stories about this plantation. Though Annie Palmer is the primary mistress at the heart and center of stories of the Rose Hall Plantation, Rose Hall's first mistress was Rosa Palmer (née Kelly), a woman of Irish descent who lived in Jamaica. In 1746, in order to establish a home for himself and his fiancée, Rosa Kelly, Englishman Henry Fanning purchased a 290-acre plot for £3,000 in St. James Parish on which to build their home; this plantation was called True Friendship. However, only a few months after they married, Henry Fanning died in 1748. In 1750 Rosa Fanning married George Ash, a prominent landowner in St. James. Ash constructed a home on the land Fanning had purchased for Rosa. Soon after the house was completed, Ash died in 1752. Again, Rosa Ash's marital status (and certainly any kind of marital bliss) would be short lived. In 1753 Rosa Ash married the Honorable Norwood Witter from Westmoreland; he died in 1765. It is often remarked that though Rosa was married to Witter for a longer period of time, this was not a blissful marriage.[26]

In 1767 Rosa married John Palmer, the custos of St. James.[27] Palmer was the owner of the neighboring Palmyra Plantation in St. James. He was a widower with two sons, both of whom resided in England. Rosa was John Palmer's second wife. John Palmer built the now-standing Georgian-style mansion between 1770 and 1780 for £30,000 on the site of the former residence built by George Ash. Although Rose Hall is often described as being named for Rosa Palmer, it is more likely that John Palmer named it Rose Hall in honor of the Rose surname, which was prominent in his family history. When Rosa Palmer died in 1790, her will dictated that her fourth husband, John Palmer, inherit Rose Hall Plantation. In 1792 John Palmer married for the third and final time; his bride was twenty-year-old Rebecca Ann James from Trelawny. In 1797 John Palmer died; though married to Rebecca Palmer at the time, he did not leave Rose Hall and Palmyra Plantations to his young widow.[28] Instead, he placed both plantations in trust to his two sons and their heirs. Neither of John Palmer's sons, James and John Palmer, had visited Jamaica, and neither had children of his own. In 1806 John Palmer's son James died, and in 1818 his second son, John, died.

Due to the dictates of his will, after the death of his two sons, John Palmer's grandnephew, Englishman John Rose Palmer, inherited Rose Hall and Palmyra Plantations.[29] John Rose Palmer moved to Jamaica in 1818. With the death of John Palmer in 1797, both plantations were in desperate need of attention and repair, so John Rose Palmer began the process of restoring Rose Hall and Palmyra Plantations.[30] If John Rose Palmer had not been informed before 1818 about the debts John Palmer had left behind, undoubtedly this information would have been revealed to him a short time after his arrival. Yet he would also have been apprised of and possibly surprised by the significant productivity of sugar and rum at Rose Hall.[31]

At some point between his arrival in 1818 and early in 1820, John Rose Palmer met Annie Mary Paterson. Annie Paterson was the daughter and only child of John Paterson, Esq., of the Baulk (an area near Lucea, the capital of the parish of Hanover) and Juliana Paterson (née Brown). Annie Paterson's maternal grandparents were the Honorable William Brown, a Scotsman who migrated to Jamaica and became custos of Hanover, and his wife, Mary Kerr James, of Kew, Jamaica, located about five kilometers or three miles east of Lucea. Her paternal grandparents were Dr. John Paterson, a Scotsman who migrated to Jamaica and settled in the parish of Hanover, and his wife, Deborah McKenzie.[32] John Paterson married Juliana Brown in 1801, but he died at the age of twenty-four before the birth of his daughter, Annie Paterson, the following year. In 1812 Juliana Paterson married Captain David Boyd, a retired naval officer and attorney. Although Annie Paterson's biological father died before she was born, she was not an orphan, as often described in the lore about her. Moreover, neither Annie Paterson nor her parents traveled to Haiti at any time. Because Annie Paterson grew up in Jamaica, her close relatives probably exerted a degree of influence over her for some time. Annie Paterson and John Rose Palmer were married on March 28, 1820, in Mount Pleasant, St. James, the town in which her mother and stepfather lived. During their honeymoon in England, they married again before returning to Jamaica. This was neither exceptional nor unusual. When her husband, John Rose Palmer, died only a few years later in 1827 at the age of forty-two, Annie Palmer could still seek the comfort and guidance of her mother, Juliana Paterson Boyd (who died in 1832), and her stepfather, Captain Boyd (who died in 1842).[33] References to any unnatural causes of John Rose Palmer's death and Annie Palmer's supposedly vile, murderous nature do not seem to emerge until the appearance of James Castello's 1868 article "The Legend of Rose Hall."[34] However, it is de Lisser's novel that provides the most significant material for the narrative presented during the Rose Hall Great House tours, with elements of Rosa Palmer's life (specifically that she had multiple husbands) being interspersed with events in the life of Annie Palmer.

After John Rose Palmer's death in 1827, Annie Palmer left Rose Hall a few years later (probably by 1830), according to limited evidence. Following Annie Palmer's departure from Rose Hall Great House in 1829 or 1830, enslaved people may have attacked the house during the Christmas Rebellion of 1831–1832 (also known as the Baptist War); it is unclear to what extent the house was damaged during the rebellion.[35] When Annie Palmer left Rose Hall Plantation, she did not leave by herself: she took a few enslaved people with her. In the "Return of Givings-In" section of the 1833 *Jamaica Almanac* for the March 1832 quarter, proprietors are listed alphabetically, and next to their names are the number of enslaved people and the number of livestock owned by the respective proprietors. Annie Palmer is one of the proprietors named living in the parish of St. James. She is listed as "Anna M. Palmer" at Bellevue; the itemized information for her includes five enslaved people and thirteen livestock. Immediately above Anna M. Palmer's name are two lines—the first one, for "Palmer, J. Rose, heirs of, Palmyra," notes eighty-three enslaved people and seventy-two livestock. Rose Hall is noted on the next line, with 112 enslaved people and 58 livestock.[36] After the abolition of slavery, "Anna Mary Palmer" also filed a claim in April 1836 for compensation for five enslaved people for the amount of £71 14s. 4d.[37]

Annie Palmer eventually settled finally at Bonavista, and she died there in 1846 at the age of forty-four.[38] Although the tours end with an elaborate story about Annie Palmer's supposed remains in the tomb on the grounds of the Rose Hall Plantation, Annie Palmer was buried in the Montego Bay churchyard, though her grave is not marked or identified in any way.[39]

EPILOGUE

somebody/anybody
sing a black girl's song
bring her out
to know herself
to know you
but sing her rhythms
carin/struggle/hard times
sing her song of life
she's been dead so long
closed in silence so long
she doesn't know the sound
of her own voice
her infinite beauty
she's half-notes scattered
without rhythm/no tune
sing her sighs
sing the song of her possibilities
sing a righteous gospel
let her be born
let her be born
& handled warmly.

—NTOZAKE SHANGE, *For Colored Girls
Who Have Considered Suicide When
the Rainbow Is Enuf*

When we left the Rose Hall Great House in the summer of 2013, one persistent thought was how many times Annie Palmer's name had been mentioned throughout the tour and the tour narrative's silence regarding the actual names of enslaved women at Rose Hall. I thought I could put my troubled mind to rest if I knew just one of their names. There was nothing in the tour that commented about these women as individual people or as a collective unit in any manner. Even the names of fictional Takoo and his fictional granddaughter Millicent (whose name is not consistently mentioned in the tours) rang hollow. I promised myself that day that I would at least try to find out if there were any records of their names. At the time of that first tour, I was not thinking in any way of a book on this topic at all; rather, I wondered if I could just find and say one name, perhaps even a few names, of those girls and women who had labored there.

These silences at Rose Hall Great House embody the extensive silences and reverberations of the afterlives of slavery in the ever-evolving national and global narratives of slavery statues, museums, and memorializations. Over the past two decades, a litany of programs and exhibitions have underscored significant commemorations of the transatlantic slave trade and the abolition of slavery. Monumental anniversaries related to slavery engender specific moments of national reflection and even transnational action.[1] In 1998, for France's sesquicentennial of the abolition of slavery, the city of Nantes announced its support for the construction of a commemorative monument to abolition. The Mémorial de l'abolition de l'esclavage opened on March 25, 2012.[2] A decade after France's sesquicentennial of the abolition of slavery, in March 2007, England marked the bicentennial of the passage of its Abolition of the Slave Trade Act, and a number of commemorative events in British cities centered on the importance of this bicentennial.[3] Bicentennial activities and other related events in England in 2007, however, did not translate into an actual monument or memorial in England itself in honor of the enslaved people of African descent of the British Empire. One response to this profound silence was the creation of the group Memorial 2007. Established in 2005, Memorial 2007 has been fundraising for a national memorial "to commemorate enslaved Africans and their descendants in the Rose Gardens of London's Hyde Park."[4] Even as this memorial or any memorial to commemorate enslaved people of African descent remains unrealized in England, in November 2004, just outside of Hyde Park, England unveiled the Animals in War Memorial. This memorial is specifically "dedicated to all the animals that served and died alongside British and Allied forces in wars and campaigns throughout time."[5]

It is important to point out that Caribbean nations, supported by African countries, encouraged the United Nations General Assembly in November 2006 "to commemorate the bicentenary of the passage of legislation in Britain calling for an end to the transatlantic slave trade."[6] As a result, in December 2007 the United Nations General Assembly declared March 25 the International Day of Remembrance of the Victims of Slavery and the Transatlantic Slave Trade.[7] The United Nations General Assembly also proclaimed 2015–2024 the International

Decade for People of African Descent.[8] In addition, the United Nations commissioned a permanent memorial in honor of the victims of the transatlantic slave trade. It was erected at the United Nations Headquarters in New York City. The United Nations unveiled the Ark of Return memorial on March 25, 2015. The memorial was designed by Rodney Leon (an American architect of Haitian descent), who was selected through an international competition and formally announced in September 2013. Leon also designed the African Burial Ground National Monument in New York City, which was dedicated in 2007.[9] Furthermore, underwater explorations of slave trade shipwrecks (such as the Diving with a Purpose projects) have also been critical in identifying these additional "grave sites" as a way of recognizing and documenting the immeasurable death toll of the transatlantic slave trade.[10]

The process of creating slavery museums still remains a tangible form of acknowledging the legacy of slavery well into the twenty-first century.[11] For example, Brazilians are currently debating the future construction of the Museum of Slavery and Liberty in Rio de Janeiro, and in December 2017 citizens of Lisbon voted affirmatively to build a monument in memory of Portuguese involvement in the transatlantic slave trade.[12] In the United States, the National Museum of African American History and Culture (established by an act of Congress in 2003 and opened to the public in 2016) prominently features the *Slavery and Freedom* exhibit. In June 2021 the Rijksmuseum, the national museum of the Netherlands in Amsterdam, opened a new exhibition entitled *Slavery* focused on Dutch participation in the transatlantic slave trade from the seventeenth century through the nineteenth century and slavery in the Dutch colonies.[13] Such museums and exhibits still serve as a particular medium and mediation for memorialization in the present day.[14]

The contested public representations of the history of slavery and their complex contemporary ramifications have permeated different institutional arenas over generations. As the movie *Gone with the Wind* (1939), the original television miniseries *Roots* (1977), and more recent films such as Steven Spielberg's *Lincoln* (2012), Quentin Tarantino's *Django Unchained* (2012), Steve McQueen's *12 Years a Slave* (2013), Kasi Lemmons's *Harriet* (2019), and Gerard Bush and Christopher Renz's *Antebellum* (2020) vividly demonstrate, cinematic ventures into the realm of slavery also contribute to the provocative conversations regarding representations and reconstructions of enslaved people's agency, resistance to bondage, and conceptions of freedom.[15]

Prominent universities in the United States and Europe (including Brown, Columbia, Georgetown, Princeton, Rutgers, the University of Virginia, and the University of Glasgow) have also publicly entered these contemporary conversations with their explorations and reports of their respective institutional and historical groundings in slavery.[16] Over the past several years, a multi-institutional collaborative project entitled Universities Studying Slavery has created opportunities for a growing list of colleges and universities to work together in order to address common objectives related to their respective institutional projects on slavery.[17] Furthermore, college and university campuses in the United States have become another battleground for renewed attention to the naming of buildings and monuments on or near their campus in honor of individuals who owned enslaved people or acted as staunch advocates of white supremacy in the Jim Crow era in the United States.[18]

The erection of slavery-related statues, memorials, and monuments has served as a catalyst for extended public discussions. The creation of slavery museums and memorials has often been in response to clarion calls for the recognition of the unrecognized, unnamed, and unmemorialized lives of incalculable enslaved people in concrete, physical, and permanent forms of remembrance. Such monuments also represent monuments of mourning for generations of people of African descent for whom the Atlantic Ocean became their physical bodies' final resting place, for whom no gravesite marker exists, for those whose remains are still part of university archival collections, and for those whose descendants can only seek solace and peace in their prayers. Even with ongoing initiatives to establish more slavery-related memorials, it is important to remember that no slavery statue or monument, no matter how exquisite, elaborate, or enormous, will ever be a sufficient memorial for generations upon generations of enslaved people of African descent who lived and labored for centuries throughout the Americas.

Renowned novelist and literary icon Toni Morrison dedicated her novel *Beloved* to "Sixty Million and More," the Africans and their descendants who died during the transatlantic slave trade and slavery writ large.[19] Her inclusion of the "and more" speaks to the impossibility of tallying the actual number of Africans who died during the Middle Passage, as well as the generations of families who lived through and beyond slavery, for whom slavery continues to reverberate in the "still unfolding aftermaths of Atlantic chattel slavery." *Beloved* itself also symbolizes a literary headstone, a marker, a memorial recognizing and commemorating lives lost, names unrecorded, and horrors untold.

Even as slavery memorials serve as partial remembrances of past injustices for generations of enslaved people of African descent, slavery's past also becomes embroiled in the afterlives of slavery in the contemporary era. In the midst of the COVID-19 global pandemic, worldwide uprisings ignited in response to acts of anti-Black state-sanctioned violence and domestic terrorism, particularly in the wake of the murders of Breonna Taylor in Louisville, Kentucky, on March 13, 2020, and George Floyd in Minneapolis on May 25, 2020. Monuments in honor of the Confederacy, including the Confederate flag itself, loomed large as overt targets of discursive and physical attacks during these uprisings in the United States.[20] Although they are often described as "Confederate monuments," the erection of most of these monuments and memorials occurred primarily in the Jim Crow era and not during the Civil War, and they have continued into the twenty-first century. According to the Southern Poverty Law Center, in February 2019, 1,747 Confederate symbols still remained standing in the United States (after the removal of 114 of these symbols in the three years following the massacre at the Mother Emanuel AME Church in Charlotte, South Carolina, on June 17, 2015).[21]

The timing of the erection and unveiling of these Confederate memorials, spanning more than a century, reflects the persistent and pervasive national presence of various manifestations of Jim Crowism and related racist systems, as well as countless violences of white supremacy not only in the South but also across the entire United States. Just as slavery was not solely a southern phenomenon but a national institution in the United States, manifestations of white supremacy permeate the entire nation, whether or not small New England towns, rural midwestern communities, or large western cities have established physical monuments to the Confederacy and white supremacy. Some have erroneously charged that the removal or destruction of these Confederate and American symbols represents acts and processes of "erasing history." Rather, such acts signify active engagement with the critical evolution of local and national narratives about slavery and the nations themselves. "To literally put the Confederacy on a pedestal," as Mitch Landrieu, mayor of New Orleans, stated in a 2017 speech, "in our most prominent places of honor is an inaccurate recitation of our full past. It is an affront to our present, and it is a bad prescription for our future."[22] Furthermore, Landrieu declared, "These statues are not just stone and metal. They are not just innocent remembrances of a benign history. These monuments purposefully celebrate a fictional, sanitized Confederacy; ignoring the death, ignoring the enslavement, and the terror that it actually stood for."[23]

In fact, histories of people of African descent in New Orleans, in the United States, and throughout the world have long been denied, ignored, and erased. The limited memorials to the struggles and achievements of enslaved people of African descent and their descendants more accurately exemplify the foundational history that has been purposefully erased from the landscape and built environment in the United States and around the world. Moreover, whether centered on the erection or removal of slavery memorials or Confederate monuments, such symbolic gestures cannot be deemed as the ultimate response, national reckoning, or "stand-in" for perceptible acts of racial justice and reparations—JEDI (Justice, Equity, Diversity, and Inclusion) practices—especially the redistribution of wealth and resources in the United States, in Jamaica, and throughout the world.

Even without controversies around Confederate monuments, the Caribbean landscape and Jamaica in particular have not been silent, still, or stark on the presence of and controversies about memorials related to slavery and abolition. Monuments regarding slavery in Caribbean countries have primarily centered on memorializing slave resistance, slave revolts, and freedom fighters. These memorials include La Nègre Marron (1967) in Port-au-Prince, Haiti; the Emancipation Statue, often referred to as Bussa (1985), the name of the freedom fighter and one of Barbados's national heroes, in Barbados; Desenkadena (unchained or unleashed), also called the Tula Monument (1998), in honor of freedom fighter Tula and others involved in the Slave Revolt of 1795, in Willemstad, Curaçao; the Anse Cafard Slave Memorial in Martinique (1998), part of the sesquicentennial commemoration of the abolition of slavery in the French Caribbean colonies; and Le memorial ACTe, Le Centre caribéen d'expressions et de mémoire de la traite et de l'esclavage (2015), at the site of the former Darboussier sugar factory and part of UNESCO'S Slave Route Project, in Pointe-à-Pitre, Guadeloupe.[24]

In Jamaica, memorials and commemorations related to slavery and abolition have engendered debates over generations. *The Gleaner* has been one site of robust public discourse over the past several years about such commemorations, as well as the removal of colonial-era statues and monuments in Jamaica.[25] Celebratory remembrances of emancipation in Jamaica commenced after the four-year apprenticeship period ended on August 1, 1838 (often referred to as the "full free" date). As historian Bridget Brereton explains, different racial and socio-economic strata of Jamaican society aligned their meanings of August First celebrations with their respective purposes and objectives. For newly emancipated Jamaicans and their descendants, their August First celebrations often involved church services, dances, parades, and other festivities, especially in rural communities.[26] One particular site for Emancipation Day celebrations, beginning in 1838, was the Kingston Race Course, initially a central venue for horse racing for much of the nineteenth century and into the mid-twentieth century. In 1953 it was renamed the George VI Memorial Park. A decade following Jamaica's Independence, in 1973, it was renamed National Heroes Park; this remains the current name of the park. In addition to the remains of Jamaica's national heroes being interred at this park, it is a prominent burial site for Jamaica's prime ministers and other distinguished national icons.[27]

In the subsequent decades following those early August First celebrations, as historians Bridget Brereton and Verene A. Shepherd clarify, commemorations related to slavery and abolition have long been criticized within Jamaica and in the broader Caribbean context.[28] Referencing critical responses in Jamaica to the fiftieth-anniversary celebration of emancipation in 1888—the Jubilee of Emancipation—Shepherd explicates how lingering perceptions concerning shame about slavery have informed the rejection expressed by some Jamaicans of African descent about such commemorative events.[29] Others, though, refused this lens of shame; instead, they pressed for the formal, annual recognition of emancipation in Jamaica, as well as Black Jamaicans' attainment of all rights and privileges afforded to lighter-complexioned and white denizens in Jamaica. For example, in the 1890s, through his newspaper, the *Jamaica Advocate*, Bahamian Dr. Robert Love rejected any notions of Black inferiority, encouraged enhanced educational opportunities for all Jamaicans, and promoted the formal recognition of Emancipation Day in Jamaica.[30] In response to the concerted efforts of Dr. Love and others, Emancipation Day was officially declared a nonworking public holiday in Jamaica in 1893, and it was observed annually on August 1 for almost seventy years in Jamaica.

When Jamaica attained political independence from Britain on August 6, 1962, the annual nonworking holiday marking Emancipation Day ended as Independence Day commenced as a nonworking public holiday. Independence Day was initially observed in Jamaica on the first Monday of August. However, due to the concerted pressure applied by many Jamaican scholars and activists in the 1980s and 1990s, in 1996 the then prime minister of Jamaica, P. J. Patterson, appointed a special committee—the National Committee of Symbols and Observances—to review and report on Jamaica's nonworking public holidays, including a reassessment of Emancipation Day. Chaired by Professor the Honourable Rex Nettleford, OM, then deputy vice chancellor of the University of the West Indies (UWI), this committee recommended the restoration of Emancipation Day as a national public holiday.[31] In September 1996, Patterson announced the reinstatement of Emancipation Day as a national public holiday. As a result, beginning in 1997, August 1 became the official day of observance of Emancipation Day. Jamaica's Independence Day public holiday then changed from the first Monday of August to August 6. Since 1997 the days between August 1 and 6 have become more elaborate celebratory days of Jamaican national heritage and pride.

Nevertheless, a decade after the restoration of Emancipation Day as a public holiday, the eminent Public Theology Forum (an ecumenical group composed of respected theologians, pastors, and laypersons in Jamaica) profoundly explained in their 2009 *Gleaner* article that there still remained resistance to the reinstate-

ment of Emancipation Day.[32] This resistance was framed as being steeped in mis-
understandings and misperceptions about slavery's past, as well as the purpose
of this day in twenty-first-century Jamaica.[33] Although lingering criticisms about
Emancipation Day may still surface, both holidays continue to be officially observed in the present day. In the past several years, this week from Emancipation
Day to Independence Day has been referred to by many Jamaicans as the port-
manteau Emancipendence. However, a letter to the editor in *The Gleaner* published on February 1, 2021, boldly stated, "Leave Emancipation Day alone!" in
response to a proposal to the actual merging of Emancipation Day and Independence Day.[34]

Almost a decade after the official reinstatement of Emancipation Day, the
bicentenary of the end of British official engagement in the transatlantic slave
trade created another inflection point for public discussion of significant anniversary milestones of slavery and abolition. Like those of other Anglophone Caribbean countries, Jamaican officials decided to observe the bicentenary of the
abolition of the transatlantic slave trade in the British Empire. In December 2005
the Jamaican government charged the newly created Jamaica National Bicentenary Committee (JNBC) with planning various events to mark this anniversary.
As had been the case before in Jamaica regarding arrangements for commemorative events concerning slavery, this bicentenary committee confronted vehement
negative responses about its purpose and objectives. Shepherd posits that over
the past several decades, extensive research on slavery and the slave trade "has
been located within a wider political project: that of producing a more liberating
narrative of self."[35] However, even with the collective work of multiple generations of scholars "about the brutality of the enslavers, the feelings of 'shame' continue to be attached firmly to the descendants of enslaved people—to the victims
of the system rather than to the perpetrators."[36]

"As cultural process," Shepherd explains, "trauma is mediated through various forms of representation and linked to the reformation of collective identity and the reworking of collective memory."[37] Shepherd further deduces that
even "though not experienced directly by today's African-descended people, the
trauma of enslavement has come to be central in our attempts to forge a collective identity out of its remembrance. As reflective process, trauma links past to
present through representations and imaginations."[38] The roots of slavery's past
penetrate the branches of the present day as some Jamaicans attempt to move
away from the projected stigmatization and perceived shame of slavery, while
others choose to recognize slavery and its afterlives as significantly influencing
contemporary Jamaican realities. The long reach of bondage cannot solely be cast
in the immediate wake of the formal abolition of slavery in Jamaica. Indeed, in

the twenty-first century, this internalized shame of slavery for some Black Jamaicans remains persistent and consistent in contemporary Jamaican society.

Given the twenty-first-century resistance of some Jamaicans to the annual recognition of Emancipation Day and invoking some sense of the roots of the "shame" Shepherd describes in her work, the Public Theology Forum asserts:

> This means that nearly 200 years after "Missis Queen Victoria" decreed that the forebears of some of us were no longer to be forced to work for those whose property they were under the law—descendants of both owners and human property are still in mental, psychological, political, and spiritual slavery. They do not wear chains around their necks, ankles or wrists, but are tied up without hope of release, by the myths and phobias which prevent them from affirming themselves as nationals of a sovereign nation, and participants in the shaping of their own personal and national destiny.[39]

This Public Theology Forum article echoes the words and sentiments spoken by Jamaican National Hero and Right Excellent Marcus Garvey in his 1937 speech in Nova Scotia, which he delivered a century after emancipation in Jamaica. Garvey declared: "We are going to emancipate ourselves from mental slavery because whilst others might free the body, none but ourselves can free the mind. Mind is your only ruler, sovereign. The man who is not able to develop and use his mind is bound to be the slave of the other man who uses his mind, because man is related to man under all circumstances for good or for ill."[40]

Commencing with the then prime minister, P. J. Patterson, these sentiments (and in some years Garvey's exact words) have been invoked by prime ministers of Jamaica during their annual "Emancipation Day Message." At the very beginning of his "Emancipation Day Message" for 2020, Prime Minister Andrew Holness recited Garvey's words.[41] Twenty-first-century recognition of Jamaica's Emancipation Day serves not only as a celebration of freedom fighters of the past and the eradication of chattel slavery but also as a stark reminder of the contemporary reckonings with iterations of systemic racism and its cousin colorism in Jamaica and beyond.

While grappling with the echoes and ripples of the afterlives of slavery, sometimes manifested in collective trauma and collective shame, Jamaicans have been purposeful about their public, official demonstrations of collective national pride centered on resistance to slavery, as well as selected freedom fighters. The first official Jamaican memorial to an enslaved freedom fighter was created in 1976, when Charles Square in downtown Montego Bay was renamed Sam Sharpe Square. As noted in chapter 5, Sam Sharpe is the most recognized leader of the Baptist War / Christmas Rebellion of 1831–1832. He is also one of the seven national heroes of Jamaica. This particular site in Montego Bay was chosen to honor Sam Sharpe, as the executions of those involved in this slave revolt (including Sam Sharpe) transpired in this square.

Sam Sharpe Square includes a sculpture of Sharpe speaking to four of his comrades associated with the Baptist War / Christmas Rebellion of 1831–1832. These five bronze sculptures were unveiled by the then prime minister, Edward Seaga, on October 16, 1983. In addition to Sharpe being named as one of Jamaica's national heroes, Sharpe's sculpture served as another way of recognizing his historical importance. Within steps of Sharpe's sculpture is "The Cage," a space that was built in 1806. In the signage at this site, "The Cage" is described as an overnight jail for vagrants, drunken sailors, and runaway slaves. Originally a wooden structure, in 1822 it was replaced by the still standing stone and brick building. With this particular configuration, a sculpture venerating Sam Sharpe and other freedom fighters of the Baptist War / Christmas Rebellion has been positioned and linked to an actual, historical, heinous remnant not only of the institution of slavery and its related violences but also of enslaved people's resistance to bondage in Jamaica.

Over the years, Sam Sharpe Square has become an expansive site for the memorialization of freedom fighters in Jamaica. In 2001 the old Montego Bay Court House, also located in Sam Sharpe Square, was restored. It had been destroyed by a fire in 1968. This courthouse was the site of the trials of Sam Sharpe and other enslaved Jamaicans who were convicted and executed for their participation in the Baptist War / Christmas Rebellion. The newly restored building, named the Montego Bay Civic Centre (also referred to as the Montego Bay Cultural Centre), includes the Museum of St. James, a theater, and an art gallery. In 2007 another monument, the Freedom Monument, was added to Sam Sharpe Square on Emancipation Day (August 1) in Jamaica. Established by the Jamaica National Heritage Trust and unveiled by the then prime minister, Portia Simpson-Miller, the Freedom Monument recognizes the unsung heroes and heroines who fought against slavery. The names of eighty-two freedom fighters are engraved in the monument as a testament to the countless enslaved persons who fought against the institution of slavery and died in the Baptist War / Christmas Rebellion of 1831–1832.

Montego Bay has not been the sole Jamaican city celebrating emancipation and honoring Jamaica's freedom fighters with such public monuments. In 2003, twenty years after the unveiling of the Sam Sharpe Monument in Montego Bay, another sculpture in recognition of the historical impact of emancipation was officially presented in the six-acre Emancipation Park in New Kingston. Emancipation Park officially opened on July 31, 2002, in commemoration of Emancipa-

tion Day in Jamaica. The Emancipation Park sculpture, created by Jamaican artist Laura Facey, is called *Redemption Song*, in honor of the popular song written
by Bob Marley, highlighting the iconic words of Marcus Garvey. This particular sculpture generated intense discussion and controversy within Jamaica, which
also extended to international news, due to the nudity of the male and female figures, the figures' seemingly passive gaze skyward, the size of the male figure's geni-
tals, and artist Facey's light-skinned physical appearance. The most recent memorials to freedom fighters in Jamaica include the busts of Nanny of the Maroons
and Sam Sharpe at Emancipation Park. Funded by the Rotary Club of Kingston, the busts of Nanny, Sam Sharpe, and the other five Jamaican national heroes were unveiled at Emancipation Park in June 2018. Even with the controversy
associated with the *Redemption Song* sculpture, Emancipation Park has become
a site of Jamaican cultural activities, run/walk events, films, and a range of entertainment activities, as well as a favorite for everyday walkers and joggers from
the early morning and continuing throughout the day.[42] Emancipation Park has
also been the venue for select special occasions. For example, when Ms. Tori-Ann
Singh was crowned Miss World in 2019, her celebratory four-day tour at home
in Jamaica included a cultural tribute and performance at Emancipation Park.[43]
Emancipation Park has become another Jamaican venue for the celebration of Jamaican heritage, pride, and achievements at home and abroad.

In addition to Montego Bay and Kingston, one other Jamaican site memori-
alizes the horrors of the transatlantic slave trade and those who perished during
the Middle Passage: the *Zong* memorial. Having left São Tomé on September
6, 1781, the *Zong* slave ship, one of countless slave ships with Jamaica as its final
destination, arrived at Black River on December 22, 1781.[44] As was common on
slave ships at the time, sixty-two enslaved people succumbed to the deleterious
conditions on board. Moreover, due to navigational mistakes and, supposedly,
concern for limited water for the survival of all on board, a couple of weeks before arrival at Black River the ship's crew had thrown a total of 132 African captives overboard in three separate instances. Ten additional African captives had
jumped overboard—a purposeful action taken by other African captives on slave
ships in resistance, in despair, in fear of what might become of them at the end of
the journey. This particular case attracted significant attention in England due to
the legal proceedings related to the insurance claimed by the *Zong*'s owners. Although the owners initially won the case for the insurance payment, when the insurance company appealed with additional evidence, the ruling was overturned,
and the final judgment substantiated the insurance company's position. Having
garnered the attention of abolitionists such as Olaudah Equiano, the murder of
these African captives heightened the outcry in England for the abolition of the

transatlantic slave trade, and the *Zong* massacre became a monumental catalyst in the movement to end England's participation in the transatlantic slave trade. On December 28, 2007, 216 years after this massacre, as part of the bicentenary of England's Abolition of the Slave Trade Act, a stone memorial was unveiled at Black River, the capital of St. Elizabeth Parish. It serves as a memorial in recognition of the 132 African souls who perished in the Atlantic Ocean. Located close to the market, positioned in an area believed to be one of the venues where enslaved people were auctioned, the monument was officially established by the Institute of Jamaica and the Jamaica National Bicentenary Committee.

Jamaica's concentration on the public recognition and memorialization of individual freedom fighters, including the countless enslaved women, men, and children who remain unnamed, represents one dimension of humanizing the fight against slavery and positioning that fight rightly in the hands of enslaved people. In slavery studies, scholars are often navigating through the conundrums of presenting the vicissitudes of slavery and the costs of bondage. Certainly, the economic dimensions of the peculiar institution remain critical vectors of analysis. In addition, we must continue to attend to the very human costs of enslavement and the detriments of racial capitalism. Even as we focus on delving further and deeper into the facts and figures of slavery, we must continue to explore multiple trajectories for presenting a sense of the humanity of enslaved people beyond numerical calculations. Although we may never be able to name each and every soul who experienced the multifarious shackles of slavery in Jamaica or in the Americas broadly, we must insist on the remembrance, recognition, and restoration of their humanity.

❧❧❧

At the very core of this overall project are telling questions and modes of inquiry regarding history-making and history-telling about enslaved people's lived experiences, as well as public memorialization and representations of slavery and enslaved people at plantation sites. I want to encourage the examination of the layered complexities of public history directly related to representations of slavery at plantation sites as I tell the human, humane story of Rose Hall Plantation. This project represents a generative initiative that not only explores particular nuances of these publicly available and accessible sites throughout the African diaspora but also yearns to serve as a catalyst for change at this tourist site (and other sites) in the contemporary daily tours and related materials.

At Rose Hall and other plantation tourist sites, we must ask, What and whom do we value as memorable, as significant enough, as valuable enough to be memorialized? In his notable work *Nothing Ever Dies: Vietnam and the Memory of*

War, Viet Thanh Nguyen reminds us that "forgetting also begets remembering (sometimes thought of as haunting). This is especially the case when forgetting is not accidental but deliberate, strategic, even malicious—in other words, disremembering."[45] He also articulates an ethics of remembering:

> Regardless of whether those we remember are saintly or all too human, the ethical force of remembering one's own reinforces the shared identities of family, nation, religion or race. In the ethics of remembering one's own, remembering those of one's side, even when they do terrible things, is better than ignoring them altogether. Nothing is worse than being ignored, erased, or effaced as the losers of any war of conflict can affirm. In memory wars, a victory is had in simply being remembered and being able to remember, even if one's self and one's own appear troubled, tortured, even demonic.[46]

Nguyen invokes one of Paul Ricoeur's often repeated (though frequently truncated) assertions of memory in his crucial book *Memory, History, Forgetting*. Ricoeur declares: "The duty of memory is the duty to do justice, through memories, to an other than the self."[47] Rose Hall Plantation represents one site of many with an opportunity to grapple with ideological, tangible, holistic, and synergistic notions of memory, memorialization, history, and justice. How do we "do justice" in the present moment in honor of enslaved people who labored at Rose Hall Plantation and their lived experiences of bondage and belonging, strife and separation, terror and trauma, and, yes, love and even levity?

As we hear the calls, pleas, appeals, and demands across the United States and the world that "Black Lives Matter," I cannot help but be reminded of the very long legacy of this war over centuries, across many waters and lands, for the very recognition of Black humanity. Now over two decades into the twenty-first century, we might believe that with all the technological advancements and "progress" we have witnessed in the past ten, twenty, thirty, forty, fifty years, we should be living in a different moment in how we recognize, value, and appreciate Black persons in our midst. Yet as the litany of names of Black people beaten, raped, and murdered continues to grow throughout the African diaspora, some have become desensitized to the horrors of this centuries-long war with the easy, effortless consumption of the latest video lynching of another Black body on YouTube, on the news, always available and easily accessible for viewing on iPads, cell phones, computers, and flat TV screens.

I was recently reminded of the valuation and devaluation of Black lives in what many might consider an unlikely venue and meeting of the minds: an annual academic conference for a scholarly organization centered on Caribbean history. To be clear, I was impressed by the degree of detail and determination necessary for the research agendas evident in some of the work presented, especially the seemingly inexhaustible time and energy already committed to such projects. Yet at a number of the sessions, I wondered how the devaluation of Black people ironically and tragically still continues to infiltrate erudite minds of historians of slavery. Was a clarion call necessary here, too, that Black Lives Matter? It was not that papers centered on slavery did not integrate bondage or enslaved people. However, some presenters seemed content not to dig too deeply into the actual stories of Black lives, of Black humanity; instead, it seemed sufficient to present their lives in a fairly cursory and peripheral manner.

Attempting to present the lives of enslaved people, most of whom did not leave behind any written narratives of their life stories, cannot be solely centered on finding and presenting "facts" and "figures" about their lives in bondage. Historian Daryle Williams beseeches us "to tell a human story, in a humane way, about a crime against humanity." In the telling of those stories we must not solely attend to the crimes and violences against humanity but also attend to the humanity of the people of African descent themselves. One of my main objectives for this project is to attempt to name as many of the enslaved people at Rose Hall as possible. When I first reviewed the actual names of enslaved people on the 1817 slave register for Rose Hall Plantation, I stopped and stared at the names of two particular women, one positioned under the other, first Cecelia (African born) and then Celia (Creole). Given the mostly alphabetic ordering of the names on this 1817 list, their names appeared toward the top of the very first page of enslaved women. It took a long time for me to move on to the names below their names. Although not directly and biologically related to any of the enslaved people at Rose Hall (as far as I know), I had not expected in reading the names of enslaved people at Rose Hall to see my own name. My inability to quickly move on to the other names on the list was not grounded in any sense of shame. Rather, my feelings and thoughts were bound up in a recognition, a reverence for these names. Over time, I began to think of this slave register of 1817 and the subsequent triennial lists not as lists of Rose Hall's "human property" but as lists of Rose Hall's founding mothers and fathers, builders, survivors, and warriors. This, too, is part of a long-overdue shift and transformation in perspective, in consciousness, in historical understanding of the enslaved people at Rose Hall and, by extension, throughout the African diaspora. The process of reconstructing and telling the stories of enslaved people involves exploring holistic possibilities of humanity and expressions of the human spirit.

By integrating, interpreting, and interrogating historical artifacts and information about enslaved people at Rose Hall, as well as creating a digital humanities project, I hope to establish additional gateways for displaying and disseminating crucial material about slavery and enslaved people to local Jamaicans, tourists, and a broader community of academics and nonacademics. Given the monetary attachments of the current owners of Rose Hall—the Rollins family—to the mythical "storyline" of this tourist attraction, with the assistance of a team, I have created a Rose Hall Project website to enable visitors to explore online selected primary and secondary source materials related to the actual history of slavery and enslaved persons at Rose Hall. One of the objectives of the website is to present a counternarrative to the particular centrality of the mythical story of Annie Palmer. I envision this overall public history project centered on Rose Hall serving as a catalyst for future interdisciplinary, collaborative programs involving multiple institutions in Jamaica (e.g., the University of the West Indies, Mona, the National Archives of Jamaica, the Institute of Jamaica, and the National Library of Jamaica), as well as institutions throughout the world. It is my hope that this overall project serves also as another way of recognizing and memorializing enslaved people at Rose Hall Plantation. This project holds space for those who were enslaved—as a memorial, as a site of mourning, and as a catalyst for the on-going remembrance, exploration, and presentation of the lives and humanity of enslaved persons in Jamaica, in the Americas, and throughout the world.

POSTSCRIPT

I am truly fortunate to have other members of my family who have been deeply motivated and committed to researching different branches of my own family tree. As I discovered more about the enslaved people at Rose Hall, I wondered more about my own Jamaican ancestors. I have names, pictures, and stories for some and for others no information at all.

My father, Cecil Anthony Naylor, enjoyed telling stories about his family, and his tales often focused on the Naylor family in Manchioneal and Port Antonio (in the current parish of Portland). He would, though, also mention as an aside that my mother's family—on her paternal side (the Hornett family)—was from Port Royal. He would always then jokingly express in the next breath that her people were "pirates from Port Royal." He particularly enjoyed conveying this in my mother's presence. Indeed, Port Royal had been a haven for pirates in the seventeenth century, though it is unlikely that my mother's family had any actual, historical connection to pirates there.

Although my father spoke fondly about his childhood holiday trips to Manchioneal, I don't remember visiting these places during my childhood. My older brother, Stuart, has memories of attending funerals and other events with my father in Portland during his early childhood. However, my memories begin with family vacations enjoyed farther west along the North Coast in Mammee Bay (only a few kilometers from Ochi / Ocho Rios). My father's stories became more evident to me several years ago when a distant cousin I have not met (Bobby Naylor) shared some genealogical information about the Naylor family. Over the years, he has devoted a great deal of time researching the Naylor family's history (including sharing one of the coat of arms for the Naylor family/name in England). In his report, the title, "Naylor Family Tree," stands out in bold letters. Immediately under that, the subtitle is "The Genealogy of John Rowland Naylor of Liverpool—Great Britain." John Rowland Naylor's parents are included at the top of the report (John Naylor and Mary Ann Fairbrother from Liverpool); they had six children. John Rowland Naylor, their second child, was born in Liverpool in 1809. He was christened on July 2, 1809, at Our Lady and Saint Nicholas Church in Liverpool. At some point in the 1830s, John Rowland Naylor and at least one additional family member traveled to Jamaica and settled in Port Antonio.

While living in Jamaica, John Rowland Naylor was probably involved in a number of personal and business relationships, and he may have engaged in intimate interactions with multiple women in Jamaica. Archival records indicate that he had a child with at least one other Jamaican woman of color before he married Elizabeth Perry. Perry was a woman of color born around 1818 in Portland. Elizabeth Perry had eight children with John Rowland Naylor between 1834 and 1850/1851: Mary Matilda Naylor (1834–1846), Helen Naylor (1838–1846), Charlotte Ann Naylor (1841–1842), John Rowland Naylor Jr. (1843–1883), William Naylor (1844–1921), Charles Parry Naylor (1844–?), George Duncan Naylor (1847–1893), and Henry Murray Naylor (1850/1851–1922). Given the birthdates of all of their baptized children, Elizabeth Perry Naylor only had free-born children for John Rowland Naylor. We do not know whether they waited until 1834, the year of abolition, to have their first child or if this was coincidental. This might have been a strategic decision on her or his part or perhaps a joint decision. During his time in Jamaica, John Rowland Naylor Sr. lived in Port Antonio from the mid- to late 1830s to 1845. He then moved in 1845 with Elizabeth Perry and their children at the time from Port Antonio to Manchioneal. John Rowland Naylor Sr. owned a store in Manchioneal, as well as a couple of plots of land in what was then included in the parish of St. Thomas in the East (now located in the parish of Portland). The Port Antonio Hospital is currently located on one of his previously owned plots of land—on a hill still known as Naylor's Hill.

Although searching further for the Naylor family's roots in Liverpool seems plausible, Elizabeth Perry's personal and family histories in Jamaica before she met John Rowland Naylor Sr. remain more difficult to explore in the records. Oral histories in our family convey that the "Naylors were all mixed up with the Maroons." The records for Elizabeth and John Rowland Naylor Sr. include baptism records of their children, John Rowland Naylor's will (dated April 10, 1855), and the deed for plots of land he owned in St. Thomas in the East. Elizabeth Perry's profession is described as a "housekeeper" (and she may also have been a seamstress). She was described as a "spinster" when she married John Rowland Naylor Sr. on April 11, 1850; this marriage occurred after the births of their eight children. It is not clear if Elizabeth Perry was born free or enslaved or whether her freedom was attained by running away, via legal manumission, or through the circumstances of her birth and parentage. What we do know is that she had been living in the same household with John Rowland Naylor Sr. in Port Antonio in the mid- to late 1830s (and possibly earlier) and that they then resettled together in Manchioneal. They had been living together for many years before they were married in 1850. What circumstances might have encouraged their formal marriage at that time are unknown. However, only a few years after they became legally married and a few months after the creation of an official will, John Rowland Naylor Sr. passed in 1855. In his will, he included one executor, George Ward, Esq., and one executrix, his wife, Elizabeth Naylor. Elizabeth Perry Naylor lived a much longer life; she passed in Manchioneal in 1888, the year of the Jubilee of Emancipation.

As an adult, one of the sons of John Rowland Sr. and Elizabeth Perry Naylor, George Duncan Naylor, married Jane Cecelia Barclay in Manchioneal. George Duncan Naylor and Jane Barclay Naylor had six children over the course of twelve years. Cecil George Naylor, one of their sons (a twin, though his twin—named Gilford—died within a year), was born on March 12, 1889, in Manchioneal. George Duncan Naylor passed in 1893, only a few years after his son Cecil George Naylor was born. Cecil George Naylor moved to Kingston as a young man, and he worked at Myrtle Bank Hotel. He married Josephine Agnes Dean in Kingston on September 6, 1923. She was from a town called Friendship, in the parish of Portland, and her family's history was deeply connected to the Maroon community of Nanny Town (now called Moore Town). Cecil George and Josephine Naylor had two sons, Cecil Anthony Naylor (April 10, 1927) and Dudley Ignatius Naylor (March 11, 1933). Cecil George Naylor, my paternal grandfather, died in Kingston on August 7, 1950, and my paternal grandmother, Josephine Dean Naylor (Granny), died in Kingston on November 30, 1981. My father, Cecil Anthony Naylor, passed in Maryland, at the age of ninety, on August 23, 2017.

I do not remember any mention of either Elizabeth Perry Naylor or John Rowland Naylor in any of my father's stories of Port Antonio and Manchioneal. My father focused on his older uncles and aunts with whom he developed loving relationships over the course of his lifetime (especially his Uncle Roy and Aunt Marie). A couple of his family members served in the position of postmaster and postmistress in multiple generations in the parish of Portland. Perhaps being in those jobs encouraged some degree of knowledge about people's personal and related business. My father was always a curious person, and I imagine as a child he posed many questions about our family's history and life in general. As a perspicacious boy, he may have been encouraged to ask more questions even as he received answers to other questions. Throughout his life, he shared and, indeed, gave life to those answers and family stories.

As the only daughter of Una Adams Hornett and Edmund Augustus Hornett, my mother's curiosity at a young age was not encouraged in a similar manner, even as her three brothers (Trevor, Dennis, and Owen, known as Bobby) became involved in all kinds of activities. Throughout the decades, though, my mother, Fay Patricia Naylor, was one of our family's vital sources for old stories about the Hornett, Adams, and Hussey families. Before she passed on March 15, 2020, my mother often reminded me that children and young folks in her time were not involved (or welcomed) in any adult conversations about the past or anything of consequence. Still, my mother held on to some of the stories she overheard as a child and young person. Although I only have one family photo of my father as a child with his brother and parents, I have several family photos of my mother's family—her parents (my grandparents), Una Cynthia Adams (1906–1970) and Edmund Augustus Hornett (1902–1998), as well as Edmund Hornett's parents (my great-grandparents), Reuben James Hornett (1871–1943) and Alberta Constancia Smith Hornett (1876–1963). On my mother's maternal side, her mother, Una Adams Hornett, was the daughter of Margaret Louise Hussey Adams and Joseph James Adams. Margaret Hussey Adams and Joseph James Adams were married on September 16, 1903. Joseph James Adams was fatally injured in the earthquake of 1907 in Jamaica. After he died, Margaret Hussey Adams married Percival Samuels. My mother remembered her grandmother Margaret Hussey Adams Samuels telling stories about her (white) father, referred to as Richard (though possibly called by the name William) Hussey. Richard/ William Hussey's father was a landowner and enslaver in St. Andrew (in the area of Mount Charles and Lawrence Tavern in the parish of St. Andrew). One of the stories passed down about Richard/William Hussey was that an enslaved playmate accidentally put something in his eye while they were in the midst of playing, and as a result Richard/William Hussey became blind in one eye. My mother also recalled her grandmother Margaret Hussey Adams Samuels telling a number of different stories about her white father, and she always spoke about him in loving ways. However, my maternal great-grandmother never mentioned any stories about her Black mother—not even her name. Her mother, most likely an enslaved woman, had twelve children (six boys and six girls) for Richard/William Hussey. There is no other information that has been passed down about her—just the name of the man with whom she had twelve children and the children she gave birth to over many years.

1. Although my book highlights aspects of the evening tour in particular at the Rose Hall Great House, for an example of the Rose Hall day tour, see "Rose Hall Great House Montego Bay Tour and Song." For more information on the day and nighttime Rose Hall Great House tours, see Rose Hall Developments Ltd., "Rose Hall Tour." This book focuses on the Rose Hall Plantation in St. James Parish. However, there was another Rose Hall Plantation in St. Thomas-in-the-Vale in Jamaica; this area is now part of St. Catherine Parish.

2. Ghosts in Jamaica and Barbados are called duppies. Duppies often play a central role in Jamaican storytelling and folktales. For a discussion of duppies within the context of Jamaican metaphysical belief systems, see "Afro-Creole Belief System I," in Moore and Johnson, *Neither Led nor Driven*, 14–50. Also see Vincent Brown's excellent historical perspective on death and the role of duppies in colonial Jamaican culture, *The Reaper's Garden*. For a few examples of Jamaican duppy stories, see Hausman, *Duppy Talk*.

3. There are other shorter published fictional versions of the story of the White Witch of Rose Hall (e.g., Henry, *Rose Hall's White Witch*).

4. Invocations and references to the White Witch of Rose Hall have appeared in a number of popular culture contexts. For example, the TV show *America's Next Top Model* cycle 19 (the College Edition) was filmed in 2012 at a couple of locations in Jamaica. The finale was filmed at Rose Hall and included a storyline that incorporated elements of the myth of the White Witch. For a clip from this episode, see "ANTM CYCLE 22 BTS: The Rose Hall Ghost Story." This YouTube clip title mistakenly identifies it as ANTM cycle 22; it was actually cycle 19. Also see "Multimillion-Dollar Earnings."

5. Spivak, "Can the Subaltern Speak?," 295. My reference to Black women being "invisibly visible" invokes the perspicacious analysis of a number of Black feminist scholars who have examined the historical conception(s) of Black female sexuality. For example, as Evelynn M. Hammonds posits, "There is a way black women's sexuality has been constructed in a binary opposition to that of white women: it is rendered simultaneously invisible, visible (exposed), hypervisible, and pathologized in dominant discourses" ("Toward a Genealogy," 93). Also see Guy-Sheftall, "The Body Politic." I would like to consider these works by Spivak, Hammonds, and Guy-Sheftall in conversation with Wynter, "'No Humans Involved.'"

6. See the Rose Hall Digital Humanities Project. For a thoughtful article on some of the critical purpose(s) and historical contextualization of Black digital practice, see Johnson, "Markup Bodies."

7. Although Rose Hall is the most popular great house in Jamaica, a number of other Jamaican great houses have become sites of interest. Many of these houses have not been preserved over the years. See Michael W. Mosley's blog, "A Tour" (started in January 2015) of Jamaican great houses, plantations, and pens (including a couple of homes in Curaçao). Although this website includes blog entries about Cinnamon Hill Great House and Greenwood Great House in St. James Parish, as of June 2021 the Rose Hall Great House has not been selected as one of the highlighted historical homes. Given that part of the reason for this project on great houses in Jamaica is to reveal and feature often ignored or unknown great houses, it is not surprising that the Rose Hall Great House has not yet been included. The Jamaica National Heritage Trust website "Greathouses (Plantation houses)" highlights thirty of the notable great houses in Jamaica. However, as Mosley's blog reflects, there were hundreds of great houses in Jamaica.

8. For an excellent anthology regarding the reconstructions of slavery in the contemporary era at selected sites in North America, West Africa, western Europe, South America, and the Caribbean, see Araujo, *Living History*. Also see Holsey, *Routes of Remembrance*; Hartman, *Lose Your Mother*; Tillet, *Sites of Slavery*; Colbert, Patterson, and Levy-Hussen, *The Psychic Hold of Slavery*; and Araujo, *Slavery*.

9. See, for example, the website devoted to weddings at Thomas Jefferson's plantation, Monticello, "Weddings"; Beck, "Disturbing Wedding Trend"; and Macgonagle, "From Dungeons."

10. I utilize the term "neocolonial," in lieu of "postcolonial," to reflect the precarious nature of Caribbean independence, especially in relation to the ongoing systemic control of transnational corporations and imperial, hierarchical forces over the socioeconomic structures throughout the Caribbean. Numerous critical works have presented these multifaceted dynamics in Jamaica and in the larger Caribbean context. For a concise article highlighting the case of Jamaica (with some discussion of Guyana and Grenada), see Edmonds, "An Elusive Independence."

11. The four hundredth anniversary commemorative activities related to the 1619 arrival of "twenty and odd" Africans near Point Comfort in the colony of Virginia have sparked a range of reflections about the history of slavery in the United States. In August 2019 the *New York Times Magazine* launched the 1619 Project "to reframe the country's history by placing the consequences of slavery and the contributions of black Americans at the very center of our national narrative." This ongoing initiative has attracted a great deal of attention and generated significant discussion. A critical letter on the project from five historians and the response/rebuttal by Jake Silverstein (*New York Times Magazine* editor in chief) appeared in the magazine's December 20, 2019, issue. For the entire letter and Silverstein's response, see Silverstein, "We Respond." Also see Guyatt, "1619, Revisited." It is important to point out that some historical sites have been involved in significant initiatives to integrate more comprehensive and historically accurate stories about slavery and enslaved people. The National Park Service has played a key role in many of these initiatives. For some examples of these efforts (and resistance to these projects), see Cohen, "Slavery in America." An article in the *Washington Post* in August 2019 highlighted the expectations of some white visitors for a safe and enjoyable passage through plantation tours in the United States; they conveyed how it troubled them to hear about the horrors of slavery. One reviewer vented: "My husband and I were extremely disappointed in this tour. We didn't come to hear a lecture on how the white people treated slaves, we came to

get this history of a southern plantation and get a tour of the house and grounds. . . . It was just not what we expected. I'll go back to Louisiana and see some real plantations that are so much more enjoyable to tour" (Brockell, "Some White People").

12. Williams, "Stop Getting Married."

13. See Murphy, "Pinterest." Also see Luongo, "Despite Everything."

14. Williams, comments.

15. For example, though the work of Marianne Hirsch and Leo Spitzer focuses on intergenerational memory (and what they define as "postmemory") in relation to the Holocaust, they proffer new ways of understanding memory, trauma, and the restoration of forgotten or erased lives. See Hirsch and Spitzer, *Ghosts of Home*; Hirsch and Miller, *Rites of Return*; and Hirsch, *The Generation of Postmemory*.

16. Sharpe, *In the Wake*, 2, 8. Sharpe invokes Saidiya Hartman's incisive analysis: "If slavery persists as an issue in the political life of black America, it is not because of an antiquarian obsession with bygone days or the burden of a too-long memory, but because black lives are still imperiled and devalued by a racial calculus and a political arithmetic that were entrenched centuries ago. This is the afterlife of slavery—skewed life chances, limited access to health and education, premature death, incarceration and impoverishment. I, too, am the afterlife of slavery" (*Lose Your Mother*, 6).

17. Sharpe, *In the Wake*, 18.

18. Ibid., author's emphasis.

19. Ibid., 19–20. Throughout her book, Sharpe critically engages with quotidian representations of Black life in what she describes as the "orthography of the wake," and "this orthography," she maintains, "makes domination in/visible and not/visceral" (ibid., 20–21). Given invocations of the "wake" being closely associated with death and mourning, Sharpe specifically distinguishes "the work of melancholia and mourning" from Black being in the wake and wake work "as a theory and praxis of the wake; a theory and a praxis of Black being in diaspora" (ibid., 19).

20. Ibid., 9.

21. See, for example, Monticello, "Slavery." From April to October, slavery at Monticello tours are conducted hourly. The Whitney Plantation in Wallace, Louisiana, has been celebrated since its grand opening in 2014 as one of the few plantation museums that focuses on slavery. For more information, see Whitney Plantation, "Whitney Plantation Guided Tours." In October 2016 Mount Vernon opened a new exhibit on slavery at Mount Vernon. The exhibit ended in July 2021. See Mount Vernon, "Lives Bound Together."

22. The silence surrounding enslaved women at Rose Hall echoes ongoing silences and gaps in the scholarly discourse on slavery studies. It is important to pay homage to Lucille Mathurin Mair's groundbreaking 1975 work, *The Rebel Woman in the British West Indies during Slavery*, and her now published 1974 dissertation (coedited by Verene A. Shepherd and Hilary McD. Beckles), entitled *A Historical Study of Women in Jamaica, 1655–1844*. Although there have been several works published on enslaved women in the Americas over the past thirty years, there still remains a dearth of studies concentrating on enslaved women of African descent in this region. Unfortunately, the high expectations in the 1990s regarding the anticipated expansion of work on enslaved women in the Americas have been thwarted in recent years. Even as the field itself has matured, the contributions have slowed. In 2022 it is clear that signifi-

cant work remains to be done on women and gender in slavery studies, as well as in Atlantic world and African diaspora studies. Some of the critical published studies, however, in the past thirty years include, for example, Beckles, *Natural Rebels* and *Centering Women*; Morissey, *Slave Women*; Bush, *Slave Women*; Gaspar and Hine, *More Than Chattel*; Fett, *Working Cures*; Camp, *Closer to Freedom*; Morgan, *Laboring Women* and *Reckoning with Slavery*; Berry, *Swing the Sickle*; Altink, *Representations*; Millward, *Finding Charity's Folk*; Fuentes, *Dispossessed Lives*; Cooper Owens, *Medical Bondage*; Turner, *Contested Bodies*; Vasconcellos, *Slavery, Childhood, and Abolition*; Johnson, *Wicked Flesh*. For a thorough list of scholarship on enslaved women in the United States and the Caribbean, see Marisa J. Fuentes's footnote on this topic (*Dispossessed Lives*, 149–152). Another detailed footnote in Fuentes's book highlights vital works in Black feminist scholarship on a range of issues, including the historical representation(s) of free and enslaved Black women and Black sexuality (ibid., 156–158).

23. As the renowned anthropologist Michel-Rolph Trouillot reminds us, "Human beings participate in history both as actors and as narrators. The inherent ambivalence of the word history in many modern languages, including English, suggests this dual participation." He explains that in "vernacular use, history means both the facts of the matter and a narrative of those facts, both 'what happened' and 'that which is said to have happened.' The first meaning places the emphasis on the sociohistorical process, the second on our knowledge of that process or on a story about the process" (*Silencing the Past*, 2). Trouillot engages in an extended sagacious discussion in chapter 1, "The Power in the Story," and throughout this groundbreaking book on historical production, historical knowledge, and power.

24. For example, Long, *History of Jamaica*, and the ten thousand pages of eighteenth-century enslaver Thomas Thistlewood's diaries.

25. The narratives of Mary Prince, James Williams, Abu Bakr al-Siddiq (written in Arabic), Ashton Warner, Archibald John Monteath/Monteith, and Juan Francisco Manzano are slave narratives of people of African descent who were enslaved in the Caribbean. See Ferguson, *The History*; Williams, *A Narrative of Events*; al-Siddiq, "The History," 183–189; al-Siddiq, "Routes in North Africa"; "Being the Narrative of Ashton Warner"; Monteith, *Archibald John Monteith*; Warner-Lewis, *Archibald Monteath*; and Luis, *Juan Francisco Manzano*. An English translation of this autobiography is Mullen, *The Life and Poems of a Cuban Slave, Juan Francisco Manzano*. Some historians and literary critics have drawn on slave narratives as a lens through which to explore enslaved perspectives of bondage and freedom in the United States and the Caribbean. In addition to examining iconic slave narratives in the United States (e.g., Jacobs, *Incidents in the Life of a Slave Girl*; Douglass, *Narrative of the Life of Frederick Douglass*), scholars have also utilized the interviews of previously enslaved people conducted in the 1930s by the Works Progress Administration to extract information regarding the quotidian experiences of enslaved people of African descent in the United States. Initially deposited in the Library of Congress, the WPA interviews of ex-slaves remained a relatively untapped source of information until Greenwood Press's publication of these interviews in the 1970s (see Rawick, *The American Slave*). In April 2001 the Library of Congress announced the release of the online collection "Born in Slavery." This online collection includes over twenty-three hundred interviews and five hundred black-and-white photographs of ex-slave interviewees. In addition, see the complete text of biographies and narratives of previously enslaved people at the University of North Carolina, Chapel Hill, North American Slave Narratives.

26. Abu Bakr al-Siddiq, who was born in Timbuktu, wrote his narrative in Arabic. In a few pages, al-Siddiq focuses on describing family members, areas he remembers of his home country, and the details regarding his captivity in Africa. He does not describe his experiences of enslavement in Jamaica in any detail. His narrative was translated by Irish doctor, abolitionist, and historian Richard Robert Madden (1798–1886). Madden included his translated narrative in his diary, which documented aspects of the transition period from slavery to apprenticeship in Jamaica. Madden traveled to different parts of the Caribbean in the 1830s. Before his arrival in the Caribbean, Madden had learned some Arabic during his previous travels to Egypt and Turkey. For his narrative, see al-Siddiq, "The History," and "Routes in North Africa." In his twenty-six-page 1837 *Narrative of Events*, James Williams focuses on his experiences during the 1834–1838 apprenticeship period in Jamaica, especially the range and severity of punishments in the penal institutions at that time. Archibald John Monteath/Monteith's narrative reflects the Moravian memorialization tradition. However, in this case, instead of a third-person narrative memorializing Archibald John Monteath/Monteith, this twelve-page narrative is a first-person account based on various conversations with Monteath/Monteith. These conversations and interviews were conducted by members of the Moravian mission at New Carmel in Westmoreland, Jamaica in the 1850s. He includes information about his Igbo home, family, community, and cultural aspects of his life in West Africa, as well as how he was captured and his transatlantic journey to Jamaica. He only briefly discusses the Middle Passage and the conditions of his enslaved life in Jamaica. He centers primarily on his spiritual experiences, the introduction to Moravians, the importance of his spiritual life, and his interactions over a thirty-year span with other Moravians in Jamaica (beginning in 1824 to the time of the memorial in 1853).

27. As Trouillot delineates, "Silences enter the process of historical production at four crucial moments: the moment of fact creation (the making of *sources*); the moment of fact assembly (the making of *archives*); the moment of fact retrieval (the making of *narratives*); and the moment of retrospective significance (the making of *history* in the final instance)" (*Silencing the Past*, 26, author's emphasis). All of these, he clarifies, "are conceptual tools, second-level abstractions of processes that feed on each other. As such, they are not meant to provide a realistic description of the making of any individual narrative. Rather, they help us understand why not all silences are equal and why they cannot be addressed—or redressed—in the same manner." He affirms that "any historical narrative is a particular bundle of silences, the result of a unique process, and the operation required to deconstruct these silences will vary accordingly" (ibid., 26–27).

28. Soumahoro, #unsilencedpast Series.

29. Often presented as coined by Bernard Bell, "neo–slave narratives" describe "residually oral, modern narratives of escape from bondage to freedom" (*The Afro-American Novel*, 289). Ishmael Reed mentioned the term "neo–slave narrative" in an interview conducted in 1983. For a transcript of the interview, see Dalkey Archive Press, "A Conversation." Ashraf H. A. Rushdy in *Neo–Slave Narratives* defines neo–slave narratives as contemporary fictional works emulating and adopting the form and conventions of first-person antebellum slave narratives. Examples of neo–slave narratives and slavery novels by African American writers include Butler, *Kindred*; Williams, *Dessa Rose*; Morrison, *Beloved*; Jones, *The Known World*; and Coates, *The Water Dancer*. Such works by writers of African Caribbean descent include D'Aguiar, *The Longest Memory* and *Feeding the Ghosts*; James, *The Book of Night Women*; Levy, *The Long Song*;

and Brand, *At the Full and Change of the Moon*. Also see the two-part special issue of *Callaloo*, "The Neo–Slave Narrative Genre," 40, no. 4 (Fall 2017) and 41, no. 1 (Winter 2018). Although not categorized in the specific genre of the neo–slave narrative, Saidiya Hartman's work, such as *Scenes of Subjection*, has critically explored many of the questions and challenges presented in slave narratives and contemporary artistic representations of slavery.

30. In addition to these novels, a few television programs have also attempted to integrate slavery within the content of their shows; some have been criticized for their problematic depiction and reimagining of bondage. See Gay, "I Don't Want to Watch"; and Serjeant, "'Confederate' Writers Defend." In 2020 the new HBO series *Lovecraft Country*, based on Matt Ruff's novel by the same title, received significant critical attention for its imaginative integration of references to slavery.

31. Morrison, "Unspeakable Things Unspoken."

32. Morrison, "The Site of Memory," 92. Morrison partakes in this process of literary archaeology, as many of the authors of nineteenth-century slave narratives often circumvented specific moments of slavery that they deemed too painful, too horrific, indeed too traumatic to relive and reveal. As Mae Henderson posits, the "'things too terrible to relate' were most often the sexual exploitation of slave women by white men. Convention allowed, indeed almost demanded, that these violations be named but not described" ("Toni Morrison's *Beloved*," 81).

33. Christiansë, *Toni Morrison*, 46.

34. Ibid., 75.

35. Walcott, "Laventille," 35. In addition, it may also be fruitful to include Du Bois's "double-consciousness" in this conversation. I am particularly thinking about the aspect of his double-consciousness that speaks of "the sense of always looking at one's self through the eyes of others, of measuring one's soul by the tape of a world that looks on in amused contempt and pity" (*The Souls of Black Folk*, 11).

36. Sharpe, *In the Wake*, 12. In this section Sharpe avers that in their archival work in the "accumulated erasures, projections, fabulations, and misnamings," scholars of slavery confront what Hortense Spillers characterizes as "the agents buried beneath" (ibid.). See also Spillers, "Mama's Baby."

37. Sharpe, *In the Wake*, 12.

38. Ibid.; and Brand, *A Map to the Door*, 25. Dionne Brand states: "The door signifies the historical moment which colours all moments in the Diaspora. It accounts for the ways we observe and are observed as people, whether it's through the lens of social injustice or the lines of human accomplishments. The door exists as an absence. A thing in fact which we do not know about, a place we do not know. Yet it exists as the ground we walk. Every gesture our bodies make somehow gestures toward this door. What interests me primarily is probing the Door of No Return as consciousness. The door casts a haunting spell on personal and collective consciousness in the Diaspora. Black experience in any modern city or town in the Americas is a haunting. One enters a room and history follows; one enters a room and history precedes. History is already seated in the chair in the empty room when one arrives. Where one stands in a society seems always related to this historical experience. Where one can be observed is relative to that history. All human effort seems to emanate from this door. How do I know this? Only by self-observation, only by looking. Only by feeling. Only by being a part, sitting in the room with history" (*A Map to the Door*, 24–25).

39. Fuentes's term "mutilated historicity" "refers to the violent condition in which enslaved women appear in the archive disfigured and violated. Mutilated historicity exemplifies how their bodies and flesh become 'inscribed' with the text/violence of slavery. As a result, the *quality* of their historicization remains degraded in our present attempts to recreate their everyday experiences" (*Dispossessed Lives*, 16, author's emphasis).

40. Ibid., 5.

41. Ibid.

42. Ibid., 116.

43. Ibid., 141. "The enslaved women's 'most dreadful cries,'" Fuentes contends, "are a momentary refusal to be historically silenced but remain inaccessible to historical articulation. Their screams do not subvert nor destroy relations of power. They demand historical attention but do not depend on our empirical collaboration or narrativization. This is the historical genre of the enslaved in the colonial archive" (ibid., 143). For incisive essays on the silence, violence, and politics of the archives of slavery, see the following articles in the special issue of *History of the Present* 6, no. 2 (Fall 2016): Connolly and Fuentes, "Introduction"; Smallwood, "The Politics"; Kazanjian, "Two Paths"; Arondekar, "What More Remains"; Moglen, "Enslaved"; Morgan, "Accounting"; and Hartman, "Response."

44. At the end of chapter 5, I provide cursory information about the families who have owned Rose Hall, including its current ownership by the Rollins family of Delaware, in order to offer one example of the present-day deployment of Rose Hall as an embodiment of American imperialism and the afterlives of slavery in Jamaica. Although not focused on Rose Hall, a number of exceptional books have already been published on slavery in Jamaica, including comprehensive examinations of enslavers connected to Jamaica. For example, see Craton and Walvin, *A Jamaican Plantation*; Higman, *Montpelier, Jamaica*; Higman, *Plantation Jamaica*; and Petley, *White Fury*. B. W. Higman includes Rose Hall in his examination of sugar estates in Jamaica. He offers an informative brief analysis of enslaved workers and "occupational allocation" for the year 1832. His demographic examination provides some sense of differences shaped by age, gender, color, age, duties/positions, and overall health conditions at Rose Hall (Higman, *Slave Population and Economy*, 193–196).

45. The voluminous papers left behind by Jamaican enslaver Thomas Thistlewood are one significant example.

46. It is important to note that partially in response to the calls for more research on white women's experiences in the Caribbean (especially planters' wives and female enslavers), Annie Palmer has recently been highlighted as an example of white female agency. See Donahue, "The Ghost." In this new work centered on the myth of Annie Palmer, questions about enslaved women remain unasked and unanswered. The experiences of white women who served as enslavers in the United States and the Caribbean remain an area in need of further comprehensive investigation. See, for example, Beckles, "White Women"; and Jones, *Engendering Whiteness*. For a critical examination of the dearth of studies in this area, also see Jones, "White Women." Two recently published scholarly works on this topic are Jones-Rogers, *They Were Her Property*; and Walker, *Jamaica Ladies*. Walker focuses not only on free white women enslavers but also on free and freed women of color in the British Empire. Some of the women enslavers of color deployed slave ownership as a tangible marker of freedom and as a way to present and maintain their status and rights as free people of color within a slavocracy.

47. Hartman, "Venus in Two Acts," 10.

48. Ibid., 11. Hartman elucidates that the "intention here isn't anything as miraculous as recovering the lives of the enslaved or redeeming the dead, but rather laboring to paint as full a picture of the lives of captives as possible." "This double gesture," she explains, "can be described as straining against the limits of the archive to write a cultural history of the captive, and, at the same time, enacting the impossibility of representing the lives of the captives precisely through the process of narration" (ibid.).

49. Ibid.

50. Ibid., 12, author's emphasis.

51. Ibid.

52. One of the plenaries of the 2019 Lapidus Center Conference at the Schomburg Center in New York, held October 10–12, 2019, highlighted aspects of speculative history. The title of the 2019 conference was "Enduring Slavery: Resistance, Public Memory, and Transatlantic Archives." The October 11 plenary was entitled "Slavery Archives and Speculation." Although not utilizing the term "speculative history" as a legitimizing process, Yvette Abrahams's article "Was Eva Raped?" begins with brief incisive comments related to the invocation of speculation in history writ large.

53. Ioannidis, "'History.'"

54. Gordon-Reed, *The Hemingses of Monticello*, 31.

55. Ibid.

56. Ibid., 31–32. Also see Gordon-Reed, "Writing Early American Lives."

57. See Reckord, "The Jamaica Slave Rebellion"; Brathwaite, "The Slave Rebellion"; and Higman, *Montpelier, Jamaica*, 262–283. Also see the recently published work of Zoellner, *Island on Fire*.

58. Established in 1819, the Office for the Register of Colonial Slaves received copies of these returns of slaves (slave registers) from the respective colonies. For more on the history of the Slave Registry Bill, see *Reasons for Establishing a Registry of Slaves in the British Colonies*; and Schuyler, "The Constitutional Claims."

59. Vasconcellos, *Slavery, Childhood, and Abolition*, 34–35.

60. John Rose Palmer's grandfather, Capt. James Palmer, was the brother of the Honorable John Palmer. See "John Rose Palmer."

61. In Jamaica, these triennial slave registers were required by the Jamaican Assembly beginning in 1817. See NA Kew, T71/202.

62. NA Kew, T71/206; JARD, 1B/11/7/40.

63. NA Kew, T71/209; JARD, 1B/11/7/66.

64. NA Kew, T71/214; JARD, 1B/11/7/85.

65. NA Kew, T71/218; JARD, 1B/11/7/100, fols. 210a, 210b, and 211a.

66. NA Kew, T71/223.

67. The Rose Hall Journal (RHJ, hereafter cited as JARD, 1B/26 PLus the volume and folio numbers) entries begin on Monday, March 17, 1817 (vol. 1, fol. 1) and end on Saturday, November 10, 1832 (vol. 3, fol. 140). The RHJ folio numbers included in this book are the pencil foliation numbers. In 2014, during my first archival trip, the record locator number for the Rose Hall Journal was 1B/26, vols. 1, 2, and 3. During my most recent archival visit to JARD in November 2019, due to the recent addition of other materials on another plantation, JARD

had renumbered the volumes of the Rose Hall Journal. Vols. 1, 2, and 3 are now vols. 5, 6, and 7, respectively. As I have utilized the original record locator volume numbers since 2014, I have decided not to renumber all of the endnotes to the current record locator volume numbers. However, future researchers at JARD should be aware of this change.

68. This was also the case for the previous white resident enslavers of Rose Hall—John Rose Palmer's great-uncle John Palmer and his wife, Rosa Palmer. They, too, had no children at Rose Hall who would have been breastfed by the enslaved women at Rose Hall.

69. For an adroit and meticulous study of the everyday routines and practices related to enslaved women and reproduction on Jamaican plantations from 1780 to 1834, see Turner, *Contested Bodies*.

70. For more on the historical contextualization and juridical aspects of this law, see Morgan, *"Partus Sequitur Ventrem."*

71. For a comparative example of the workings and lived experiences on a plantation in Jamaica (Mesopotamia Plantation in Savanna-la-Mar, Westmoreland) and a plantation in the United States (Mount Airy Plantation in Virginia), see Dunn, *A Tale of Two Plantations*. For an exceptional study of marriage for enslaved and free Blacks in the nineteenth century in the United States, see Hunter, *Bound in Wedlock*.

72. My thanks to my colleague Professor Dorothy Ko for guiding me to this particular understanding of my book.

73. Cohen, *No Tea, No Shade*, xii.

74. Daisy's birth is noted in JARD, 1B/11/7/40. Panella's birth of a female child is also recorded in JARD, 1B/26, RHJ, Monday, December 22, 1817, vol. 1, fol. 33. This female child is Daisy.

75. In the daily notes for Friday, August 27, 1824, the overseer mentioned that "Kate Delivered of a Still Born child" (JARD, 1B/26, RHJ, August 27, 1824, vol. 2, fol. 63b).

76. Celia's son Lewis's fatal accident is mentioned in the Rose Hall Journal. When a Rose Hall wagon was in the process of running errands (including transporting shingles from another site to Rose Hall), Lewis was noted as "falling under the Wheel it Crush'd him so much as to cause his death" (JARD, 1B/26, RHJ, December 8, 1818, vol. 1, fol. 81). The 1820 slave register notes Lewis's death at the age of twenty-five. Peachy's death is recorded in the journal during the week of March 2–7, 1817, RHJ, March 4, 1818, vol. 1, fol. 43.

77. Here I am invoking what Professor Mame-Fatou Niang posited in the Barnard College #unsilencedpast event with Professor Maboula Soumahoro. Niang pensively noted the "harnessing of silences," the "noisy silences that have haunted me," and the ways "silences can be as eloquent as the noises of the French national narrative." Mame-Fatou Niang, #unsilencedpast Online Series.

CHAPTER 1. In the Wake of the Archive

1. JARD, 1B/26, RHJ, Monday, March 17, 1817, vol. 1, fol. 1, and Saturday, November 10, 1832, vol. 3, fol. 140.

2. The following citations are all from JARD, 1B/26, RHJ. For example, on Monday, August 21, 1820, it is noted that Jno. Slater "Removed to Palmyra as Book-Keeper" and Jno. Hallilay "Removed to Rose Hall from P.M." (vol. 1, fol. 166b). On Wednesday, May 1, 1822, "Wm.

Donaldson Employed as second Book keeper" (vol. 1, fol. 254b). On Wednesday, July 30, 1824, "William Townshend Employed as Book keeper" (vol. 2, fol. 59b). Two years later, on Saturday, July 8, 1826, "William Townshend discharged" (vol. 2, fol. 158a). Soon after, on Monday, July 17, 1826, "Employed Charles Skeatsas bookkeeper" (vol. 2, fol. 160a). Three months later, on Friday, October 27, 1826, "Employed Mr. James Marks as bookkeeper" (vol. 2, fol. 173b). On Thursday, September 17, 1829, "Thomas Wilkinson Employed as Bookeeper [sic] by the Honble. W. Miller and Mr. R Blair Removed to the [unclear wording]" (vol. 3, fol. 55a). After John Rose Palmer's death in November 1827, William Miller (custos of Trelawny) and William Heath (solicitor) served as receivers of Rose Hall. On April 11, 1832, "Charles Stewart Employed as Bookkeeper" (vol. 3, fol. 121a). On Saturday, August 18, 1832, there is a note at the bottom of the left page stating, "August 16th John Gunson discharged" (vol. 3, fol. 129b). As he is not mentioned as an overseer in the Rose Hall crop accounts, he was probably employed as a bookkeeper.

3. Even though the names of overseers and bookkeepers are infrequently mentioned in the three volumes of the journal, the names of the overseers—William Kerr, James McFarlane, Lawrence Lowe, and Robert Scott—are consistently included in the archival record in Rose Hall's annual crop accounts. In 1822 and 1823 resident owner John Rose Palmer signed the crop accounts for Rose Hall. The crop accounts for most of the years between 1818 and 1832 are housed at JARD, 1B/11/4. These reports specify the number of hogsheads and tierces (wooden barrels) of sugar, as well as hogsheads and puncheons (wooden barrels) of rum produced at Rose Hall, which were then primarily shipped to London and Liverpool (including specific ship names and individuals), with a limited amount being noted as sold in Jamaica and also for consumption at Rose Hall itself. See, for example, the crop accounts signed by Lawrence Lowe as overseer at Rose Hall Estate from 1826 to 1831 (and possibly for some months in 1832) before Robert Scott assumed that position in 1832 (JARD, 1B/11/4/63, 1B/11/4/66, 1B/11/4/68, 1B/11/4/69, 1B/11/4/71, 1B/11/4/72).

4. This format of the journal (JARD, 1B/26, RHJ) remains essentially the same from March 17, 1817, vol. 1, fol. 1, to Saturday, January 17, 1829, vol. 3, fol. 37. The new format included each week's "Distribution of Negroes" and the "Daily Occurrences" on one page (instead of the "Distribution of Negroes" being on the left side of the page and the "Daily Occurrences" on the right side of the page). This shift transpired on Sunday, January 18, 1829, vol. 3, fol. 38, and this new format continued to the end of the journal entries on Saturday, November 10, 1832, vol. 3, fol. 140.

5. In this small group of employed whites at Rose Hall is an alphabetical list of the most recent overseer, Robert Scott, who started in this position on January 5, 1832, as well as the two most recent bookkeepers, Thomas Jessop, who started in this position on August 19, 1832, and Charles Stewart, who started as a Rose Hall bookkeeper on April 11, 1832 (JARD, 1B/26, RHJ, vol. 3, fol. 130b). It is not clear which of these three white men recorded this journal entry, because, consistent with the other journal entries, the recorder did not sign or initial the page.

6. For more on these laws, see Hall, "Some Aspects." See also Higman, *Plantation Jamaica*.

7. Nicholas Crawford's current book project, entitled "Sustaining Slavery: Food Provisioning, Power, and Protest in the British Caribbean," will offer critical insights about the impact of enslaved people's sustenance and related activism on colonial and imperial policies from the

American Revolution to abolition in the British Caribbean. Thurston, interview with Nicholas Crawford. Provision grounds in Jamaica were often located in rocky plots of land, sometimes in mountainous areas that were positioned at some distance from plantations. Enslaved people cultivated tuberous root vegetables such as cassava, yam, and sweet potatoes, as well as callaloo and various herbs for seasoning and medicinal purposes.

8. Higman, *Slave Populations*, 181–182.

9. The Consolidated Slave Law in Jamaica was not exceptional to this colony. Other British slave colonies, including Barbados and Grenada, also enacted consolidated, ameliorative laws.

10. B. W. Higman notes that the provision grounds for enslaved people at Rose Hall were located at the neighboring Palmyra Plantation (*Jamaica Surveyed*, 236). This would have been the case only after Rose Palmer married John Palmer in 1767, as John Palmer owned Palmyra Plantation. The location of the provision grounds for enslaved people at Rose Hall before 1767 is not clear from the records; some part of the Rose Hall Estate might have been designated for this particular use. In the Rose Hall Journal, overseers also indicated that enslaved people worked provision grounds in the mountains, as was often the case at other Jamaican plantations. In 1828 one overseer noted, "Negro Day No. 24. in their Grounds in Sunderland Mountains" (JARD, 1B/26, RHJ, Saturday, January 10, 1829, vol. 3, fol. 36). Although there is no extant plan or map for Rose Hall Estate before abolition, in 1838 William Miller, one of the receivers of Rose Hall Estate, arranged for a survey of Rose Hall; the survey was conducted by Richard Wilson. Part of the plan is reproduced in Higman, *Jamaica Surveyed*, 235, fig. 8.11.

11. In November 1826 an overseer noted, "Negro Day No. 15," reflecting a recognition of the 1826 Jamaican law regarding twenty-six of these days per year (JARD, 1B/26, RHJ, Saturday, November 4, 1826, vol. 2, fol. 174). In June 1828 a overseer started tracking and noting the number of "Negroes Days" throughout the year. He noted, "Negro Day No. 1" (JARD, 1B/26, RHJ, Saturday, June 28, 1828, vol. 3, fol. 6).

12. A number of scholars have examined the critical role of provision grounds for both enslaved people and enslavers in Jamaica and throughout the Caribbean. See, for example, Parry, "Plantation"; Marshall, "Provision Ground"; Sheridan, "From Chattel"; and Higman, *Slave Population and Economy*. Ahmed Reid revisits previous hypotheses and proposes a direct relationship between labor productivity and provision grounds, specifically that "on estates where the enslaved population grew provisions, the level of labor productivity was high relative to those estates where no such incentive was present." As a result, he argues, "an increase in provision acres led to an increase in the number of hogsheads produced per slave" (Reid, "Sugar, Slavery," 169–170). Also see DeLoughrey, "Yam, Roots, and Rot." Invoking the significance of the provision grounds in Jamaica, a recent cookbook pays homage to the women of Jamaica and the Caribbean who worked those provision grounds during slavery and presents a range of contemporary vegetarian recipes in this spirit; see Rousseau and Rousseau, *Provisions*.

13. "Grasscutters" as a separate category are sometimes listed under the gangs. The categories for first gang, second gang, and third gang are always at the top of the columns of duties/positions. The first and second gangs are often grouped together with a combined total number for enslaved people working in these gangs. Also, due to the overseers reporting the numbers, there are journal entries that list the three gangs combined in one total number, and they are listed as "The Gangs" or "The Three Gangs."

14. JARD, 1B/26, RHJ, vol. 1, fol. 1b.

15. JARD, 1B/26, RHJ, vol. 1, fol. 1a.

16. For more on meanings of mortuary and mourning beliefs, practices, and politics in eighteenth- and early nineteenth-century Jamaica, see Brown, *The Reaper's Garden*.

17. A range of illnesses are recorded in the documents, for example, "affection of the brains," dysentery, venereal disease, tuberculosis (referred to as "consumption" at that time), worms, yaws, palpitation of the heart, dropsy, and poisoning from ingesting substances, especially parts of the nightshade plant. In addition to these diseases, other listed reasons for death include "natural decay," "old age," "debility," and "visitation of God."

18. See historian Stephanie E. Smallwood's critical analysis of slave trade–related ledgers and notes on African captives in the marginalia of these ledgers in *Saltwater Slavery*.

19. Edward Mountague served as receiver of Rose Hall Estate in 1817. When Rose Hall owner John Palmer passed in 1797, the estate was inherited by his two sons, James and John, who resided in England. In 1817, in their absence, Edward Mountague was charged with submitting the slave register for Rose Hall for 1817. By the next year, both of John Palmer's sons had died, and John Rose Palmer, John Palmer's grandnephew, inherited Rose Hall Plantation and the neighboring Palmyra Plantation. From John Rose Palmer's arrival at Rose Hall in 1818, as the new plantation owner and receiver, until his death in November 1827, he endorsed these triennial returns for Rose Hall Plantation. Following John Rose Palmer's death, William Heath and the Honorable William Miller served as the receivers for the final 1829 and 1832 returns. See "Edward Mountague"; "William Heath"; and "Hon. William Miller (attorney)."

20. NA Kew, T71/202. The 1817 list of enslaved people at Rose Hall was also dated as officially confirmed on September 16, 1817. Between Isaac's passing on March 19, 1817, and the date of the 1817 slave register on June 28, 1817, two other enslaved people had died. One of them was "J.O." The first letter is somewhat blurred but is probably a J. J.O. is recorded as dead on Monday, April 28, 1817. At the bottom of the page of the "Distribution of Negroes" for the week of April 28 to May 3, J.O. is described as dying "of natural decay being an Invalid for many years." There is no indication about whether J.O. was categorized as a man or woman, and there is no note about whether J.O. was African born or Creole. The total number of enslaved people at Rose Hall is changed in this entry from 154 (minus 1) to 153. The adjustment in the number on the "Distribution of Negroes" page, however, includes a reduction of one in the total number of people working in the combined first and second gangs. As a result, J.O. most likely worked primarily in the cane fields in either the first or second gang (JARD, 1B/26, RHJ, vol. 1, fol. 3a). The next week of the journal (May 5–10) is missing. The next journal entry is for the following week (May 12–17), and the total number of enslaved people beginning on Monday, May 12, is 152, indicating that another enslaved person probably died during the week of May 5. There are no other deaths of enslaved people recorded in the journal from May 12, 1817, until the first Rose Hall slave register dated June 28, 1817, and the total number of 152 enslaved people remains constant during this time period.

21. Nadia Ellis's conception of "queer" in her article on Jamaican dancehall provides a useful, generative way of conceptualizing the fluidity that I would suggest we consider in holding this imaginative space for enslaved persons: "*Queer* functions for me as a signifier of sexual and gender nonnormativity, a break in the line of gender. This may include erotic exchanges between people of the same gender, but is not limited to them. It is very often bound up with the homo-

erotic, though it need not be sexual. *Queer* emphasizes practice, action, not categorical state. *Queer* shifts, it moves, it does not rest. It names a practice, it names a moment, it names a person, sometimes all three simultaneously. It might name a different practice, a different person in another moment. Crucially, in my analysis *queer* does not depend on knowing in any assured way what a person feels about his or her sexual orientation. Indeed, it refuses the sense that 'orientation' tells us anything concrete or stable about who we are and what we do. It *does* depend on there being a discursive field, a social matrix, that defines normative sexual and social practices against which the queer stands" ("Out and Bad," 12).

22. There are other racial- and color-centered terms that are not utilized in either the Rose Hall Journal or the slave registers for Rose Hall but that appear in other plantation and general records during this time (e.g., mustee, mustiphini, quinteroon, and octoroon). While touring the Caribbean and in his notes about his time in Jamaica, Dr. Richard Robert Madden described the "various classes of free persons of colour." In *A Twelvemonth's Residence in the West Indies* he includes definitions for sambos, mulattos, quadroons, and mestees (89).

23. JARD, 1B/26, RHJ, vol. 3, fols. 2–4.

24. This item is entitled "List of Slaves on Rose Hall Estate Served with Clothing by the Honble. William Miller, This 18th August, 1832." One of the subsequent reprintings in 1952 (most often housed in libraries) mistakenly identifies the list for the Rose Hill Estate (instead of the Rose Hall Estate). Shortened citations to Shore, *In Old St. James*, refer to the 1952 edition and its "List of Slaves on Rose Hall Estate, August 18, 1832," plus the page number.

25. Osnaburg fabrics, named for the city of Osnabrück, Germany, were worn by both enslaved people and poor working-class whites in the eighteenth and nineteenth centuries. In the eighteenth century, it was made from linen fibers, and in the nineteenth century, it was primarily made from cotton. Osnaburg fabric was also utilized for industrial purposes. Today it is still used for upholstery and draperies due to its durable qualities. Peniston/Pennystone is a coarse heavy woolen cloth from England worn from the sixteenth to the nineteenth century. It presumably also was named in relation to a town—Penistone in southern Yorkshire in England. Penistone was known for its native sheep, which produced a strong, durable wool, with coats from this area sometimes referred to as Penistones.

26. The madras/bandana silk cloth was initially from India. However, the silk Indian version was not utilized for enslaved people. Instead, a cotton version of this style was produced in England and then exported to Jamaica. This madras/bandana cloth was utilized for blouses, dresses, and head wraps. Although this fabric had long been associated with slavery (or country folk generally) in Jamaica, when Jamaican icon Louise Bennett-Coverley ("Miss Lou") began wearing this cloth in the 1960s in a purposeful manner for her performances, she celebrated this cloth as an item to be reclaimed as part of Jamaican cultural history. Her incorporation of this cloth shifted perceptions of it, and this transformed its integration into other Jamaican cultural performances as a visible, tangible marker of Jamaican cultural and national history. For one examination of Jamaican clothing and style, see McKenzie, "Jamaican Ethnic Dress."

27. An English ell equals 1.25 yards; however, the Scottish and Flemish ells equal slightly less yardage. This fabric could have been calico, which was another cloth often allocated to enslaved people in the Caribbean, or some other kind of mixed inexpensive fabric.

28. Camp, *Closer to Freedom*.

29. At the bottom of the 1832 list of males at Rose Hall is a note: "N.B.—Jack, to the Estate

of Mr. Kerr, a Negro." Although I have included Jack here, it is not absolutely clear whether at the time of the list Jack was an enslaved person at Rose Hall working at Mr. Kerr's estate, a "hired negro" of Mr. Kerr's working at Rose Hall, or an enslaved person involved in some other arrangement. I have included Jack in the total number of enslaved people, as he appears on this 1832 clothing allowance list. However, I have no other descriptive information regarding Jack's country of origin or duties or other distinguishing characteristics.

30. Although the journal and my study are focused on Rose Hall Plantation, it is important to note that this enslaved community probably extended to Palmyra Plantation (a nearby plantation owned by John Palmer). Even before John Palmer married Rosa Palmer, enslaved people at both plantations might have developed relationships based on kin and kith. There are several references to Palmyra in the Rose Hall Journal. Although there are triennial slave registers for Palmyra, there is no extant plantation journal for Palmyra, so it is not possible to reconstruct and confirm details of individual enslaved people's lives at Palmyra and their connections to enslaved people at Rose Hall.

31. The term "fictive" kin/kinship has long been utilized in scholarly work. Instead of describing these connections as "fictive" kinship relationships, I suggest utilizing "expansive" kinship relationships. These relationships between people who were not related by blood or marriage did not make them contrived or fictitious in any way.

32. See, for example, the arguments presented in Goveia, *Slave Society*; Besson, *Transformations*; Patterson, "From Endo-deme to Matri-deme"; Higman, "The Slave Family"; and Craton, "Changing Patterns." For one example of an excellent study of the complicated relationships and marital structures between African Americans in bondage and in freedom, see Hunter, *Bound in Wedlock*.

33. For example, the Queering Slavery Working Group, co-organized by professors Jessica Marie Johnson at Johns Hopkins University and Vanessa Holden at the University of Kentucky, "was formed to discuss issues related to reading, researching, and writing histories of intimacy, sex, and sexuality during the period of Atlantic slavery. Guided by the question, 'What would it mean to Queer Slavery?,' the group seeks out queer encounters in slavery's archive. Operating across page and screen, the Queering Slavery Working Group brings discussions happening in black queer studies, queer of color studies, and histories of enslaved and free people of African descent across the diaspora into lurid and profane contact" ("About, Queering Slavery Working Group"). Also see Aidoo, *Slavery Unseen*.

34. NA Kew, T71/214, fol. 33. Although not done consistently, the placement of names on the triennial slave registers often reflects the particular timing of births and deaths at Rose Hall; the names listed at the top are associated with the first part of the time period for the register and additional names following a sequential pattern.

35. JARD, 1B/26, RHJ, vol. 2, fols. 33b, 52b.

36. As noted earlier, over the course of the journal, from 1817 to 1832, the notes related to the passing of enslaved people at Rose Hall appear more frequently in the marginalia of these weekly reports.

37. Renny, *An History of Jamaica*, 172. Shipmates of the Middle Passage are referenced in a number of sources. In *An History of Jamaica* in 1807, Robert Renny, Esq., states: "A *ship-mate* is one of their most endearing appellations; and they who have been wafted across the Atlantic ocean in the same vessel, ever after look upon each other as brethren: So natural is it for part-

ners in misfortune, to become dear to each other!" (ibid., author's emphasis). See also Herman Bennett's critical work regarding the close relationships developed between shipmates during the Middle Passage and how these connections extended to the selection of godparents for enslaved Africans and free Blacks in colonial Mexico (*Colonial Blackness*).

38. NA Kew, T71/202, fol. 544.

39. It is extremely difficult to read the journal entry for the week of April 29, 1822, due to the worn, weathered condition of the page. In fact, the "Distribution of Negroes" side of the page (on the left) is mostly blank as a result of the damage to this page. The "Daily Occurrences," on the right side of the page, is somewhat legible. It is in the notes for Saturday, May 4, that someone is mentioned as dying of old age. It is clear that the name is a short one and part of the reason that it could well be Jreen/Green. In addition, given the older enslaved people at Rose Hall in that year and the timing of their recorded deaths before or after this date, it is most likely that the person who was noted as dying "of old age" on Saturday, May 4, 1822, is Jreen/Green (JARD, 1B/26, RHJ, vol. 1, fol. 254b).

40. NA Kew, T71/202, fols. 544, 543, 544, 540, 541.

41. In the 1817 slave register, Janet is listed as Janet and Creole (NA Kew, T71/202, fol. 543). However, she is listed as Jannet and African in the 1828 list for clothing allowance in the Rose Hall Journal, as well as in the *Old St. James* 1832 clothing allowance list (JARD, 1B/26, RHJ, vol. 3, fol. 3; and Shore, *In Old St. James*, 110). As she is listed in both of the final clothing allowance lists as African, I have included her as part of the group of African-born women at Rose Hall.

42. It is important to note his position as a watchman at Rose Hall, as he had absconded multiple times from Rose Hall in 1820, 1826, and even in 1832.

43. The position of "driveress" was not exceptional on Jamaican sugar plantations. See Richard S. Dunn's discussion of the positions of enslaved persons (including driveress) at the Mesopotamia sugar plantation in Jamaica (*A Tale of Two Plantations*, esp. chap. 4, "'Dreadful Idlers' in the Mesopotamia Cane Fields," 131–180).

44. Shore, *In Old St. James*, 106–109.

45. JARD, 1B/26, RHJ, vol. 1, fol. 102; JARD, 1B/11/7/40, fol. 160ba.

46. JARD, 1B/26, RHJ, vol. 2, fol. 52b; JARD, 1B/11/7/85, fol. 155a.

CHAPTER 2. Bondage, Birthing, and
Belonging at Rose Hall Plantation

1. Morgan, *Laboring Women*, 40.
2. Ibid.
3. Vasconcellos, *Slavery*, 8.
4. Ibid., 9.
5. Ibid.
6. Ibid.
7. Ibid., 16.
8. Ibid., 10. As Vasconcellos also states, "The nature of girls' work became more complex as planters increasingly linked gender to reproductive potential, and enslaved girls' work summarily took on a reproductive component as a result" (ibid.).

9. I invoke this notion of African-born women in Jamaica being a new "Eve" of the Creole population in the Caribbean in conversation with historian Jennifer L. Morgan's analysis of how some European male travelers described African women as experiencing pain-free childbirth. Morgan includes an excerpt from English-born Jamaican planter and historian Edward Long's statement in his 1774 text *History of Jamaica* that Black women "delivered with little or no labour. . . . Thus they seem exempted from the course [*sic*] inflicted upon Eve and *her daughters*" (Long as quoted in Morgan, *Laboring Women*, 189, Morgan's emphasis). Morgan asserts: "If African women gave birth without pain, they somehow sidestepped God's curse upon Eve. It they were not her descendants, they were not related to Europeans and could therefore be forced to labor on England's overseas plantations with immunity" (ibid.). As she affirms, "In the case of England's contact with Africa and the Americas, the crisis in European identity was mediated by constructing an image of pain-free reproduction that diminished Africa's access to certainly and civilization, thus allowing for the mass appropriation that was the transatlantic slave trade" (ibid., 190).

10. JARD, 1B/26, RHJ, December 22, 1817, vol. 1, fol. 33.

11. As previously mentioned, Julina is noted as Creole in the 1817 slave register and then as African in the 1832 clothing allowance list (NA Kew, T71/202, fol. 543; and Shore, *In Old St. James*, 110). Parts of the 1828 list for clothing allowance have been torn or have deteriorated over time, and in the list (arranged by age), Julina's name would have been included at the very bottom of one of these torn-out/deteriorated pages. As a result, I do not have that additional list in order to confirm whether Julina was African-born or Creole. Jannet is also described as Creole in the 1817 slave register (name spelled in 1817 as Janet). However, she is categorized as African in the 1828 list for clothing allowance in the Rose Hall Journal and in the Old St. James 1832 clothing allowance list (name spelled as Jannet) (JARD, 1B/26, RHJ, vol. 3, fol. 3; and Shore, *In Old St. James*, 110). As she is listed in both of the clothing allowance lists as African, I have included her as part of the group of African-born women at Rose Hall.

12. Names of enslaved people that included "Sambo" or "Mulatto" were not particular to Rose Hall. Instead, these monikers emerge in other plantation records.

13. Doshy's name is also spelled as Doshey in the Rose Hall Journal.

14. See, for example, Morgan, *Laboring Women*; Turner, *Contested Bodies*; and Morgan, "Slave Women."

15. See, for example, Bush, "Hard Labor"; Bush, "The Family Tree." See also Schiebinger, "Agnotology" (on the poinciana tree as an abortifacient in the Caribbean), and Fett, *Working Cures*, regarding herbal knowledge and medical practices of enslaved women in the southern United States.

16. Turner, *Contested Bodies*, 203.

17. Denaud, "Renegade Gestation." Denaud is a doctoral candidate in Africana studies at Brown University. She is currently working on her dissertation, "At the Vanishing Point of the Word: Blackness, Imperium, and the Unnameable War."

18. See, for example, Craton, *Searching*; Higman, *Slave Population and Economy*; Morgan, "Slave Women"; Forster and Smith, "Surviving Slavery"; Vasconcellos, *Slavery*; and Turner, *Contested Bodies*.

19. For a thoughtful, comprehensive analysis of the myriad factors shaping the shifting notions, values, and strategies associated with enslaved motherhood, pregnancy, childbirth,

and child-rearing in Jamaica from the late 1700s into the early decades of the 1820s, see Turner, *Contested Bodies*.

20. Ibid., 170–171.

21. Whether or not enslaved children were named in the journal shortly after birth, my close analysis of the records enabled me to identify and name all of the enslaved children if their individual names appeared in at least one of the archival documents. For a detailed discussion of neonatal complications and the precarity of enslaved newborns, as well as enslaved mothers' strategies and responses in their pregnancy, childbirth, and child-rearing practices in Jamaica, see chap. 5, "'Dead before the Ninth Day': Struggles over Neonatal Care," in ibid., 151–181.

22. JARD, 1B/26, RHJ, March 27, 1824, vol. 2, fol. 41b.

23. JARD, 1B/11/7/85, fol. 155a.

24. JARD, 1B/26, RHJ, September 9, 1832, vol. 3, fol. 132a, and September 23, 1832, vol. 3, fols. 133a, 134a.

25. JARD, 1B/26, RHJ, August 27, 1824, vol. 2, fol. 63b. In only a couple of years, another child of Kate was recorded in the 1826 register; her name is Leddy. The 1826 register notes her age as six months. The next slave register, of 1829, lists Leddy's death at eight months. These are the only children named as being Kate's children at Rose Hall.

26. JARD, 1B/26, RHJ, July 2, 1823, vol. 2, fol. 4b. This is the only child of Gift/Giss who appears in the extant records.

27. JARD, 1B/26, RHJ, September 28, 1825, vol. 2, fol. 120a. Gift/Giss's death is also recorded in JARD, 1B/11/7/85, fol. 155a.

28. There is some disagreement among scholars about the extent to which enslavers in Jamaica consistently recorded information about stillborn infants and infants who passed within days and weeks after their birth. See, for example, Higman, *Slave Population and Economy*. In his work, historian Kenneth Morgan argues that "it is likely that spontaneous miscarriage (before twenty-eight weeks of pregnancy) and stillbirths (after twenty-eight weeks) rather than calculated abortions were responsible for high rates of foetal loss. Indeed, what were alleged as self-induced abortions might equally have been spontaneous miscarriages: on plantations it would have been difficult to distinguish these two causes of prematurely terminated pregnancy" ("Slave Women," 246).

29. NA Kew, T71/202, fol. 545; and Shore, *In Old St. James*, 112–113.

30. JARD, 1B/11/7/85, fol. 155a.

31. At the bottom of the "Distribution of Negroes" in the journal for the week of June 1, 1818, the overseer noted that "Dorinda deliv'd of a male ch'd, Morris." In the column for Monday, June 1, 1818, the total number of enslaved people is listed as 153 with the addition of one and the new total of 154 (JARD, 1B/26, RHJ, vol. 1, fol. 56a). Morris's birth and death are listed in JARD, 1B/11/7/40, fol. 160. Morris's death and related circumstances are not included in the pages of the Rose Hall Journal. Although Morris's name is recorded at the time of his birth, the recording of names of newborns in the Rose Hall Journal is not consistently included.

32. John's birth and death (JARD, 1B/11/7/66, fol. 74).

33. In the "Daily Occurrences" for the week of April 15, 1822, the overseer's notes for Tuesday, April 16, 1822, include the statement "Mary Delivered of a Male Childe." As in most of the notations regarding births of enslaved children at Rose Hall, John's name is not mentioned (JARD, 1B/26, RHJ, vol. 1, fol. 252b).

34. Matilda, NA Kew, T71/202, fol. 543.

35. JARD, 1B/11/7/85, fol. 155a; and Shore, *In Old St. James*, 108–109.

36. JARD, 1B/26, RHJ, note regarding Sylvia's birth, June 2, 1831, vol. 3, fol. 102. She is listed as one year and one month old in the 1832 slave register, NA Kew, T71/223, fol. 91.

37. NA Kew, T71/218, no folio number noted on document; and JARD, 1B/11/7/100, fol. 215.

38. NA Kew, T71/218, no folio number noted on document; and JARD, 1B/11/7/100, fol. 215. Given the timing of the deaths of Marcus and Maxwell, their deaths were probably recorded in the missing pages of the Rose Hall Journal in 1827 and 1828.

39. NA Kew, T71/218, no folio number noted on document; and JARD, 1B/11/7/100, fol. 215.

40. Mary's age is listed in NA Kew, T71/202, fol. 544.

41. JARD, 1B/11/7/40, fol. 160ba; and Shore, *In Old St. James*, 108–109.

42. JARD, 1B/11/7/66, fol. 74a; and Shore, *In Old St. James*, 112–113.

43. JARD, 1B/11/7/85, fol. 155a; and Shore, *In Old St. James*, 108–109 (listed under the name "Jennie," a possible misspelling of "Jemmie").

44. JARD, 1B/11/7/66, fol. 74a; and see JARD, 1B/26, RHJ, note regarding John's birth (though unnamed in the journal), August 29, 1820, vol. 1, fol. 167b.

45. NA Kew, T71/218, no folio number noted on document; and JARD, 1B/11/7/100, fol. 215. Note regarding Allick's death in JARD, 1B/26, RHJ, February 24, 1832, vol. 3, fol. 117b.

46. Allick's birth is recorded in the journal on Monday, September 4, 1820; it is noted that "Dorinda delivered of Male Child Sept 3d" (JARD, 1B/26, RHJ, vol. 1, fol. 168b). The journal entry for Monday, January 8, 1821 notes, "Allick, young child of Dorinda's died of Yaws" (vol. 1, fol. 186b). Although a number of Dorinda's other children's names are included in the notations of their respective births in the journal, this is not the case for Allick or Surry. The entry for Wednesday, December 12, 1821, states, "Dorinda delivered of a Male Child" (vol. 1, fol. 234b). This is in reference to Surry's birth. The overseer mentioned on Tuesday, February 19, 1822, that "Surry died suddenly Verdict Visitation of God" (vol. 1, fol. 244b). Both Allick's and Surry's births and deaths are recorded on the same page in 1823 (JARD, 1B/11/7/66, fol. 74).

47. Eliza's birth (JARD, 1B/11/7/66, fol. 74a) and Eliza's death at four (JARD, 1B/11/7/85, fol. 155a).

48. Sam is included in the 1817 slave register as age eleven, negro, Creole, and son of Dorinda (NA Kew, T71/218, fol. 542) and in the 1832 list of enslaved people as Sam (Christian name Sam Ellis), age twenty-five, negro, Creole, a cooper, of good disposition, with a sore leg, and valued at £100 (Shore, *In Old St. James*, 106–107).

49. Anthony is included in the 1817 slave register as age seven, negro, Creole, and son of Dorinda (NA Kew, T71/218, fol. 542) and in the 1832 list of enslaved people as Anthony (Christian name Jas. Ellis), age twenty-one, negro, Creole, a muleman, of good disposition, able and healthy, and valued at £100 (Shore, *In Old St. James*, 106–107).

50. William is included in the 1817 slave register as age two, negro, Creole, and son of Dorinda (NA Kew, T71/218, fol. 542) and in the 1832 list of enslaved people as Wm Kerr, age sixteen, negro, Creole, a cattleboy, able and healthy, and valued at £100 (Shore, *In Old St. James*, 108–109). He is also noted as a runaway at that time.

51. Venus is listed as age one, negro, Creole, and daughter of Dorinda (JARD, 1B/11/7/85, fol. 155a) and in the 1832 list of enslaved people as Venus (Christian name Eliza Stennet), age six, negro, Creole, the hogmeat gang, of good disposition, healthy, and valued at £40 (Shore, *In*

Old St. James, 112–113). Venus's birth is noted along the left margin of the "Daily Occurrences" for the week of July 11, 1825: "1825, July 3rd Dorinda Delivered of a Female Child Named Venus" (JARD, 1B/26, RHJ, vol. 2, fol. 109a).

52. John is listed as three weeks old, negro, Creole, and son of Dorinda (NA Kew, T71/218, no folio number noted on document; and JARD, 1B/11/7/100, fol. 215), as well as in the 1832 list of enslaved people as John (Christian name John Rose Palmer), age two, negro, Creole, not at work, of good disposition, able and healthy, and valued at £30 (Shore, *In Old St. James*, 106–107). John's birth is noted in the journal along the left margin for the weekly entry of May 31–June 6: "Dorinda delivered of a Male Child Named John on the 1st" (JARD, 1B/26, RHJ, vol. 3, fol. 47b).

53. JARD, 1B/26, RHJ, vol. 3, fol. 72a.

54. At the very beginning of the journal, for the week of March 17–22, 1817, there is a category titled "Doctress & Gardner" (JARD, 1B/26, RHJ, vol. 1, fol. 1). The title "doctress" remains within the listed duties until November 3, 1817 (fol. 26). The following week, the week beginning on November 10, 1817, the category changes to "Doctor & Gardner" (fol. 27). On Monday, March 16, 1818, it changes to "Doctorman" and then back to "Doctor" (fol. 45). In February 1820, "Gardner" is deleted, and only "Doctor" remains for this category (fol. 140). In March 1820 the category changes to "In Hospital and Attendants" (fol. 146). This category remains until the end of the journal in 1832. No specific person is named as the doctress or doctor between 1817 and 1820.

55. As historian Tara Inniss explains, midwifery during slavery was a contested racial, gendered, and classed profession in the British Caribbean. Enslaved and free midwives, as Inniss notes, "received monetary payments for their attendance of enslaved women. Enslaved midwives were one of the few enslaved, female-dominated occupational groups in plantation society to receive cash payments from estate managers. . . . In addition to small sums of money, enslaved midwives were also given non-monetary consideration for their work. It is unclear, however, to what extent enslaved midwives received cash payments exclusively for the unique service they offered" ("'Any Elderly,'" 45). See Paugh, *The Politics of Reproduction*, 122–153, for one example of the politics of midwifery in the Caribbean, with specific references to the midwives at the Newton Plantation in Barbados (primarily between 1770 and 1804). Given Paugh's description and discussion of the midwives at Newton Plantation (including the Afro-Barbadian midwife Doll), it is clear that definite differences existed in terms of the benefits extended to midwives in different circumstances across plantations in the British Empire. Neither Doll's nor Dorinda's experiences should be utilized as exemplary of midwifery on a Caribbean plantation. See Turner, *Contested Bodies*, for a thoughtful and extensive analysis of midwives and the practice of midwifery in Jamaica from the 1780s to the 1830s.

56. For an insightful discussion of childbirth practices and the critical roles of pregnant enslaved women and midwives in these practices and processes, see Turner, *Contested Bodies*, especially chap. 3, "When Workers Become Mothers, Who Works? Motherhood, Labor, and Punishment," 68–111, and chap. 4, "'Buckra Doctor No Do You No Good': Struggles over Maternal Health Care," 112–150.

57. JARD, 1B/26, RHJ, April 22, 1830, vol. 3, fol. 72a. This incident with Dorinda is also briefly mentioned in Vasconcellos, *Slavery*, 35.

58. JARD, 1B/26, RHJ, December 11, 1830, vol. 3, fol. 88b. This sentence ends with the ini-

tials L.L., most likely for Lawrence Lowe, who was overseer at Rose Hall from 1826 to 1831 (and possibly for some months in 1832), before Robert Scott assumed that position. Elizabeth Palmer's baby was born on December 5 and died on December 8. As with the previous examples noted earlier in this chapter, the passing of Elizabeth Palmer's newborn in 1830 (who died within the first nine days of life) remains unrecognized and unnamed in the 1832 slave register.

59. Her two children included in the 1832 clothing allowance list were Othello (fifteen in 1832) and Hope (four in 1832) (Shore, *In Old St. James*, 108–109, 112–113). Another son, Robert, who was born in October 1832, is not on that clothing allowance list; instead, his birth is included in the journal and the 1832 slave register (JARD, 1B/26, RHJ, note regarding Robert's birth, October 26, 1832, vol. 3, fol. 138a; NA Kew, T71/223, fol. 91).

60. JARD, 1B/26, RHJ, note regarding Cecelia's birth (unnamed in journal entry), February 5, 1822, vol. 1, fol. 242b; and JARD, 1B/11/7/66, fol. 74a.

61. JARD, 1B/11/7/66, fol. 74a.

62. JARD, 1B/26, RHJ, note regarding Lydia's birth on May 3, 1824, vol. 2, fol. 47.

63. JARD, 1B/26, RHJ, note regarding death of Juno's child (unnamed in journal entry), January 6, 1826, vol. 2, fol. 134.

64. NA Kew, T71/223, fol. 91.

65. JARD, 1B/26, RHJ, note regarding Susan's death, September 26, 1831, vol. 3, fol. 111b. Her death should also have been included in this 1832 slave register, but she is not included in the death section.

66. NA Kew, T71/218, no folio number noted on document; and JARD, 1B/11/7/100, fol. 215.

67. Shore, *In Old St. James*, 112–113.

68. JARD, 1B/11/7/85, fol. 155a.

69. Shore, *In Old St. James*, 112–113.

70. Henry's birth and death at the age of two are both listed in the same register (NA Kew, T71/218, no folio number noted on document; and JARD, 1B/11/7/100, fol. 215). Henry is classified as negro in the birth section but then reclassified as mulatto in the death section. It is possible that he was misclassified at birth and then correctly classified at the time of his death at two or vice versa.

71. Shore, *In Old St. James*, 112–113.

72. NA Kew, T71/202, fol. 544; and JARD, 1B/11/7/66, fol. 74a.

73. NA Kew, T71/202, fol. 544; and Shore, *In Old St. James*, 110–111.

74. NA Kew, T71/202, fol. 543; and T71/223, fol. 91.

75. NA Kew, T71/202, fol. 544; and Shore, *In Old St. James*, 112–113.

76. NA Kew, T71/202, fol. 542; and Shore, *In Old St. James*, 108–109.

77. JARD, 1B/26, RHJ, JANUary 6, 1819, vol. 1, fol. 85a.

78. Shore, *In Old St. James*, 108–109.

79. NA Kew, T71/202, fol. 544.

80. NA Kew, T71/202, fols. 543, 542.

81. JARD, 1B/26, RHJ, note regarding Doshy's death, November 8, 1823, vol. 2, fol. 21; and JARD, 1B/11/7/85, fol. 155a.

82. NA Kew, T71/218, no fol. number noted on document; and JARD, 1B/11/7/100, fol. 215.

83. A number of entries of the Rose Hall Journal are missing and unreadable (especially due

to the deterioration of the pages) for this time period, so the recording of Exeter's death is not included in the extant pages of the journal.

84. JARD, 1B/26, RHJ, note regarding Rebecca's death, July 15, 1828, vol. 3, fol. 9a, and her death at sixty-three is included in NA Kew, T71/218, no fol. number noted on document; and JARD, 1B/11/7/100, fol. 215.

85. NA Kew, T71/202, fol. 545.

86. JARD, 1B/11/7/85, fol. 155a.

87. Shore, *In Old St. James*, 112–113.

88. Augusta was thirty-eight years old in 1817 and is noted as having died at age fifty-two in 1832 (NA Kew, T71/202, fol. 542; and Shore, *In Old St. James*, 110–111). Augusta was the mother of five children: Ben, son who is seventeen in 1817 and thirty-one in 1832 (NA Kew, T71/202, fol. 542; and Shore, *In Old St. James*, 106–107); Pitt, son who is fourteen in 1817 and twenty-eight in 1832 (NA Kew, T71/202, fol. 542; and Shore, *In Old St. James*, 106–107); Brown, daughter who is eleven in 1817 and twenty-eight in 1832—probably closer to twenty-six in 1832 (NA Kew, T71/202, fol. 545; and Shore, *In Old St. James*, 110–111); Clarinda, daughter who is five in 1817 and nineteen in 1832 (NA Kew, T71/202, fol. 545; and Shore, *In Old St. James*, 112–113); and Oliver, son who is two in 1817 and sixteen in 1832 (NA Kew, T71/202, fol. 542; and Shore, *In Old St. James*, 108–109). Although Augusta and her five children were still alive in 1832, in the 1829 slave register Augusta's granddaughter Charity—Brown's daughter—dies at three months old (NA Kew, T71/218, no fol. number noted on document; and JARD, 1B/11/7/100, fol. 215).

89. African-born Polly was forty in 1817 and then dead at the age of forty-nine. Polly's son Scipio was fifteen in 1817 and twenty-nine in 1832 (NA Kew, T71/202, fol. 542; and Shore, *In Old St. James*, 106–107).

90. African-born Rachel is sixty-two in 1817; however, she died a few years later in 1822 at the age of sixty-six (NA Kew, T71/202, fol. 544). Rachel's death of old age is noted in JARD, 1B/26, RHJ, Monday, June 17, 1822, vol. 1, fol. 261b; and in JARD, 1B/11/7/66, fol. 74a. Her son Peter is eighteen in 1817, and he remained alive at age thirty-two in 1832 (NA Kew, T71/202, fol. 541; and Shore, *In Old St. James*, 106–107).

91. African-born Stella is thirty-two in 1817 (NA Kew, T71/202, fol. 544). The overseer recorded her death in the journal on March 16, 1818, and her death at the age of forty-three is also noted in the 1829 slave register (JARD, 1B/26, RHJ, note regarding Stella Williams's death, May 3, 1829, vol. 3, fol. 45b, in the marginalia; NA Kew, T71/218, no fol. number noted on document; and JARD, 1B/11/7/100, fol. 215). Stella's daughter Flora is twelve years old in 1817 and twenty-six in 1832 (NA Kew, T71/202, fol. 544; and Shore, *In Old St. James*, 110–111).

92. Creole Bessy, also known as Bessy McLaren, was twenty-seven years old in 1832. She is noted as mulatto, and in 1832 she was a washerwoman (Shore, *In Old St. James*, 110–111). She had two sons described as quadroon: Richard/Richard Mabon, who is one in 1823 and nine in 1832 (JARD, 1B/11/7/66, fol. 74a; and Shore, *In Old St. James*, 108–109), and Robert, who is one in 1829 and three in 1832 (NA Kew, T71/218, no fol. number noted on document; JARD, 1B/11/7/100, fol. 215; and Shore, *In Old St. James*, 108–109).

93. Creole Chance was thirty-three years old in 1832 (Shore, *In Old St. James*, 110–111). Her one daughter, Frances, is one in 1820 and twelve in 1832 (JARD, 1B/11/7/40, fol. 160ba; and Shore, *In Old St. James*, 112–113).

94. Creole Cynthia was twenty-five years old in 1832 (Shore, *In Old St. James*, 112–113). Her one daughter, Lizzy, Elizabeth / Elizabeth Chambers, is described as sambo and noted as six months old in the 1826 slave register; Lizzy Elizabeth is noted as six years old in the 1832 list (JARD, 1B/11/7/85, fol. 155a; and Shore, *In Old St. James*, 112–113).

95. Delia was forty-four years old in 1832 (Shore, *In Old St. James*, 110–111). Her son Quaco is thirteen years old in 1817 and twenty-seven in 1832 (NA Kew, T71/202, fol. 542; and Shore, *In Old St. James*, 106–107).

96. Creole Dianna is described as negro and five years old in 1817, and in 1832 she is described as sambo and nineteen years old (NA Kew, T71/202, fol. 545; and Shore, *In Old St. James*, 112–113). Her son James was born in January 1831, and he is noted as one year and five months old in the 1832 list (NA Kew, T71/223, fol. 91).

97. When Hope died in December 1828 at the age of fifty-six, both of her adult children were still alive (Hope's death due to "debility" noted in JARD, 1B/26, RHJ, December 7, 1828, vol. 3, fol. 28b). In fact, they both remained alive in 1832—Juno is forty in 1832, and George is thirty-nine in 1832 (Shore, *In Old St. James*, 106–107, 110–111). Hope, however, also lived to witness two of her daughter Juno's children die between the ages of one and three.

98. Jeany/Jeanie is thirty-four in 1832 (JARD, 1B/26, RHJ, December 7, 1828, vol. 3, fol. 28b; and Shore, *In Old St. James*, 110–111). She was the mother of two young daughters: Bess, two and a half in 1826 and seven in 1832, and Suckey/Suckie, six months old in 1826 and five in 1832 (JARD, 1B/11/7/85, fol. 155a; and Shore, *In Old St. James*, 112–113).

99. Maphe is fifty-nine in 1832 (Shore, *In Old St. James*, 108–109). She was the mother of one daughter, Mary, who is twenty-three in 1817 and thirty-seven in 1832 (NA Kew, T71/202, fol. 544; and Shore, *In Old St. James*, 110–111).

100. Nancy is a fifty-four-year-old field worker in 1832 (Shore, *In Old St. James*, 110–111). She was the mother of three daughters: Kate, twenty-four in 1817 and thirty-eight in 1832 (NA Kew, T71/202, fol. 543; and Shore, *In Old St. James*, 110–111); Frankey/Frankie, eighteen in 1817 and thirty-two in 1832 (NA Kew, T71/202, fol. 544; and Shore, *In Old St. James*, 110–111); and Matilda, eighteen in 1817 and thirty-two in 1832 (NA Kew, T71/202, fol. 543; and Shore, *In Old St. James*, 110–111). Frankey and Matilda may well have been twins; if not twins, they were born quite close in time to each other.

101. Memmy Jun was fourteen in 1817 (NA Kew, T71/202, fol. 544). Isaac's name is not included in the notation in the Rose Hall Journal regarding his birth. The journal entry states, "Mimmy deliver'd of a Male Child" (JARD, 1B/26, RHJ, April 13, 1820, vol. 1, fol. 148). Memmy Jun is also called "Mimmy" in the journal.

102. JARD, 1B/11/7/66, fol. 74a.

103. The journal notes that "Panella delivered of a [missing word—probably "Female"] Chd Nd Daizy" (JARD, 1B/26, RHJ, December 22, 1817, vol. 1, fol. 33). Panella is listed as twenty-three years old in 1817 (NA Kew, T71/202, fol. 544).

104. JARD, 1B/11/7/40, fol. 160ba.

105. Panella's death of consumption noted in JARD, 1B/26, RHJ, June 15, 1822, vol. 1, fol. 260b. For information on Daizy, see Shore, *In Old St. James*, 112–113.

106. See Vasconcellos, *Slavery*, for an extended discussion of different kinship groups and "slave villages" on Jamaican plantations that might have served to assist young enslaved children who had been separated from their biological mothers and extended family networks.

107. JARD, 1B/26, RHJ, note regarding Daphney's death on May 12, 1818, vol. 1, fol. 53.

108. NA Kew, T71/202, fol. 544.

109. Fanny's age recorded in NA Kew, T71/202, fol. 544. Fanny's death of dropsy (or edema) noted in JARD, 1B/26, RHJ, May 5, 1821, vol. 1, fol. 202.

110. Rosannah is listed as thirty in 1817 (NA Kew, T71/202, fol. 544). Her death is recorded in JARD, T71/218, no fol. number noted on document; and JARD, 1B/11/7/100, fol. 215.

111. Mary James is noted as fourteen in 1817 (NA Kew, T71/202, fol. 544). She is listed as twenty-eight in 1832 (Shore, *In Old St. James*, 110–111).

112. NA Kew, T71/202, fol. 544.

113. NA Kew, T71/202, fol. 543; and Shore, *In Old St. James*, 110–111.

114. NA Kew, T71/202, fol. 542; and Shore, *In Old St. James*, 106–107.

115. NA Kew, T71/202, fol. 544; and Shore, *In Old St. James*, 112–113.

116. NA Kew, T71/202, fol. 545; and Shore, *In Old St. James*, 112–113.

117. JARD, 1B/11/7/85, fol. 155a; NA Kew, T71/218, no fol. number noted on document; and JARD, 1B/11/7/100, fol. 215.

118. For works on the particular experiences of enslaved girls and women, including sexual violence, in the Caribbean and in the United States, see, for example, Beckles, *Natural Rebels*; Berry, *Swing the Sickle*; Berry, *The Price*; Bush, *Slave Women*; Camp, *Closer to Freedom*; Cooper Owens, *Medical Bondage*; Fett, *Working Cures*; Fuentes, *Dispossessed Lives*; Glymph, *Out of the House of Bondage*; Mair, *The Rebel Woman* and *A Historical Study*; Millward, *Finding Charity's Folk*; Morgan, *Laboring Women*; Morissey, *Slave Women*; and Turner, *Contested Bodies*. Although focused on the sexual violation and exploitation of enslaved girls and women here, recently scholars have begun to explore more thoughtfully the sexual violation of enslaved boys and men. For two critical books in this area, see Aidoo, *Slavery Unseen*; and Foster, *Rethinking Rufus*.

119. Some attention has been focused on one particular Jamaican enslaver, especially his detailed records of his sexual exploitation and violation of enslaved girls and women. Indeed, one historian tallied the number of sexual acts that this enslaver described in his diaries and how many women were mentioned in these acts, including a calculation regarding the average number of acts of sexual violation by this enslaver in different periods of his life. See Burnard, *Mastery*, 156. A necessary intervention to Burnard's analysis regarding the rapes of enslaved women by Thistlewood has been offered by Vermeulen, "Thomas Thistlewood's."

120. Although the records do not specify the white fathers associated with Sarah Spence's family, it is telling that Sarah's daughter Bessy's surname was McLaren. Robert McLaren was one of the overseers at Rose Hall (and possibly also partly at Palmyra Plantation). From 1803 to June 1808, McLaren submitted the annual crop accounts report for Rose Hall until a new overseer, Thomas Forsyth, was hired in that position. McLaren also submitted the annual crop accounts for Palmyra Plantation in 1821 (JARD, 1B/11/4/56, fol. 41). It is possible that Bessy's father was Robert McLaren. Bessy's son Robert's Christian name was listed as "Lawrence Low." Lawrence Lowe was one of the overseers at Rose Hall Plantation. The invocation of this name may have reflected a biological association between Lawrence Lowe and Robert.

121. Recent works on multiracial people and interracial sex in the British Empire during slavery include Newman, *A Dark Inheritance*; and Livesay, *Children of Uncertain Fortune*.

122. James, *The Book of Night Women*, 156–158. For an especially discerning examination of

this scene, as well as the multifarious layers of Lilith's character, see the recent work of literary scholar Kaiama L. Glover, *A Regarded Self*, 188–217. Although a novel, the venue for *The Book of Night Women* is Montpelier Plantation, an actual sugar plantation in Jamaica also located, like Rose Hall, in the parish of St. James. Marlon James weaves layers of complexities of slavery and sexuality within this novel. Lilith, the protagonist and the character raped in this excerpt from the novel, is not only the child resulting from the rape of her enslaved mother and a white overseer but also engaged in a complicated relationship with another white overseer (for whom she has a daughter after he is killed during a slave revolt). For an excellent historical study of Montpelier Plantation, see Higman, *Montpelier, Jamaica*.

123. Vasconcellos, *Slavery*, 44.

124. Ibid., 44–45. Enslaver Thomas Thistlewood is the usual example, given his documented sexual abuse of enslaved girls and women in Jamaica.

125. For a couple of examples, see Crowley, "Naming Customs"; Higman, "The Slave Family"; Handler and Jacoby, "Slave Names"; Craton, *Searching*; Thornton, "Central African Names"; Burnard, "Slave Naming Patterns"; and Vasconcellos, *Slavery*, 63–67.

126. For a more extensive discussion about Yoruba names, see Babalola and Alaba, *A Dictionary*. Also see Barber, *I Could Speak*.

127. For more on Akan naming practices, see Agyekum, "The Sociolinguistic."

128. The selection of the eighth day for Yoruba naming ceremonies is often connected partially to Islamic influences on Yoruba cultural practices. It is important to note that there are also some Yoruba groups that have naming ceremonies on the sixth day after the baby's birth. Depending on whether twins are fraternal or identical, naming ceremonies for twins may also occur on the seventh, eighth, or ninth day after birth.

129. For a detailed discussion of some of the historical and linguistic elements of names of enslaved people in Jamaica focusing on Mona and Papine Estates, see West, "Slave Names Memorialized."

130. See Agyekum, "The Sociolinguistic," 214.

131. NA Kew, T71/202, fol. 542.

132. JARD, 1B/26, RHJ, October 30, 1824, vol. 2, fol. 73.

133. JARD, 1B/11/7/85, fol. 155a.

134. Miranda's name is spelled Maranda in this list (Shore, *In Old St. James*, 110–111).

135. Elder Cecelia was also described as the mother of Liddy (listed as twenty-five in 1817 and dead in 1823 at age thirty), Smith (listed as twenty-three in 1817 and thirty-seven in 1832), Harry (listed as twenty-one in 1817 and thirty-five in 1832), and grandmother of Pastora (Liddy's daughter listed as eleven in 1817 and twenty-five in 1832), grandmother of North (Liddy's son listed as six in 1817 and twenty in 1832), Parish/Paris (Liddy's son listed as four in 1817 and dead in 1823 at age four).

136. JARD, 1B/26, RHJ, February 5, 1822, vol. 1, fol. 242b.

137. JARD, 1B/11/7/66, fol. 74a.

138. JARD, T71/218, no fol. number noted on document; and JARD, 1B/11/7/100, fol. 215.

139. JARD, 1B/26, RHJ, December 7, 1828, vol. 3, fol. 28b.

140. See Vasconcellos, *Slavery*, for more on the range of duties of the "children's gang" (30–33).

141. JARD, 1B/26, RHJ, May 3, 1824, vol. 2, fol. 47.

142. JARD, 1B/26, RHJ, January 6, 1826, vol. 2, fol. 134.

143. JARD, 1B/26, RHJ, December 8, 1818, vol. 1, fol. 81.

144. JARD, 1B/26, RHJ, May 11, 1829, vol. 3, fol. 46a.

145. JARD, 1B/26, RHJ, March 6, 1832, vol. 3, fol. 118b.

146. JARD, 1B/11/7/40, fol. 160ba.

147. JARD, 1B/26, RHJ, April 13, 1820, vol. 1, fol. 148.

148. JARD, 1B/26, RHJ, October 28, 1828, vol. 3, fol. 23a. The word "poisonous" is blurred and misspelled in the journal, and the exact name of the fish may have been included but was not legible.

149. In the 1829 slave register, Patrick is listed as dead at the age of fifty-six (JARD, T71/218, no fol. number noted on document; and JARD, 1B/11/7/100, fol. 215).

150. JARD, 1B/26, RHJ, September 8, 1818, vol. 1, fol. 69.

151. Although I have emphasized naming at Rose Hall as a process primarily involving enslaved people, there may have been instances of white denizens naming enslaved people or influencing the naming processes at Rose Hall as an extension and demonstration of their authority, power, and entitlement. The overseers note, in the margin, that on June 1, 1829, Dorinda gave birth to a son (JARD, 1B/26, RHJ, June 1, 1829, vol. 3, fol. 47b). This son is later identified in the 1829 slave register as John. In the 1832 clothing allowance list, John's Christian name is noted as John Rose Palmer. As resident enslaver John Rose Palmer passed in 1827, this child was probably given this name in memory of him. However, it is entirely unclear whether Dorinda or other enslaved members of the Rose Hall community decided on that name or whether that honor was realized without any particular consideration of Dorinda, John's father, or any other family members. As both Dorinda and John are identified as negro in the records and as John Rose Palmer passed before John was conceived, John Rose Palmer was certainly not the biological father of John. However, the Christian name of Bessy/Betsy's son Robert may offer additional information regarding his paternity. Bessy/Betsy, also noted as Betsy McLaren in the records, is described as a thirteen-year-old mulatto in the 1817 slave register and also in the 1832 clothing allowance list as twenty-seven years old with the primary duty of a washerwoman. She was the daughter of Sarah (often referred to as Sambo Sarah in the journal). Bessy/Betsy's listed children at Rose Hall are Richard Mabon (listed as a one-year-old quadroon in the 1823 slave register and nine in the Old St. James list in 1832) and Robert (listed as one in the 1829 slave register and three in the Old St. James list in 1832). Richard's primary duty in 1832 is listed as "overseer's house," and due to his age, Richard is "not at work." In the *Old St. James* list of 1832, Robert's Christian name is noted as being "Lawrence Low." Given that Robert was identified as a quadroon and with this Christian name, it is certainly feasible that his father was one of Rose Hall's white overseers, Lawrence Lowe.

CHAPTER 3. "Till Shell Blow"

1. Senior, *Shell*, 51–52. In her "Author's Note," Jamaican writer Olive Senior states that she wanted to complete this book "by 2007, the 200th anniversary of the abolition of the slave trade by Britain." She highlights that the "huge labour force required by the sugar cane plantations was the driving force behind the slave trade by which millions of Africans were captured and brought in chains to forced labour across the sea.... The sugar plant itself is a hard shell

imprisoning the gold within. But that shell has to be beaten and crushed to release its sweet juice, the first step in making sugar, a chilling metaphor for the way millions of human beings were beaten and crushed in order to produce it" (ibid., 95).

2. The annual crop accounts for Rose Hall delineate in columns the specific number of hogsheads and tierces of sugar, as well as puncheons and gallons of rum produced at Rose Hall (sometimes listed for part of the year, usually from the last day of December to the beginning of June or for an entire year). For the period from January to June 1819, the crop accounts include the specific persons associated with receiving respective quantities of sugar and rum (and their location as Bristol). The crop accounts also include the amount of sugar and rum "Sold in the Country" and "Reserved for Estates Use." See, for example, JARD, 1B/11/4/55, fol. 152. In the years immediately before abolition and during the four-year apprenticeship period between 1834 and 1838, the annual crop accounts for Rose Hall Plantation specify the names of ships, the names of the masters of ships, and the names of the consignees. See, for example, JARD, 1B/11/4/71, fol. 25.

3. As noted previously, even though there is no extant plan or map of Rose Hall Estate before abolition, a survey of the Rose Hall Estate was conducted by Richard Wilson in 1838. See Higman, *Jamaica Surveyed*, 234–236.

4. There were also instances when an enslaved person at Rose Hall was hired out to another plantation. The Rose Hall Journal infrequently includes the category "Hired off the estate" and "Hired from the estate." For example, from the last few months in 1823 and continuing into 1824, one carpenter from Rose Hall was employed at another plantation for approximately one year (JARD, 1B/26, RHJ, week of July 26, 1824, vol. 2, fol. 21, to the week of July 16, 1825, vol. 2, fol. 109a). The journal also includes references to enslaved carpenters from Rose Hall working at the nearby Palmyra Plantation on specific jobs, as Palmyra was also owned by John Palmer (and later John Rose Palmer).

5. The first mention in the journal of "Mr. Ridley's Negroes" appears the week of April 28 to May 3, 1817 (JARD, 1B/26, RHJ, vol. 1, fol. 3). These are "hired negroes" who work at Rose Hall (and possibly other plantations) during different periods of the harvesting season. These hired enslaved people worked every day of the week. So during the periods when enslaved people at Rose Hall were granted a Friday or Saturday to work in their provision grounds (usually noted as "Negroes Taking Day" or "Negroes in Their Grounds"), hired negroes are noted as engaged in the usual work on those days. Mr. Ridley is mentioned (though not consistently) as Mr. Ridley, Esq., and Joseph Ridley. The Legacies of British Slave-Ownership database includes fairly basic information for him. He is noted as having married Lydia Ridley (née Hine) on May 23, 1816 ("Joseph Ridley"). In the Return of Givings-In for the March quarter, 1832, in the *Jamaica Almanac*, the listing is for the heirs of Lydia Ridley, probably indicating that at that time both Joseph Ridley and his spouse, Lydia Ridley, had passed, and the number of enslaved people associated with the family at Mount Pleasant is listed as sixteen (Jamaican Family Search Genealogy, "1833 Jamaica Almanac").

6. Vasconcellos, *Slavery*, 30.

7. Ibid., 32.

8. Turner, *Contested Bodies*, 73. A number of scholars have highlighted the significant presence of enslaved women as field workers on sugarcane plantations in Jamaica and throughout the Caribbean. See, for example, Richard Dunn's discussion of enslaved women's duties at Mes-

opotamia sugar plantation in the Westmoreland Parish of Jamaica (*A Tale of Two Plantations*, chap. 4, "'Dreadful Idlers' in the Mesopotamia Cane Fields," 131–180). Also see Bush, *Slave Women*; and Moitt, *Women and Slavery*.

9. For a good summary of enslaved children's experiences in the Anglophone Caribbean, see Teelucksingh, "The 'Invisible Child.'" Also see Vasconcellos, *Slavery*; and Sasha Turner's chapter regarding enslaved childhood on Jamaican plantations, "Raising Hardworking Adults: Labor, Punishment, and the Slave Childhood," in *Contested Bodies*, 211–248.

10. Although "skilled labor" at plantations often translated to duties and positions held by men, Dorinda's midwifery abilities involved "skilled labor." As Darlene Clark Hine and Kathleen Thompson assert, "Almost all historians make a distinction between 'skilled' work and the sort of work that women did—nursing, midwifing, cooking, spinning, weaving, seamstressing. The fact is that these are clearly forms of skilled labor. We may lose sight of this fact because so many women acquired these skills, but it is a very important one" (*A Shining Thread*, 76–77).

11. One enslaved man referred to as "Smith" in the slave register of 1817 and in the Rose Hall Journal is also specifically noted in the clothing allowance list in 1832 as the only blacksmith at Rose Hall. It is unclear whether he was frequently called "Smith" due to his work as the blacksmith but also had other names that were not associated with his job at Rose Hall at all (NA Kew, T71/202, fol. 541; and Shore, *In Old St. James*, 106–107).

12. As Sasha Turner explains, enslaved boys were often selected by planters for "highly disciplined and skilled roles. Tending cattle and mules was a specialized position reserved for males." Cattleboys and muleboys were responsible for leading and yoking cattle and riding mules in the process of carrying and transporting sugarcane, manure, and other items on the plantation. They were also charged with controlling cattle and mules in order to keep these animals in designated areas so that they could not ruin canefields or provision grounds. Turner, *Contested Bodies*, 231.

13. As Sasha Turner describes in her book, some enslaved women nursed other enslaved women's babies due to their beliefs about the milk of mothers being compromised for the first few days after childbirth (ibid., 121–122).

14. Vasconcellos, *Slavery*, 17. Also see Turner, *Contested Bodies*.

15. Ibid.

16. Turner, *Contested Bodies*.

17. JARD, 1B/26, RHJ, week of March 17, 1817, vol. 1, fol. 1.

18. JARD, 1B/26, RHJ, week of November 3, 1817, vol. 1, fol. 26.

19. JARD, 1B/26, RHJ, week of November 10, 1817, vol. 1, fol. 27.

20. JARD, 1B/26, RHJ, week of March 16, 1818, vol. 1, fol. 45.

21. JARD, 1B/26, RHJ, week of November 9, 1818, vol. 1, fol. 78.

22. JARD, 1B/26, RHJ, week of March 20, 1818, vol. 1, fol. 145.

23. JARD, 1B/26, RHJ, beginning the week of August 26, 1832, and ending the week of November 4, 1832, vol. 3, fols. 130–140.

24. Vasconcellos, *Slavery*, 29. See also Turner, *Contested Bodies*.

25. See Turner, *Contested Bodies*; and Vasconcellos, *Slavery*.

26. Turner, *Contested Bodies*, 113. Also see Paugh, *The Politics of Reproduction*.

27. Turner, *Contested Bodies*, 113.

28. Ibid., author's emphasis. See also Vasconcellos, *Slavery*.

29. For an examination of midwives at the Newton Plantation in Barbados, see Paugh, *The Politics of Reproduction*, 122–153. In Paugh's work she discusses some of the rights and responsibilities granted to white midwives in early modern England. She also focuses on the only Afro-Barbadian midwife, Doll, and the white (primarily "poor and middling") midwives at the Newton Plantation in order to explore some of the interracial power dynamics and struggles between white and Afro-Barbadian midwives and other members of the managerial staff at the Newton Plantation. As Paugh notes, Doll received payment for her midwifery services; however, she was not remunerated in the same way the white midwives at Newton Planation were. Doll either received payment in currency that was less than half of what white midwives received or she received payment in rum. It is unclear whether the payment in rum was her preference in all cases (ibid., 124–126).

30. NA Kew, T71/218, no fol. number noted on document; and JARD, 1B/11/7/100, fol. 215.

31. JARD, 1B/26, RHJ, note on Jane's birth, January 23, 1831, vol. 3, fol. 93a; and Shore, *In Old St. James*, 112.

32. As previously stated, Lawrence Lowe was overseer at Rose Hall from 1826 to 1831 (and probably for some months in 1832). Bessy McLaren's son Richard Mabon is listed as at the overseer's house, that is, Lawrence Lowe's house. In addition, her youngest son, Robert, three years old at the time of the 1832 clothing allowance, was given the Christian name "Lawrence Low." It is possible that Robert was given this Christian name reflecting paternity and the name of his father—overseer Lawrence Lowe.

33. As mentioned earlier, Robert McLaren was one of the overseers at Rose Hall between 1803 and 1808. In 1821 he was working at the neighboring Palmyra Plantation (owned by John Palmer and then passed on to John Rose Palmer), as he submitted and signed the annual crop accounts report for Palmyra Plantation that year (JARD, 1B/11/4/56, Palmyra Estate, Crop Accounts, fol. 41, January 1820–December 1820).

34. For one probing analysis of the representations of forms of disability in Jamaican and Barbadian runaway slave advertisements between 1718 and 1815, see Hunt-Kennedy, "'Had His Nose Cropt.'" Also see Hunt-Kennedy, *Between Fitness and Death*.

35. Senior, *Shell*, 34.

36. Individual and group stories of runaway slaves are often highlighted in the published narratives of previously enslaved people in the United States (e.g., Harriet Tubman, Frederick Douglass, Harriet Jacobs, Henry Bibb, Henry Box Brown, William Wells Brown, and William and Ellen Craft). The Underground Railroad has also attracted a great deal of attention; the 2019 film *Harriet* reignited interest in this topic in the United States and elsewhere. Runaway attempts and revolts, as well as Maroon societies in the Caribbean and quilombos in Brazil during slavery and in the contemporary era, have been of particular interest to scholars. For critical works published over the past several decades, see James, *The Black Jacobins*; Price, *Maroon Societies*; Gaspar, *Bondmen and Rebels*; Heuman, *Out of the House of Bondage*; Reis, *Slave Rebellion in Brazil*; Franklin and Schweninger, *Runaway Slaves*; Dubois, *A Colony of Citizens*; Dubois, *Avengers of the New World*; Thompson, *Flight to Freedom*; Geggus, *Haitian Revolution Studies*; Geggus, *The Haitian Revolution*; Diouf, *Slavery's Exiles*; Scott, *The Common Wind*; Brown, *Tacky's Revolt*; and Kars, *Blood on the River*. Also, in June 2018, the *William and Mary Quarterly* published its inaugural born-digital article by historian Simon P. Newman; it was entitled "Hidden in Plain Sight: Escaped Slaves in Late Eighteenth- and Early Nineteenth-

Century Jamaica." A published forum on this article appeared in the January 2019 issue of the *William and Mary Quarterly*, which included review essays by invited scholars and a formal response from Newman to these essays.

37. See, for example, Cornell University's Freedom on the Move project; the Marronnage in Saint-Domingue project; the University of Southern Mississippi's Documenting Runaway Slaves (DRS) PROJect; and the University of Glasgow's Runaway Slaves in Britain project.

38. For a first-person enslaved person's account of experiences in a penal institution (specifically, workhouses in Jamaica), see Williams, *A Narrative of Events*. For a critical, comprehensive historical analysis of penal institutions in Jamaica, see Paton, *No Bond*.

39. The following information is from JARD, 1B/26, RHJ. William's name is included in the "Runaways" column (Wednesday, April 25, 1821, vol. 1, fol. 201). The overseer noted, "Cooper William brought home" (Saturday, April 28, 1821, vol. 1, fol. 201). In the next notation about him running away, he is described as "Cooper William" (Monday, April 30, 1821, vol. 1, fol. 202). His position is again mentioned in the journal with the statement "Cooper William come home" (Monday, May 21, 1821, vol. 1, fol. 205).

40. Entry regarding Adonis running away (JARD, 1B/26, RHJ, Saturday, May 29, 1830, vol. 3, fol. 74). Adonis is described as a twenty-five-year-old Creole in 1817 (NA Kew, T71/202, fol. 540).

41. In the 1832 clothing allowance list, Adonis is noted as a thirty-nine-year-old Creole whose position was "Head Cooper" and who suffered from the disease yaws (Shore, *In Old St. James*, 106–107).

42. JARD, 1B/26, RHJ, Friday, July 10, 1829, vol. 3, fol. 50.

43. Vasconcellos, *Slavery*, 33.

44. JARD, 1B/26, RHJ, Thursday, November 4, 1830, vol. 3, fol. 85.

45. JARD, 1B/26, RHJ, Tuesday, September 1, 1818, vol. 1, fol. 68.

46. Ibid.

47. JARD, 1B/26, RHJ, Monday, January 5, 1829, vol. 3, fol. 36.

48. JARD, 1B/26, RHJ, Sunday, March 27, 1831–Sunday, April 3, 1831, vol. 3, fol. 97.

49. For one critical examination of slavery and notions of disabilities in the British Caribbean, see Hunt-Kennedy, *Between Fitness and Death*.

50. The following information is from JARD, 1B/26, RHJ. Entry regarding Mark running away (Thursday, October 15, 1818, vol. 1, fol. 74). Mark's return date is not mentioned; however, he was back by Monday, October 26, 1818, as he is not included in the named runaways on that date (vol. 1, fol. 76). Entry regarding March running away at the age of sixty-two (Sunday, February 1, 1829, vol. 3, fol. 39). Three months later, on Tuesday, May 5, 1829, the overseer noted that March was "Brot home" (Tuesday, May 5, 1829, vol. 3, fol. 45).

51. For example, the journal notes July running away on February 6, 1831, being "caught" on February 29, 1831, and then "went away next day" (JARD, 1B/26, RHJ, Sunday, March 27, 1831–Sunday, April 3, 1831, vol. 3, fol. 97).

52. See JARD, 1B/26, RHJ: entries regarding Mark's runaway attempts appear on Monday, April 24, 1820, vol. 1, fol. 150 (back by May 1, 1820, vol. 1, fol. 151); May 29, 1820, vol. 1, fol. 155 (listed as one of the runaways, though unclear what specific date he ran away, back by June 19, 1820, vol. 1, fol. 158); June 26, 1820, vol. 1, fol. 157 (back by Monday, July, 31, 1820, vol. 1, fol. 163); Tuesday, August 7, 1821, vol. 1, fol. 216 ("brought home" on Thursday, August 16, 1821, vol. 1,

fol. 217); Monday, September 10, 1821, vol. 1, fol. 221 (back by Monday, September 17, 1821, vol. 1, fol. 222); Wednesday, January 30, 1822, vol. 1, fol. 241 ("brought home" on Thursday, March 21, 1822, vol. 1, fol. 248); Tuesday, May 15, 1822, vol. 1, fol. 256 ("brought home" on Monday, June 10, 1822, vol. 1, fol. 260); Tuesday, July 29, 1823, vol. 2, fol. 8 ("Brt home" on Friday, August 1, 1823, vol. 2, fol. 8); Monday, August 4, 1823, vol. 2, fol. 9 ("Brot home" on Friday, August 8, 1823, vol. 2, fol. 9); Monday, September 25, 1826, vol. 2, fol. 169 (back by Monday, October 30, 1826, vol. 2, fol. 174); and Sunday, April 15, 1832, vol. 3, fol. 121. Mark remains listed as a "runaway" on the 1832 clothing allowance list (Shore, *In Old St. James*, 106–107). This runaway attempt in April 1832 might have concluded with his successful attempt to free himself.

53. On Monday, March 5, 1821, both Bolton and Pitt are noted as runaways (JARD, 1B/26, RHJ, March 5, 1821, vol. 1, fol. 194). A month later, on Tuesday, April 10, 1821, Bolton was "brought home" (April 10, 1821, vol. 1, fol. 199).

54. This change in the "Runaways" columns to "Runaways and Looking for dº" appears the week of December 5, 1825 (JARD, 1B/26, RHJ, vol. 2, fol. 130a). "Dº" is an abbreviation for "ditto."

55. The week of December 12, 1825, the overseers created the separate category of "Looking for Runaways" (JARD, 1B/26, RHJ, December 12, 1825, vol. 2, fol. 130a). For the next few months, several pages are badly weathered and are unreadable. In February 1826, this separate column still appears; however, in July 1826, it is no longer included (the week of July 26, 1826, vol. 2, fol. 169). During this time, a different overseer began to use the term "Absentees" instead of "Runaways."

56. The record of March's runaway attempts begins in 1820 (JARD, 1B/26, RHJ, Monday, April 24, 1820, vol. 1, fol. 150 [back by Monday, July 31, 1820, vol. 1, fol. 163] and Sunday, February 1, 1829, vol. 3, fol. 39 ["Brot home" on Tuesday, May 5, 1829, vol. 3, fol. 45]).

57. Washington is named in the "Runaways" column as "Washenton" (JARD, 1B/26, RHJ, Monday, April 8, 1822, vol. 1, fol. 251). Due to the weathered condition of this section of the journal, most of the weekly entries in April 1822 are unreadable or blank. However, on May 6, 1822, there are no runaways listed, so Washington had returned or had been brought back to Rose Hall by that time (Monday, May 6, 1822, vol. 1, fol. 255).

58. Joe's runaway attempt (JARD, 1B/26, RHJ, Sunday, June 10, 1832, vol. 3, fol. 125 [not noted when Joe returned]).

59. Shemoon's runaway attempt (JARD, 1B/26, RHJ, March 15, 1822, vol. 1, fol. 247 [returned, Thursday, March 28, 1822, vol. 1, fol. 249]).

60. JARD, 1B/26, RHJ, Monday, August 21, 1826, vol. 2, fol. 164.

61. Anthony was eleven years old when overseers recorded his first runaway attempt (JARD, 1B/26, RHJ, Monday, September 17, 1821, vol. 1, fol. 222 ["Antony brought home," Friday, September 21, 1821, vol. 1, fol. 222]). Anthony absconded six months later (Wednesday, March 5, 1822, vol. 1, fol. 246). Antony/Anthony's date of return is not noted in the journal. However, given that he is listed as a runaway that week but not listed as such on Monday, March 11, 1822, he probably returned on March 9 or 10. Three months later, Anthony, Hercules, and Pitt are listed as runaways (Wednesday, June 5, 1822, vol. 1, fol. 259 ["Anthony brought home," Tuesday, June 11, 1822, vol. 1, fol. 260]).

62. Ben and Pitt would have returned by Friday, August 25, 1826, given the changing num-

ber of runaways over the course of that week and the named runaways at that time (JARD, 1B/26, RHJ, the week of August 21, 1826, vol. 2, fol. 164).

63. JARD, 1B/26, RHJ, Monday, September 18, 1826, vol. 2, fol. 168.

64. JARD, 1B/26, RHJ, Wednesday, June 5, 1822, vol. 1, fol. 259.

65. "Anthony Absent from work since the 16th Inst.," note at the bottom of the "Daily Occurrences" page for the week of July 14, 1828 (JARD, 1B/26, RHJ, vol. 3, fol. 9 ["Anthony Brot home this day," Thursday, August 7, 1828, vol. 3, fol. 12]); "Anthony and Gloster absconded on the 24th April," note at the bottom of the "Daily Occurrences" page for the week of April 19, 1829 (vol. 3, fol. 44 ["Anthony Brot home on the 24th June," note at the bottom of the "Daily Occurrences" page for the week of June 22, 1829, vol. 3, fol. 49]); "Anthony absconded on the 17th Inst.," note at the bottom of the "Daily Occurrences" page for the week of July 12, 1829 (vol. 3, fol. 50 [Anthony's date of return is not noted in the journal]).

66. Shore, *In Old St. James*, 108–109.

67. It is also possible that the cattleboys' access to livestock provided opportunities for another manifestation of resistance. In the journal, overseers reported the death of cattle at Rose Hall (often referring to the cows by specific names). This information is included in the format overseers utilized to report the death of enslaved people, with the one difference being that the deaths of animals are not noted in the marginalia. In a similar vein, the *Royal Gazette* newspaper of Kingston often combines its section(s) listing "runaways and strays"; the strays include a range of animals (horses, mules, and cows). See, for example, *Royal Gazette*, January 20–27, 1821, 8. In the final years leading up to abolition, overseers reported particular incidents of livestock being poisoned. The poison frequently identified with these incidents was the poisonous plant nightshade (*Atropa belladonna*). In May 1830 the overseer recorded that "Patrice Cow died this day from eating Nightshade" (JARD, 1B/26, RHJ, Friday, May 7, 1830, vol. 3, fol. 73a). The overseer noted on July 1, 1830: "This evening died Margaret cow from a supposition of poison but in a [word unclear] the body it was found she was choked with a [two words unclear]" (Thursday, July 1, 1830, vol. 3, fol. 77a). No additional comments were included regarding the circumstances of her choking. Three months later, at the beginning of October 1830, the overseer recorded, "[Name unclear] Steer died of poison" (with a total of 138 livestock remaining) (Friday, October 8, 1830, vol. 3, fol. 83a). At the end of October, a few weeks later, the overseer indicated that another "Steer died from the effects of Poison," with the livestock number changed to 137 (bottom of page for the week of October 25, 1830, vol. 3, fol. 84). A year later, in the month of September alone, the overseers reported four separate instances of the death of four steers. Three of the four died due to their ingestion of nightshade (Friday, September 2, 1831, Wednesday, September 7, 1831, and Tuesday, September 20, 1831, vol. 3, fols. 109a, 109b, and 111b). The fourth steer reportedly died due to "purging" (Sunday, September 18, 1831, vol. 3, fol. 110b). In October 1831, a steer named Peter died from an unreadable reason (though not due to poison) (Thursday, October 27, 1831, vol. 3, fol. 113b). In 1832 the overseer recorded two steers poisoned by "eating nightshade" in June and July (Tuesday, June 19, 1832, vol. 3, fol. 126a, and Tuesday, July 3, 1832, vol. 3, fol. 127a). In October 1832, the overseer noted (in a newly created box at the bottom of the weekly entry entitled "Increase and Decrease of Stock"), "Hannah a breeding Cow died by eating Nightshead [*sic*]" (Monday, October 1, 1832, vol. 3, fol. 135a). Given the frequency and timing of these poisonings, it is certainly possible that

the cattleboys either fed the nightshade to the cows or purposefully allowed the cows to ingest parts of the plant while grazing. Other enslaved people who were not cattleboys also could have poisoned the cows with nightshade.

68. Scott is listed as running away in JARD, 1B/26, RHJ, Thursday, March 15, 1821, vol. 1, fol. 195, and then he was "brought home from the Spring" (Monday, April 23, 1821, vol. 1, fol. 201). The exact departure date of his second runaway attempt in April or May 1822 is not included in a readable section of the journal. However, Scott is listed in the "Runaways" column for Monday, May 20, 1822, vol. 1, fol. 257. His third runaway attempt is noted for Monday, May 26, 1823, vol. 2, fol. 1. In June 1823, it is noted "Scott Brot home" (Wednesday, June 4, 1823, vol. 2, fol. 2).

69. Scott's death is noted in JARD, 1B/26, RHJ, July 26, 1823, vol. 2, fol. 7b. The 1826 slave register also records his death at the age of forty-eight (JARD, 1B/11/7/85, fol. 155a).

70. NA Kew, T71/202, fols. 540 and 543, for Charlie/Charley and Beck, respectively.

71. JARD, 1B/26, RHJ, Sunday, February 15, 1829, vol. 3, fol. 39.

72. JARD, 1B/26, RHJ, Tuesday, February 24, 1829, vol. 3, fol. 40.

73. Beck's death is noted in JARD, 1B/26, RHJ, Friday, December 4, 1829, vol. 3, fol. 60. The 1832 slave register also records her death at the age of fifty-two (NA Kew, T71/223, fol. 91).

74. JARD, 1B/26, RHJ, Monday, April 21, 1817, vol. 1, fol. 2 (not sure of the exact date Charley ran away, but he is noted as "still away" and "brought home" [Monday, May 12, 1817, vol. 1, fol. 4]); Monday, February 9, 1818, vol. 1, fol. 40 ("Charley retd," Monday, May 25, 1818, vol. 1, fol. 55); Monday, February 21, 1820, vol. 1, fol. 141 ("Charley brought home," Wednesday, April 19, 1820, vol. 1, fol. 149); Tuesday, May 8, 1821, vol. 1, fol. 203 ("Charley came home," Wednesday, May 9, 1821, vol. 1, fol. 203); and Friday, May 24, 1822 vol. 1, fol. 257—"Charley brought home" (not stated when he ran away).

75. JARD, 1B/26, RHJ, Monday, August 1, 1825, vol. 2, fol. 112.

76. JARD, 1B/26, RHJ, Wednesday, November 9, 1825, vol. 2, fol. 126. For more information on colonial inquests for enslaved people in Jamaica, see Brown, *Reaper's Garden*, 77–81.

77. NA Kew, T71/202, fol. 540.

78. JARD, 1B/26, RHJ, Monday, January 12, 1818, vol. 1, fol. 36. There is no record of the date that Caesar initially ran away.

79. JARD, 1B/26, RHJ, Tuesday, January 13, 1818, vol. 1, fol. 36.

80. JARD, 1B/26, RHJ, Monday, June 8, 1818, vol. 1, fol. 57.

81. JARD, 1B/26, RHJ, Monday, July 6, 1818, vol. 1, fol. 61.

82. JARD, 1B/26, RHJ, Tuesday, July 21, 1818, vol. 1, fol. 63. Caesar's passing at the age of twenty-five is also listed in the slave register of 1820.

83. The overseer noted that Elizabeth Palmer (a.k.a. Susannah Johnston) in a "State of Pregnancy absconded" (JARD, 1B/26, RHJ, Tuesday, July 27, 1830, vol. 3, fol. 79). It is unclear when Elizabeth Palmer returned to Rose Hall. However, on Monday, August 16, 1830, the overseer noted again, "Elizabeth Palmer (pregnant) absconded" (Monday, August 16, 1830, vol. 3, fol. 80). Elizabeth Palmer's return to Rose Hall is noted on October 24, 1830 (Sunday, October 24, 1830, vol. 3, fol. 84).

84. JARD, 1B/26, RHJ, week of December 5, 1830, vol. 3, fol. 88b. As discussed in the previous chapter, Dorinda was implicated in this baby's death (due to Dorinda's "neglect" of her duties as midwife).

85. JARD, 1B/26, RHJ, Saturday, July 31, 1830, vol. 3, fol. 79.

86. The overseer noted that Juno absconded in November 1826 (JARD, 1B/26, RHJ, Monday, November 6, 1826, vol. 2, fol. 175 [date of her return not mentioned in extant entries]). Juno also ran away in August 1829 (Monday, August 10, 1829, vol. 3, fol. 52 [date of return not noted in extant entries]).

87. JARD, 1B/26, RHJ, Sunday, December 10, 1826, vol. 2, fol. 180.

88. NA Kew, T71/218, no fol. number noted on document; and Slave Register of 1829, 1B/11/7/100, fol. 215.

89. JARD, 1B/26, RHJ, Thursday, July 16, 1829, vol. 3, fol. 50.

90. JARD, 1B/26, RHJ, Tuesday, March 30, 1830, vol. 3, fol. 70.

91. JARD, 1B/26, RHJ, Thursday, April 1, 1830, vol. 3, fol. 70.

92. The overseer noted that "Dorrinda the midwife being orderd to the field for general neglect in the performance of her duty thot proper to abscond" (JARD, 1B/26, RHJ, Wednesday, April 21, 1830, vol. 3, fol. 72). Dorinda returned to Rose Hall the following evening (Thursday, April 22, 1830, vol. 3, fol. 72).

93. JARD, 1B/26, RHJ, Saturday, May 29, 1830, vol. 3, fol. 74.

94. Cynthia ran away at least two other times. The overseer stated that Cynthia was brought home on February 24, 1829; however, the specific date she ran away is not recorded (JARD, 1B/26, RHJ, Tuesday, February 24, 1829, vol. 3, fol. 40). And her third recorded runaway attempt occurred less than a month after she had run away to avoid punishment for late rising (Friday, June 18, 1830, vol. 3, fol. 76). Four days later Cynthia was "brot home" (Tuesday, June 22, 1830, vol. 3, fol. 76).

95. JARD, 1B/26, RHJ, Tuesday, May 25, 1830, vol. 3, fol. 74.

96. JARD, 1B/26, RHJ, Thursday, May 27, 1830, vol. 3, fol. 74.

97. JARD, 1B/26, RHJ, Thursday, June 10, 1830, vol. 3, fol. 75.

98. The overseers recorded James's runaway attempt in August 1829 (JARD, 1B/26, RHJ, Tuesday, August 11, 1829, vol. 3, fol. 52), though it is possible that additional attempts were mentioned in unreadable damaged sections of the journal. James was brought home two days later (Thursday, August 13, 1829, vol. 2, fol. 52). His second recorded attempt on June 10, 1830, was the "late rising" incident. After James "returned home" on June 12, 1830, he "absconded without cause" on June 14, 1830. Hercules also absconded on the same day (Monday, June 14, 1830, vol. 3, fol. 76). James was "brot home" a week later (Monday, June 21, 1830, vol. 3, fol. 76). His final runaway attempt occurred in March 1832 (Tuesday, March 20, 1832, vol. 3, fol. 119). James was still on the run during the clothing allowance distribution in 1832. His final attempt may have ended successfully with his self-emancipation.

99. The journal indicates that Doshey ran away at least sixteen times in five years: JARD, 1B/26, RHJ, Monday, April 21, 1817, vol. 1, fol. 2 ("brought home" on Tuesday, April 22, 1817, vol. 1, fol. 2); Monday, September 15, 1817, vol. 1, fol. 19 (back by Monday, September 22, 1817, vol. 1, fol. 20); Monday, October 6, 1817, vol. 1, fol. 22 ("returned" on Monday, October 13, 1817, vol. 1, fol. 23); Tuesday, April 21, 1818, vol. 1, fol. 50 ("brought home" on Saturday, April 25, 1818, vol. 1, fol. 50); Monday, May 29, 1820, vol. 1, fol. 155 (back by Monday, June 5, 1820, vol. 1, fol. 156); Monday, August 28, 1820, vol. 1, fol. 167 ("come home" on Thursday, August 31, 1820, vol. 1, fol. 167); Monday, January 15, 1821, vol. 1, fol. 187 ("brought home" on Wednesday, February 7, 1821, vol. 1, fol. 190); Thursday, April 5, 1821, vol. 1, fol. 198 (back by Monday, April 9, 1821); Friday, April 27, 1821, vol. 1, fol. 201 (not noted when she returned or was brought back);

Monday, July 16, 1821, vol. 1, fol. 213 ("brought home" on Friday, July 20, 1821, vol. 1, fol. 213); Wednesday, October 10, 1821, vol. 1, fol. 225 ("brot home" on Saturday, October 13, 1821, vol. 1, fol. 225); Monday, December 10, 1821, vol. 1, fol. 234 (back by Monday, December 24, 1821, vol. 1, fol. 236); Monday, January 7, 1822, vol. 1, fol. 238 (and probably returned that day or soon after, as she was not recorded as a runaway in any of the columns that week until January 11, 1822); Friday, January 11, 1822, vol. 1, fol. 238 (back by Monday, January 14, 1821); Wednesday, April 3, 1822, vol. 1, fol. 250 ("brought home" on Thursday, April 4, 1822, vol. 1, fol. 250); and Monday, June 17, 1822, vol. 1, fol. 261—"Doshey Ranaway" (not noted when she returned).

100. When Doshey ran away on Friday, January 11, 1822, given that no runaways are recorded on Monday, January 14, 1822, she probably returned to Rose Hall over the weekend (JARD, 1B/26, RHJ, Friday, January 11, 1822, vol. 1, fol. 238). However, the following Monday, January 21, 1822, the overseer entered a new, separate category entitled "Runaways in confinement" (Monday, January 21, 1822, vol. 1, fol. 240). The number two appears in this category; however, no specific names are listed. Given Doshey's fairly recent return and her numerous runaway attempts, it is certainly possible that Doshey was one of the two in confinement in the jail cells of Rose Hall. Even though it is not clear whether the same two enslaved people were held in confinement for this entire week, it is likely they were the same two people held in this position for the entire week.

101. Doshey's death is mentioned in JARD, 1B/26, RHJ, November 8, 1823, vol. 2, fol. 21.

102. Arabella ran away at least thirteen times from Rose Hall: JARD, 1B/26, RHJ, Wednesday, April 23, 1817, vol. 1, fol. 2 ("brought home," Monday, May 12, 1817, vol. 1, fol. 4); Monday, June 23, 1817, vol. 1, fol. 8—"Arrabella still away," missing pages in journal, so not sure of the exact date Arabella ran away between mid-May and mid-June ("Arabella returned," Tuesday, September 30, 1817, vol. 1, fol. 21); Tuesday, April 21, 1818, vol. 1, fol. 50 ("Arrabella came home to Day," Monday, September 21, 1818, vol. 1, fol. 71); Monday, October 19, 1818, vol. 1, fol. 75 ("Mercury and Arabella got away at shell blow!," Monday, February 1, 1819, vol. 1, fol. 89; "Arabella still away" is crossed out—assume, though not noted, she has been away and just returned that Monday, February 1, or over the weekend); Monday, April 24, 1820, vol. 1, fol. 150 (back by Monday, May 1, 1820, vol. 1, fol. 151); Wednesday, October 17, 1821, vol. 1, fol. 226 (back by Monday, October 22, 1821, vol. 1, fol. 227); Monday, May 20, 1822, vol. 1, fol. 257 (Arabella named in "Runaways" column, though exact date of departure not specified; exact date of return also not noted in extant pages); Monday, December 6, 1824, vol. 2, fol. 78 (back by Tuesday, January 18, 1825, vol. 2, fol. 84); Monday, October 23, 1826, vol. 2, fol. 174 (back by Monday, November 6, 1826, vol. 2, fol. 175); Monday, April 20, 1829, vol. 3, fol. 44 ("Brot home" on Thursday, April 23, 1829, vol. 3, fol. 44); Monday, June 20, 1830, vol. 3, fol. 76 ("returned," Monday, July 5, 1830, vol. 2, fol. 77); Monday, October 18, 1830, vol. 3, fol. 84 (exact date of return not noted in extant pages); and Sunday, June 3, 1832, vol. 3, fol. 125 (and still on the run for the 1832 clothing allowance list).

103. Paton, *No Bond*, 22. See Williams, *A Narrative of Events* for a first-person enslaved man's account of his experiences in workhouses in Jamaica.

104. Paton, *No Bond*, 22.

105. Ibid.

106. Ibid., 22–23.

107. Ibid., 23.

108. Ibid., 19.

109. As Paton explains, the "Jamaican prison population thus differed from that of a typical prison in a contemporary 'free' society such as Britain in two important ways. First, it included large numbers of people committed without judicial procedures. Second, the majority of the prisoners were held for life at a time when the longest prison sentence in Britain was three years" (ibid.).

110. Ibid., 21.

111. As Paton postulates, "One consequence of the establishment of a large-scale prison system in Jamaica may have been the facilitation of communication among some of the most persistently oppositional slaves from different estates and areas by forcing them to spend time in the same space. . . . As they could in daily life outside of prisons, enslaved people in prison could twist and transform—but not completely overturn—technologies aimed at their domination" (ibid., 22).

112. The regularity of Jamaican newspapers began in the early 1700s, including, for example, the *Weekly Jamaican Courant* (est. 1718) and the *Jamaican Gazette* (est. 1745).

113. I did not find any references to either Doshey or Arabella in the lists of enslaved people in the St. James Parish workhouse in Montego Bay in any of the issues of the *Royal Gazette* during the time period of this study. However, other enslaved women appear in the newspaper's listing of those held in the St. James Parish workhouse. For example, the newspaper mentions "RACHEL, a yellow-complexioned elderly Eboe negro woman, 5 feet ½ inch; sent in by her owner, Alex. Milne, Esq." She is recorded as in the St. James workhouse on April 17, 1826 (*Royal Gazette*, Supplement, week of April 29–May 6, 1826, 463). Rachel remains on the list of enslaved people held in that workhouse until the beginning of June 1826. Her name appears in the weekly list for the week of May 27–June 3, 1826, but not for the week of June 3–10, 1826 (*Royal Gazette*).

114. JARD, 1B/26, RHJ, Monday, February 9, 1818, vol. 1, fol. 40.

115. JARD, 1B/26, RHJ, Friday, August 21, 1818, vol. 1, fol. 67.

116. JARD, 1B/26, RHJ, Monday, October 19, 1818, vol. 1, fol. 75.

117. JARD, 1B/26, RHJ, Monday, February 7, 1820, vol. 1, fol. 139.

118. JARD, 1B/26, RHJ, Saturday, April 22, 1820, vol. 1, fol. 149.

119. Mercury is listed as a runaway in JARD, 1B/26, RHJ, for the week of June 19, 1820, vol. 1, fol. 158 (back by July 3, 1820, vol. 1, fol. 160); Monday, August 28, 1820, vol. 1, fol. 167 (not stated when Mercury returned); and Monday, October 30, 1820, vol. 1, fol. 176—"Mercury runaway" ("brought home," Thursday, November 23, 1820, vol. 1, fol. 179).

120. JARD, 1B/26, RHJ, Monday, January 15, 1821, vol. 1, fol. 187. Doshey also ran away at the same time that Mercury was sent to the Montego Bay jail.

121. JARD, 1B/26, RHJ, Tuesday, January 30, 1821, vol. 1, fol. 189.

122. Archey ran away at least eleven times before he was sent to the Falmouth workhouse in August 1823: (JARD, 1B/26, RHJ, Monday, November 19, 1821, vol. 1, fol. 231—"Archy Runaway" ["brought home, Friday, November 23, 1821, vol. 1, fol. 231]); Monday, November 26, 1821, vol. 1, fol. 232 ("Brought home," Tuesday, November 27, 1821, vol. 1, fol. 232); Wednesday, November 28, 1821, vol. 1, fol. 232 (not stated when Archey returned); Wednesday, January 30, 1822, vol. 1, fol. 241 ("brought home," Friday, February 8, 1822, vol. 1, fol. 242); week of February 18, 1822, vol. 1, fol. 244—"Runaways in confinement" with one person listed in

this category (though the person is not named). Without any names specifically mentioned, it is unclear whether it was Archey who was in confinement or someone else. Given that the other runaway at this time (Mark) returned in March 1822, it was probably Archey who was in confinement. JARD, 1B/26, RHJ, Monday, March 4, 1822, vol. 1, fol. 246 (incorrectly dated as March 3 and date of return not stated, though probably over the weekend of March 9 and 10); Saturday, March 16, 1822, vol. 1, fol. 247 ("brought home," Monday, March 18, 1822, vol. 1, fol. 248); Thursday, March 28, 1822, vol. 1, fol. 249—"brought home" (not stated when he ran away); Monday, May 13, 1822, vol. 1, fol. 256 ("brought home," Wednesday, May 15, 1822, vol. 1, fol. 256); Monday, July 14, 1823, vol. 2, fol. 6 (not stated when he returned); and Wednesday, August 6, 1823, vol. 2, fol. 9 ("Brot home," Monday, August 18, 1823, vol. 2, fol. 11).

123. JARD, 1B/26, RHJ, Monday, November 19, 1821, vol. 1, fol. 231.

124. JARD, 1B/26, RHJ, Monday, August 18, 1823, and Wednesday, August 20, 1823, vol. 2, fol. 11.

125. JARD, 1B/26, RHJ, Monday, October 6, 1823, vol. 2, fol. 17.

126. JARD, 1B/26, RHJ, Tuesday, November 11, 1823, vol. 2, fol. 22.

127. JARD, 1B/26, RHJ, Tuesday, November 11, 1823, vol. 2, fol. 22.

128. JARD, 1B/26, RHJ, October 11–14, 1824, vol. 2, fol. 70.

129. JARD, 1B/26, RHJ, Monday, February 28, 1825, vol. 2, fol. 90.

130. JARD, 1B/26, RHJ, Tuesday, October 11, 1825, vol. 2, fol. 122. This is exactly one year after his runaway attempt on October 11, 1824. The fact that Archey ran away on this same date may not be coincidental; it may reflect the significance of this date for him and/or a loved one.

131. JARD, 1B/26, RHJ, Monday, December 26, 1825, vol. 2, fol. 133.

132. JARD, 1B/11/7/85, fol. 155.

133. JARD, 1B/26, RHJ, Tuesday, August 11, 1829, vol. 3, fol. 52, and Sunday, March 27, 1831–Sunday, April 3, 1831, vol. 3, fol. 97. The journal notes that James was caught on April 11, 1831. This particular combined list of runaways' movements includes dates from the beginning of February 1831 to the end of April 1831.

134. JARD, 1B/26, RHJ, Tuesday, March 20, 1832, vol. 3, fol. 119.

135. Though not identified as a "notorious runaway," in the clothing allowance list for 1832, he is characterized as having a "bad" disposition (Shore, *In Old St. James*, 106–107).

136. JARD, 1B/26, RHJ, Tuesday, July 31, 1821, vol. 1, fol. 215 ("Hercules brought home," Wednesday, August 8, 1821, vol. 1, fol. 216); Wednesday, August 22, 1821, vol. 1, fol. 218 (Hercules ran away only for that day); Wednesday, August 29, 1821, vol. 1, fol. 219 (returned or was brought back by Monday, September 17, 1821, vol. 1, fol. 222); Monday, September 24, 1821, vol. 1, fol. 223 ("Hercules brought home," Friday, September 28, 1821, vol. 1, fol. 223); Monday, October 15, 1821, vol. 1, fol. 226 ("Hercules brought home," Wednesday, October 31, 1821, vol. 1, fol. 228); Wednesday, December 26, 1821, vol. 1, fol. 236—"Hercules brought home" (not stated when he ran away); week beginning on Monday, March 11, 1822, Hercules named in the "Runaways" column, though not stated when he ran away, Monday, March 11, 1822, vol. 1, fol. 247 ("Hercules and Archey brought home," Monday, March 18, 1822, vol. 1, fol. 248); Wednesday, May 22, 1822, vol. 1, fol. 257 (Hercules brought home, though not stated when he ran away); Thursday, May 30, 1822, vol. 1, fol. 258 (not stated when he returned or was brought back); Wednesday, June 5, 1822, vol. 1, fol. 259, "Hercules, Anthony & Pitt Runaway" ("Hercules brought home," Monday June 17, 1822, vol. 1, fol. 261); Thursday, July 17, 1823, vol. 2, fol. 6

("Hercules Brot home," Sunday, August 24, 1823, vol. 2, fol. 11); Wednesday, October 12, 1825, vol. 2, fol. 122 (Hercules brought home, October 15, 1825, vol. 2, fol. 122); Thursday, November 10, 1825, vol. 2, fol. 126 (not stated when he returned or was brought back); Monday, August 28, 1826, vol. 2, fol. 165—Hercules and Anthony absent this week (date of return not stated but returned by Monday, September 11, 1826, vol. 2, fol. 167); Thursday, December 28, 1826, vol. 2, fol., 182 (not stated when he returned or was brought back); Monday, October 6, 1828, vol. 3, fol. 20 (back by Monday, October 13, 1828, vol. 2, fol. 21); Saturday, December 13, 1828, vol. 2, fol. 29—"Hercules absconded on the 13th Inst. from Peter in consequence of which Peter has likewise absented himself" ("Hercules Brought home," Tuesday, December 30, 1828, vol. 3, fol. 32); Wednesday, March 24, 1830, vol. 3, fol. 70 (Hercules "returned home this day," Sunday, March 28, 1830, vol. 3, fol. 70); Monday, May 10, 1830, vol. 3, fol. 73 ("Hercules Brot home," Monday, May 17, 1830, vol. 3, fol. 74); Thursday, May 27, 1830, vol. 3, fol. 74 ("Hercules returned was forgive," Sunday, May 30, 1830, vol. 3, fol. 74); Monday, June 14, 1830, vol. 3, fol. 76—"Hercules & James once more absconded without cause" ("Hercules Brot home," Monday, June 28, 1830, vol. 3, fol. 77); Monday, September 13, 1830, vol. 3, fol. 81—"Hercules absconded cause unknown" (not stated when he returned or was brought back); Sunday, October 24, 1830, vol. 3, fol. 84—"Hercules made his Escape from Confinement" (not stated when he returned or was brought back); Tuesday, November 16, 1830, vol. 3, fol. 86—"Hercules after being pardond for his last offence again made his exit without cause" (not stated when he returned or was brought back); Sunday, March 27, 1831–Sunday, April 3, 1831, vol. 3, fol. 97 (ran away on March 29, 1831 and caught on April 4, 1831); week of February 6, 1832, vol. 3, fol. 116; note at the end of weekly entry that Hercules ran away on January 24, 1832, vol. 3, fol. 116 (not stated when he returned).

137. NA Kew, T71/202, fol. 542.

138. Ibid. Mark and Gloster also ran away multiple times. As previously discussed, Mark ran away at least twelve times; those instances are included in a previous endnote. Gloster ran away at least twice (JARD, 1B/26, RHJ, Friday, April 24, 1829, vol. 3, fol. 44 [not stated when he returned], and Wednesday, March 24, 1830, vol. 3, fol. 70 ["Glouster brot home," Thursday, March 25, 1830, vol. 3, fol. 70]).

139. Hercules (and Gloster) absconded in March 1830 "without cause" (JARD, 1B/26, RHJ, Wednesday, March 24, 1830, vol. 3, fol. 70). Four days later, the overseer noted that Hercules "returned home this day" (Sunday, March 28, 1830, vol. 3, fol. 70). Hercules absconded in May 1830 (Thursday, May 27, 1830, vol. 3, fol. 74). Three days later, the overseer noted that "Hercules returned was forgive" (Sunday, May 30, 1830, vol. 3, fol. 74).

140. In the 1832 clothing allowance list, Hercules is described as twenty-five years old and a field worker (Shore, *In Old St. James*, 106–107).

141. JARD, 1B/26, RHJ, Thursday, May 27, 1830, vol. 3, fol. 74.

142. JARD, 1B/26, RHJ, Sunday, May 30, 1830, vol. 3, fol. 74.

143. JARD, 1B/26, RHJ, Monday, June 14, 1830, vol. 3, fol. 76.

144. JARD, 1B/26, RHJ, Monday, June 28, 1830, vol. 3, fol. 77.

145. JARD, 1B/26, RHJ, Monday, September 13, 1830, vol. 3, fol. 81.

146. JARD, 1B/26, RHJ, Sunday, October 24, 1830, vol. 3, fol. 84.

147. JARD, 1B/26, RHJ, Tuesday, November 16, 1830, vol. 3, fol. 86.

148. Higman, *Montpelier, Jamaica*, 262.

149. For more on the Baptist War / Christmas Rebellion, see Reckord, "The Jamaica Slave Rebellion"; Brathwaite, "The Slave Rebellion"; Higman, *Montpelier, Jamaica*, 262–283; and Zoellner, *Island on Fire*.

150. JARD, 1B/26, RHJ, the week of December 12, 1831, vol. 3, fol. 115. The journal pages are missing for the two-week period from November 27, 1831, to December 12, 1831.

151. JARD, 1B/26, RHJ, the week of December 12, 1831, vol. 3, fol. 115.

152. JARD, 1B/26, RHJ, the week of December 19, 1831, vol. 3, fol. 116a.

153. JARD, 1B/26, RHJ, the week of February 6, 1832, vol. 3, fol. 116b.

154. Ibid.

155. Camp, *Closer to Freedom*, 7. As Camp mentions, this term "rival geography" was coined by Edward Said, though it has been utilized by scholars in their analyses of resistance to colonial structures.

156. As in other countries, women did not vote in Jamaica until the enactment of full adult suffrage; in 1944 suffrage was granted without regard to race, gender, or socioeconomic status in Jamaica.

157. For more on the Morant Bay Rebellion, see Heuman, *The Killing Time*.

158. The United Fruit Company also owned significant acres of land dedicated to banana production in other parts of the Caribbean and in Central America: Costa Rica, Colombia, the Dominican Republic, Honduras, and Panama. When Marcus Garvey migrated to Costa Rica in 1910, it was while being employed as a timekeeper at one of the banana plantations owned by the United Fruit Company that he witnessed and published articles regarding the exploitation of workers.

CHAPTER 4. The Fictional Fabrication of
the Myth of the White Witch

1. The limited administrative files housed at the Rose Hall Great House concerning the script for the tours do not mention the person(s) who created the script and when the original script was crafted for the tours. It is also unclear from the documents at the Rose Hall Great House what changes to the script have been made over the decades.

2. Even with all of Herbert G. de Lisser's writings in multiple genres and his long-standing appointment at *The Gleaner* in Jamaica, a comprehensive biography has not been penned for him. For an overview of his writing with a few biographical details, see Cobham, "The Literary Side." Also see Cobham, "Herbert George de Lisser." Cobham only discusses *The White Witch of Rosehall* in a few lines in both essays. For more on de Lisser's professional career, see Morris, "H. G. de Lisser." Also see Rosenberg, "Herbert's Career." De Lisser did not compose any autobiographical account for public consumption. His personal papers are not housed in a specific depository, and it is unclear what sources he utilized for this novel. However, in her work, Laura Lomas explores different oral stories and perspectives that may have influenced aspects of de Lisser's novel. She also examines the role(s) and processes of oral history and mythmaking in relation to the mythological elements of Annie Palmer's story. See Lomas, "Mystifying Mystery."

3. For a critical discussion of this labor movement and rebellion, see Palmer, *Freedom's Children*.

4. De Lisser, *The White Witch of Rosehall*, 1. Hereafter cited parenthetically in the text.

5. For example, historian Jennifer L. Morgan explores the supposedly compromised character, fortitude, and mores of European men when they became intimately connected not only to African women but also to Indigenous women in the Americas. See Chapter 1, "'Some Could Suckle over Their Shoulder': Male Travelers, Female Bodies, and the Gendering of Racial Ideology," in Morgan, *Laboring Women*, 50–68. In specific reference to (white) Creole degeneracy in the British Caribbean, Elise A. Mitchell notes: "The sexual availability of the black female body became a trap that ensnared Englishmen and white creoles, resulting both in their own degeneracy and the degeneracy of their mixed racial progeny" ("Tainted Bodies," 32). Mitchell includes in her essay sections of her undergraduate thesis, "Infectious Blackness." Mitchell recently completed her dissertation on smallpox and slavery at New York University. See also chapter 3, "Deviant and Dangerous: Slave Women's Sexuality," in Altink, *Representations*, 65–90. For a more general discussion of (white) Creole identities and notions of degeneracy compared to notions of (white) Creole regeneracy in the British colonies in North America, see Goudie, *Creole America*. See Livesay, *Children of Uncertain Fortune*, for an exploration of the intimate and familial dynamics of selected migrants of color as they navigated the particular sociocultural and juridical British terrain in the metropole and the colony of Jamaica.

6. See, for example, the critical discussion of the complexities of the seasoning processes in Smallwood's landmark work, *Saltwater Slavery*.

7. Williamson, *Medical and Miscellaneous Observations*, 49.

8. Nugent, *Lady Nugent's Journal*, 87.

9. Due to the nature and limitations of the archival record, elite women of color have been the primary population of free women of color in the Americas explored by historians. For example, in her article on free women of color in colonial Jamaica, Erin Trahey analyzes a sample of forty-two wills and related documents of elite property-owning free women of color in Jamaica between 1750 and 1834 (Trahey, "Among Her Kinswomen"). Also see Fuentes, *Dispossessed Lives*; Landers, *Against the Odds*; Hanger, *Bounded Lives*; and Johnson, *Wicked Flesh*.

10. Lizabeth Paravisini-Gebert examines different aspects of the power dynamics between Annie Palmer and Millicent, as well as the gendered dimensions of de Lisser's portrayal of a white mistress of a Jamaican plantation ("The White Witch").

11. Bilby and Handler, "Obeah," 153. Although Handler and Bilby disagree with this etymological connection to Obeah, it is important to note that other scholars such as Fernández Olmos and Paravisini-Gebert trace the origins of the word Obeah "to the Ashanti terms *Obayifo* or *obeye*, meaning, respectively, wizard or witch, or the spiritual beings that inhabit witches. The term was creolized in the Caribbean over the years as *Obeah, obi*, or *obia*" (*Creole Religions*, 155–156). Fernández Olmos and Paravisini-Gebert also note that in "recent decades, because of widespread migration of West Indians to metropolitan centers like New York, London, Toronto, and Miami (among others), Obeah practices have come into contact with other Caribbean belief systems like Vodou, Santería, and Espiritismo, contributing to the richness of healing and spiritual offerings available in the Diaspora" (ibid., 156). Also see Frye, "'An Article of Faith.'" Although the Asante Twi language is often referenced as a possible source for the word "obeah," some scholars have explored other African-based languages and language groups, including Efik, Igbo, and Ibibio, as well as other foundational purposes of Obeah. See Handler and Bilby, "On the Early Use"; and Crosson, "What Obeah Does Do." For other extensive

examinations of Obeah, see Handler and Bilby, *Enacting Power*; Paton, *The Cultural Politics*; and Turner, "The Art of Power."

12. Bilby and Handler, "Obeah," 153–154.

13. Ibid., 154.

14. Bilby and Handler highlight "two fundamental characteristics" of Obeah: (1) "the manipulation and control of supernatural forces, usually through the use of material objects and recitation of spells," and (2) a focus on "divination (e.g., foretelling, finding lost or stolen goods, ascertaining the cause of illness), healing and bringing good fortune, and protection from harm—although it was sometimes used malevolently to harm others" (ibid.).

15. Brown, *The Reaper's Garden*, 145. Also see chaps. 3 and 4 in Brown, *Tacky's Revolt*.

16. Powell, "Obeah." Powell noted that her forthcoming book incorporates Obeah as a central aspect of the narrative. In her keynote address, Powell also described Obeah as "our sacred connection to ourselves . . . [w]hat enabled us to carry on . . . our divine source . . . our divine mystic." Also see the novel *Myal*, by renowned Jamaican writer and sociologist Erna Brodber.

17. Fernández Olmos and Paravisini-Gebert, *Creole Religions*, 171.

18. Ibid., 173.

19. Jean-Jacques Dessalines and Henri Christophe were significant leaders in the Haitian Revolution, and both were formerly enslaved in Saint-Domingue. Dessalines was the first ruler of Haiti, initially naming himself governor general for life of Haiti and later emperor of Haiti. After Dessaline's assassination, Christophe retreated to the Plaine-du-Nord in February 1807. He was elected president of the state of Haiti (the moniker he used for that area of Haiti). In March 1811 Christophe established a kingdom and was proclaimed Henry I, king of Haiti. For more on the Haitian Revolution, see James, *The Black Jacobins*; Dubois, *Avengers*; and Scott, *The Common Wind*.

20. For more on the particular lore and presence of "Old Hige" and the deployment of diasporic female vampire lore (specifically the soucouyant) in various parts of the Caribbean, see Anatol, *The Things That Fly*. Although the characters in this novel discuss Old Hige within Jamaican and Obeah frameworks, Monika Mueller examines Old Hige as a hybrid iteration of European vampirism and Voodoo ("Hybridity Sucks").

21. For a discussion of Obeah practices in the elimination of Old Hige (or Old Higue), see Moore and Johnson, *Neither Led nor Driven*. Moore and Johnson elaborate on the particular importance of Obeah practices as specific acts of resistance to British cultural customs and religiosity overall. They assert that as an Afro-Creole belief system, Obeah served as a vital avenue in preserving and confirming "their intention to determine *for themselves* what was culturally appropriate and what was not. It was a positive assertion of cultural self-determination in the face of hostile pressure from above" (Moore and Johnson, *Neither Led nor Driven*, authors' emphasis, 46).

22. De Lisser later reveals that the youth was carrying a sacrificial "young white goat."

23. Fernández Olmos and Paravisini-Gebert, *Creole Religions*, 174.

24. Dawes, "An Act," 3. Also see Harkins, "'Spells of Darkness.'"

25. This slave revolt is often referred to as the Christmas Rebellion or the Baptist War; it began on December 27, 1831, during the Christmas holiday period and continued into the first month of 1832. For more on the Baptist War / Christmas Rebellion, see Reckord, "The Jamaica

Slave Rebellion"; Brathwaite, "The Slave Rebellion"; Higman, *Montpelier, Jamaica*, 262–283; and Zoellner, *Island on Fire*.

26. The trope of notorious women (also known as "femmes fatales" or monster women) inhabits a particular space in the Western literary canon. A couple of iconic literary examples include H. Rider Haggard's novel *She: A History of Adventure* (initially serialized in *The Graphic* magazine between October 1886 and January 1887), as well as selected authors and their respective works discussed in Gilbert and Gubar, *The Madwoman in the Attic*. In addition to considering the "madness" and hysteria associated with (white) women in the Western literary canon, it is also important to examine how "madness" emerges and operates within Caribbean literary aesthetics. Recent critical works on this subject include Josephs, *Disturbers of the Peace*; Ledent, O'Callaghan, and Tunca, *Madness in Anglophone Caribbean Literature*; and Brown and Garvey, *Madness in Black Women's Diasporic Fictions*.

CHAPTER 5. The White Witch and Enslaved Ghosts

1. "Rose Hall Deal Sealed." Before John Rollins Sr. bought the Rose Hall property, one of the notable families that owned Rose Hall was the Barrett family—the family of eminent poet Elizabeth Barrett Browning. Although focused on Rose Hall's current ownership by the Rollins family, records at Jamaica's National Land Agency in Kingston include shared and overlapping ownership of sections of the Rose Hall property by the Henderson, Jarrett, and Barrett families.

2. The Rollins's family hotels in Montego Bay include the Holiday Inn Resort, the Hilton Rose Hall Resort and Spa (formerly the Wyndham Beach Resort), the Hyatt Ziva Rose Hall, Zilara Rose Hall (formerly the Ritz-Carlton), and the Iberostar Rose Hall Beach Hotel. Over the past few years, the Rollins family has sold some of its properties in Montego Bay. For example, in 2013 the Rollins family sold the five-thousand-acre Ritz-Carlton Rose Hall Resort to Playa Hotels and Resorts. For *The Gleaner*'s article on this sale, see Silvera, "Ritz-Carlton."

3. Over the past several years, Michele Rollins has begun the process of transferring her duties and responsibilities with Rollins Jamaica Ltd. to the next generation. In 2011 Michael Rollins (one of the children of John and Michele Rollins), who had been actively involved in his family's business operations as vice president of Rose Hall Developments Ltd., became the president of Rollins Jamaica Ltd. Over the past several years while working on this book, I have sent formal letters and emails addressed to Mrs. Rollins, as well as called and left messages with various Rose Hall Developments Ltd. staff members in order to speak with Mrs. Rollins. I have not received any responses from Mrs. Rollins, other members of the Rollins family, or any staff members responding on behalf of a member of the Rollins family.

4. See "White Witch of Rose Hall." Michele Rollins and other members of the Rollins family are fully engaged in current and future business ventures related to the marketing of Rose Hall and the legend of the "White Witch of Rose Hall." In 2014, for example, Arthur Wylie (Global Renaissance Entertainment Group) and Michael Rollins (director of Rose Hall Developments Ltd.) announced plans for an epic trilogy of films based on the legend of Annie Palmer as the White Witch of Rose Hall. See CaribPr Wire, "Press Release."

5. Given the 2019 presidential impeachment process in the United States and discussions

related to the withholding of aid to Ukraine, it is important to note that such withholding tactics also permeated John Rollins Sr.'s negotiations with the Jamaican government in the 1980s over one of the Rollins hotel properties in Montego Bay. Rollins's particular relationship with Representative Charles Wilson of Texas, who served on the House Appropriations Committee, resulted in the United States withholding aid to Jamaica for a housing project until the government of Jamaica agreed to concede to John Rollins Sr.'s requests. For more on these negotiations, see, for example, Powers and Trento, "Rollins Finds a Nightmare"; "For a Friend"; Green, "Move to Block Aid"; "Govt. Bows to Rollins' Pressure"; "Funds Freed in Rollins Row?"; "Rollins 'Laughing to the Bank'"; Milford, "Rollins' Dream"; Morris, "Whither the Rose Hall Deal?"; and Ritch, "Civil Society under Attack."

6. Rose Hall Great House is a popular destination wedding venue. Until recently, it was described on its main website as a glorious setting for prospective clients: "Rose Hall is a mystical island destination for any bride or groom seeking to have that dream destination wedding. There is not a location in the Caribbean that could compare to the intimacy, service and scenery of Rose Hall for the wedding of your dreams. Rose Hall is home to ancient ruins, panoramic views of the Caribbean Sea, a private beach, a tranquil waterfall, a majestic great house and fairways of a beautifully manicured golf course. Overlooking the sapphire blue Caribbean Sea or emerald green rolling mountains, the bride & groom, family & friends will remember a magnificent wedding for years to come" ("Rose Hall Wedding Events"). Some of this wording still remains in other Rose Hall–related wedding information. Recently revised language regarding weddings on the main Rose Hall Great House website states: "Rose Hall abounds with history and beauty that can be matched by nowhere in the world. Lush green landscapes, exquisite panoramas, secret waterfalls, beach escapes, historic ruins and majestic great houses— there is a Rose Hall Signature location that is perfect for your dream wedding. Our team of expert wedding planners will ensure that your day is rooted as deep as the rich and vibrant heritage of the land. You bring the love! We will take care of the rest!" There is, of course, no mention of Rose Hall as a site of slavery in either the older or current descriptions ("Rose Hall Weddings"). Members of the Rollins family also have utilized Rose Hall for their weddings and wedding receptions. For two recent examples of their use of the Rose Hall Great House and their other properties for family weddings, see *The Gleaner*'s articles and pictures regarding the 2011 wedding of Marc Rollins (one of the children of John Rollins Sr. and Michele Rollins) ("What a Wedding") and the 2018 wedding of Kate Searby, one of the grandchildren of John Rollins Sr. ("A Great Love Story").

7. Wilkes, *Whiteness*.

8. The marketing extends beyond the Rose Hall Great House and hotels owned by the Rollins family. On December 6, 2019, the Miss Jamaica Universe Organization revealed the national costume to be worn by Miss Jamaica 2019, Iana Tickle Garcia; Garcia is from Montego Bay in St. James Parish. It was not the elaborate fashion and adornments of the white costume that incited an uproar on Twitter over the weekend; rather, what most complained about centered on the name of Jamaica's national costume to be worn by Garcia. It was called "Annie Palmer—Legend of Rose Hall." Unsurprisingly, the sponsor for the 2019 Miss Jamaica Universe was the Rollins family's organization, Rose Hall Developments Ltd. The banner with the name of the organization is draped on Garcia for most of the marketing shots about her

on social media. On December 7, 2019, the Rose Hall organization sent a tweet announcing and applauding the costume and Garcia in it, with pictures of Garcia dressed in the costume in front of Rose Hall Great House: "Miss Universe Jamaica's Costume Name: Annie Palmer—Legend of Rose Hall Iana Tickle Garcia is rocking this!" Needless to say, countless tweets and other messages criticized the invocation of Annie Palmer as an appropriate national representative of Jamaica. See, for example, Wright, "Outrage"; and "Social Media Split."

9. For one example of a cruise company highlighting the Rose Hall Great House tour, see "Rose Hall Great House." This MSC cruise company website, however, in 2021 did mention "slaves" in its overview of the Rose Hall Great House: "Enjoy a thrilling adventure through the Rosehall Mansion where stories of witchcraft, black magic, murder and slaves exacting revenge on their masters abound! . . . Legend has it that the White Witch Annie Palmer murdered her four husbands in addition to numerous slaves who worked at the plantation" (ibid.).

10. Tourism Product Development Company, "History."

11. Tourism Product Development Company, "TPDCo Expanding."

12. The specific information about the Rose Hall tour guides and volunteers was offered and confirmed by Rose Hall Great House staff members in July 2020.

13. As previously stated, my first tour was in the summer of 2013. Over the past several years, I have taken the group tours (both in the day and at night) with different tour guides. The tour narrative has been fairly consistent over the years. The quotes from the tour narrative in this chapter are from my most recent Rose Hall Great House tour on November 11, 2019, with Miss S. I have not included her full name in order to protect her identity. I had previously been on a group tour with her, and we had discussions about different aspects of the tour. However, for this most recent tour in November 2019, it was a solo tour with her, and I was able to discuss to a greater extent items included and excluded from the standard tour. For example, we discussed the possible sites for enslaved people's dwellings at Rose Hall. This kind of information is not included in the official tour script. In this chapter, I have only included quotes from the tour narrative that are in the standard tours for guests to the Rose Hall Great House.

14. Rose Hall Great House, tour narrative, November 11, 2019.

15. Marlon James's fictional representation of a white woman being savaged by unruly enslaved men is vividly presented in his novel *The Book of Night Women*. Although James characterizes Miss Isobel as someone who has been engaged with multiple sexual partners and who has been deeply affected by a range of herbs and alcohol, the scene at the end presents the caricature of "Black brutes." In the midst of the slave revolt at Montpelier, as enslaved people in his novel move throughout a chaotic plantation, one enslaved woman, Pallas, opens the door to Miss Isobel's bedroom. James writes, "She go in to see a light-skin nigger fuckin' Miss Isobel hard while the chocolate-skin nigger hold her up and cussing that he taking till Judgement Day fi cum. Miss Isobel don't look like she living. They holding her up by the arm while the chocolate nigger have her two leg on him shoulder and him breeches at him knees. Pallas fire a shot and they drop Miss Isobel" (James, *The Book of Night Women*, 404–405). It is important to note that there are a number of aspects of the myth of Annie Palmer and de Lisser's novel embedded in Marlon James's *The Book of Night Women*.

16. For additional information about John Palmer and John Rose Palmer, see the brief summary at the end of this chapter.

17. The "Annee's Pub" sign had been positioned inside the bar area, but within the past couple of years, it was moved to the outside of the bar and is now permanently placed on the outside wall of the bar and dungeon area. This bar had been operated with Rose Hall Great House staff; this has changed in the past couple of years, so that the bar is now operated by an independent businessman via a special arrangement with Rose Hall Developments Ltd.

18. Johnny Cash wrote and recorded a song called "The Ballad of Annie Palmer," https://www.youtube.com/watch?v=YOSU5WMkOpo. Recently, daily tours of this previous home of Johnny Cash and June Carter-Cash, Cinnamon Hill Great House, have been formally organized through Rose Hall Developments Ltd. For more information about these tours, see Rose Hall Developments Ltd., "Cinnamon Hill."

19. Miles, *Tales from the Haunted South*, 11. Miles's illuminating book centers on three main sites: the Sorrrel-Weed House haunting in Savannah, Georgia; the Madame Lalaurie House haunting in New Orleans, Louisiana; and the Myrtles Plantation haunting in St. Francisville, Louisiana. For another insightful exploration of the complexities of haunting within historical, literary, and sociocultural contexts, see Gordon, *Ghostly Matters*. In chapter 4, Gordon's analysis of haunting within Toni Morrison's *Beloved* is of particular relevance in understanding the interconnections of history, haunting, and slavery.

20. Miles, *Tales from the Haunted South*, 15.

21. Ibid., 16, author's emphasis.

22. Ibid., 123–124. As Miles posits, such ghost stories often "seek to engage and yet also avoid the troubling memory of slavery. Why? Because slavery and the racial ideology that justified the practice are cultural wounds that have never healed." Ghost stories particularly related to "the enslaved dead bring those wounds to the surface of awareness, allowing tourists of the former slaveholding South to stare and pick at them. But seeing these wounds, acknowledging that they still fester, is uncomfortable in a would-be post-racial society. Recognition must therefore be a *misrecognition* that diminishes the harsh realities of America's peculiar institution" (ibid., 17, author's emphasis).

23. See, for example, the interactions between *Scientific American Frontiers* host Alan Alda and the reenactors at Colonial Williamsburg, Virginia, in *Scientific American Frontiers*, "Unearthing Secret America" episode.

24. Thanks to Professor Modupe Labode for raising this question regarding my talk at the Berks Conference at Hofstra University in June 2017. I appreciate her query of whether or not Rose Hall represented a museum or a pretense of a museum, as well as her suggestion that I consider this issue in my analysis of the tours.

25. Hartman, *Scenes of Subjection*, 4.

26. For more information, see Hakewill, *A Picturesque Tour*, 92–96; Black, *Tales of Old Jamaica*, 11–17; and Shore, *In Old St. James*, 42–48. Also see Yates, "Death of a Legend"; and Yates, "The Rose Hall Legend." For an online version of Yates's articles, see Yates, "Rose Hall: Death of a Legend"; and DuQuesnay, "Rose Hall Great House."

27. The custos (or custos rotulorum), or keeper of the rolls in Jamaica (and throughout the United Kingdom except for Scotland), was often designated as the chief magistrate of a specific parish in Jamaica.

28. After John Palmer's death, Rebecca Palmer returned to England. She later married Dr. Nathaniel Weeks of Barbados. Although she was not granted ownership of either Rose Hall

Plantation or Palmyra Plantation, after John Palmer's death she received an annuity from the profits of these two plantations until her death in 1846/1847 (Yates, "Death of a Legend").

29. For more information, see Black, *Tales of Old Jamaica*, 11–17; Shore, *In Old St. James*, 42–48; Yates, "Death of a Legend"; and Yates, "The Rose Hall Legend." Also see "John Rose Palmer."

30. It is important to note that like many other eighteenth- and nineteenth-century plantation owners, John Palmer struggled with his overwhelming debts. As a result of his increasing debt, his creditors foreclosed on both plantations in 1792, and he mortgaged both Rose Hall and Palmyra Plantations. He then moved to his other residence, called Brandon Hill. Eventually, after John Palmer's death and with the properties in trust to John Palmer's sons (James and John Palmer), the Court of Chancery administered both estates. The Court of Chancery officially appointed specific receivers for administering both plantations; Hon. William Miller (custos of Trelawny) and solicitor William Heath served in this capacity for Rose Hall and Palmyra Plantations. Even as John Rose Palmer arrived in Jamaica and began the process of repairing Rose Hall and Palmyra Plantations, he could not claim outright ownership of these plantations. Instead, he mortgaged the receivership to Henry Ancrum (who was based in London) (Yates, "Rose Hall: Death of a Legend").

31. In 1822, with an enslaved population of between 142 (in 1820) and 135 (in 1823), Rose Hall Plantation produced 194 hogsheads of sugar (with 193 hogsheads being shipped to England and 1 hogshead being used on the estate) and 131 puncheons and 1 hogshead of rum (with 129 puncheons being shipped to England, 2 puncheons of this total being used on the estate, and 1 hogshead being sold in Jamaica) (JARD, 1B/11/4/58, fol. 220). For one comparison, Richard Dunn notes that in 1810 Mesopotamia Sugar Plantation in Westmoreland, Jamaica, with an enslaved population that year between 332 and 355 (well over twice the size of the enslaved population of Rose Hall), produced a record crop of 361 hogsheads and 45 tierces of sugar and 164 puncheons of rum (*A Tale of Two Plantations*, 94). Moreover, Mesopotamia's acreage specifically for sugar was also twice the size of Rose Hall.

32. Yates, "Death of a Legend."

33. Shore, *In Old St. James*, 48–49; Yates, "Death of a Legend"; Yates, "The Rose Hall Legend?"; and DuQuesnay, "Rose Hall Great House." The *Royal Gazette* noted John Palmer's death in November 1827.

34. Castello's article was also published in the October 1894 issue of the *Trifler Magazine*, 7/74/1, fols. 12–19, JARD. A number of letters to the editor appeared in 1895 in *The Gleaner* regarding the legend and facts about the various Mrs. Palmers. Selected clippings are available at JARD, files 7/74/1 to 7/74/7. As Laura Lomas discusses in her critical work, Castello's version of events, selected notes and letters printed in *The Gleaner* in 1868 and 1895, and oral testimonies provide the fodder for the legend of Annie Palmer ("Mystifying Mystery").

35. For one telling account of the unfolding of events of this Christmas Rebellion, see Sherlock and Bennett, *The Story of the Jamaican People*, 212–228. Also see Higman, *Montpelier*, 262–283. Fred W. Kennedy's novel, based on the life of Samuel Sharpe (the most recognized leader of this rebellion and one of the national heroes of Jamaica), is entitled *Daddy Sharpe: A Narrative of the Life and Adventures of Samuel Sharpe, a West Indian Slave Written by Himself, 1832*. Also see Zoellner, *Island on Fire*.

36. JARD, *Jamaica Almanac*, 1833. An online version of the *Jamaica Almanac* for 1833 is

available on the Jamaica Family Search Genealogy Research Library website. For the list of proprietors in the St. James Parish, see Jamaican Family Search Genealogy, "1833 Jamaica Almanac."

37. See the listing for Anna M. Palmer's claim, "Jamaica St. James 275."

38. Bonavista is located about ten kilometers or about six miles southwest of Rose Hall
Plantation. While she was in Bonavista, Annie Palmer's living expenses were taken care of by
William Augustus Dickson, who was married to her aunt Ann Robina Brown. See "Anna Mary
Palmer (née Paterson)."

39. Yates, "Death of a Legend"; Yates, "The Rose Hall Legend." Also see Robertson, "The
Rose Hall Legend." The Legacies of British Slave-Ownership Project also includes some
biographical information about Anna (Annie) Mary Palmer. See "Anna Mary Palmer (née
Paterson)."

EPILOGUE

The epigraph is from pages 4–5 of Shange's poetry collection, *For Colored Girls Who Have
Considered Suicide When the Rainbow Is Enuf.* Reprinted by the permission of Russell &
Volkening as agents for Ntozake Shange, copyright © 1974 by Ntozake Shange.

1. See, for example, Araujo, *Politics of Memory*; and Araujo, *Slavery*.

2. For more on this memorial in Nantes, France, see "Mémorial de l'abolition de l'esclavage."

3. The British Parliament passed this abolition act on March 25, 1807. For more on the range
of commemorative events in Great Britain, see Cubitt, "Museums and Slavery." For specific
information about the bicentennial events at the International Slavery Museum in Liverpool,
see Benjamin, "Museums." Also see Moody, *The Persistence of Memory*; and Araujo, *Museums
and Atlantic Slavery.*

4. For more on this project and movement, see "Memorial 2007." Also see Hirsch, "Britain
Was Built."

5. Animals in War Memorial.

6. *Nation Newspaper* (Barbados), March 25, 2007, as quoted in Shepherd, "Slavery, Shame
and Pride," 1–2.

7. For more information on the background and events associated with its declaration of
March 25 as the International Day of Remembrance of the Victims of Slavery and the Transatlantic Slave Trade, see United Nations, "Remember Slavery."

8. In 2015 the theme for the year was "Women and Slavery"; in 2016 the theme was
"Remember Slavery: Celebrating the Heritage and Culture of the African Diaspora and Its
Roots"; in 2017 the theme was "Remember Slavery: Recognizing the Legacy and Contribu-
tions of People of African Descent"; in 2018 the theme was "Remember Slavery: Triumphs
and Struggles for Freedom and Equality"; in 2019 the theme was "Remember Slavery: The
Power of the Arts for Justice"; in 2020 the theme was "Confronting Slavery's Legacy of Racism
Together"; and in 2021 the theme was "Ending Slavery's Legacy of Racism: A Global Imperative for Justice." See the individual sites at United Nations, "Remember Slavery."

9. For more information about Rodney Leon's design, see "African Burial Ground Ancestral
Chamber."

10. For more information about the Diving with a Purpose (DWP) organization, see

https://divingwithapurpose.org/. The six-part documentary series entitled *Enslaved*, released in September 2020, includes highlights of the work of Diving with a Purpose in searches for selected wrecks of ships of the transatlantic slave trade. DWP is also engaged in a range of environmental dimensions in their work (e.g., protecting, monitoring, and restoring coral reefs). Although often assumed to be an underwater memorial related to the transatlantic slave trade and enslaved persons, the Molinere Bay Underwater Sculpture Park, located off the west coast of Grenada, was not conceived with this purpose in mind.

11. Although not specifically a monument to slavery, the *I Am Queen Mary* statue in Copenhagen, Denmark, a collaborative work of Danish artist Jeannette Ehlers and Virgin Islander artist La Vaughn Belle, is part of this transnational discourse. For more on this statue, see the *I Am Queen Mary* website. See also "The Three Rebel Queens"; "Fireburn"; *Smithsonian Magazine*, "New Statue"; and Barnard College, "Break This Down."

12. For some of the issues in Brazil and Portugal, see Freelon, "Rio Is Debating"; Charr, "Rio Slavery Museum"; and Ames, "Portugal Confronts." In addition to the discussions about the creation of a slavery museum in Brazil, it is important to note the existence of the Instituto de Pesquisa e Memória Pretos Novos, or the Instituto Pretos Novos (IPN), in Rio de Janeiro. See "IPN." Also see the Passados Presentes project on sites of memory of slavery in Brazil.

13. For more on this exhibit, including its centerpiece video presentation of "ten true stories," see Rijksmuseum, "Slavery."

14. The sesquicentennial of the Civil War in the United States (2011–2015) ushered in copious and even controversial programs highlighting the Civil War and different perspectives on the significance of slavery in the war. See National Park Service, "The Civil War."

15. For some of the critical concerns about the representations of slavery and enslaved people in the 2012 films *Django Unchained* and *Lincoln*, see Masur, "In Spielberg's 'Lincoln'"; Downs, "Our Lincoln"; Leveen, "Is 'Django Unchained'"; Gates, "Tarantino 'Unchained'"; and Bobo, "Slavery on Film." For insightful comments on the 2013 film *12 Years a Slave*, see, for example, Davies, "12 Years a Slave"; George, "An Essentially American Narrative"; and Gilroy, "12 Years a Slave." On *Harriet*, see, for example, a number of the issues presented in France, "'Harriet' Controversies." For examples of the mixed reviews of *Antebellum*, see Debruge, "'Antebellum' Review"; and Searles, "'Antebellum' Film Review."

16. See, for example, the award-winning critical book by Craig S. Wilder, *Ebony & Ivy*. For specific university websites on their respective institutions and historical connections to slavery, see, for example, Brown University, "Brown University Steering Committee"; Georgetown University, "Georgetown University"; Columbia University, "Columbia University & Slavery"; Rutgers University, "Rutgers Scarlet and Black Project"; and Princeton University, "The Princeton & Slavery Project." Some colleges and universities have also been exploring monuments or memorials related to slavery to be positioned on their respective campuses. As one of the initiatives of its Lemon Project (focused on the college's history related to slavery and enslaved people at the college), the College of William & Mary has decided to create a memorial. See College of William & Mary, "Memorial to African Americans." The University of Virginia's work in this area includes a memorial for enslaved laborers, which was completed in 2020. For more about this memorial, see the University of Virginia, President's Commission on Slavery and the University. For an excellent online presentation in October 2020 about the history, design, and

process regarding this memorial, see "Memorial to Enslaved Laborers." Regarding the recent actions of the University of Glasgow related to slavery, see Belam, "Glasgow University"; and University of Glasgow, "Slavery." One of the catalysts for such responses from the University of Glasgow has been the CARICOM Reparations Commission (CRC). For more information on the CRC, which was launched in July 2013, see CARICOM Reparations Committee, "Ten Point Action Plan."

17. For more on Universities Studying Slavery (USS), see the University of Virginia, President's Commission. As of October 2021, the USS membership included eighty-three colleges and universities based in the United States, Canada, Ireland, and the United Kingdom. Also see the University of Mississippi's Slavery Research Group.

18. For example, a few days after the protests in Charlottesville, including attacks on the monument of Confederate general Robert E. Lee, Duke University decided to remove the statue of Lee from the entrance of Duke's chapel on August 17, 2017. See Neuman, "Duke University Removes." In response to the Charlottesville protests, the University of Texas at Austin also decided to remove three Confederate monuments in August 2017: Confederate generals Robert E. Lee and Albert Sidney Johnston and Confederate cabinet member John Reagan. See Bromwich, "University of Texas." In addition to the removal of statues, several universities have chosen to rename buildings of prominent Americans who promulgated racist statements and policies. In June 2020, for example, Princeton University decided to change the name of the School of Public and International Affairs and Wilson College; both were named for President Woodrow Wilson. The official statement explained that "the trustees concluded that Woodrow Wilson's racist thinking and policies make him an inappropriate namesake for a school or college whose scholars, students, and alumni must stand firmly against racism in all its forms" (Princeton University, Office of Communications, "President Eisgruber's Message").

19. Morrison, *Beloved*.

20. In the spring and summer of 2020, these uprisings and attacks on Confederate monuments culminated in symbolic changes in a range of racist-inspired American food brands, sports mascots, and other realms of popular culture (e.g., the decision to get rid of the Aunt Jemima brand name, to change the name of the Washington Redskins, and to change the group names of the Dixie Chicks and Lady Antebellum).

21. Southern Poverty Law Center, "Whose Heritage?"

22. "Mitch Landrieu's Speech."

23. Ibid.

24. For a general overview of these Caribbean memorials and other related African, European, North American, and South American sites, see Freelon, "Look at All."

25. Statues of Christopher Columbus, Admiral George Rodney, and Queen Victoria have been particular targets in this discussion. See, for example, Reid, "Topple Columbus' Statue"; Hyman and Rodney, "Update."

26. For more on the various ways Jamaicans (and freedpeople in other British colonies in the Caribbean) celebrated August First in the first few decades following abolition, see Brereton, "A Social History." Also see an abridged summary of aspects of Emancipation Day by the Jamaica Information Service (JIS), "Emancipation."

27. See Rhoden, "Evolution of National Heroes Park."

28. Brereton, "A Social History"; Shepherd, "Slavery, Shame and Pride."

29. Shepherd, "Slavery, Shame and Pride."

30. For a brief summary of Dr. Robert Love's life, see the National Library of Jamaica's profile, "Robert Love (1839–1914)." One of the many people inspired by Dr. Love's journalism, political work, and overall achievements was Marcus Garvey.

31. After serving as deputy vice chancellor of the University of the West Indies (UWI), Nettleford would serve as vice chancellor from 1998 to 2004. For a brief summary of the life of Professor the Honourable Ralston "Rex" Milton Nettleford, see the National Library of Jamaica's profile, "Nettleford, Rex." This site includes a number of links to articles about and tributes to Nettleford.

32. Although the specific members of this forum are not included in the 2009 article, in another article submitted by the Public Theology Forum in 2017, the individual names of members at that time are mentioned at the end of the article: Anna Kasafi Perkins, Marvia Lawes, Verna Cassells, Doreen Wynter, Christine Gooden-Benguche, Burchell Taylor, Richmond Nelson, Stotrell Lowe, Garnett Roper, Devon Dick, Garth Minott, Ashley Smith, Wayneford McFarlane, Gary Harriott, Stanley Clarke, Oral Thomas, Glenroy Lalor, and Byron Chambers (coordinator). Public Theology Forum, "Is It Just a Little Sex."

33. Public Theology Forum, "Emancipation Observance."

34. Assata, "Leave Emancipation Day Alone!"

35. Shepherd, "Slavery, Shame and Pride," 14.

36. Ibid., 16.

37. Ibid.

38. Ibid., 16–17.

39. Public Theology Forum, "Emancipation Observance."

40. Marcus Garvey's speech "The Work That Has Been Done." For an online transcription of this speech, see Henrietta Vinton Davis's Weblog.

41. Emancipation Day Message 2020 (transcript), the Office of the Prime Minister Andrew Holness, August 1, 2020. For a video of Prime Minister Holness's message, see "Emancipation Day Message." In his recent annual Emancipation Day messages, Prime Minister Holness often begins with a brief look back at slavery and slavery's freedom fighters and then transitions to critical present-day issues and initiatives concerning unity and forward movement in Jamaica. Having been reelected in September 2020 as prime minister, he will indubitably continue this tradition of Emancipation Day messages and the invocation of Marcus Garvey's words. Indeed, in his Emancipation Day message on August 1, 2021, he highlighted different forms of violence inflicted on enslaved people and then connected these examples to the eradication of various contemporary forms of violence, including child abuse, domestic violence, corporal punishment, and gang violence.

42. Cooke, "Emancipation Park Marks a Decade."

43. "Miss World Tori-Ann Singh."

44. The Zong Massacre has been the subject of a number of recent scholarly works, including Philip, *Zong!*; and Walvin, *The Zong*. Also see Myers, "The Zong Massacre"; and Clarke, "Remembering the 'Zong Massacre.'"

45. Nguyen, *Nothing Ever Dies*, 40.

46. Ibid., 32–33.
47. As quoted in ibid., 68.

POSTSCRIPT

Thanks to my colleague Professor Premilla Nadasen for encouraging me to include some details about my own family's history in Jamaica.

BIBLIOGRAPHY

UNPUBLISHED PRIMARY SOURCES

Jamaica Archives and Records Department, Spanish Town, Jamaica (JARD)

1b/11/4/55 Rose Hall Estate, Crop Accounts, fol. 152, December 31, 1818–June 8, 1819.

1b/11/4/58, Rose Hall Estate, Crop Accounts, fol. 220, January 1–December 31, 1822.

1b/11/4/63, Rose Hall Estate, Crop Accounts, fol. 144, January–December 1826.

1b/11/4/66, Rose Hall Estate, Crop Accounts, fol. 56, January–November 1827.

1b/11/4/68, Rose Hall Estate, Crop Accounts, fol. 211, September 1828–September 1829.

1b/11/4/69, Rose Hall Estate, Crop Accounts, fol. 133, September 1829–September 1830.

1b/11/4/71, Rose Hall Estate, Crop Accounts, fol. 25, September 1830–September 1831.

1b/11/4/72, Rose Hall Estate, Crop Accounts, fol. 180, September 1831–September 1832.

1b/11/7/40, Rose Hall Estate List of Slaves, Registers of Returns of Slaves, St. James, June 28, 1820, John Rose Palmer as receiver and proprietor, fols. 160a and 160b.

1b/11/7/66, Rose Hall Estate List of Slaves, Registers of Returns of Slaves, St. James, June 28, 1823, John Rose Palmer as owner and receiver for Rose Hall Estate, fol. 74a.

1b/11/7/85, Rose Hall Estate List of Slaves, Registers of Returns of Slaves, St. James, June 28, 1826, John Rose Palmer as owner and receiver for Rose Hall Estate, fol. 155a.

1b/11/7/100, Rose Hall Estate List of Slaves, Registers of Returns of Slaves, St. James, June 28, 1829, in the possession of William Miller and William Heath as receivers of Rose Hall Estate, fol. 215.

1b/26, Rose Hall Journal (RHJ), vols. 1–3 (recently renumbered by JARD, vols. 5–7).

1b/11/4/56, Palmyra Estate, Crop Accounts, fol. 41, January 1820–December 1820.

National Archives, Kew Gardens, London (NA Kew)

t71/202, Rose Hall Estate List of Slaves, Registers of Returns of Slaves, St. James, June 28, 1817, Edward Mountague as receiver for Rose Hall Estate, fols. 540–545.

t71/206, Rose Hall Estate List of Slaves, Registers of Returns of Slaves, St. James, June 28, 1820, John Rose Palmer as receiver and proprietor for Rose Hall Estate, fol. 195.

t71/209, Rose Hall Estate List of Slaves, Registers of Returns of Slaves, St. James, June 28, 1823, John Rose Palmer as owner and receiver for Rose Hall Estate, fols. 279–280.

t71/214, Rose Hall Estate List of Slaves, Registers of Returns of Slaves, St. James, June 28, 1826, John Rose Palmer as owner and receiver for Rose Hall Estate, fols. 33–34.

t71/218, Rose Hall Estate List of Slaves, Registers of Returns of Slaves, St. James, June 28, 1829, in the possession of William Miller and William Heath as receivers of Rose Hall Estate, no folio numbers listed.

t71/223, Rose Hall Estate List of Slaves, Registers of Returns of Slaves, St. James, June 28, 1832, in
    the possession of William Miller and William Heath as receivers of Rose Hall Estate, fol. 91.

NEWSPAPERS AND PERIODICALS

The Gleaner, Kingston, Jamaica.
New York Times, New York, New York.
Royal Gazette, Kingston, Jamaica.
Sunday News Journal, Wilmington, Delaware.

PUBLISHED PRIMARY SOURCES

al-Siddiq, Abu Bakr. "The History of Abon Becr Sadika, known in Jamaica by the name of
    Edward Donlan." In *A Twelvemonth's Residence in the West Indies*. By Richard Robert Mad-
    den. Vol. 2: 183–189. Philadelphia: Carey, Lea and Blanchard, 1835.
———. "Routes in North Africa, by Abu Bekr es Siddik." Translated by G. C. Renouard. *Jour-
    nal of the Royal Geographical Society of London* 6 (1836): 100–113.
Douglass, Frederick. *Narrative of the Life of Frederick Douglass, an American Slave*. Boston:
    Anti-Slavery Office, 1845.
Ferguson, Moira, ed. *The History of Mary Prince*. 1831; repr., Ann Arbor: University of Michi-
    gan Press, 1997.
Hakewill, James. *A Picturesque Tour of the Island of Jamaica, with Drawings Made in the Years
    1820 and 1821*. London: Hurst and Robinson, 1825.
Higman, B. W. *Jamaica Surveyed: Plantation Maps and Plans of the Eighteenth and Nineteenth
    Centuries*. Kingston: Institute of Jamaica Publications, 1988.
Jacobs, Harriet. *Incidents in the Life of a Slave Girl*. Boston: Published for the Author, 1861.
Long, Edward. *History of Jamaica*. London: T. Lowndes, 1774.
Luis, William, ed. *Juan Francisco Manzano: Autobiografía del esclavo poeta y otros escritos*. 1835;
    repr., Madrid: Iberoamericana Vervuert, 2007.
Madden, Richard Robert. *A Twelvemonth's Residence in the West Indies*. Vol. 1. Reprint of 1835
    ed. Westport, Conn.: Negro Universities Press, 1970.
———. *A Twelvemonth's Residence in the West Indies*. Vol. 2. Philadelphia: Carey, Lea and
    Blanchard, 1835.
Monteith, Archibald John. *Archibald John Monteith: Native Helper and Assistant in the
    Jamaica Mission at New Carmel*. Edited by Vernon H. Nelson. In *Transactions of the Mora-
    vian Historical Society*. 21, no. 1 (1966): 29–52.
Mullen, Edward J., ed. *The Life and Poems of a Cuban Slave, Juan Francisco Manzano, 1797–
    1854*. New York: Palgrave, 2014.
North American Slave Narratives. Documenting the Old South. https://docsouth.unc.edu/
    neh/.
Nugent, Maria. *Lady Nugent's Journal of Her Residence in Jamaica from 1801–1805*. Edited by
    Philip Wright. Kingston, Jamaica: University of the West Indies Press, 2002.
Rawick, George P., ed. *The American Slave: A Composite Autobiography*. Westport, Conn.:
    Greenwood Press, 1973.

———. *The American Slave: A Composite Autobiography*. Supplement Series 2. Westport, Conn.: Greenwood Press, 1979.

Reasons for Establishing a Registry of Slaves in the British Colonies: A Report of a Committee of the African Institution. London: Ellerton and Henderson, 1815.

Renny, Robert. *An History of Jamaica*. London: Printed for J. Cawthorn, 1807.

Shore, Joseph, comp. *In Old St. James, Jamaica: A Book of Parish Chronicles*. Kingston, Jamaica: Aston W. Gardner & Co., 1911.

Shore, Joseph, comp. *In Old St. James, Jamaica: A Book of Parish Chronicles*. Edited by John Stewart. Kingston, Jamaica: Sangster's Book Stores Ltd. in association with the Bodley Head, London, 1952.

Williams, James. *A Narrative of Events, Since the First of August, 1834, by James Williams, an Apprenticed Labourer in Jamaica*. London: J. Rider, 1837.

Williamson, John. *Medical and Miscellaneous Observations, Relative to the West Indian Islands*. Vol. 1. Edinburgh: Printed by Alex Smellie, 1817.

PUBLISHED SECONDARY SOURCES

Abrahams, Yvette. "Was Eva Raped? An Exercise in Speculative History." *Kronos*, no. 23 (November 1996): 3–21.

Agyekum, Kofi. "The Sociolinguistic of Akan Personal Names." *Nordic Journal of African Studies* 15, no. 2 (2006): 206–235.

Aidoo, Lamonte. *Slavery Unseen: Sex, Power, and Violence in Brazilian History*. Durham, N.C.: Duke University Press, 2018.

Altink, Henrice. *Representations of Slave Women in Discourses on Slavery and Abolition, 1780–1838*. New York: Routledge, 2007.

Anatol, Giselle Liza. *The Things That Fly in the Night: Female Vampires in Literature of the Circum-Caribbean and African Diaspora*. New Brunswick, N.J.: Rutgers University Press, 2015.

Anim-Addo, Joa, and Maria Helena Lima, eds. "The Neo–Slave Narrative Genre." Special issues, *Callaloo* 40, no. 4 (Fall 2017) and 41, no. 1 (Winter 2018).

Araujo, Ana Lucia, ed. *Living History: Encountering the Memory of the Heirs of Slavery*. Newcastle: Cambridge Scholars Publishing, 2009.

———. *Museums and Atlantic Slavery*. New York: Routledge, 2021.

———, ed. *Politics of Memory: Making Slavery Visible in the Public Space*. New York: Routledge, 2012.

———. *Slavery in the Age of Memory: Engaging the Past*. New York: Bloomsbury, 2021.

Arondekar, Anjali. "What More Remains: Slavery, Sexuality, South Asia." *History of the Present* 6, no. 2 (Fall 2016): 146–154.

Babalola, Adeboye, and Olugboyega Alaba. *A Dictionary of Yoruba Personal Names*. Lagos, Nigeria: West African Book Publishers, 2006.

Barber, Karin. *I Could Speak Until Tomorrow: Oriki, Women and the Past in a Yoruba Town*. Washington, D.C.: Smithsonian, 1991.

Beckles, Hilary McD. *Centering Women: Gender Discourses in Caribbean Slave Society*. Princeton, N.J.: Markus Wiener, 1999.

———. *Natural Rebels: A Social History of Enslaved Women in Barbados*. New Brunswick, N.J.: Rutgers University Press, 1989.

———. "White Women and Slavery in the Caribbean." In *Caribbean Slavery in the Atlantic World: A Student Reader*, edited by Verene Shepherd and Hilary McD. Beckles, 659–669. Princeton, N.J.: Markus Wiener, 2000.

Bell, Bernard W. *The Afro-American Novel and Its Tradition*. Amherst: University of Massachusetts Press, 1987.

Benjamin, Richard. "Museums and Sensitive Histories: The International Slave Museum." In *Politics of Memory: Making Slavery Visible in the Public Space*, edited by Ana Lucia Araujo, 178–196. New York: Routledge, 2012.

Bennett, Herman. *Colonial Blackness: A History of Afro-Mexico*. Bloomington: Indiana University Press, 2009.

Berry, Daina Ramey. *The Price for Their Pound of Flesh: The Value of the Enslaved, from Womb to Grave, in the Building of a Nation*. Boston: Beacon Press, 2017.

———. *Swing the Sickle for the Harvest Is Ripe: Gender and Slavery in Antebellum Georgia*. Champaign: University of Illinois Press, 2007.

Besson, Jean. *Transformations of Freedom in the Land of the Maroons: Creolization in the Cockpits Jamaica*. Kingston, Jamaica: Ian Randle Publishers, 2015.

Bilby, Kenneth M., and Jerome S. Handler. "Obeah: Healing and Protection in West Indian Slave Life." *Journal of Caribbean History* 38, no. 2 (2004): 158–183.

Black, Colin V. *Tales of Old Jamaica*. 1966; repr., London: Collins Sangster, 1979.

Brand, Dionne. *A Map to the Door of No Return: Notes to Belonging*. Toronto: Vintage, 2001.

———. *At the Full and Change of the Moon*. Toronto: Knopf, 2011.

Brathwaite, Edward Kamau. "The Slave Rebellion in the Great River Valley of St. James 1831/32." *Jamaican Historical Review* 13 (1982): 11–30.

Brereton, Bridget. "A Social History of Emancipation Day in the British Caribbean: The First Fifty Years." In *Inside Slavery: Process and Legacy in the Caribbean Experience*, edited by Hilary McD. Beckles, 78–95. Kingston, Jamaica: University of the West Indies Press, 2002.

Brodber, Erna. *Myal*. Long Grove, Ill.: Waveland Press, 2014.

Brown, Caroline A., and Johanna X. K. Garvey, eds. *Madness in Black Women's Diasporic Fictions: Aesthetics of Resistance*. New York: Palgrave Macmillan, 2017.

Brown, Vincent. *The Reaper's Garden: Death and Power in the World of Atlantic Slavery*. Cambridge, Mass.: Harvard University Press, 2010.

———. *Tacky's Revolt: The Story of an Atlantic Slave War*. Cambridge, Mass.: Harvard University Press, 2020.

Burnard, Trevor. *Mastery, Tyranny, and Desire: Thomas Thistlewood and His Slaves in the Anglo Jamaican World*. Chapel Hill: University of North Carolina Press, 2004.

———. "Slave Naming Patterns: Onomastics and the Taxonomy of Race in Eighteenth-Century Jamaica." *Journal of Interdisciplinary History* 31, no. 3 (Winter 2001): 325–346.

Bush, Barbara. "The Family Tree Is Not Cut: Women and Cultural Resistance in Slave Family Life in the British Caribbean." In *In Resistance: Studies in African, Caribbean, and Afro-American History*, edited by Gary Y. Okihiro, 117–127. Amherst: University of Massachusetts Press, 1986.

———. "Hard Labor: Women, Childbirth, and Resistance in British Caribbean Slave Societies." In *More Than Chattel: Black Women and Slavery in the Americas*, edited by David Barry Gaspar and Darlene Clark Hine, 193–217. Bloomington: Indiana University Press, 1996.

———. *Slave Women in Caribbean Society, 1650–1838*. Bloomington: Indiana University Press, 1990.

Butler, Octavia. *Kindred*. New York: Doubleday, 1979.

Camp, Stephanie. *Closer to Freedom: Enslaved Women and Everyday Forms of Resistance in the Plantation South*. Chapel Hill: University of North Carolina Press, 2004.

Castello, James. "The Legend of Rose Hall." *Falmouth (Jamaica) Post*, 1868.

Christiansë, Yvette. *Toni Morrison: An Ethical Poetics*. New York: Fordham University Press, 2013.

Coates, Ta-Nehisi. *The Water Dancer*. New York: One World, 2019.

Cobham, Rhonda. "Herbert George de Lisser." In *Fifty Caribbean Writers: A Bio-bibliographical Critical Sourcebook,* edited by Daryl C. Dance, 166–177. Westport, Conn.: Greenwood Press, 1986.

———. "The Literary Side of H. G. de Lisser (1878–1944)." *Jamaica Journal* 17, no. 4 (1984): 2–9.

Cohen, Cathy J. *No Tea, No Shade: New Writings in Black Queer Studies*. Durham, N.C.: Duke University Press, 2016.

Colbert, Soyica Diggs, Robert J. Patterson, and Aida Levy-Hussen, eds. *The Psychic Hold of Slavery: Legacies in American Expressive Culture*. New Brunswick, N.J.: Rutgers University Press, 2016.

Connolly, Brian, and Marisa Fuentes. "Introduction: From Archives of Slavery to Liberated Futures?" *History of the Present* 6, no. 2 (Fall 2016): 105–116.

Cooper Owens, Deirdre. *Medical Bondage: Race, Gender, and the Origins of American Gynecology*. Athens: University of Georgia Press, 2017.

Craton, Michael. "Changing Patterns of Slave Families in the British West Indies." *Journal of Interdisciplinary History* 10, no. 1 (Summer 1979): 1–35.

———. *Searching for the Invisible Man: Slaves and Plantation Life in Jamaica*. Cambridge, Mass.: Harvard University Press, 1978.

Craton, Michael, and James Walvin. *A Jamaican Plantation: A History of Worthy Park, 1670–1970*. Toronto: University of Toronto Press, 1970.

Crosson, J. Brent. "What Obeah Does Do: Healing, Harm, and the Limits of Religion." *Journal of Africana Religions* 3, no. 2 (2015): 151–176.

Crowley, Daniel J. "Naming Customs in St. Lucia." *Social and Economic Studies* 5, no. 1 (March 1956): 87–92.

Cubitt, Geoffrey. "Museums and Slavery in Britain: The Bicentenary of 1807." In *Politics of Memory: Making Slavery Visible in the Public Space*, edited by Ana Lucia Araujo, 159–177. New York: Routledge, 2012.

D'Aguiar, Fred. *Feeding the Ghosts*. New York: Ecco Press, 1999.

———. *The Longest Memory*. Cheltenham, Australia: Insight Publications, 1998.

Davies, Carole Boyce. "12 Years a Slave Fails to Represent Black Resistance to Enslavement." *The Guardian*, January 10, 2014.

Dawes, Kwame S. N. "An Act of 'Unruly' Savagery: Re-writing Black Rebellion in the Language of the Colonizer: H. G. de Lisser's *The White Witch of Rosehall*." *Caribbean Quarterly* 40, no. 1 (March 1994): 1–12.

de Lisser, Herbert G. *The White Witch of Rosehall*. 1929; repr., Oxford: Macmillan, 2007.

DeLoughrey, Elizabeth. "Yam, Roots, and Rot: Allegories of the Provision Grounds." *Small Axe* 51 (March 2011): 58–75.

Diouf, Sylviane A. *Slavery's Exiles: The Story of the American Maroons*. New York: New York University Press, 2014.

Donahue, Jennifer. "The Ghost of Annie Palmer: Giving Voice to Jamaica's 'White Witch of Rose Hall.'" *Journal of Commonwealth Literature* 49, no. 2 (June 2014): 243–256.

Dubois, Laurent. *Avengers of the New World: The Story of the Haitian Revolution*. Cambridge, Mass.: Harvard University Press, 2004.

———. *A Colony of Citizens: Revolution & Slave Emancipation in the French Caribbean, 1787–1804*. Chapel Hill: University of North Carolina Press, 2004.

Du Bois, W. E. B. *The Souls of Black Folk*. 1903; repr., New York: Norton, 1999.

Dunn, Richard S. *A Tale of Two Plantations: Slave Life and Labor in Jamaica and Virginia*. Cambridge, Mass.: Harvard University Press, 2014.

Ellis, Nadia. "Out and Bad: Toward a Queer Performance Hermeneutic in Jamaican Dancehall." *Small Axe* 35 (July 2011): 7–23.

Fernández Olmos, Margarite, and Lizabeth Paravisini-Gebert. *Creole Religions of the Caribbean: An Introduction from Vodou and Santería to Obeah and Espiritismo*. 2nd ed. New York: New York University Press, 2011.

Fett, Sharla M. *Working Cures: Healing, Health, and Power on Southern Slave Plantations*. Chapel Hill: University of North Carolina Press, 2002.

Forster, Martin, and S. D. Smith. "Surviving Slavery: Mortality at Mesopotamia, a Jamaican Sugar Estate, 1762–1832." *Journal of the Royal Statistical Society* 174, no. 4 (October 2011): 907–929.

Foster, Thomas A. *Rethinking Rufus: Sexual Violations of Enslaved Men*. Athens: University of Georgia Press, 2019.

Franklin, John Hope, and Loren Schweninger. *Runaway Slaves: Rebels on the Plantation*. New York: Oxford University Press, 1999.

Frye, Karla Y. E. "'An Article of Faith': Obeah and Hybrid Identities in Elizabeth Nunez-Harrell's *When Rocks Dance*." In *Sacred Possessions: Vodou, Santería, Obeah, and the Caribbean*, edited by Margarite Fernández Olmos and Lizabeth Paravisini-Gebert, 195–215. New Brunswick, N.J.: Rutgers University Press, 1997.

Fuentes, Marisa J. *Dispossessed Lives: Enslaved Women, Violence, and the Archive*. Philadelphia: University of Pennsylvania Press, 2016.

Gaspar, David Barry. *Bondmen and Rebels: A Case Study of Master-Slave Relations in Antigua, with Implications for Colonial British America*. Baltimore, Md.: Johns Hopkins University Press, 1985.

Gaspar, David Barry, and Darlene Clark Hine, eds. *More Than Chattel: Black Women and Slavery in the Americas*. Bloomington: Indiana University Press, 1996.

Gay, Roxanne. "I Don't Want to Watch Slavery Fan Fiction." *New York Times*, July 25, 2017.

Geggus, David, ed. *The Haitian Revolution: A Documentary History*. Indianapolis: Hackett Publishing Company, 2014.

———. *Haitian Revolutionary Studies*. Bloomington: Indiana University Press, 2002.

George, Nelson. "An Essentially American Narrative: A Discussion of Steve McQueen's Film '12 Years a Slave.'" *New York Times*, October 11, 2013.

Gilbert, Sandra, and Susan Gubar. *The Madwoman in the Attic: The Woman Writer and the Nineteenth-Century Literary Imagination*. New Haven, Conn.: Yale University Press, 1980.

Gilroy, Paul. "12 Years a Slave: In Our 'Post-racial' Age the Legacy of Slavery Lives On." *The Guardian*, November 10, 2013.

Glover, Kaiama L. *A Regarded Self: Caribbean Womanhood and the Ethics of Disorderly Being*. Durham, N.C.: Duke University Press, 2021.

Glymph, Thavolia. *Out of the House of Bondage: The Transformation of the Plantation Household*. New York: Cambridge University Press, 2008.

Gordon, Avery F. *Ghostly Matters: Haunting and the Sociological Imagination*. 1996; repr., Minneapolis: University of Minnesota Press, 2008.

Gordon-Reed, Annette. *The Hemingses of Monticello: An American Family*. New York: W. W. Norton, 2009.

———. "Writing Early American Lives as Biography." *William and Mary Quarterly* 71, no. 4 (October 2014): 491–516.

Goudie, Sean X. *Creole America: The West Indies and the Formation of Literature and Culture in the New Republic*. Philadelphia: University of Pennsylvania Press, 2006.

Goveia, Elsa V. *Slave Society in the British Leeward Islands at the End of the Eighteenth Century*. New Haven, Conn.: Yale University Press, 1965.

Guy-Sheftall, Beverly. "The Body Politic: Black Female Sexuality and the Nineteenth-Century Euro-American Imagination." In *Skin Deep, Spirit Strong: The Black Female Body in American Culture*, edited by Kimberly Wallace-Sanders, 13–35. Ann Arbor: University of Michigan Press, 2002.

Haggard, H. Rider. *She: A History of Adventure*. Originally serialized in *The Graphic* magazine, October 1886 and January 1887.

Hall, N. A. T. "Some Aspects of the Deficiency Question in Jamaica in the Eighteenth Century." *Caribbean Studies* 14, no. 1 (1975): 5–19.

Hammonds, Evelynn M. "Toward a Genealogy of Black Female Sexuality: The Problematic of Silence." In *Feminist Genealogies, Colonial Legacies, Democratic Futures*, edited by M. Jacqui Alexander and Chandra Talpade Mohanty, 93–104. New York: Routledge, 1997.

Handler, Jerome S., and Kenneth M. Bilby. "On the Early Use and Origin of the Term 'Obeah' in Barbados and the Anglophone Caribbean." *Slavery & Abolition* 22, no. 2 (August 2001): 87–100.

Handler, Jerome S., and JoAnn Jacoby. "Slave Names and Naming in Barbados 1650–1830." *William and Mary Quarterly*, 3rd ser., 53, no. 4 (October 1996): 685–728.

Hanger, Kimberly S. *Bounded Lives, Bounded Places: Free Black Society in Colonial New Orleans, 1769–1803*. Durham, N.C.: Duke University Press, 1997.

Harkins, Patricia. "'Spells of Darkness': Invisibility in the White Witch of Rosehall." *Journal of the Fantastic in the Arts* 4, no. 2 (1992): 49–64.

Hartman, Saidiya. *Lose Your Mother: A Journey along the Atlantic Slave Route*. New York: Farrar, Straus and Giroux, 2007.

———. "Response: The Dead Book Revisited." *History of the Present* 6, no. 2 (Fall 2016): 208–215.

———. *Scenes of Subjection: Terror, Slavery and Self-Making in Nineteenth-Century America*. New York: Oxford University Press, 1997.

———. "Venus in Two Acts," *Small Axe* 12 (June 2008): 1–14.

Hausman, Gerald. *Duppy Talk: West Indian Tales of Mystery and Magic*. Miami, Fla.: Irie Books, 1999.

Henderson, Mae. "Toni Morrison's *Beloved*: Re-membering the Body as Historical Text." In *Toni Morrison's "Beloved": A Casebook*, edited by William L. Andrews and Nellie Y. McKay, 79–106. New York: Oxford University Press, 1999.

Henry, Mike. *Rose Hall's White Witch: The Legend of Annie Palmer*. Kingston, Jamaica: LMH Publishing, 2006.

Heuman, Gad. *The Killing Time: The Morant Bay Rebellion in Jamaica*. Knoxville: University of Tennessee Press, 1994.

———, ed. *Out of the House of Bondage: Runaways, Resistance, and Marronage in Africa and the New World*. London: Frank Cass, 1986.

Higman, B. W. *Montpelier, Jamaica: A Plantation Community in Slavery and Freedom, 1739–1912*. Kingston, Jamaica: University of the West Indies Press, 1998.

———. *Plantation Jamaica, 1750–1850: Capital and Control in a Colonial Economy*. Kingston, Jamaica: University of the West Indies Press, 2005.

———. "The Slave Family and Household in the British West Indies, 1800–1834." *Journal of Interdisciplinary History* 6, no. 2 (Autumn 1975): 261–287.

———. *Slave Population and Economy in Jamaica, 1807–1834*, with a new introduction. 1976; repr., Kingston, Jamaica: University of the West Indies Press, 1995.

———. *Slave Populations of the British Caribbean, 1807–1834*. Baltimore, Md.: Johns Hopkins University Press, 1984.

Hine, Darlene Clark, and Kathleen Thompson. *A Shining Thread of Hope: The History of Black Women in America*. New York: Broadway Books, 1998.

Hirsch, Marianne. *The Generation of Postmemory: Writing and Visual Culture after the Holocaust*. New York: Columbia University Press, 2012.

Hirsch, Marianne, and Nancy K. Miller, eds. *Rites of Return: Diaspora Poetics and the Politics of Memory*. New York: Columbia University Press, 2011.

Hirsch, Marianne, and Leo Spitzer. *Ghosts of Home: The Afterlife of Czernowitz in Jewish Memory*. Oakland: University of California Press, 2011.

Holsey, Bayo. *Routes of Remembrance: Refashioning the Slave Trade in Ghana*. Chicago: University of Chicago Press, 2008.

Hunter, Tera W. *Bound in Wedlock: Slave and Free Black Marriage in the Nineteenth Century*. Cambridge, Mass.: Harvard University Press, 2017.

Hunt-Kennedy, Stefanie. *Between Fitness and Death: Disability and Slavery in the Caribbean*. Champaign: University of Illinois Press, 2020.

———. "'Had His Nose Cropt for Being Formerly Runaway': Disability and the Bodies of

Fugitive Slaves in the British Caribbean." *Slavery & Abolition*. DOI 10.1080/0144039X .2019.1644886.

Inniss, Tara A. "'Any Elderly, Sensible, Prudent Woman': The Practice and Practitioners of Midwifery during Slavery in the British Caribbean." In *Health and Medicine in the Circum-Caribbean*, edited by Juanita De Barros, Steven Palmer, and David Wright, 40–52. New York: Routledge, 2009.

James, C. L. R. *The Black Jacobins: Toussaint L'Ouverture and the San Domingo Revolution*. 1938; repr., New York: Random House, 1963.

James, Marlon. *The Book of Night Women*. New York: Riverhead Books, 2009.

Johnson, Jessica Marie. "Markup Bodies: Black [Life] Studies and Slavery [Death] Studies at the Digital Crossroads." *Social Text* 36, no. 4 (December 2018): 57–79.

———. *Wicked Flesh: Black Women, Intimacy, and Freedom in the Atlantic World*. Philadelphia: University of Pennsylvania Press, 2020.

Jones, Cecily. *Engendering Whiteness: White Women and Colonialism in Barbados and North Carolina, 1627–1865*. Manchester: Manchester University Press, 2007.

Jones, Edward P. *The Known World*. New York: Amistad Press, 2003.

Jones-Rogers, Stephanie E. *They Were Her Property: White Women as Slave Owners in the American South*. New Haven, Conn.: Yale University Press, 2019.

Josephs, Kelly Baker. *Disturbers of the Peace: Representations of Madness in Anglophone Caribbean Literature*. Charlottesville: University of Virginia Press, 2013.

Kars, Marjoleine. *Blood on the River: A Chronicle of Mutiny and Freedom on the Wild Coast*. New York: New Press, 2020.

Kazanjian, David. "Two Paths Through Slavery's Archives." *History of the Present* 6, no. 2 (Fall 2016): 133–145.

Kennedy, Fred W. *Daddy Sharpe: A Narrative of the Life and Adventures of Samuel Sharpe, a West Indian Slave Written by Himself, 1832*. Kingston, Jamaica: Ian Randle Publishers, 2008.

Landers, Jane G., ed. *Against the Odds: Free Blacks in the Slave Societies of the Americas*. London: Frank Cass & Co., 1996.

Ledent, Bénédicte, Evelyn O'Callaghan, and Daria Tunca, eds. *Madness in Anglophone Caribbean Literature: On the Edge*. New York: Palgrave Macmillan, 2018.

Leveen, Lois. "Is 'Django Unchained' Shackled to Hollywood's Past?" *Wall Street Journal*, December 20, 2012.

Levy, Andrea. *The Long Song*. London: Headline Review, 2011.

Livesay, Daniel. *Children of Uncertain Fortune: Mixed-Race Jamaicans in Britain and the Atlantic Family, 1733–1833*. Chapel Hill: University of North Carolina Press, 2018.

Lomas, Laura. "Mystifying Mystery: Inscriptions of the Oral in the Legend of Rose Hall." *Journal of West Indian Literature* 6, no. 2 (May 1994): 70–87.

Macgonagle, Elizabeth. "From Dungeons to Dance Parties: Contested Histories of Ghana's Slave Forts." *Journal of Contemporary African Studies* 24, no. 2 (May 2006): 249–260.

Mair, Lucille Mathurin. *The Rebel Woman in the British West Indies during Slavery*. Kingston: Institute of Jamaica, 1975.

————. *A Historical Study of Women in Jamaica, 1655–1844*. Edited by Verene A. Shepherd and Hilary McD. Beckles. Kingston: University of the West Indies Press, 2006.

Marshall, Woodville K. "Provision Ground and Plantation Labour in Four Windward Islands: Competition for Resources during Slavery." In *The Slaves' Economy: Independent Production by Slaves in the Americas*, edited by Ira Berlin and Phillip D. Morgan, 48–67. Portland, Ore.: Frank Cass & Co., 1991.

Masur, Kate. "In Spielberg's 'Lincoln,' Passive Black Characters." *New York Times*, November 12, 2012.

McKenzie, Jennifer Otholene. "Jamaican Ethnic Dress: An Evolution of Cultures from Post Emancipation 1838 to Independence 1962." Master's thesis, University of Wisconsin–Stout, 2003.

Miles, Tiya A. *Tales from the Haunted South: Dark Tourism and Memories of Slavery from the Civil War Era*. Chapel Hill: University of North Carolina Press, 2015.

Millward, Jessica. *Finding Charity's Folk: Enslaved and Free Black Women in Maryland*. Athens: University of Georgia Press, 2015.

Mitchell, Elise A. "Infectious Blackness: Slavery, Englishness, and Representations of the Body in the British West Indies (c. 1770–1807)." BA thesis, University of Pennsylvania, 2014.

————. "Tainted Bodies: Gendered Representations of Racial Mixing and Creole Degeneracy in the British West Indies (1770–1812)." *Penn History Review* 21, no. 1 (Spring 2014): 31–63.

Moglen, Seth. "Enslaved in the City on a Hill: The Archive of Moravian Slavery and the Practical Past." *History of the Present* 6, no. 2 (Fall 2016): 155–183.

Moitt, Bernard. *Women and Slavery in the French Antilles, 1635–1848*. Bloomington: Indiana University Press, 2001.

Moody, Jessica. *The Persistence of Memory: Remembering Slavery in Liverpool, "Slaving Capital of the World."* Liverpool: Liverpool University Press, 2020.

Moore, Brian L., and Michele A. Johnson. *Neither Led nor Driven: Contesting British Cultural Imperialism in Jamaica, 1865–1920*. Kingston, Jamaica: University of the West Indies Press, 2004.

Morgan, Jennifer L. "Accounting for 'The Most Excruciating Torment': Gender, Slavery, and Trans-Atlantic Passages." *History of the Present* 6, no. 2 (Fall 2016): 184–207.

————. *Laboring Women: Reproduction and Gender in New World Slavery*. Philadelphia: University of Pennsylvania Press, 2004.

————. "*Partus Sequitur Ventrem*: Law, Race and Reproduction in Colonial Slavery." *Small Axe* 55 (March 2018): 1–17.

————. *Reckoning with Slavery: Gender, Kinship, and Capitalism in the Early Black Atlantic*. Durham, N.C.: Duke University Press, 2021.

Morgan, Kenneth. "Slave Women and Reproduction in Jamaica, 1776–1834." *History* 91, no. 2 (April 2006): 231–253.

Morissey, Marietta. *Slave Women in the New World: Gender Stratification in the Caribbean*. Lawrence: University Press of Kansas, 1989.

Morris, Mervyn. "H. G. de Lisser: The First Competent Caribbean Novelist in English." *Carib* 1 (1979): 18–26.

Morrison, Toni. *Beloved*. New York: Alfred Knopf, 1987.

———. "The Site of Memory." In *Inventing the Truth: The Art and Craft of Memoir*, edited by William Zinsser, 83–102. 2nd ed. Boston: Houghton Mifflin Company, 1995.

———. "Unspeakable Things Unspoken: The Afro-American Presence in American Literature." *Michigan Quarterly Review* 28, no. 1 (Winter 1989): 1–34.

Mueller, Monika. "Hybridity Sucks: European Vampirism Encounters Haitian Voodoo in *The White Witch of Rosehall*." In *Vampires and Zombies: Transcultural Migrations and Transnational Interpretations*, edited by Dorothea Fischer-Hornung and Monika Mueller, 130–146. Jackson: University Press of Mississippi, 2016.

Murphy, Heather. "Pinterest and the Knot Pledge to Stop Promoting Plantation Weddings." *New York Times*, December 5, 2019.

Myers, Garfield. "The Zong Massacre." *Jamaica Observer*, August 6, 2017.

Naylor, Celia E. "Imagining and Imagined Sites, Sights, and Sounds of Slavery." *William and Mary Quarterly*, 3rd ser., 76, no. 1 (January 2019): 25–32.

Newman, Brooke N. *A Dark Inheritance: Blood, Race, and Sex in Colonial Jamaica*. New Haven, Conn.: Yale University Press, 2018.

Newman, Simon P. "Breaking Free: Digital History and Escaping from Slavery." *William and Mary Quarterly*, 3rd ser., 76, no. 1 (January 2019): 33–40.

Nguyen, Viet Thanh. *Nothing Ever Dies: Vietnam and the Memory of War*. Cambridge, Mass.: Harvard University Press, 2016.

Palmer, Colin A. *Freedom's Children: The 1938 Labor Rebellion and the Birth of Modern Jamaica*. Chapel Hill: University of North Carolina Press, 2014.

Paravisini-Gebert, Lizabeth. "The White Witch of Rosehall and the Legitimacy of Female Power in the Caribbean Plantation." *Journal of West Indian Literature* 4, no. 2 (November 1990): 25–45.

Parry, John H. "Plantation and Provision Ground: An Historical Sketch of the Introduction of Food Crops into Jamaica." *Revista de Historia de América*, no. 39 (June 1955): 1–20.

Paton, Diana. *A Cultural Politics of Obeah: Religion, Colonialism, and Modernity in the Caribbean World*. Cambridge: Cambridge University Press, 2015.

———. *No Bond but the Law: Punishment, Race, and Gender in Jamaican State Formation, 1780–1870*. Durham, N.C.: Duke University Press, 2004.

Patterson, Orlando. "From Endo-deme to Matri-deme: An Interpretation of the Development of Kinship and Social Organization among the Slaves of Jamaica, 1655–1830." In *Eighteenth-Century Florida and the Caribbean*, edited by Samuel Proctor, 50–59. Gainesville: University Press of Florida, 1976.

Paugh, Katherine. *The Politics of Reproduction: Race, Medicine, and Fertility in the Age of Abolition*. New York: Oxford University Press, 2017.

Petley, Christer. *White Fury: A Jamaican Slaveholder and the Age of Revolution*. New York: Oxford University Press, 2018.

Philip, M. NourbeSe. *Zong!* Toronto: Mercury Press, 2008.

Powell, Patricia. "Obeah, Spiritual Technologies and Social Justice." Keynote speech presented at the Association of Caribbean Women Writers and Scholars, Zoom conference. January 15, 2021.

Powers, Jacqueline, and Joe Trento. "Rollins Finds a Nightmare in His Jamaican Dream." *Sunday News Journal*, August 5, 1979.

Price, Richard, ed. *Maroon Societies: Rebel Slave Communities in the Americas*. Baltimore, Md.: Johns Hopkins University Press, 1979.

Reckord, Mary. "The Jamaica Slave Rebellion of 1831." *Past and Present* 40, no. 1 (July 1968): 108–125.

Reid, Ahmed. "Sugar, Slavery and Productivity in Jamaica, 1750–1807." *Slavery & Abolition* 37, no. 1 (2016): 169–170.

Reis, João José. *Slave Rebellion in Brazil: The Muslim Uprising of 1835 in Bahia*. Translated by Arthur Brakel. Baltimore, Md.: Johns Hopkins University Press, 1993.

Rosenberg, Leah Reade. *Nationalism and the Formation of Caribbean Literature*. New York: Palgrave, 2007.

Rousseau, Michelle, and Suzanne Rousseau. *Provisions: The Roots of Caribbean Cooking*. New York: Da Capo Press, 2018.

Rushdy, Ashraf H. A. *Neo–Slave Narratives: Studies in the Social Logic of a Literary Form*. New York: Oxford University Press, 1999.

Schiebinger, Londa. "Agnotology and Exotic Abortifacients: The Cultural Production of Ignorance in the Eighteenth-Century Atlantic World." *Proceedings of the American Philosophical Society* 149, no. 3 (September 2005): 316–343.

Schuyler, Robert Livingston. "The Constitutional Claims of the British West Indies." *Political Science Quarterly* 40, no. 1 (March 1925): 1–36.

Scott, Julius S. *The Common Wind: Afro-American Currents in the Age of the Haitian Revolution*. New York: Verso, 2018.

Senior, Olive. *Shell*. Toronto: Insomniac Press, 2007.

Shange, Ntozake. *For Colored Girls Who Have Considered Suicide When the Rainbow Is Enuf*. New York: Scribner, 1997.

Sharpe, Christina. *In the Wake: On Blackness and Being*. Durham, N.C.: Duke University Press, 2016.

Shepherd, Verene A. "Slavery, Shame and Pride: Debates over the Marking of the Bicentennial of the Abolition of the British Trans-Atlantic Trade in Africans in 2007." *Caribbean Quarterly* 56, no. 1/2 (March–June 2010): 1–21.

Sheridan, Richard B. "From Chattel to Wage Slavery in Jamaica, 1740–1860." In *The Wages of Slavery: From Chattel Slavery to Wage Labour in Africa, the Caribbean, and England*, edited by Michael Twaddle, 13–40. New York: Frank Cass & Co., 1993.

Sherlock, Philip, and Hazel Bennett. *The Story of the Jamaican People*. Kingston, Jamaica: Ian Randle Publishers, 1998.

Smallwood, Stephanie E. "The Politics of the Archive and History's Accountability to the Enslaved." *History of the Present* 6, no. 2 (Fall 2016): 117–132.

———. *Saltwater Slavery: A Middle Passage from Africa to American Diaspora*. Cambridge, Mass.: Harvard University Press, 2007.

Spillers, Hortense. "Mama's Baby, Papa's Maybe: An American Grammar Book." In *Black, White, and in Color: Essays on American Literature and Culture*, edited by Hortense Spillers, 203–229. Chicago: University of Chicago Press, 2003.

Spivak, Gayatri Chakravorty. "Can the Subaltern Speak?" In *Marxism and the Interpretation of Culture*, edited by Cary Nelson and Lawrence Grossberg, 271–316. Urbana: University of Illinois Press, 1988.

Teelucksingh, Jerome. "The 'Invisible Child' in British West Indian Slavery." *Slavery & Abolition* 27, no. 2 (August 2006): 237–250.

Thompson, Alvin O. *Flight to Freedom: Runaways and Maroons in the Americas*. Kingston, Jamaica: University of the West Indies Press, 2006.

Thornton, John. "Central African Names and African-American Naming Patterns." *William and Mary Quarterly* 50, no. 4 (October 1993): 727–742.

Tillet, Salamishah. *Sites of Slavery: Citizenship and Racial Democracy in the Post–Civil Rights Imagination*. Durham, N.C.: Duke University Press, 2012.

Trahey, Erin. "Among Her Kinswomen: Legacies of Free Women of Color in Jamaica." *William and Mary Quarterly* 76, no. 2 (April 2019): 257–288.

Trouillot, Michel-Rolph. *Silencing the Past: Power and the Production of History*. 1995; repr., Boston: Beacon Books, 2015.

Turner, Sasha. "The Art of Power: Poison and Obeah Accusations and the Struggle for Dominance and Survival in Jamaica's Slave Society." *Caribbean Studies* 41, no. 2 (December 2013): 61–90.

———. *Contested Bodies: Pregnancy, Childrearing, and Slavery in Jamaica*. Philadelphia: University of Pennsylvania Press, 2017.

Vasconcellos, Colleen A. *Slavery, Childhood, and Abolition in Jamaica, 1788–1838*. Athens: University of Georgia Press, 2015.

Vermeulen, Heather V. "Thomas Thistlewood's Libidinal Linnaean Project: Slavery, Ecology, and Knowledge Production." *Small Axe* 22 (March 2018): 18–38.

Walcott, Derek. *The Castaway, and Other Poems*. London: Jonathan Cape, 1965.

Walker, Christine. *Jamaica Ladies: Female Slaveholders and the Creation of Britain's Atlantic Empire*. Chapel Hill: University of North Carolina Press, 2020.

Walvin, James. *The Zong: A Massacre, the Law and the End of Slavery*. New Haven, Conn.: Yale University Press, 2011.

Warner-Lewis, Maureen. *Archibald Monteath: Igbo, Jamaican, Moravian*. Kingston, Jamaica: University of the West Indies Press, 2007.

West, Diane M. "Slave Names Memorialized: A Historical-Linguistic Analysis of Monumented Slave Names in Jamaica." MA thesis, University of the West Indies, Mona Campus, 2017.

Wilder, Craig S. *Ebony & Ivy: Race, Slavery, and the Troubled History of America's Universities*. New York: Bloomsbury, 2013.

Wilkes, Karen. *Whiteness, Weddings, and Tourism in the Caribbean: Paradise for Sale*. New York: Palgrave, 2016.

Williams, Daryle. Comments presented at the "Slavery, Heritage and Tourism" panel, "Slave Pasts in the Present: Narrating Slavery through the Arts, Technology, and Tourism" symposium. King Juan Carlos of Spain Center, New York University, April 28, 2018.

Williams, Patricia J. "Stop Getting Married on Plantations." *The Nation*, September 26, 2019.

Williams, Sherley Anne. *Dessa Rose*. New York: HarperCollins, 1986.

Yates, Geoffrey S. "Death of a Legend: The True Tale of the 'White Witch of Rose Hall.'" *The Gleaner*, November 21, 1965.

———. "The Rose Hall Legend: Was It Really Annie?" *The Gleaner*, December 5, 1965.

Zoellner, Tom. *Island on Fire: The Revolt That Ended Slavery in the British Empire*. Cambridge, Mass.: Harvard University Press, 2020.

ONLINE SOURCES

"About, Queering Slavery Working Group." https://qswg.tumblr.com/about.

"African Burial Ground Ancestral Chamber." https://www.nps.gov/afbg/learn/historyculture/ancestral-chamber.htm.

Ames, Paul. "Portugal Confronts Its Slave Trade Past." *Politico.eu*. https://www.politico.eu/article/portugal-slave-trade-confronts-its-past/.

Animals in War Memorial. https://www.royalparks.org.uk/parks/hyde-park/things-to-see-and-do/memorials,-fountains-and-statues/animals-in-war-memorial.

"Anna Mary Palmer (née Paterson)." Legacies of British Slave-Ownership Project. https://www.ucl.ac.uk/lbs/person/view/21929.

"ANTM CYCLE 22 BTS: The Rose Hall Ghost Story." https://www.youtube.com/watch?v=4d4gikpWq90.

Assata, Nzingha. "Leave Emancipation Day Alone!" *The Gleaner*, February 1, 2021. http://jamaica-gleaner.com/article/letters/20210201/leave-emancipation-day-alone?utm_source=newsletter&utm_medium=email&utm_campaign=am_newsletter.

Barnard College. "Break This Down: 'I Am Queen Mary' at Barnard." Created October 15, 2019. https://barnard.edu/news/break-down-i-am-queen-mary-barnard.

Beck, Koa. "Disturbing Wedding Trend: Getting Married at a Plantation." *Salon*, January 5, 2014. http://www.salon.com/2014/01/05/disturbing_wedding_trend_getting_married_at_a_plantation/.

"Being the Narrative of Ashton Warner." https://docsouth.unc.edu/neh/warner/summary.html.

Belam, Martin. "Glasgow University to Make Amends over Slavery Profits of Past." *The Guardian*, September 17, 2018. https://www.theguardian.com/education/2018/sep/17/glasgow-university-to-make-amends-over-slavery-profits-of-past.

Bobo, Laurence D. "Slavery on Film Sanitized No More." *The Root*, January 9, 2013. https://www.theroot.com/slavery-on-film-sanitized-no-more-1790894819.

Brockell, Gillian. "Some White People Don't Want to Hear about Slavery at Plantations Built by Slaves." *Washington Post*, August 8, 2019. https://www.washingtonpost.com/history/2019/08/08/some-white-people-dont-want-hear-about-slavery-plantations-built-by-slaves/.

Bromwich, Jonah Engel. "University of Texas at Austin Removes Confederate Statues in Overnight Operation." *New York Times*, August 21, 2017. https://www.nytimes.com/2017/08/21/us/texas-austin-confederate-statues.html.

Brown University. "Brown University Steering Committee on Slavery and Justice." http://www.brown.edu/Research/Slavery_Justice/.

CaribPr Wire. "Press Release." http://caribpr.com/arthur-wylie-and-rollins-family-commit-90
‑million-to-produce-epic-film-trilogy-in-jamaica-with-creator-of-final-destination/.

CARICOM Reparations Committee. "Ten Point Action Plan." http://caricomreparations
.org/.

Charr, Manuel. "Rio Slavery Museum Raises Questions." *Museum Next*, August 27, 2019.
https://www.museumnext.com/article/rio-slavery-museum-raises-questions/.

Clarke, Paul. "Remembering the 'Zong Massacre.'" *The Gleaner*, December 20, 2019. http://
jamaica-gleaner.com/article/news/20191220/remembering-zong-massacre.

Cohen, Max. "Slavery in America: Some Historical Sites Try to Show the Horrors. Others Are
Far Behind." *USA Today*, October 16, 2019. https://www.usatoday.com/in-depth/news
/education/2019/10/16/slavery-racism-black-history-historical-sites-historic-places-field
-trip/1905346001/.

College of William & Mary. "Memorial to African Americans Enslaved by William & Mary."
https://www.wm.edu/sites/enslavedmemorial/slavery-at-wm/index.php.

Columbia University. "Columbia University & Slavery." https://columbiaandslavery.columbia
.edu/.

Cooke, Mel. "Emancipation Park Marks a Decade." *The Gleaner*, July 29, 2012. http://jamaica
-gleaner.com/gleaner/20120629/ent/ent2.html.

Dalkey Archive Press. "A Conversation with Ishmael Reed by Reginald Martin." July
1983. http://www.dalkeyarchive.com/a-conversation-with-ishmael-reed-by-reginald
-martin/.

Debruge, Peter. "'Antebellum' Review: Janelle Monáe Stands Up to the Horrors of Slavery in
Mind." *Variety*, August 31, 2020. https://variety.com/2020/film/reviews/antebellum
-review-janelle-monae-slavery-1234754308/.

Denaud, Felicia. "Renegade Gestation: Writing Against the Procedures of Intellectual History."
Journal of the History of Ideas Blog. October 23, 2020. https://jhiblog.org/2020/10/23
/renegade-gestation/

Diving with a Purpose. https://divingwithapurpose.org/.

Downs, Jim. "Our Lincoln, Ourselves: Rethinking Slavery and Abolition." *The Huffington Post*,
The Blog, December 12, 2012. http://www.huffingtonpost.com/jim-downs/lincoln
-historical-accuracy_b_2285718.html.

DuQuesnay, Frederick J. "Rose Hall Great House" (1964). http://www.jamaicanfamilysearch
.com/Samples/fred03.htm.

Edmonds, Kevin. "An Elusive Independence: Neocolonial Intervention in the Caribbean."
International Socialism: A Quarterly Review of Socialist Theory, no. 146 (Spring 2015).
http://isj.org.uk/neocolonial-intervention-in-the-caribbean/.

"Edward Mountague." Legacies of British Slave-Ownership Database. https://wwwdepts-live
.ucl.ac.uk/lbs/person/view/2146644311.

Emancipation Day Message 2020. Transcript of message. The Office of the Prime Minister
Andrew Holness. August 1, 2020. https://opm.gov.jm/speech/emancipation-day
-message-2020/.

Emancipation Day Message 2020. YouTube video of message. July 31, 2020. https://www
.youtube.com/watch?v=qfJaOVwGLII.

Emancipation Day Message 2021. YouTube video of message. August 1, 2021. https://www
    .youtube.com/watch?v=L—njMvTmek.
"Fireburn: The Uprising of 1878." https://en.natmus.dk/historical-knowledge/historical
    -themes/danish-colonies/the-danish-west-indies/fireburn/.
"For a Friend, Lawmaker Bars Aid to Jamaica." *New York Times*, March 3, 1988. https://www
    .nytimes.com/1988/03/03/world/for-a-friend-lawmaker-bars-aid-to-jamaica.html.
France, Lisa Respers. "'Harriet' Controversies Didn't Stop Box Office Success." *CNN Enter-
    tainment*, November 4, 2019. https://www.cnn.com/2019/11/04/entertainment/harriet
    -controversies-box-office/index.html.
Freelon, Kiratiana. "Look at All These Monuments from Around the World That Honor Those
    Who Fought Against Slavery." *The Root*, August 24, 2017. https://www.theroot.com/look
    -at-all-these-monuments-from-around-the-world-that-1798358305.
———. "Rio Is Debating Creation of a Slavery Museum." *Next City*, August 31, 2017. https://
    nextcity.org/daily/entry/new-rio-slavery-museum-name-debate.
"Funds Freed in Rollins Row?" *The Gleaner*, September 7, 1988. https://newspaperarchive.com
    /kingston-gleaner-sep-07-1988-p-1/.
Gates, Henry Louis, Jr. "Tarantino 'Unchained,' Part 1: 'Django' Trilogy?" *The Root*, December 23,
    2012. https://www.theroot.com/tarantino-unchained-part-1-django-trilogy-1790894626.
Georgetown University. "Georgetown University: Slavery, Memory, and Reconciliation."
    http://slavery.georgetown.edu/.
"Govt. Bows to Rollins' Pressure: Talks Said Opened over Property Claim." *The Gleaner*,
    August 20, 1988. https://newspaperarchive.com/kingston-gleaner-aug-20-1988-p-1/.
"A Great Love Story." *The Gleaner*, February 13, 2018. https://jamaica-gleaner.com/article
    /outlook/20180218/great-love-story.
Green, Andrew. "Move to Block Aid to J'ca: Dispute over Property in St. James at Issue." *The
    Gleaner*, March 5, 1988. https://newspaperarchive.com/kingston-gleaner-mar-05-1988-p-1/.
Guyatt, Nicholas. "1619, Revisited." *New York Times*, October 19, 2020. https://www.nytimes
    .com/2020/10/19/opinion/1619-nikole-hannah-jones-bret-stephens.html.
Henrietta Vinton Davis's Weblog. https://henriettavintondavis.wordpress.com/2010/03/24
    /redemption-song/.
Hirsch, Afua. "Britain Was Built on the Backs of Slaves. A Memorial Is the Least They
    Deserve." *The Guardian*, October 23, 2019. https://www.theguardian.com/commentisfree
    /2019/oct/23/memorial-2007-enslaved-africans-black-history-britain.
"Hon. William Miller (attorney)." Legacies of British Slave-Ownership Database. https://
    wwwdepts-live.ucl.ac.uk/lbs/person/view/2146637296.
Hyman, Danae, and Dave Rodney. "Update: Statue Rage—Government Opens Debate on
    Removing Monuments to Colonial-Era Icons." *The Gleaner*, June 11, 2020. http://jamaica
    -gleaner.com/article/lead-stories/20200611/update-statue-rage-government-opens
    -debate-removing-monuments-colonial.
I Am Queen Mary. https://www.iamqueenmary.com/.
Ioannidis, Sakis. "'History Is, Above All, an Exercise in Imagination.'" June 30, 2018. http://
    www.ekathimerini.com/230207/article/ekathimerini/life/history-is-above-all-an-exercise
    -in-imagination-mazower-tells-kathimerini.

"IPN: Black New Research and Memory Institute on Facebook." https://www.facebook.com
/ipn.museumemorial/.

Jamaica Information Service. "Emancipation." Edited by Patrick Bryan. https://jis.gov.jm
/information/emancipation/.

Jamaica National Heritage Trust. "Greathouses (Plantation houses)." http://www.jnht.com
/greathouses.php.

Jamaican Family Search Genealogy. "1833 Jamaica Almanac." http://www.jamaicanfamily
search.com/Members/AL33James.htm.

"Jamaica St. James 275." Legacies of British Slave-Ownership database. https://wwwdepts-live
.ucl.ac.uk/lbs/claim/view/22102.

The Johnny Cash Show. "Johnny Cash—The Ballad of Annie Palmer." YouTube. January 2,
2009, 3:06. https://www.youtube.com/watch?v=YOSU5WMkOpo.

"John Rose Palmer." Legacies of British Slave-Ownership Database. https://wwwdepts-live.ucl
.ac.uk/lbs/person/view/2146637407.

Jones, Cecily. "White Women in British Caribbean Plantation Societies (Topical Guide)."
H-Slavery LISTSERV. Posted on May 3, 2016. https://networks.h-net.org/node/11465
/discussions/123038/white-women-british-caribbean-plantation-societies-topical
-guide.

"Joseph Ridley." Legacies of British Slave-Ownership Database. https://www.ucl.ac.uk/lbs
/person/view/2146652809.

Library of Congress. "Born in Slavery: Slave Narratives from the Federal Writers' Project,
1936–1938." http://memory.loc.gov/ammem/snhtml.

Luongo, Michael T. "Despite Everything, People Still Having Weddings at 'Plantation' Sites."
New York Times, October 17, 2020. https://www.nytimes.com/2020/10/17/style/despite
-everything-people-still-have-weddings-at-plantation-sites.html.

"Memorial 2007: Remembering Enslaved Africans and Their Descendants." http://www
.memorial2007.org.uk/about.

"Mémorial de l'abolition de l'esclavage." http://memorial.nantes.fr/en/.

"Memorial to Enslaved Laborers." https://www.youtube.com/watch?v=b14yuObEJaE.

Milford, Maureen. "Rollins' Dream May Come True: Finally Reaches Accord on Jamaican
Plantation." *Sunday News Journal*, October 15, 1989. https://www.newspapers.com/image
/155207945/.

"Miss World Tori-An Singh to Perform at Emancipation Park Concert on Saturday." *The
Gleaner*, December 18, 2019. http://jamaica-gleaner.com/article/news/20191218/miss
-world-toni-ann-singh-perform-emancipation-park-concert-saturday.

"Mitch Landrieu's Speech on the Removal of Confederate Monuments in New Orleans."
New York Times, May 23, 2017. https://www.nytimes.com/2017/05/23/opinion/mitch
-landrieus-speech-transcript.html.

Monticello. "Slavery at Jefferson's Monticello: Paradox of Liberty." https://www.monticello
.org/slavery-at-monticello.

———. "Weddings." http://www.monticello.org/site/visit/weddings-monticello.

Morris, Margaret. "Whither the Rose Hall Deal?" *The Gleaner*, January 2, 1991. https://
newspaperarchive.com/kingston-gleaner-jan-02-1991-p-1/.

Mosley, Michael W. "A Tour of Jamaica's Great Houses, Plantations, & Pens." Created in January 2015. https://thelastgreatgreathouseblog.wordpress.com/.

Mount Vernon. "Lives Bound Together: Slavery at George Washington's Mount Vernon." https://www.mountvernon.org/plan-your-visit/calendar/exhibitions/lives-bound -together-slavery-at-george-washingtons-mount-vernon/.

"Multimillion-Dollar Earnings from America's Next Top Model." *The Gleaner*, November 11, 2012. http://jamaica-gleaner.com/gleaner/20121111/ent/ent9.html.

National Library of Jamaica. "Nettleford, Rex—Choreography, Education (1933–2010)." https://nlj.gov.jm/project/nettleford-rex-choreography-education-1933-2010/.

———. "Robert Love (1839–1914)." https://nlj.gov.jm/project/robert-love-1839-1914/.

National Park Service. "The Civil War: 150 Years—Confronting Slavery." https://www.nps .gov/features/waso/cw150th/reflections/confronting-slavery.

Neuman, Scott. "Duke University Removes Robert E. Lee Statue from Chapel Entrance." *NPR: The Two-Way*, August 19, 2017. https://www.npr.org/sections/thetwo-way/2017/08 /19/544678037/duke-university-removes-robert-e-lee-statue-from-chapel-entrance.

New York Times Magazine. The 1619 Project. https://www.nytimes.com/interactive/2019/08 /14/magazine/1619-america-slavery.html.

Niang, Mame-Fatou. ##unsilencedpast Online Series. Barnard College, Digital Humanities Center. Session with Professors Maboula Soumahoro and Mame-Fatou Niang, July 23, 2020. https://vimeo.com/441413700.

Passados Presentes. http://passadospresentes.com.br/site/Site/index.php/principal/index.

Princeton University. "The Princeton & Slavery Project." https://slavery.princeton.edu/.

Princeton University. Office of Communications. "President Eisgruber's message to community on removal of Woodrow Wilson name from public policy school and Wilson College." https://www.princeton.edu/news/2020/06/27/president-eisgrubers-message-community -removal-woodrow-wilson-name-public-policy.

Public Theology Forum. "Emancipation Observance: A Time for Reflection." *The Gleaner*, August 2, 2009. http://old.jamaica-gleaner.com/gleaner/20090802/focus/focus5.html.

———. "Is It Just a Little Sex: Church, Sex and Power." *The Gleaner*, August 2, 2009. http:// jamaica-gleaner.com/article/commentary/20170219/public-theology-forum-it-just-little -sex-church-sex-and-power.

Reid, Ahmed. "Topple Columbus' Statue." *The Gleaner*, November 2, 2018. http://jamaica -gleaner.com/article/focus/20181104/ahmed-reid-topple-columbus-statue.

Rhoden, Sheree. "Evolution of National Heroes Park." *The Gleaner*, October 18, 2020. http:// jamaica-gleaner.com/article/art-leisure/20201018/evolution-national-heroes-park.

Rijksmuseum. "Slavery." https://www.rijksmuseum.nl/en/whats-on/exhibitions/slavery?gclid =CjwKCAjwtdeFBhBAEiwAKOIy5xWP4jjCsw9X_l-xzeQgkEhijstHvqsrE1BVPowZr7D 7IHskm3OOAxoC_YIQAvD_BwE.

Ritch, Dawn. "Civil Society under Attack." *The Gleaner*, July 30, 2000. http://old.jamaica -gleaner.com/gleaner/20000730/Cleisure/Cleisure2.html.

"Rollins 'Laughing to the Bank.'" *The Gleaner*, August 12, 1989. https://newspaperarchive.com /kingston-gleaner-aug-12-1989-p-5/.

"Rose Hall Deal Sealed: Purchase Price £850,000." *The Gleaner* March 19, 1957. https://
    newspaperarchive.com/kingston-gleaner-mar-19-1957-p-1/.
Rose Hall Developments Ltd. "Cinnamon Hill." https://rosehall.com/cinnamon-hill/.
———. "Rose Hall Tour." https://rosehall.com/rose-hall/.
Rose Hall Digital Humanities Project. rosehallproject.columbia.edu.
"Rose Hall Great House." https://www.msccruisesusa.com/en-us/Cruise-Destinations
    /Caribbean-Antilles/Jamaica/Montego-Bay.aspx.
"Rose Hall Great House Montego Bay Tour and Song." Posted by garvey200 on YouTube,
    March 20, 2015. https://www.youtube.com/watch?v=X8vTzU8pjWA.
"Rose Hall Wedding Events." https://rosehall.com/wedding-events/destination-weddings
    -in-jamaica.
"Rose Hall Weddings." https://rosehall.com/weddings/.
Rutgers University. "Rutgers Scarlet and Black Project." http://scarletandblack.rutgers.edu/.
Scientific American Frontiers. "Unearthing Secret America" episode, October 8, 2002. http://
    www.chedd-angier.com/frontiers/season13.html.
Searles, Jourdain. "'Antebellum' Film Review." *Hollywood Reporter*, September 18, 2020.
    https://www.hollywoodreporter.com/news/antebellum-film-review.
Serjeant, Jill. "'Confederate' Writers Defend Modern U.S. Slavery Show as Scary but Real."
    Entertainment News, July 21, 2017. https://www.reuters.com/article/us-television
    -confederate/confederate-writers-defend-modern-u-s-slavery-show-as-scary-but-real
    -idUSKBN1A628Y.
Silvera, Janet. "Ritz-Carlton Rose Hall Sold to Playa." *The Gleaner*, April 7, 2013. https://
    jamaica-gleaner.com/gleaner/20130407/business/business1.html.
Silverstein, Jake. "We Respond to the Historians Who Critiqued the 1619 Project." *New York
    Times Magazine*, December 20, 2019. https://www.nytimes.com/2019/12/20/magazine
    /we-respond-to-the-historians-who-critiqued-the-1619-project.html.
Smithsonian Magazine. "New Statue Immortalizes Mary Thomas." Created April 4, 2018.
    https://www.smithsonianmag.com/smart-news/denmark-unveils-monument-queen-mary
    -thomas-who-led-revolt-against-danish-colonial-rule-180968661/.
"Social Media Split over Jamaica Costume at Miss Universe Pageant." http://www.jamaica
    observer.com/latestnews/Social_media_split_over_Jamaica_costume_at_Miss_Universe
    _pageant#disqus_thread.
Soumahoro, Maboula. #unsilencedpast Series. Barnard College, Digital Humanities Cen-
    ter. Session with Professors Maboula Soumahoro and Mame-Fatou Niang, July 23, 2020.
    https://vimeo.com/441413700.
Southern Poverty Law Center. "Whose Heritage? Public Symbols of the Confederacy."
    February 1, 2019. https://www.splcenter.org/20190201/whose-heritage-public-symbols
    -confederacy#methodology.
"The Three Rebel Queens." https://www.virgin-islands-history.org/en/history/fates/the
    -three-rebel-queens/.
Thurston, Thomas. Interview with Nicholas Crawford. Gilder Lehrman Center for the Study
    of Slavery, Resistance, and Abolition. Podcast audio. March 2, 2020. https://slaveryand

itslegacies.yale.edu/news/nicholas-crawford-plantation-provisioning-and-politics-health
-british-caribbean.

Tourism Product Development Company. "History." https://www.tpdco.org/history/.

———. "TPDCo Expanding Team Jamaica Programme." https://www.tpdco.org/tpdco
-expanding-team-jamaica-programme/.

United Nations. "Remember Slavery." https://www.un.org/en/events/slaveryremembranceday/.

University of Glasgow. "Slavery, Abolition and the University of Glasgow: Report and Recommendations of the University of Glasgow History of Slavery Steering Committee, September 2018." https://www.gla.ac.uk/media/Media_607547_smxx.pdf.

University of Mississippi. University of Mississippi Slavery Research Group. https://slavery
researchgroup.olemiss.edu/slavery-at-um/.

University of Virginia. President's Commission on Slavery and the University. https://slavery
.virginia.edu/memorial-for-enslaved-laborers/.

"What a Wedding." The Gleaner, December 16, 2011. http://jamaica-gleaner.com/gleaner
/20111216/social/social1.html.

"White Witch of Rose Hall, as Told by Michelle Rollins." https://www.youtube.com/watch
?v=0rFypxa3ZEE.

Whitney Plantation. "Whitney Plantation Guided Tours of Whitney Plantation Museum."
http://www.whitneyplantation.com/.

"William Heath." Legacies of British Slave-Ownership Database. https://wwwdepts-live.ucl
.ac.uk/lbs/person/view/22955.

Wright, Bruce D. T. "Outrage after Miss Universe Jamaica's Costume Named for Slave Owner
'Legend' Annie Palmer." https://newsone.com/playlist/miss-universe-jamaica-annie
-palmer-costume-controversy/item/2/.

Wynter, Sylvia. "'No Humans Involved': An Open Letter to My Colleagues." https://libcom
.org/library/%E2%80%9Cno-humans-involved%E2%80%9D-open-letter-my-colleagues.

Yates, Geoffrey S. "Rose Hall: Death of a Legend" (1965). http://www.jamaicanfamilysearch
.com/Samples2/mpalmer.htm.

INDEX

Note: Italicized page numbers indicate illustrations.

Underground Railroad, 206n36
UNESCO, 164
unionization, 119
United Fruit Company (UFC), 116–117, 216n158
United Nations, 160–161, 224nn7–8
Unite the Right Rally (Charlottesville, 2017), 226n18
Universities Studying Slavery (USS), 226n17

Vasconcellos, Colleen A., 51–52, 83, 87
Viet Thanh Nguyen, 170–171
violence, 3, 81, 123, 153, 168; epistemic, 12; Shepherd on, 166. *See also* rape
Virginia, slavery in, 180n11
Vodou, 134–137, 146, 217n11. *See also* Obeah practices

"wake work," 6–7, 181n19
White Witch Golf Course, 2
White Witch of Rose Hall. *See* Palmer, Annie Paterson

Whitney Plantation (La.), 181n21
Wilkes, Karen, 144
Williams, Daryle, 6, 172
Williams, James, 9, 183n26
Williams, Patricia J., 6
Williams, Robert (a.k.a. Quaco) (Creole), 73–74, 77
Williamson, John, 126–127
Wilson, Charles, 220n5
Wilson, Richard, 204
Witter, Norwood, 156
"women-girls," 51–52
"worker-mothers," 60, 65, 66, 86–91
workhouses, 106–109, *108*, 213n109, 213n111

yaws, 37, 96
yellow fever, 146, 147
Yoruba, 135; naming practices of, 71–73, 202n128

Zong massacre, 169–170

CPSIA information can be obtained
at www.ICGtesting.com
Printed in the USA
LVHW041301100822
725608LV00004B/339

9 780820 362151